Labour Markets in Europe

Labour Markets in Europe:

Issues of Harmonization and Regulation

Edited by

John T. Addison and W. Stanley Siebert

The Dryden Press

Harcourt Brace & Company Limited
London   Fort Worth   New York   Orlando
Philadelphia   San Diego   Toronto   Sydney   Tokyo

The Dryden Press
24/28 Oval Road,
London NW1 7DX

A catalogue record for this book is available from the British Library
ISBN 0-03-099046-7

Typeset by Servis Filmsetting Ltd, Manchester
Printed in Great Britain at WBC Book Manufacturers, Bridgend, Mid Glamorgan

Contents

Contributors

John T. Addison	Professor of Economics at the University of Hull and the University of South Carolina, and John M. Olin Visiting Professor of Labor Economics, Center for the Study of American Business, Washington University in St Louis, USA
Antonio Argandoña	Professor of Economics at the Instituto de Estudios Superiores de la Empresa, University of Navarra, Spain
Richard Barrett	Senior Lecturer in Economics at the University of Birmingham
Simon Deakin	Fellow of Peterhouse College, Cambridge, and Assistant Director ESRC Centre for Business Research at the University of Cambridge
David Marsden	Reader in Industrial Relations at the London School of Economics
Jami Mirka	Graduate Assistant in the Department of Economics at the University of North Carolina at Greensboro, USA
Karl-Heinz Paqué	Professor and Head of Department I (Growth and Structural Policy) at the Institute of World Economics in Kiel, Germany
Christopher J. Ruhm	Professor of Economics at the University of North Carolina at Greensboro, and research associate National Bureau of Economic Research, USA
W. Stanley Siebert	Reader in Labour Economics in the Department of Commerce, University of Birmingham.
Rüdiger Soltwedel	Professor and Head of Department III (Regional Economics and Infrastructure) at the Institute of World Economics in Kiel, Germany

1

Introduction

John T. Addison and W. Stanley Siebert

Despite the focus on the purely economic in the treaties establishing the common market, namely, the Treaty of Rome and the Single European Act, it is now clear that an active 'social policy' – the European term for the various forms of support and protection to be provided for workers – is part and parcel of the process of European integration. If that was ever in doubt, it no longer is. Tangible evidence in the form of the Community 'social charter', and the recent 'social chapter' is there for all to see. Indeed, there can be few individuals who are unaware of particular pieces of Community social legislation on such matters as hours regulation and worker participation, even if their details are only vaguely discerned and knowledge of the broader thrust of policy incomplete.

Social policy in the new European Union is a matter of controversy, however, both with respect to individual measures and the breadth of actual and proposed intervention (the Community 'blueprint'). Given this controversy and the failure of the initiating agency, the European Commission, to establish a clear case for its measures or otherwise offer a consistent economic assessment of their impact on the labour market, the time is ripe to take a closer look at Community-level mandates. This is the task of the essays in this volume.

We have assembled a cast of ten authors to address these contentious issues. The reader will not find a unified set of interpretations since the state of our knowledge is such that there are no hard and fast answers. Instead, there is a diversity of response that mirrors that of public opinion. But there are important commonalities, chiefly in the recognition of the array of factors that may be expected to influence the efficacy of policy, some positive others negative, even if this is not always explicitly stated. The essays thus provide a framework for evaluating Community social policy as well as no small volume of detail that can be slotted into this framework to provide insights into the consequences of social policy mandates. As a result, the reader should come away with a sharper understanding of the basis of the controversies that surround even well-meaning attempts to improve the lot of workers in the Union and hence the uncertainties that attach to such attempts.

Our first substantive chapter (Addison and Siebert) largely confines itself to the nuts and bolts of actual and prospective Community legislation. It describes the course of policy from the 1970s onwards and the key markers along that road. Although close attention is paid to all of the binding (and indeed much of the nonbinding) legislation stemming from the social charter, we are concerned to point out that its shape and content were established long before 1989. Similarly, the erection of new machinery for pursuing social policy made possible by the 1993 Treaty on European Union (the so-called 'social chapter' route) may be seen as the teleological outcome of a long history of attempted legislation set in the context of ill-defined Community authority or 'competence'. The main message of this chapter is that social policy has a long and chequered history in the Community, and that its success owes much to the commitment and persistence of that part of the Commission responsible for framing social policy, Directorate General V. Bluntly put, this activist directorate has outmanoeuvred and outlived its principal antagonists. Nevertheless, and to repeat, it is our contention that DGV's justification for intervention has never been clearly set out, and that its analysis of impact effects has been cursory.

Chapter 3 (Addison, Barrett and Siebert) is therefore devoted to an analysis of the justifications for labour market regulation, together with an assessment of likely impact effects. In this chapter the standard neoclassical model of labour markets is honestly confronted with the main forms of 'market failure': problems of asymmetric information (relevant for mandates with insurance elements such as maternity benefits), externalities, and the existence of monopoly/monopsony power. If there is such market failure, then it can be shown that mandates may be efficient, that is, raise average 'full' earnings. (Full earnings are the sum of earnings and fringes plus the worker's valuation of the mandated benefit.)

The chapter shows how a mandate need not necessarily be prescribed even when a market failure has been diagnosed. Other policies, for example direct transfers, might be more appropriate. Moreover, even where a mandate is worth considering, two further questions arise. First, other components of the payment package must be flexible downwards when a mandate is imposed. In other words, as the 'social wage' rises, workers' pay must be free to fall. Otherwise employment will fall. Second, mandates can be *inequality-increasing* even if they are efficient. For example, minimum wages might increase efficiency because of monopsony problems, but result in firms raising their hiring standards. The unskilled, who are least able to meet the higher standards would find their job opportunities and incomes falling. So inequality would increase. Not much research has been conducted into the inequality aspects of mandates, but this is clearly important, and the relevant arguments are rehearsed here.

Chapter 3 devotes equal attention to assessing the empirical evidence on job protection mandates. Here, as indeed elsewhere, the research results are mixed, though there is some evidence that these laws are associated with reduced employment as well as higher and lengthier unemployment. It is interesting to note that while the inflexibilities associated with job protection can be alleviated by hours variation, there has at the same time to be some means of subsidising short-time working hours, otherwise weekly pay falls to an unacceptably low level. But then, however, a reduced number of favoured workers (the 'insiders') is likely to end up enjoying greater job security, leaving other groups less protected. Here, once again, we have an example of how mandates may serve to widen inequality.

The extension of maternity insurance in the USA may have lessons for the European Union. As is reported in Chapter 3, the compensation package of married women aged 20 to 40 did alter in composition in states that passed such laws relative to those that did not: the value of the insurance component rose, but pay fell approximately in the same amount, suggesting a full shifting of the costs of the mandate. It appears that weekly hours worked also rose by 5% for the affected group, but numbers employed fell by 2%. These findings imply that the mandate is valued by the target group, but that it also disadvantages part-time labour, perhaps because pregnancy insurance is a fixed cost which is a higher proportion of pay for low hours workers. Thus it is evident from the US analysis that, even where wages are flexible, mandates can have disemployment effects. Where wages are less flexible, as is likely to be the case in Community member states, the employment costs could be much higher.

In an important sense Community mandates appear to be fashioned on German institutions. This is of course most clearly evident in the case of the many proposals seeking to extend worker participation. Interestingly, however, our two German contributors to this volume stand most opposed to Community-level mandates. In the first of these contributions, in Chapter 4, Karl-Heinz Paqué argues forcefully that the web of rules governing the social protection of workers in a nation state are a determinant of that country's competititive position no less than its endowments of raw materials, human capital, and so on. The Community seeks to harmonize employment protection rules among other things, while leaving the other dimensions of a country's competitive position intact. For Paqué this position is not only illogical but also, and more importantly, damaging. He argues that the social systems of individual countries are put up for adoption by the market. That is, they have to stand a market test. Those systems that survive (and adapt) are competitive. He writes that 'the cultural space of Europe provides enough leeway for a broad social search process which may lead to very different results depending on the mentality of the population and the particular local conditions'. On this view, harmonization places a straightjacket on experimentation with different social systems and labour relations.

For Paqué the notion of social dumping that underpins much of the pro-harmonization argument is a 'semantic misfit'. If the argument has any force it must be reformulated as 'unfair competition' and judged according to an ethical standard, in the patent absence of any absolute standard. Specifically, is a national welfare state supported by a 'democratically legitimized consensus'? He argues that the income level of a nation is the best clue as to the existence of this consensus, given the tendency toward higher standards in richer nations. The poorer nations are unwilling to countenance financing a more generous welfare state at their present levels of per capita incomes. Forcing them to do so would prejudice the very growth from which higher standards would naturally evolve. He thus writes that 'harmonization is not the moral precondition of economic integration, but its final consequence'.

Ultimately, therefore, Paqué is led to consider another rationale for harmonization, namely, a political justification. (And it is here that one begins to see that German attitudes to harmonization are increasingly being shaped by the experience of a post-unified Germany.) While accepting that the social dimension is part of a 'politically motivated rush into federalism', Paqué doubts that it will lower the likelihood of political conflicts among the member states. Despite the political problems caused by heightened competitive pressures (loosely, social dumping), the soothing balm of devices to lessen the forces of competition through harmonization of standards at once removes a potent advantage of the poorer member states, namely, their lower labour costs. As a result, the latter will inevitably be led to demand large increases in subsidies through the structural funds apparatus (for example, the European Regional Development Fund and European Social Fund –

both described in Chapter 2). This in turn may be expected to produce political conflict that would prejudice integration, unless there is social consensus in the Union
for an extensive redistribution system. Such consensus, he warns, is coming under
stress even within member states, noting in particular the difficulties being experienced in his own nation in integrating the five new *Länder* – the former German
Democratic Republic. The stress is likely to be heightened further with the future
accession of eastern European nations to the Union. In sum, the pursuit by the
Community of a social dimension is at best premature.

Chapter 5, by Simon Deakin, analyses the legal bases for Community social
policy: the Treaty of Rome as it has been amended over the years, the case law developed by the European Court of Justice, and the emerging doctrine of 'subsidiarity'.
In his analysis of the Treaty of Rome, Deakin describes the limits which the Treaty
originally placed – and continues to place – on social policy. The base was widened
somewhat with the admission of majority voting for certain labour regulations (primarily health and safety) under the Single European Act in 1986. This allowed the
Commission to play the 'Treaty base game' of choosing the less restrictive majority
voting articles of the Treaty to introduce social policy directives, and thereby avoid
a UK veto. Most recently, of course, the base has widened further with the Treaty
on European Union and its annexed Protocol on Social Policy. However, Deakin
emphasizes that there are doubts as to the legal status of the Protocol; in particular,
as to whether it is merely an agreement between states, or instead an integral part of
Community law in the sense that Community citizens can assert it in their national
courts. He takes the view that 'the present state of Community labour and social
legislation is inadequate, and its legal basis uncertain'.

Deakin also shows that the European Court of Justice has played a more subtle
role in the development of social policy than is usually realized. The Court has both
strengthened and weakened harmonization of labour standards among member
states. As far as strengthening goes, the Court has developed the doctrine of 'direct
effect', which confers rights against the state on individuals. For example, the far-
reaching *Barber* case on equality in occupational pensions was decided on the basis
that Article 119 (equal pay) had direct effect. Community directives can also be used
to give purposive interpretation to national legislation – the principle of 'indirect
effect'. Moreover, the European Court of Justice has permitted individuals to sue
the state for failing to implement a directive – an example being the *Francovich* case
concerning the Italian government's failure to implement the directive on protection
of employee rights in insolvency.

Going the other way, however, Deakin points out how the European Court of
Justice has also held that different social standards are permissible among states –
even if this interferes with trade – if the standards can be justified on 'public policy'
grounds. He illustrates this point using the *Oebel* case, in which the Court upheld
German regulations on nightwork in bakeries. Deakin sees the powerful European
Court of Justice as not simply aiming for harmonization (still less uniformity), but
rather as working to create a floor of rights. Such a floor, Deakin argues, will not
involve the imposition of uniformity or parity of costs, but rather will aim to
'promote labour as a productive resource'.

In Chapter 6, David Marsden takes up the industrial relations implications of
Community labour regulation. Marsden believes that the internationalization of
firms and industrial restructuring brought about by the Single European Market
'may destabilize worker–employer cooperation and so undermine economic performance'. Within this context, he sees an important role for the social dimension

because certain measures – such as works councils, and the social dialogue – can help maintain worker–employer cooperation.

Cooperation can be analysed in the framework of the prisoner's dilemma model. Although cooperation has obvious benefits for both sides in the form of improved flexibility and increased information exchange, it also brings the threat of opportunism. As Marsden emphasizes, an atmosphere of 'trust' within the firm is needed to neutralize this threat. But trust requires wider institutional support. He argues, for example, that a centralized pay bargaining system helps maintain trust by providing a framework for acceptable company bargains. Again, a system of works councils, as in Germany, is said to encourage worker–management cooperation by providing an effective power base for workers, and (just as important) worker–worker cooperation by virtue of its inclusiveness (i.e. including all worker groups).

Marsden sees the threat to cooperation becoming stronger with the widening of the European market, and believes the 'social dimension' is therefore needed to counteract this threat. As the market widens, firms become more international, the fear of relocation becomes more real (a classic example is the relocation of the Hoover factory from Dijon in France to Cumbernauld in Scotland), and the rewards to cooperation diminish. Moreover, as governments attempt to bring down deficits, there are threats to government spending and the welfare state. Yet the welfare state, according to the author's analysis, has played an important role in anchoring the post-war development of cooperation. Thus, Chapter 5 provides the reader with a basis for conceptualizing the 'social dimension' as promoting trust. Most important here, in Marsden's view, is the Community's encouragement of the 'social dialogue', and its emphasis on maintaining workers' acquired rights when businesses are transferred. In this way, the social dimension is defended as part of the Single European Market, and necessary if the benefits of that market are not to be frittered away through workplace conflicts.

Turning from this broad-based legal and economic analysis, the remaining chapters of the book focus on particular countries. Thus, the second German contribution to this volume (Chapter 7) by Rüdiger Soltwedel, has a more specifically German focus. German corporatism, notes Soltwedel, was initially at one with the active social policy agenda of the Community, subject to some nervousness on the subsidiarity issue. Indeed, both sides of German industry were able to issue a joint declaration on the need for a social dimension to the Community, the text of which Soltwedel appends to his chapter.

But the keynote of Soltwedel's essay is the peculiar schizophrenia that characterizes German attitudes to the Union. These stem from the desire to preserve the corporatist nature of German institutions – and what might appear to outsiders to be the near-mystical notion of social peace – in an increasingly competitive international economy. The accepted wisdom in Germany, we are told, is that its labour market is not to be exposed to competition from without (the so-called 'country of destination' principle) even if trade in goods is to be unfettered (the 'country of origin' principle). Such ambiguity also attaches to the position of other member states of course, but it is particularly noticeable in Germany given this formalization of apparent contradictions. The shifting nature of political coalitions tracked by Soltwedel is quite understandable in this milieu.

Soltwedel also notes particular sources of tension that harmonization is currently posing for Germany. Interestingly, these stem not from the actions of the Commission but, rather, from the decisions of the European Court of Justice and its perceived disregard for the 'systemic structure of German labour and social law'.

Such anxiety may appear marginal to Anglo-Saxon readers (but see Chapter 5's discussion of the European Court), more concerned perhaps with the increased authority of the Commission, but considerations such as the export of social benefits loom large in a country with more than six million foreign workers and a social security system that is coming under increasing pressure.

If Germans are currently much exercised by the subsidiarity issues noted above, Soltwedel discerns a more fundamental change in attitudes towards social cohesion in the wake of the formal unification of the two Germanies on 3 October 1990. In particular, he argues that the inherent contradictions of the 'cosy corporatism', that has long predisposed Germany to favour harmonization, albeit within limits, has come under severe strain because of the truly massive costs of unification. Soltwedel contends that this is all too the good and will lead to what he terms a loosening of the 'tight corporatist straightjacket'. Even if this conclusion is controversial – note that Soltwedel gives chapter and verse on the costs of German corporatism – there can be little disagreement that the empty public coffers in Germany at least threaten to slow down the introduction of new social policy measures post-Maastricht where these have to be purchased through increased subsidies to the poorer member states of the Union.

In Chapter 8, by Antonio Argandoña, we turn to Spain. Spain makes an important case study because its labour market is at once one of the most rigidly regulated in the Community (the Franco legacy), and also among the poorest performing. Unemployment rates in Spain are the highest in the Community, and this coincides with the lowest rates of private sector per capita employment growth (see Chapter 10). Thus the issue of whether there is a connection between labour market regulation and unemployment confronts us in stark form in the Spanish case.

In Chapter 8 the reader will find details of the form taken by Spain's labour market regulations. Most important seems to be the 'minute regulation' of dismissal of workers on full-time, open-ended contracts. Indeed, dismissals of such workers (including dismissals on grounds of redundancy) generally require official authorization if they are contested, and carry a severance payment that averages in practice about 40 months' salary. Spain's partially publicly-financed and powerful central union federations firmly support these dismissals laws. In the effort to sidestep the perceived adverse employment effects of such regulation, the Spanish government has, however, been able to permit the development of fixed-duration contracts. Argandoña reports that these contracts have been so attractive that virtually all new contracts are fixed-term in nature. Overall, they cover 30% of the Spanish workforce, compared with only 10% in other Community states.

Centralized collective bargaining, and a form of social dialogue between the two main union federations and the central employer's federation are also a feature of the Spanish system. Such corporatism, according to Argandoña, underlies the retention of dismissals regulation in Spain, and also that country's inappropriately high rates of real wage growth. Spain thus appears as something of a counter-argument to Marsden (in Chapter 6), who sees the social dialogue as productive of cooperation and increased labour productivity. Argandoña's analysis itself leads him to the conclusion that the regulations which the Community's social dimension seeks to impose would reinforce Spain's rigidities, and support the position of those who resist reform.

In the penultimate contribution, Jami Mirka and Christopher Ruhm offer an American perspective. They use the North American Free Trade Agreement (NAFTA) as a point of comparison. The major differences between this entity and the Community are detailed – one notable example of which is the use of economic integration to stem the flow of labour from Mexico to the USA – as well as some similarities to do with social dumping. In the latter context, it is argued that side agreements under NAFTA will be overtly more protectionist in nature than is the case in Europe given the much lower level of integration. (Social policy is not contained in the basic NAFTA agreement and will have to be given force under separate agreements, called 'side agreements'.) In another sense of course the more pressing problems of cross-border pollution offer a clearer economic case for harmonization along this dimension.

The authors document the very different attitude toward labour market regulation in the USA than in Europe, which may be expected nevertheless to limit social charter-like initiatives under future NAFTA side agreements. In their documenting the cases for and against regulation (examined in much greater detail in Chapter 3), however, there are indications that US attitudes are changing, even if they remain several standard deviations away from the European model. Mirka and Ruhm take three specific types of legislation – advance notice, parental leave, and unjust dismissal – to make comparisons between the two systems and to indicate our knowledge of the consequences of such policies. Although more sympathetic to some (but by no means all) Community mandates than certain of our European authors, Mirka and Ruhm are concerned to emphasize the need for explicit efficiency audits. Without such an evaluation, policy is quite simply hamstrung. The sting of the Mirka–Ruhm analysis thus lies in the tail.

The final chapter offers a brief overview of European labour markets. It has a basis in a tabular presentation of labour market data for the Community member states, plus the USA and Japan. Comparative evidence is provided on aspects of the wage-fixing machinery (minimum wages, union density, and extension of collective agreements), dismissals protection, and laws affecting labour contracts such as restrictions on working hours and the operation of temporary work agencies. The main point raised by this institutional review is the dissonance between Anglo-American and continental European practices, with Portugal, Greece and Spain appearing as the most restrictive among the latter group.

The main aim of the final chapter is to provide empirical material relevant to the debate on the links between the regulatory framework and labour market outcomes. The chapter therefore also offers comparative data on labour market outcomes, including employment statistics (employment growth, unemployment, self-employment, and part-time and temporary employment), earnings and income information (average earnings, trends in earnings for the top and bottom percentiles, and Gini coefficients for income distributions), and trends in unemployment inequality by education. Some of the more interesting results of the covariation of institutions and performance are the apparent discouragement of part-time work in the highly regulated countries, the higher degree of self-employment in such regimes, and a possible line of causation running from regulation to low incomes and sluggish private sector employment growth. Interestingly, there is little suggestion in this aggregative data of any link between the strength of regulation and developments in either income inequality or unemployment inequality.

Overall, the essays in this volume confirm that the move towards labour market harmonization in Europe is substantive and of consequence. The Commission, backed up by the European Court of Justice, is proceeding on a very broad front, having secured a slew of legislation covering most aspects of working conditions. The fundamental logical question is whether government regulation in general and supranational regulation in particular can improve on the outcomes arrived at by individuals freely contracting with each other. A related question is the extent to which government regulation improves the labour market opportunities of some workers while prejudicing the prospects of yet others. The authors in this book clearly take contrasting or opposing positions on either or both of these questions. Both sides can bring forward countries that illustrate their position. Thus, for example, Spain might be regarded as a case study of the debilitating effects of regulation and corporatism. Germany, on the other hand, can be cited as the exemplar of what can be achieved under an interlocking system that confers responsibilities and not just rights, although we are conscious of the reservations of our German contributors on the deficiencies of what is termed 'cosy corporatism' in an increasingly competitive product market.

Similarly, the broad empirical evidence can be interpreted as offering support to both sides. That said, we believe that the predominant thrust of the evidence on dismissals protection in particular points to both reduced employment and elevated joblessness, even if the precise contribution of legislation to observed changes in these two outcome indicators is clouded because of likely omitted variables bias. And there are indeed signs that many observers once favourable to such mandates are beginning to question the longer-term impacts of job protection on the process of labour reallocation. We also believe that empirical research has highlighted the fact that mandates such as maternity benefits have acted to the disadvantage of part-timers and unskilled workers, thereby exacerbating existing income distribution problems.

Given the large potential effects of labour market mandates, a thorough examination of these effects should precede the introduction of any directive. Our discussion has indicated all too clearly that this has not been the case in the Community. The strategy of introducing a mandate and then fine-tuning or otherwise modifying it in the light of experience would appear to be naive from a public choice perspective, given the largely unmodelled endogeneity of laws and the constituencies ranged against any subsequent downward revisions of standards. Moreover, from a theoretical perspective the use of mandates to establish default values has received insufficient attention. As a practical matter, European-wide mandates, where modified, have only ever subsequently been revised upwards, although the Commission would argue that this has only occurred where its original proposals were much attenuated in Council. Our point would be that more analytical attention be accorded all mandates despite the inevitable shading of precision introduced during the legislative process. Hopefully the essays contained in this volume will in their different ways serve to focus attention on the variety of issues involved by different mandates and in so doing assist in securing this necessary development.

2

The Course of European-Level Labour Market Regulation

John T. Addison and W. Stanley Siebert

2.1. Introduction

In this chapter we trace the development of labour policy at Community level from its inception in the early 1970s through the 'social charter' to the recently ratified Treaty on European Union. Our intention is to set down the facts, and not at this stage to offer much in the way of interpretation. Analytical issues concerning the justification for Community mandates and their associated adjustment costs are tackled in the next chapter. The themes investigated in Chapter 3 are of course also taken up by other contributors to this volume.

It is perhaps not widely recognized that the Community actively pursued the goal of social harmonization long before the adoption in 1989 of the Community Charter of the Fundamental Social Rights of Workers, or 'social charter' as we have termed it. Section 2.2 considers the pre-social charter era successes and failures of DGV, the Commission directorate for employment, industrial relations and social affairs which is mainly responsible for framing social legislation. This provides the necessary background to subsequent social policy developments.

Section 2.3 addresses the social charter, and offers a detailed description of the status and content of the actual legislation stemming from its Action Programme. All the binding instruments are identified, as well as the more important of the non-binding measures. Since the passage of legislation is linked to increased subsidies from the richer to the poorer member states, the expansion of the Community's structural funds is also examined in Section 2.3.

At the same time as the Commission was seeking to implement the social charter, it also pursued a number of separate initiatives, most notably in the area of worker participation, including, for example, the European Company Statute. These 'ancillary' measures are reviewed in Section 2.4.

The procedural and substantive changes introduced under the Treaty on European Union, are next discussed in Section 2.5. One important objective of the Commission has been to involve the two sides of industry, or 'social partners' as they are known, in the design and implementation of policy in the quest for a more flexible though no less comprehensive approach to the harmonization of labour standards. Section 2.6 considers this process of 'social dialogue' and the important role of Community legislation in its evolution. The current and future course of social policy are discussed in Section 2.7. The chapter concludes with a brief summary.

2.2.   Initial Developments

The origins of modern Community social policy can be said to date from October 1972. At a conference of heads of state in Paris, the European Council gave support to a 'vigorous' social policy, having the same importance as the achievement of economic union. The Commission, which had up to this point been preoccupied with the development of the Common Agricultural Policy, responded by putting forward in 1973 an ambitious Social Action Plan that sought to advance the rights of workers by strengthening the role of trade unions, and by imposing social obligations upon employers in such areas as health and safety at work, minimum wages ('to promote Community concertation between governments and Social Partners to bring about a selective and progressively harmonized upgrading of low wages'), working hours and paid vacations, employee participation including asset formation, and the hiring of contract labour (Commission, 1974). This Social Action Plan also called for improved cooperation between national employment agencies, a more dynamic Community policy on vocational training, improvement in the position of women at work in addition to equal pay, adequate income maintenance for workers during retraining and job search, improved coordination of national social security schemes, a long-term programme for the social integration of the handicapped, and the extension of social protection to include linking social security benefits to the industrial wage.

The Council of Ministers issued a Resolution on 21 January 1974, guardedly endorsing the Social Action Plan (*OJ* C13 of 12.2.74). It cautioned that a standard solution to all social problems should not be attempted, and that there should be no transfer to Community level of responsibilities assumed more effectively at other levels – the subsidiarity principle. Although the Council's Resolution amounted to a declaration of general principles rather than a *carte blanche* (Roberts, 1989: 43), it provided a foundation for Community social policy. It should be read in conjunction with Articles 117 and 100 of the Treaty establishing the common market. Article 117 is one of a limited number of social provisions contained in the Treaty of Rome (see Appendix 1). Article 117 expresses the agreement of member states 'to promote improved working conditions and an improved standard of living for workers, so as to make possible their harmonization while the improvement is being maintained', further noting that 'such a development will ensue not only from the functioning of the common market ... but also from the procedures provided for in this Treaty ...'. Article 100 is one such procedure and concerns the approximation (or harmonization) of laws:

> The Council shall, acting unanimously on a proposal by the Commission, issue directives for the approximation of such provisions laid down by law, regulation and administrative action in the Member States as directly affect the establishment or functioning of the common market.

The Commission was in fact able to achieve some early success in enacting social legislation. Thus, three Council directives designed to strengthen job rights in the event of collective redundancies, transfers of business, and firm insolvency were adopted between 1975 and 1980.[1] Somewhat more substantive equal opportunities legislation was also introduced. Thus, for example, an *equal pay directive*[2] introduced the principle of equal pay for work of equal value – that is, comparable worth – and sought to abolish discriminatory clauses in collective agreements. Inasmuch as Article 119 of the Treaty of Rome (see Appendix 1) established the principle that men and women should receive equal pay for equal work, this new directive extended the definition of equal pay. Shortly thereafter, an *equal treatment in employment directive*[3] addressed gender discrimination in hiring especially in areas where women were judged to be segregated by gender into low-paid work. It also tackled discrimination in vocational training and in promotion and working conditions. Finally, an *equal treatment in social security directive*[4] required that there be no discrimination against women in contributing to or receiving benefits relating to sickness, workplace health and safety, and unemployment.

These gender directives had a discernible impact on member states. As a case in point, the UK was forced in 1983 to amend its Equal Pay Act (1970) to comply with the comparable worth doctrine and in 1986 to amend its Sex Discrimination Act (1975) when this was adjudged to be in violation of the equal treatment directive (see Mazey, 1988).

Substantial progress was also made in the area of health and safety, despite the fact that there was no explicit Treaty basis providing for such intervention – at least until the ratification and implementation of the Single European Act in 1987. Between 1978 and 1987 – a period encompassing two Community safety action programmes – some 11 directives were adopted by the Council of Ministers. Additional protection was extended to workers under the 1980 *hazardous agents framework directive*[5] and its specific 'daughter' directives covering the risks occasioned by exposure to lead, asbestos and noise. Passage of all these measures required unanimity in Council via Article 100. The success of Community legislation in this area reflects reluctance on the part of member states to permit labour market competition on the basis of lower health standards.

Article 118A of the Single European Act marks the beginning of a firm Treaty basis for health and safety measures, and also provides for qualified majority voting (see Appendix 2). It is important to note as well that Article 100A(3) of the Act requires the Commission 'to take as a base a high level of protection' – there are to be no concessions for the poorer countries. Following the Act, the development of Community law affecting health and safety accelerated with a *workplace health and safety framework directive,*[6] whose preamble affirmed that 'the improvement in workers' safety, hygiene and health at work is an objective which should not be subordinated to purely economic considerations'.

The directive required employers to assess risks to workers in the choice of work equipment, the chemical substances used, and the design and fitting out of workplaces, and to introduce protective measures. It also established extensive worker rights to information and consultation, much on the German pattern (Walters, 1990: Table IV). The directive moreover provided for the adoption of further individual measures under its umbrella, including measures on minimum standards at the workplace, work equipment, personal protective equipment, the manual handling of loads, and work with display screen units. Three such directives were adopted immediately prior to the social charter, bringing to 17 the number of health and safety directives. The remaining directives were adopted in May 1990 (*EIRR*, 1990).

Although the Commission succeeded in obtaining Council's approval of the above measures, it was blocked on the remainder of the important initiatives foreshadowed under the 1973 Social Action Plan. In particular, impasse was reached on the Commission's proposals dealing with worker involvement in their companies, the regularization of part-time work and temporary contracts of employment, and parental leave. By the middle-to-late 1980s, therefore, a considerable backlog of draft legislation had built up.

Beginning with worker rights to information, consultation, and participation, the Commission had proceeded on three main fronts: the so-called 'Vredeling' initiative; the European Company Statute; and the draft Fifth Directive on company law. The Vredeling proposal[7] called for employees to be given regular information on a wide range of economic, financial, business and employment issues plus consultation on decisions likely to affect their interests (such as plant closures or transfers) in multinational corporations and firms with subsidiaries employing 100 or more workers. Confronted by major opposition from employer groups, the Commission was forced to amend its proposal. A new draft directive provided for less frequent information on a narrower range of issues, and elevated the firm size threshold to 1000 workers.[8] Notwithstanding these and other modifications, the draft directive was to remain stalled in Council.

Given that the two other draft directives on worker involvement sought to proceed beyond information provision and consultation, it should come as no surprise to learn that they too remained blocked, with even longer lags describing their legislative history. The European Company Statute, which was first introduced in 1970, provided for employee representation on obligatory supervisory boards for those organizations that elected to form a 'European Company'.[9] As full board members, employee representatives would participate in all matters concerning the management and progress of the company, as dealt with by the supervisory board. In addition, the draft legislation also called for directly elected European Works Councils (EWCs) in every European Company having at least two establishments in different member states, each with at least 50 employees. The management board of the European Company was to meet regularly with its EWC, and in any event at least four times a year, to report among other things on the economic and financial position of the company, production and marketing, the investment programme, new working methods, and rationalization plans. The EWC was to be consulted on such matters as job evaluation and piecework rates. And it had codetermination rights – that is, the management board could only proceed with its agreement – with respect to rules on recruitment, vocational training, the fixing of terms of remuneration, measures relating to safety and health, and holiday schedules, *inter alia*. The influence of the German 'model' in shaping the draft legislation is apparent.

The draft Fifth Directive on company law also proposed obligatory worker representation on the supervisory boards of all public limited companies with 500 or more employees. The legislation was amended in 1983, however, to take account of the reality of unitary board systems in some member states and to permit a somewhat wider menu of choice than worker directors alone – and at the same time the employment size threshold was raised to 1000 or more employees.[10] But in all cases employee representatives were to be given regular information and consulted on all aspects of the company's situation, progress and prospects, including investment plans. Consultation was to be necessary in respect of plant closures, substantial changes in the organization of production, and substantial curtailment or expansion of the company's activities. (We note that the ECS was also amended in 1989 (*OJ* C263 of 16.10.89) to allow for participation options other than worker directors. The options are considered in Section 2.4 in the light of further amendments to both pieces of legislation.)

Despite this movement towards more flexible systems of participation, the reality of yet more diverse pratices and legislation across the Community (see Industrial Relations Services, 1990b) were to militate against adoption of the ECS and Vredeling. As we now know, similar diversity and the continuing active opposition of the UK were also to snag the Commission's intiatives on part-time work, temporary employment, and parental leave.

The Commission's 1982 and 1983 proposals on part-time work sought to ensure that such workers were offered the same treatment as their full-time counterparts.[11] Part-time work was not to be used to justify differences in working conditions, rules governing dismissal, and access to either promotion or training. Remuneration, holiday pay, and redundancy payments were furthermore to be calculated on the same basis as those of full-timers and in the same proportion. Part-timers were also to be covered by statutory or occupational social security schemes, subject to thresholds in force in member states, and to be informed of the nature of the employment contract upon request. Finally, any introduction of part-time working was to be preceded by consultation with the full-time workers through existing machinery.

The Commission's 1982 proposals on temporary employment agencies and fixed duration contracts of employment reflected its view that the diversity of such contracts distorted competition and hindered the development of the common market (on the diversity of employment contracts see Industrial Relations Services, 1990a).[12] To ensure that agencies would not be concentrated in those countries with the most permissive legislation, the Commission proposed a tight set of licensing curbs on their operation. For their part, temporary workers were to receive detailed written contracts of employment and were to be subject to the same terms as employees of the user company with respect to working conditions established by law, regulations, and collectively agreed or customary practices. The temporary workforce was also to be included by the user firm in calculating its size for employment security laws. (The limitations placed upon fixed-term contracts broadly paralleled those established for temporary worker contracts and are not discussed separately.)

Finally, the Commission's then abortive parental leave proposals established rights to leave attendant upon the birth of a child during the period following maternal leave.[13] Parental leave covered fathers as well as mothers. Its length was fixed at a minimum of 3 months and ceased when the child was two years of age, or five years in the case of a disabled child. (On the diversity of practice among member states in this regard see *EIRR*, 1989a, b.)

In sum, the Commission's successes outside of gender equality and health and safety were few and far between. After some initial success, the Commission encountered major resistance when it sought to stray too far beyond existing national practice. Indeed, by the mid-1980s much of its legislation was blocked by British opposition. And it was the British who in December 1986 with the support of the Irish and Italian governments, secured adoption in Council of what appeared to be radical redirection of policy. Community policy was henceforth to be redirected toward freeing up the labour market, and existing legislation was to be streamlined to accommodate small-to-medium sized enterprises that provided the source of job growth. The Commission was supposed to develop flexibility measures and issue regular progress reports. This British proposal was in part a response to the initiative taken by the new head of the Commission, Jacques Delors, who in 1985 had advocated the corporatist notion of a 'social dialogue' as a solution to the stalemate in Council over social policy. His intention was to encourage the two sides of industry at European level to conclude joint agreements on social policy that would then serve as the basis for Community legislation. (On the progress of the social dialogue, see below.)

Acceptance of the British initiative has to be seen against the backdrop of misgivings at this time about the employment-retarding effects of well-intentioned job regulation legislation (see, for example, Dahrendorf, 1986) and the reality of deregulatory moves in a number of European countries (Emerson, 1987). But despite such disenchantment with labour market regulation, the success in redirecting Community policy was to prove short-lived. As noted by Teague (1989: 73), in its response to the Council resolution, the Commission (1987a) was to portray the British initiative as adding 'merely a new dimension to the long-standing goal of obtaining the free movement of workers inside the Community rather than part of a deregulatory programme for the European labour market'. Shortly thereafter, the Commission (1987b) reasserted its intention to put forward new initiatives to promote social cohesion.

A number of developments proved favourable to the Commission's position. First, under the Single European Act, the British had in effect conceded ground on qualified majority voting in order to speed up the removal of obstacles to economic union. Second, opinion within the Community became less hostile to regulatory measures at European level with the accession of Spain and Portugal in 1986. With three distinctly low-wage countries in the Community (Greece having been a member since 1981) fears of a competitive erosion of social standards in the more advanced nations – 'social dumping' – were elevated. Third, opposition to social measures became more muted with the resumption of net job creation after 1987.

2.3.   The Community Charter of the Fundamental Social Rights of Workers

In his address before the May 1988 Congress of the European Trade Union Confederation, the President of the Commission announced his intention to press the European Council to make an explicit commitment to a 'social dimension' for the Single Market. No such commitment is of course contained in the Treaty of Rome or the Single European Act, the thrust of both of which is unequivocally economic. Jacques Delors outlined a platform of social rights, having much in common with the European Social Charter,[14] to be backed up by an action programme. In May 1989 the Commission issued a draft Community Charter of Fundamental Social Rights for Workers. After several iterations, a 'compromise text' was adopted by Council on 30 October 1989, and subsequently endorsed at the Strasbourg Summit on 8–9 December 1989 (Commission, 1989a). As is well known, having earlier given warning of its outright opposition, the UK did not endorse this 'solemn proclamation of fundamental social rights'.

The Community social charter set down a series of worker rights under 12 headings. The text of this declaratory agreement is reproduced in Appendix 3. It will be seen that Title II addresses the issue of implementation: the Commission is invited by the European Council to submit initiatives 'as soon as possible'. In fact, the Commission (1989b) had already issued a detailed Action Programme in November 1989 containing no less than 47 separate initiatives.[15] The Action Programme was silent on the question of Treaty basis, but in discussing its proposals on procedures for informing and consulting workers in European-scale organizations – Vredeling in new clothes – the Commission (1989b: 32) provided the broadest of hints in noting that 'in the field of health and safety at the workplace, participation is now an established Community fact'. (Again it will be recalled that health and safety initiatives now had a basis in Article 118A of the Single European Act and were thus subject to qualified majority voting.)

As we shall see, the social charter and its accompanying Action Programme resurrect many of the Commission's hitherto unsuccessful initiatives. Reflecting the Commission's long-standing commitment to an active social policy, the parallels with the 1973 Social Action Plan are therefore close. On this occasion, however, the Commission was to prove much more successful.

Binding Measures

Table 2.1 shows the salient features and current status of the binding instruments – in the form of regulations, decisions, and directives – stemming from the social charter. (Table 2.2 in the following section repeats this exercise for the non-binding measures.) As is readily apparent from Table 2.1, the large majority of the measures have either been adopted by Council or appear close to passage. Only on four measures has there been no progress under the social charter route, although one of these (item 25 on European Works Councils) has already been enacted into law under the Agreement on Social Policy of the Treaty on European Union, described below. To all intents and purposes, therefore, this particular phase of active social policy has drawn to a close. That said, some of the more contentious social charter measures have inevitably been subject to modification or 'dilution', as we shall see. If past experience is any guide these measures will be revisited by the Commission.

Not all the adoptions cited in panel A of Table 2.1 have proved controversial. Thus, modifications to existing Community vocational training and employment information programmes (items 14 and 16, respectively), and broad action programmes for the elderly and the disabled (items 15 and 17) have occasioned little debate, and the unanimity requirement has not been a barrier to their speedy adoption. Much the same is true of the health and safety initiatives (items 6 through 13). As we saw in Section 2.2, there was a slew of health and safety legislation in effect well before the social charter, and a specific Treaty basis for such measures, namely, Article 118A. Indeed, virtually all the health and safety proposals announced in the Action Programme have a basis in the pre-social charter framework directive on workplace health and safety. The remaining health and safety measures (items 20 to 22) also seem destined to pass into law. That said, there are signs of increasing resistance to further legislation of this type. Thus, for example, the seven deregulation task forces set up by the UK Department of Trade and Industry have each identified health and safety as an area in which deregulation would be desirable. Given this resistance and the Commission's (1989b: 43) own acknowledgement in the Action Programme that here exists 'a series of binding provisions which ensure fairly broad protection for workers' health and safety at the workplace', it is

Table 2.1. Basic Initiatives Under the Social Charter/Action Programme

Measure	Subject Area	Content	Status/Implementation
A. ADOPTED 1. Council Directive of 25 June 1991 supplementing the measures to encourage improvements in the safety and health at work of workers with a fixed duration employment relationship or a temporary employment relationship, 91/383/EEC (*OJ* L206 of 29.7.91).	Employment and Remuneration	Agency workers and those on fixed term contracts to be informed of job risks and to be trained in light thereof. The health and safety authorities have to be informed of their deployment.	Qualified majority.[a] First submitted to Council in June 1990. Implementation required by 31 December 1992.
2. Council Directive of 14 October 1991 on an employer's obligation to inform employees of the conditions applicable to the contract or employment relationship, 91/533/EEC (*OJ* L288 of 18.10.91).	Improvement of Living and Working Conditions	Workers to be provided a written contract or statement detailing the employment relation. Information to include job description, duration (if temporary), details of pay, paid leave, normal hours, and length of notice. Workers also to be given the name of the body determining the collective agreement (if any) governing the firm's pay and conditions. Member states can elect to exclude casual labour or those working less than 8 hours a week or for under 1 month.	Unanimity (Article 100). First submitted to Council in December 1990. Implementation by 30 June 1993.
3. Council Directive 93/104/EC of 23 November 1993 concerning certain aspects of the organization of working time (*OJ* L307 of 13.12.93).	As above	Establishes principle of the 48-hour maximum working week, but workers have right to work more than the limit if they choose. (This concession is to be reviewed 7 years after the implementation of the directive.) Maximum reference period over which 48-hour week to be calculated is 4 months, but is extended to 6 months where certain 'derogations' apply and up to 12 months under collective agreements. A number of exemptions allowed (e.g. work at sea, and doctors in training).	Qualified majority. First submitted to Council in August 1990. General implementation date by 23 November 1996.

Table 2.1. (*continued*)

Measure	Subject Area	Content	Status/Implementation
		Also maximum working week need not apply for workers with 'autonomous decision-making powers' and family workers. Directive also sets daily (weekly) rest periods of 11 (35) hours and fixes a 3 week paid holiday entitlement. Normal hours of night workers are not to exceed an average of 8 hours in any 24-hour period. This limit may again be averaged over a reference period – to be decidedby member states after consultation with the two sides of industry or via collective agreements. Night workers to be given free health assessments prior to assignment and regularly thereafter. Transfer to day work in the event of health problems recognized to be connected with night work.	
4. Council Directive 92/56/EEC of 24 June 1992 amending Directive 75/129/EEC on the approximation of the laws of the member states relating to collective redundancies (*OJ* L245 of 26.8.92).	As above	Main modification to the 1975 directive is a *de facto* widening of the employer to encompass the controlling undertaking or central administration of multi-establishment entity. Other changes include a widening of information disclosure provisions, and a requirement to consult with worker representatives in 'good time' with a view to 'minimizing' layoffs and mitigating their consequences through 'social measures'.	Unanimity (Article 100). First submitted to Council in September 1991. Implementation by 24 June 1994.
5. Council Directive 92/85/EEC of 19 October 1992 on the introduction of measures to encourage improvements in the safety and health at work of pregnant	Equal Treatment for Men and Women	Individual directive under the 1989 safety and health framework directive (89/391/EEC) as well as social charter. Pregnant women to receive sick pay. National eligibility requirements for	Qualified majority. First submitted to Council in September 1990. Implementation by

Table 2.1. (*continued*)

Measure	Subject Area	Content	Status/Implementation
workers and workers who have recently given birth or are breastfeeding (*OJ* L348 of 28.11.92).		entitlement to paid leave not to exceed 12 months of service. Employers to provide risk assessment. Where risks to worker's health and safety revealed, working conditions/ hours to be adapted and transfer or leave when this not practicable. Absolute ban on working with specific list of agents, processes, and working conditions. General prohibition of nightworking.	19 October 1994.
6. Council Directive 92/29/EEC of 31 March 1992 on the minimum safety and health requirements for improved medical treatment on board vessels (*OJ* L113 of 30.4.92).	Health Protection and Safety at the Workplace	Unless otherwise specified, all vessels to carry specific medical supplies, equipment, and antidotes. All seafarers to receive basic training in medical and emergency measures. Designated personnel to receive special and continuing training.	Qualified majority. First submitted to Council in July 1990. Implementation by 31 December 1994.
7. Council Directive of 25 June 1991 amending Directive 83/447/EEC on the protection of workers from the risks related to exposure to asbestos at work, 91/382/EEC (*OJ* L206 of 29.7.91).	As above	Lower action levels and lower limit values set for asbestos. A 'plan for work' in the case of asbestos removal to be submitted to authorities.	Qualified majority. First submitted to Council in June 1990. Implementation by 1 January 1993 (with later dates set for asbestos mining and Greece).
8. Council Directive 92/57/EEC of 24 June 1992 on the implementation of minimum safety and health requirements at temporary or mobile construction sites (*OJ* L245 of 26.8.92).	As above	Individual directive under 89/391/EEC. Directive requires designation of a health and safety coordinator, establishment of 'safety and health' plan and prior notice to authorities. Minimum standards set for work sites. Workers to have information, consultation, and participation rights.	Qualified majority. First submitted to Council in July 1990. Implementation by 31 December 1993.

Table 2.1. (*continued*)

Measure	Subject Area	Content	Status/Implementation
9. Council Directive 92/58/EEC of 24 June 1992 on the minimum requirements for the provision of safety and/or health signs at work (*OJ* L245 of 26.8.92).	As above	Individual directive under 89/391/EEC. Safety signs to be improved and standardized among member states.	Qualified majority. First submitted to Council in December 1990. Implementation by 24 June 1994.
10. Council Directive 92/91/EEC of 3 November 1992 concerning the minimum requirements for improving the safety and health protection of workers in the mineral extracting industries through drilling (*OJ* L348 of 28.11.92).	As above	Individual directive under 89/391/EEC. Detailed specification of minimum safety and health requirements. Employer to draw up 'safety and health document', and provide appropriate fire protection procedures, escape and rescue facilities, and warning and alarm systems. Health surveillance before assignment to duties and thereafter.	Qualified majority. First submitted to Council in December 1990. Implementation by 3 November 1994.
11. Council Directive 92/104/EEC of 3 December 1992 concerning minimum requirements for improving the health and safety protection of workers in surface and underground mineral extracting industries (*OJ* L404 of 31.12.92).	As above	Individual directive under 89/391/EEC. Similar content to item 10, including detailed code of safety and health protection practices.	Qualified majority. First submitted to Council in January 1992. Implementation by 3 December 1994.
12. Council Regulation (EC) No. 2062/94 of 18 July 1994 establishing a European Agency for Safety and Health at Work (*OJ* L216 of 20.8.94).	As above	The Agency, set up in Bilbao, aims to create networks for information exchange on safety and health, train experts, and provide technical and scientific information to the Commission.	Unanimity (Article 235). Submitted to Council in September 1991.
13. Council Directive 93/103/EEC of 23 November 1993 concerning minimum safety and health requirements for work	As above	Individual directive under 89/391/EEC. Sets obligations concerning the use of and alterations to vessels, and the training of fishermen.	Qualified majority. First submitted to Council in December 1991.

Table 2.1. (*continued*)

Measure	Subject Area	Content	Status/Implementation
on board fishing vessels (*OJ* L307 of 13.12.93).		Minimum safety and health standards set for new and existing vessels, including stability of structures, electrical installations, emergency escape routes, ventilation, temperatures, layout of workstations, accommodation, and sanitary facilities.	Implementation by 23 November 1995.
14. Council Decision of 22 July 1991 amending Decision 87/569/EEC concerning an action programme for the vocational training of young people and their preparation for adult and working life (Petra), 91/387/EEC (*OJ* L214 of 2.8.91).[b]	Vocational Training	To support national policies geared to providing young people with 1 or, if possible, 2 years' vocational training following compulsory schooling. Measure focuses on youth vocational training/work experience placement in other member states. Support also given to transnational training partnerships and cooperation in sphere of vocational information and guidance.	Unanimity (Article 128). First submitted to Council in October 1990. Implementation by 1 January 1992.
15. Council Decision of 26 November 1990 on Community actions for the elderly, 91/49/EEC (*OJ* L28 of 2.2.91).	The Elderly	Transfer of knowledge and experience on preventative strategies to meet the economic and social problems of an ageing population, including their social and economic integration.	Unanimity (Article 235). Submitted to Council in April 1990.
16. Council Regulation (EEC) No. 2434/92 of 27 July 1992 amending Part II of Regulation (EEC) No. 1612/68 on freedom of movement for workers within the Community (*OJ* L245 of 26.8.92).	Labour Market	Updating of existing European system for Community clearing of vacancies and applications (Sedoc). Simplification of procedures. All vacancies that could be filled by nationals of other member states to be circulated by national authorities. The latter to give same priority to workers from member states as is accorded national workers over workers from non-EC countries.	Unanimity (Article 235). Submitted to Council in April 1990.

Table 2.1. (continued)

Measure	Subject Area	Content	Status/Implementation
17. Council Decision of 25 February 1993 establishing a third Community action programme to assist disabled people (Helios II 1993 to 1996), 93/136/EEC (*OJ* L56 of 9.3.93).	The Disabled	Programme seeks the functional and employment rehabilitation, educational integration, and vocational training of disabled people. Focus on effective technologies, the exchange of information and experiences between Member States, evaluation and updating of the existing computerized information and documentation system (Handynet), and encouraging the disabled to participate in Community programmes.	Unanimity (Articles 128 and 235). First submitted to Council in October 1991.
18. Council Directive 94/33/EC of 22 June 1994 on the protection of young people at work (*OJ* L216 of 20.8.94).	Protection of Children and Adolescents.	Directive seeks in principle to ban child labour. (A child is defined as a person under 15 years of age or subject to compulsory full-time schooling.) Exceptions to the ban include apprenticeship-like schemes and 'light work', where the following limits apply: (1) 8 hours a day and 40 hours a week for apprentice programmes; (2) light work is restricted to 2 hours a day and 12 hours a week during the school year, with a daily maximum of 7 hours a week (8 hours for those over 14); (3) light work in school holidays is limited to 7 hours a day and between 35 and 40 hours a week, the threshold age again being 14 years of age; (4) a limit of 7 hours a day and 35 hours a week is set for light work performed by those children no longer in full-time compulsory schooling. Outside of light work, the hours of adolescents (15- to 17-year-olds) not subject to compulsory full-time schooling are limited to 8 hours a day and 40	Qualified majority. Submitted to Council in March 1992. Implementation by 22 June 1996.

Table 2.1. (*continued*)

Measure	Subject Area	Content	Status/Implementation
		hours a week. Night work is in principle prohibited. Separate health and safety regulations analogous to those established for pregnant workers (item 5). UK has secured a 4 year opt-out from three provisions, at the end of which period its position will be determined by majority vote in Council.	
B. ADOPTION PENDING 19. Proposal for a Council Directive concerning the posting of workers in the framework of the provision of services (*OJ* C187 of 9.7.93).[c,d]	Freedom of Movement	Workers temporarily posted to another country for over 1 month to receive same terms and conditions as obtain for work of the same character in the host country. These include, in addition to 'minimum' wages, limitations on working hours, health and safety obligations, holiday entitlements, including public holidays, restrictions on use of temporary workers, and protective measures in respect of pregnant women. Note that minimum wages may be prevailing union wage scales. Directive covers not only subcontractors but also moves between countries for the same firm.	Qualified majority (Articles 57(2) and 66). Submitted to Council in June 1991. European Parliament Opinion in February 1993. Amended proposal submitted to Council in June 1993.
20. Proposal for a Council Directive concerning the minimum safety and health requirements for transport activities and workplaces on means of transport (*OJ* C294 of 30.10.93).	Health Provision and Safety at the Workplace	Individual directive under 89/391/EEC. Establishes minimum workplace standards similar to those set under item 16.	Qualified majority. Submitted to Council in November 1992. Amended proposal submitted in October 1993.
21. Proposal for a Council Directive on the minimum health and safety requirements	As above	Individual directive under 89/391/EEC. Establishes standards to reduce risks of	Qualified majority. Submitted to Council in

Table 2.1. (*continued*)

Measure	Subject Area	Content	Status/Implementation
regarding the exposure of workers to the risks arising from physical agents (*OJ* C230 of 19.8.94).		exposure of workers to noise, mechanical vibration, optical radiation, and electric and/or magnetic fields. Sets exposure limit values and action levels at which specified measures, including health surveillance, must be initiated.	February 1993. Amended version submitted in July 1994.
22. Proposal for a Council Directive on the protection of the health and safety of workers from the risks related to chemical agents at work (*OJ* C191 of 14.7.94).	As above	Individual directive under 89/391/EEC. Employers to draw up 'safety and health document' that includes risks assessment and measures taken to protect workers. Workers to be provided with detailed information on chemical agents, risks, occupational exposure levels, and precautions taken. Prohibitions on use of certain chemical agents. Occupational exposure and biological limit values set for lead. Health surveillance to be appropriate to risks incurred.	Submitted to Council in May 1993. Amended proposal submitted in June 1994.
C. NO PROGRESS UNDER SOCIAL CHARTER ROUTE			
23. Proposal for a Council Directive on certain employment relationships with regard to working conditions (*OJ* C224 of 8.9.90).	Employment and Remuneration	Part-timers working more than 8 hours a week and fixed-term contract workers are to have employment conditions comparable to full-timers. Such conditions include vocational training, company pension schemes, and social security benefits (and corresponding taxes). Employee representatives to be informed in good time of recourse to such workers. Formal reports necessary in undertakings employing over 1000 workers.	Unanimity (Article 100). First submitted to Council in June 1990. Treaty basis challenged by European Parliament, seeking instead qualified majority voting. Considered as a consolidated directive with item 24, below, in October 1993 and again in December 1994. Now to be withdrawn and reconsidered under the

Table 2.1. (*continued*)

Measure	Subject Area	Content	Status/Implementation
24. Proposal for a Council Directive on certain employment relationships with regard to distortions of competition (*OJ* C305 of 5.12.90).	As above	Part-timers working more than 8 hours a week, fixed-term contract workers, and agency workers to have protection under statutory and occupational social security schemes that is 'rooted in the same foundations and the same criteria' as that offered full-timers, account being taken of hours of work and level of pay. Also they are to be entitled to the same annual holidays, dismissal allowances, and seniority allowances in proportion to hours worked.	Agreement on Social Policy. Qualified majority (Article 100A). First submitted to Council in June 1990. Amended proposal submitted in November 1990. Treaty basis subsequently challenged. See item 23 above.
25. Council Directive 94/45/EC of 22 September 1994 on the establishment of a European Works Council or a procedure in Community-scale undertakings and Community-scale groups of undertakings for the purposes of informing and consulting employees (*OJ* L254 of 30.9.94).	Information Consultation and Participation.	Transnational European Works Councils (EWCs) to be established in undertakings with at least 1000 employees having 150 or more employees in each of at least 2 member states. A 'special negotiating body' (SNB) of elected worker representatives to negotiate powers of EWC with central management. To trigger negotiations requires the written agreement of at least 100 workers or their representatives in at least 2 undertakings in at least 2 member states, unless central management initiates negotiations. The SNB may ultimately decide by a two-thirds majority not to open negotiations or terminate them. If negotiations are successfully concluded, there are no minimum requirements *per se* although the agreement has to cover the scope, composition, membership, role, and powers of	Unanimity (Article 100). First submitted to Council in December 1990. Amended proposal submitted in September 1991. Discussed by Council in December 1991, April 1992, and June 1993. Stalled. Subsequently adopted under the Agreement on Social Policy. Implementation by 22 September 1996.

Table 2.1. (*continued*)

Measure	Subject Area	Content	Status/Implementation
		the EWC as well as the number of meetings and financial resources allocated to it. Where no agreement is reached, 'subsidiary requirements' apply in respect of the size of the EWC, the content of information and consultation, and the number of meetings.	
26. Proposal for a Council Directive on minimum requirements to improve the mobility and safe transport to work of workers with reduced mobility (*OJ* C15 of 21.1.92).	The Disabled	Member States to ensure provision of accessible and interchangeable means of transport. Directive sets minimum accessibility standards, and on-board facilities and safety conditions. Signs to be harmonized and to accord with special needs of the disabled. Member states to provide the necessary training for the disabled and transport personnel.	Qualified majority. First submitted to Council in February 1991. Amended proposal submitted in December 1991.

Notes:

a Unless otherwise stated, 'qualified majority' refers to legislation based on Article 118A (health and safety). Qualified majority voting – requiring 54 (now 62) votes out of 76 (now 87) to secure the adoption of legislation in the Council of Ministers – was introduced under the Single European Act (SEA) of 1986. Such voting also applies in respect of Articles 100A (the establishment and functioning of the internal market), and 57(2) and 66 (concerning the coordination of laws and regulations).

b See also Council Decision of 6 December 1994 establishing an action programme for the implementation of a European Community vocational training policy (94/19/EEC) (*OJ* L340 of 29.12.94). This new initiative, known as the Leonardo da Vinci programme, is funded at ECU 620 million and is to be implemented over the period 1.1.95 – 31.12.99. It is aimed at supporting the actions of member states, and facilitating the emergence of an open European area for vocational training. It contains a 27–element list of objectives to promote a coherent development of training and 4 'strands' of measures.

c The Action Programme (p. 22) also proposed legislation on the introduction of a labour clause into public contracts. This is now subsumed under the posting of workers directive. Note, however, that contracting agencies may require tenderers to meet ruling employment protection practices and working conditions under a Council Directive on the procurement procedures of entities operating in the water, energy, transport and telecommunications sector, 90/531/EEC (*OJ* L297 of 29.10.90).

d Also under the 'freedom of movement' heading, the Council adopted 3 regulations on social security for migrant workers: Council Regulation (EEC) No. 1945/93 of 30 June 1993 amending Regulation (EEC) No. 1408/71 on the application of social security schemes to employed persons, to self-employed persons and to members of their families moving within the Community; Regulation (EEC) No. 574/72 laying down the procedure for implementing Regulation (EEC) No. 1408/71; and Regulation (EEC) No. 1247/92 amending Regulation (EEC) No. 1408/71 (*OJ* L181 of 23.7.93).

arguably the case that the social charter marks the end of an era of health and safety legislation or at least heralds an interval of consolidation. (The fourth action programme on health and safety due soon will establish whether this conjecture is correct.)

Two other measures identified in panel A of Table 2.1 have also smoothly negotiated the legislative process. The directive dealing with the safety and health of temporary workers (item 1) is of interest mainly because it is the only one of three separate 'atypical worker' directives to have been adopted. The directive dealing with the employer's obligation to inform employees of the conditions of employment (item 2) may similarly be viewed as a fairly anodyne piece of legislation, but note that the written contract by its very nature makes it easier to enforce minimum wages and indeed the provision of other directives. Among the information to be given to the worker is the 'extended' collective agreement governing the employee's conditions of work. The practice whereby firms which are not parties to a collective agreement have its terms extended to them is fairly widespread in Europe – though not in the UK where such extension was revoked under the 1980 Employment Act. This directive will make it easier to enforce such *'erga omnes'* agreements.

The balance of the adopted measures described in Table 2.1 have proved altogether more controversial, and here the Commission has been forced to accept what it would see as a watering down of its draft directives. Thus, the initial collective redundancies (or mass layoffs) proposal, item 4, had called for such redundancies to be declared null and void in the event that its information and consultation requirements had been breached. This draft directive also required provision for workers' representatives in establishments employing 50 or more workers. Both 'offending' clauses had to be dropped to secure adoption of the measure in Council. Similarly, the pregnant workers draft directive (item 5) had initially called for maternity leave to be paid at 100% of normal earnings. This had to be trimmed back to the amount the worker would have received if absent from work on grounds of sickness.

Finally, an earlier draft of the working time directive (item 3) sought to establish a maximum working week of 48 hours, in addition to setting minimum rest periods and placing limitations on patterns of work. The actual legislation now allows workers to elect to work more than 48 hours – though with the proviso that there be no discrimination against workers choosing not to work more than 48 hours. Moreover, it increases modestly the number of exemptions from the directive and allows company or local collective agreements to derogate from its main provisions.

While there has been dilution of some clauses of these three directives, in all cases amendments have also been introduced that work in the opposite direction to strengthen their reach. Changes subsequently made to the collective redundancies proposal have made it easier to reach the employment threshold that defines a collective redundancy, and the consultation requirements of the directive now obligate firms to discuss 'social measures' designed to mitigate the consequences of displacement through redeployment and retraining, *inter alia*. Similarly, the pregnant workers directive now explicitly denies member states the right to set eligibility requirements for paid leave that exceed one year's length of service. Moreover, the original draft of the working time directive contained no reference to its most contentious clause: the 48–hour maximum working week.

Note that the maternity rights and working time directives have both been given a basis in health and safety, that is, Article 118A of the Single European Act. However, both contain terms that have no well determined link with health and safety. The advantage of using the Article 118A Treaty basis is of course that it permits qualified majority voting.[16] And, as a matter of record, the UK's challenge to the health and safety basis of the working time directive, has been rejected by the European Court of Justice. The advocate general of the Court has stated that health and safety should be given a broad interpretation 'far removed from an approach confined to the protection of workers against the influence of physical and chemical factors alone' (*Financial Times*, 1996).

The protection of young workers directive (item 18) might also have been expected to occasion much controversy given its Treaty basis (Article 118A) and major differences between the UK and its continental neighbours in the utilization of young workers. On this occasion, however, the passage of the measure was secured when the UK obtained a 4-year opt-out from certain of its terms. At the end of this interval, the UK position will be decided upon via a qualified majority vote in Council. Not without relevance in explaining the success of the measure is the high level of youth unemployment in Europe – such that there may be a certain political attraction to all countries in eliminating groups of younger workers from the unemployment count. There is also the difficulty of building a coalition in opposition to a measure that can be defended on the emotive issue of child exploitation.

Turning to the pending social charter measures in panel B of Table 2.1, we have already noted the progress of the remaining health and safety proposals has been slower than might have been anticipated. Less surprising is the slow progress of the posted workers directive (item 19) since its labour clause represents the closest the Commission has yet come to regulating wages. We nonetheless note that the European Court of Justice (1990) has already ruled that member states have the right to extend their legislation or collective agreements to cover all workers, no matter where the employing firm is based.

Finally, just four of the 26 binding instruments described in Table 2.1 can be said to be either dormant or to have reached deadlock under the social charter. But, as is immediately apparent from the table, this is emphatically not the end of the story. Indeed, as noted earlier, the European Works Council directive (item 25) is already on the statute books. This directive was enacted into law not via the social charter, but rather under a new procedure made possible under the Treaty on European Union, namely, the Agreement on Social Policy. As a result of this arrangement, further discussed in Section 2.5, policy initiatives can be pursued among 11 rather than 12 member states, the UK having opted out. The Works Council directive was to all intents and purposes blocked by the British under the social charter – it is an Article 100 measure requiring unanimity – for reasons associated with the disproportionate representation of multinationals in the UK (Sisson *et al.*, 1991), and that country's commitment to voluntarism as a means of achieving employee involvement in their companies. Faced with this impasse, the other 11 member states decided on this occasion to pursue the measure under the new option, and the somewhat watered-down directive was duly adopted by the Council in September 1994.

As for the two atypical worker directives (items 23 and 24), they have subsequently been withdrawn following the new social action programme announced by the Commission in April 1995 (see below). Their fate is unclear because they seek to reduce the size of the temporary and part-time worker sector which is growing in most member states. In its initial guise, the item 23 measure sought to 'prevent any spread in the increasing prevalence of insecurity and segmentation of the labour market' (Commission, 1990: 27), while the item 24 measure sought to tackle 'distortions of competition' arising from differences in social costs and indirect costs of employing atypicals *vis-à-vis* full-timers. The two draft directives sought to make the employment conditions offered part-timers and temporary workers 'proportional' (in the case of item 24) or 'comparable' (in the case of item 23) to those of full-time employment. Despite their re-introduction in Council as a composite directive, items 23 and 24 were to remain stalled.

Non-binding Measures

In addition to the directives and decisions already considered, the action programme proposed several measures which were not intended to bind the member states, but which would serve to guide opinion in the states, or which would alter the Community's own budgetary priorities. Most of these measures have now also been adopted, and are listed in Table 2.2 augmented by more recent changes where relevant.

We will start with item 4 (equitable wages) in Table 2.2, considering the general labour market measures (items 1, 2 and 3) in the later section on the Community budget, concerning the funding for these measures. The Opinion on minimum wages stems from the social charter's pledge that 'workers shall be assured of an equitable wage, namely a wage sufficient to enable them to have a decent standard of living'. The Opinion notes that minimum wage setting is a matter for the member states, and calls upon them to protect 'the right to an equitable wage'. The states are called upon to introduce legislation against discrimination, to strengthen collective bargaining, and to improve education and training (see below for discussion of training measures). Somewhat contradictorily, however, the measures taken should not 'force low-paid workers into the informal economy'.

The Opinion on minimum wages does not actually call for minimum wage setting. However, France, the Netherlands, Portugal, Spain, Belgium and Greece all have national minimum wages; Italy, Germany and Denmark effectively have national minimum wages via the extension of collective agreements; and Ireland has binding Employment Regulation Orders (IDS, 1993a). As the UK is the only member state which does not have a system of minimum wages, perhaps such explicit provision is not thought necessary.

The Opinion on minimum wages should be taken in conjunction with (and indeed refers to) the Recommendation on common criteria concerning sufficient resources in social assistance (item 5). As can be seen, the Recommendation lays down the principle that individuals have sufficient resources to live in a manner compatible with human dignity. The Recommendation applies primarily to those out of the workforce, and hence complements the Opinion on minimum wages which applies to those in the workforce. Article 51 of the Treaty of Rome requires coordination of social security arrangements so that freedom of mobility of workers is facilitated. Such coordination of social security schemes is presently primarily governed by Regulation 1408/71 – and the new recommendations on convergence of social protection objectives (items 6 and 7) aim to advance this objective. (For a description of social security regulation see *Social Europe*, 1992.)

Turning next to the recommendation on profit sharing (item 8), the Action Programme had proposed a Community instrument on equity sharing and financial participation by workers under the heading of worker information, consultation and participation. Financial participation was seen as assisting in growth, and as 'a

Table 2.2. Non-binding Labour Policy Measures

Measure	Content
1. Documentation of the labour market.	'Employment in Europe' annual report (beginning 1989); Network of Employment Coordinators (starting April 1990); System of Documentation on Employment (SYSDEM) (launched October 1989). Note also the European Employment System (EURES) (*OJ* L274 of 6.11.93) which updates the old SEDOC system, and circulates job vacancies among member states.
2. Action programmes on employment creation.	ERGO: to improve knowledge on the long-term unemployed (beginning 1989); Local employment development initiatives: the most recent of these dates from June 1995 (*Social Europe*, 1995: 142) and aims to 'boost the employment intensity of growth' for example by identifying jobs which 'cater for new needs' especially in the environment and social services; SPEC: support programme for employment creation (beginning 1990); ELISE: European network on local employment initiatives (set up 1985); ESSEN: Community action for research, cooperation and action in the field of employment (set up 1995); ADAPT: Community initiative for programmes and grants to assist adaptation of the workforce to technical change (set up June 1994 with a budget of ECU 1.4 billion, 1994–99 (*OJ* C180 of 1.7.94).
3. Monitoring and evaluation of the European Social Fund (ESF):	The ESF was established by the Treaty of Rome in 1957 to improve employment possibilities and geographic mobility. Since then funds for agricultural guidance, for regional development and, most recently, social cohesion have been established. In 1987 it was decided to double the structural funds in real terms, to reach 25% of the EC budget. At the Edinburgh Summit of December 1992 a further increase to 33% by 1999 was agreed.
Communication from the Commission on the future of Community initiatives under the structural funds (COM (93) 282 of 16.6.93); Proposals for new Council regulations for the Community's structural fund operations 1994–99 (COM (93) 67 of 10.3.93 and COM (93) 124 and COM (93) 124 of 7.4.93).	The Communication proposes that at least 10% of the structural funds subsidies be channelled via Community initiatives rather than direct to the member states. It also proposes a 'framework human resources initiative' (see item 16) to assist in training and employment-intensive growth. The new proposed regulations put forward tightened procedures for dealing with the increased fund spending, including a new definition of additionality. Also a new 'objective 4' for the funds was introduced: facilitating the adaptation of workers to industrial changes.
4. Commission opinion on the introduction of an equitable wage (COM (93) 388 of 1.9.93).	Calls on member states to protect 'the right to an equitable wage' (permitting a 'decent' standard of living). The measures proposed seek to strengthen collective bargaining, legislation against discrimination, action against 'unlawful employment practices', and investment in education and training.

Table 2.2. *(continued)*

Measure	Content
5. Council recommendation of 24 June 1992 on common criteria concerning sufficient resources and social assistance in social protection systems, 92/441/EEC (*OJ* L245 of 26.8.92).	Member states are to recognize 'the basic right of a person to sufficient resources and social assistance to live in a manner compatible with human dignity'. The right is however to be subject to active availability for work or for vocational training where relevant.
6. Council recommendation of 27 July 1992 on the convergence of social protection objectives and policies, 92/442/EEC (*OJ* L245 of 26.8.92).	Social protection in the areas of sickness, maternity, unemployment, incapacity for work, the elderly, and the family is addressed. Member states should 'guarantee a level of resources in keeping with human dignity'. The aim is to promote an eventual convergence in levels of social protection, without which mobility between states will be impeded.
7. Commission communication of 17 July 1991 on supplementary social security schemes (SEC (91) 1332).	Aims to set in motion a debate on supplementary retirement pensions with a view to improving transferability of such rights between member states. Social security regulations 1408/71 at present exclude supplementary pensions (because of their diversity).
8. Council recommendation of 27 July 1992 concerning the promotion of participation by employed persons in profits and enterprise results (including equity participation), 92/443/EEC (*OJ* L245 of 26.8.92).	Member states are called on to encourage the introduction of profit sharing and employee share ownership schemes by offering fiscal or other financial advantages. The aim is not however to seek harmonization of 'the existing wide range' of schemes. Advances principles that schemes should observe – for example, that they should 'avoid wide fluctuations in income'.
9. Council resolution of 21 May 1991 on the third Community action programme on equal opportunities for women and men (1991 to 1995), 91/C 142/01 (*OJ* C142 of 31.5.91).	The resolution gives effect to the Commission's communication on the third action programme on equal opportunities for women and men (COM (90) 449 of 6.11.90). Actions proposed include: defining the scope of the concepts of equal pay for work of equal value and of indirect discrimination so as to encourage their inclusion in the collective bargaining process; financing the training of women via the New Opportunities for Women (NOW) initiative, the IRIS information network on training projects, and the Local Employment Initiatives (LEI) programme on creation of employment and setting up of small businesses by women; and the promotion of affordable childcare. In addition, all the programmes financed by the structural funds will require an equal opportunities dimension.

Table 2.2. *(continued)*

Measure	Content
	A fourth such programme is scheduled for the period 1996–2000. See Proposal for a Council Decision on the fourth medium-term Community action programme on equal opportunities for women and men (1996 to 2000), 95/C 306/02 (*OJ* C306 of 17.11.95).
10. Council resolution of 27 March 1995 on the balanced participation of men and women in decision-making, 95/C 168/02 (*OJ* C168 of 4.7.95).	The member states are invited to 'develop an integrated global strategy for promoting the balanced participation of women and men in decision-making' by developing research and promoting awareness. In the Commission's accompanying draft recommendation, equal opportunity programmes (for example, in the civil service) are called for.
11. Resolution of the Council and of the representatives of the governments of the member states meeting within the Council of 6 December 1994 on equal participation by women in an employment intensive growth strategy within the European Union, 94/C 368/02 (*OJ* C368 of 23.12.94).	Member states are invited, *inter alia*, to facilitate greater involvement of men in domestic life, and to promote part-time employment for men as well as women because this can have positive implications for employment. The social partners are invited to hold collective bargaining on the subject of equal opportunities, and in particular to ensure that women are adequately represented on in-service training courses.
12. Council resolution of 22 June 1994 on the promotion of equal opportunities for men and women through action by the European Structural Funds, 94/C 231/01 (*OJ* C231 of 20.8.94).	Member states are invited to establish specific measures targeted at women in projects co-financed by the European Social Fund. These measures are to be linked with the NOW initiative.
13. Council recommendation of 27 November 1991 on the protection of the dignity of women and men at the workplace, 92/141/EEC (*OJ* L49 of 24.2.92).	Companies are recommended to have a policy commitment to eradicate sexual harassment at work; supervisors are to have a positive duty to prevent harassment; and, when harassment is proved, disciplinary procedures are to be invoked.
14. Commission memorandum on equal pay for work of equal value (COM (94) 6 of 23.6.94).	Seeks to reinforce the concept of equal pay for work of equal value introduced in the 1975 equal pay directive 75/117/EEC: data on women's pay and on ECJ equal value case law is to be better disseminated, with the threat of Commission action before the ECJ if necessary.

Table 2.2. *(continued)*

Measure	Content
15. Council recommendation of 31 March 1992 on child care, 92/241/EEC (*OJ* L123 of 8.5.92).	Recommends that member states encourage initiatives to provide: 'affordable' childcare services for working parents, the state and/or firms to make a financial contribution; special leave for employed parents with children; and an increased male share of child upbringing responsibilities.
16. Council recommendation of 30 June 1993 on access to continuing vocational training, 93/404/EEC (*OJ* L181 of 23.7.93).	Recommends that member states 'raise awareness' among firms of the benefits of vocational training, and provide support for firms' analysis of their training needs. Firms should also inform workers of the training opportunities available in the firm, and provide a confidential training assessment. The ESF and the Community training programmes are to be used to facilitate international exchanges of know-how.
17. Updating of the 1963 proposal for a Council decision on the general principles for implementing a common vocational policy.	This proposal is not yet scheduled. However the Commission has issued a memorandum on vocational training in the EC in the 1990s (COM (91) 397). This emphasizes the setting of 'common objectives' for training – in accordance with the 1963 Council decision – and foresees the gradual emergence of a European space for training and qualifications. The three training initiatives set up in July 1990 – EUROFORM (ECU 300 m, 1990–93, for new qualifications), NOW (ECU 120 m, for women), and HORIZON (ECU 180 m, for the disabled) – are seen as the main Community instruments. These programmes have been updated by a Community initiative on employment and development of human resources (*OJ* C180 of 1.7.94) under which NOW is to receive ECU 370 m over 1994–99, HORIZON, ECU 730 m, and the new programme for youth training, YOUTHSTART, ECU 300 m. Note also the PETRA programme for youth exchanges and training (ECU 177 m, 1992–94), and the LEONARDO programme on an open European Area for vocational training (ECU 620 m, 1995–99).
18. Memorandum on the rationalization and coordination of vocational training programmes at Community level (COM (90) 334 of 21.8.90).	The Memorandum calls for the separate Community programme committees to be grouped into 5 categories, and in some cases for the committees to be merged since they represent a substantial administrative and financial responsibility for the member states and the Commission. The categories suggested are: initial training (e.g. PETRA); higher education and training (e.g. ERASMUS, COMETT and TEMPUS); continuing education and training (e.g. FORCE, launched 1991, on transnational training partnerships); teaching of foreign languages (LINGUA); and cooperation with third countries.
19. Communication on the role of the social partners in collective bargaining.	This has been superseded by the Communication on the application of the agreement on the promotion of social dialogue (COM (95) 600 of 14.12.93). (See *Social Europe* 1995: 193–208.) The Communication lays down the details of the process for consulting the social partners in terms of the Agreement on Social Policy.

device for a fairer distribution of wealth' (*Social Europe*, 1990: 66). The Action Programme had also called for 'a strengthening of coherence' in the member states' methods of promoting equity-sharing. In fact, the Recommendation, as it has been adopted, does not call for any harmonization, and is somewhat vague as to what is required of the member states. Mention of particular attributes of schemes, present in earlier drafts – for example, schemes which facilitate a more equitable distribution of income and wealth, or which include both part-time and full-time employees (see Commission, 1992c: 5) – has been dropped, as has reference to the role of the social partners in drawing up schemes. It seems unlikely therefore that the measure will have much discernible impact.

The third and fourth action programmes (1991–95 and 1996–2000) on equal gender opportunities (item 9) follow on the programmes of 1982–85, and 1986–90. These programmes essentially coordinate the various measures put forward to advance women's labour market position (items 10 to 15). The social charter had called for intensification of efforts to ensure equality in employment, wages and working conditions, including training and career development, and also for measures to reconcile work and family obligations. The action programmes use measures such as 'local employment initiatives for women', which subsidize women who start up in business and create at least two full-time jobs. Other subsidies are channelled via the NOW (new opportunities for women) initiative. This began in November 1990, with a budget of ECU 120 million for 1990–93 (to be matched by member states' co-financing) with the aim of supporting small businesses for women, to provide counselling for long-term unemployed women, and providing grants to cover the operating costs of childcare centres. The funding for NOW has since been increased to ECU 370 million for 1994–99 (item 17).

The childcare recommendation (item 15) naturally accompanies the equal opportunities action programme. It enters under the social charter clause requiring measures 'to enable men and women to reconcile their occupational and family obligations'. As noted above, childcare provision is part of the community's NOW initiative. In practice, publicly funded childcare provision for the under-2s in the member states accommodates only 2–3% of this age group, though France, Belgium and Denmark are exceptional with over 20% accommodated (50% in the case of Denmark) (Commission, 1991: Annex 2).[17] The Commission sees the unevenness of provision among member states as hampering mobility.

The childcare recommendation goes further than childcare as such, however, and calls for an increased male share of child upbringing responsibilities via paternity and parental leave policies (see also item 11). The justification for venturing into the field of parental leave is not so much to improve mobility as to relieve the 'impossible choices' that women face and their 'double burden' (Commission, 1991: 5). As we will see below, this thread of community policy is now being pursued via the Agreement on Social Policy, and binding legislation on parental leave will shortly be adopted.

Turning next to training, the Commission has issued many guidance notes and memoranda. The chief of these is the recommendation on access to continuing training (item 16), which gives the direction for future policy. This recommendation should be read together with the memoranda on vocational training (item 17), and on rationalization of Community training programmes (item 18). The recommendation is based on the social charter article requiring states to ensure workers have access to training throughout their working lives, through leave for training purposes. To this end, member states are 'to raise awareness among undertakings about the links between worker skills and the competitiveness of undertakings', and to provide support for advice on training and analysis of training needs. (The objection that this amounts to second-guessing business will be taken up in later chapters.) Companies are also to inform employees of the firm's policies with respect to vocational training, and provide a confidential 'assessment of training needs' for workers. The European Social Fund (ESF) and the Community's own training action programmes (see items 17 and 18) are to be used to facilitate exchanges of experience, and the two sides of industry are to discuss training and attempt to reach framework agreements.

As items 17 and 18 of Table 2.2 indicate, the Commission has been able to encourage a variety of its own ESF-funded training initiatives. In particular, starting in July 1990, three initiatives, NOW (for women), HORIZON (for the disabled) and EUROFORM (for adults) were drafted by the Commission. NOW and HORIZON have been expanded, and the YOUTHSTART thread added under the Employment and Development of Human Resources programme of July 1994.

It is important to note that the the Community's training initiatives and programmes only form a part of its influence in the training arena; the other aspect of Community influence depends on ESF funding of the member states' own training programmes. We consider the workings of the ESF in the next section. Suffice it to say here that the extra monies made available to the ESF with the expansion of the structural funds in 1988 (and again in 1993 with the Treaty on European Union) have given the Community more influence over member states' expenditures on government training schemes. Whether such large-scale schemes can achieve their objectives of improving worker productivity and helping adaptation to industrial change is a question we will have to consider later.

As for the final item of Table 2.2, the main point to be made is that the communication on the role of the social partners in collective bargaining has not yet been published. The Community has remained silent on the contentious issues of union membership and the right to strike. However, one important strand of the social charter's article on freedom of association and collective bargaining – promotion of the social dialogue – is being achieved. The Agreement on Social Policy under the Treaty on European Union builds a central role for agreements between the social partners in designing and implementing Community directives. As Table 2.2 shows, the Commission has now fleshed out the details of the way in which the social partners will be consulted, and how the fruits of their negotiations will be enforced. We take up the growing role of the Agreement on Social Policy in Section 2.7.

Economic and Social Cohesion

The Commission's general labour market measures are summarized at the beginning of Table 2.2 (items 1 to 3). These relate mainly to the way in which the Community's role is to be altered so as to accommodate the enhanced social dimension – and particularly the greater emphasis to be placed on training, which is linked to the fight against unemployment and 'social exclusion'. The foundation here is item 3, monitoring and evaluation of the ESF (and the other structural funds). The structural funds increased following the agreement at the Edinburgh summit of December 1992. The bulk of the increase has gone to the 'objective 1' (lagging) regions, Ireland, Portugal, Greece and Spain, which have experienced almost a doubling in their subsidies, to reach a flow of about ECU 19 billion (in 1992 prices) by 1999 (Commission,

Table 2.3. Expenditures on structural funds, 1987–99 (1992 prices, ECU billion)

	1987	1993	1999[b]
CAP	32.7	35.3	
Structural	9.1	21.3	27.4
funds:[a]	(–)	(1.5)	
of which objective 1		12.0	19.3
Total EC Budget[b]	51.0	70.0	
% GNP[c]	1.05	1.19	1.27

Notes:

[a] Figures in parenthesis indicate estimated 'Cohesion Fund' components of structural funds.

[b] Total includes allocations for internal/external policies, administrative expenditure, and allocations to reserves.

[c] Payment appropriations required as percentage of Community GNP – a further 0.03% addition is permitted as a margin for revision. At the Edinburgh Summit it was agreed that the Community budget would gradually rise to 1.27% of Community GNP by 1999.

Sources: Commission (1992b: 39), Commission (1992a: 39), Commission (1993b: 49), IDS (1993b: 3).

1993b: Annex 2). Part of this increase is to be accommodated by the new 'Cohesion Fund' set up by the revised Article 130D of the Treaty of European Union.

The structural fund figures are placed in the context of the Community budget in Table 2.3. In fact, the planned increase in the structural funds for 1994–99 represents a scaling down of the original plans (which envisaged a figure of ECU 29.3 billion for the structural funds by 1997, rather than only ECU 27.4 billion by 1999). However, this itself follows on a large increase in the funds over 1987–93, from ECU 9.1 to ECU 21.3 billion, consequent on the reform of Community finances when the new heading of 'Economic and Social Cohesion' was introduced under Title V of the Single European Act. In 1992 Portugal, Greece and Ireland were receiving annually from the structural funds as much as 3.5%, 2.9% and 2.3% of their respective GDPs (Commission 1992d: 67). These flows will become even larger in the future, since funding for Objective 1 regions is projected to increase as a proportion of the EC budget, as can be seen from Table 2.3. In addition, the European Investment Bank (EIB) has been provided with a new European Investment Fund with ECU 2 billion of capital. This Fund is to be directed to infrastructure projects in the poorer regions, and also 'to facilitate loans to small businesses' (*OJ* C125 of 6.5.93, 3).

The new funding has several objectives. It is to provide a financial contribution to trans-European 'transport infrastructure' (Article 130D), it is to prevent 'excessive public sector deficits' (Commission, 1993b, 26), and it is to finance new training and job creation initiatives. Such training initiatives are important, since the Treaty on European Union adds a full chapter (Title VIII) to the Treaty of Rome specifically devoted to education, vocational training and youth. The structural funds have therefore been reorganized, setting up a new objective for the ESF. Initially these funds had five objectives:

(1) to promote the development and adjustment of regions whose development is lagging behind;

(2) to convert regions seriously affected by industrial decline;

(3) to combat long-term unemployment (over-25s jobless for more than 12 months);

(4) to assist in occupational integration of young people (job seekers under 25); and
(5) to promote development in rural areas.

Objectives (3) and (4) have now been run together, to become objective (3), and the new task for the ESF is an objective (4) 'to facilitate the adaptation of workers to industrial changes through vocational training and re-training' (Commission, 1993b: 10). The aim is 'to anticipate the evolving needs over the medium term of industrial change' and 'ensure the appropriate training measures'. To assist in the achievement of the training objectives the Commission proposes an increase – from 3% to 10% – in the proportion of the structural funds being channelled via its own initiatives (rather than simply funding the member states' efforts) (Commission, 1993c: 11).[18] Hence the new ADAPT and employment initiatives mentioned in Table 2.2 (items 2 and 17).[19]

The question is why there are such large and increasing financial flows to the poorer countries. We have argued elsewhere that such flows can be explained as being necessary if the poorer countries are to accept the higher labour standards required by the social charter and its allied measures (Addison and Siebert, 1994a). In other words, since labour standards reduce the possibility of Greece, Spain and Portugal competing on the basis of lesser wages and working conditions, employment is threatened in these countries. The ESF, the Cohesion Fund, and the EIB represent attempts to mop up any unemployment by improving transport infrastructures, for example, and training programmes.

It has been argued by Lange (1992: 41), on the other hand, that the large subsidies to the poorer countries are mainly attributable to monetary union – namely, the convergence criteria set for currency stability and national budget deficits – rather than the social dimension. The difficulty with this argument is that the requirements of monetary union, such as low inflation, should reduce unemployment. Thus, for example, the promise of greater financial stability in the poorer member states should promote foreign investment in these countries, thereby reducing unemployment. Even if the movement toward a financially stable regime were to produce detrimental shock effects, as is plausible, such an outcome could not account for the steady, long-term rise in subsidies that we observe. The cause must be found elsewhere; for example, in the disruption of labour markets caused by labour standards rising faster than productivity.

To summarize, the large majority of the binding measures proposed under the social charter have either been enacted into law or are close to achieving that status. In addition, a slew of non-binding instruments that are not entirely without legal force has also been issued. Major expansion of the Community's structural funds preceded the social charter, in part to compensate the poorer member states for the erosion of their competitive position implied by the harmonization principle. Notwithstanding the ancillary measures discussed below, one phase of social policy that has its origins in the Commission's 1973 Social Action Plan has undoubtedly come to an end.

2.4.   Associated Measures

The plethora of measures contained in the social charter do not represent the sum total of Commission activity on the social policy front during this interval. As we have seen, not only does health and safety have the character of an on-going programme, but also the Commission has continued its work on other pre-social charter measures such as the burden of proof draft directive. Here, however, we propose to focus on the theme of worker participation, the main labour policy initiative pursued in parallel with the social charter. The initiatives described below complement the collective redundancies directive and the European Works Council directive (items 4 and 25 of Table 2.1), and of course also figure in the Commission's current agenda (see Section 2.7).

The two main measures in question are the proposed European Company Statute (ECS) and the draft Fifth Company Law Directive, encountered earlier in Section 2.2. It will be recalled that each has a long legislative history, reaching back to 1970 in the case of the former and 1972 for the latter. And, as also shown, the initial drafts of each piece of legislation sought to mandate worker representation on obligatory supervisory boards – although revisions to the Fifth Company Law Directive in 1983 allowed greater flexibility. We now consider the belated revisions made to the ECS in 1989, and further amendments to the Fifth Company Law directive introduced later that year.

Beginning with the draft ECS directive, a company may voluntarily incorporate as a European Company (or *Societas Europaea*), and thereby benefit from a simplified financial and tax regime, if it has a minimum capital of ECU 100 000 and if it establishes itself by merger, formation of a holding company, or creation of a joint subsidiary.[20] Under the 1989 revisions to the ECS, a European Company may also be created by the conversion of an existing public limited company. In each case, of course, the company must operate in more than one member state and have its head office in the Community. Incorporation automatically carries with it rules for employee involvement. The legislation has two Treaty bases, both relying on majority voting: the first takes the form of a regulation (based on Article 54, right of establishment) dealing with the company law aspects; and the second being a directive (based on Article 100A, approximation of laws) that establishes the rules for employee participation.

The new draft legislation provides for four types of compulsory worker participation:

(a) election by employees or their representatives of worker directors to the administrative board in unitary systems or to the supervisory board in two-tier systems, where they are to make up at least one third and not more than one half of board membership;

(b) cooption by the administrative/supervisory board of worker directors nominated by representatives of the employees;

(c) the creation of a 'separate body' akin to a works council made up of employee representatives; or

(d) some 'other model' to be jointly agreed by the administrative/supervisory board and employee representatives.

Although participation is inevitably wider where worker directors are appointed, the directive nevertheless seeks to align information and consultation rights across the various options. Thus, management will have to provide employee representatives in options (c) and (d) with the sort of information a director would have, specifically: three-monthly reports on the current situation and future prospects of the company, taking account of any information on any undertaking controlled by the company which might have an appreciable impact on the progress of the new company's business. Furthermore, employee representatives are to be supplied with any information which may have significant implications for the situation of the European Company, and they may at any time call for information or a special report on any matter concerning conditions of employment. Similarly, just as the prior authorization of the administrative or supervisory board is required for a specific set of operations, employee representatives must be informed and consulted prior to any decision being reached by the administrative/management board.

The procedure for deciding upon a participation model requires brief amplification. The precise model is determined through an agreement between the management (of the founder companies) and the representatives of workers (in those companies). In the event that no agreement can be reached, the general meeting convened to approve the formation of the European company chooses the model. Note, however, that the member state can restrict the choice of model *ab initio* and even make a single model compulsory for all European Companies having their registered office in its territory. Finally, if agreement is reached on a collectively bargained solution – where this option is not preempted by the member state – but this subsequently proves impossible to negotiate, then a 'standard model' is to apply. This fall-back model is to be provided by the law of the relevant member state and has to meet the minimum information and consultation rights noted earlier.

The draft legislation also caters for participation rights in the event of the transfer of the registered office of the European Company to another member state. Here the model applied prior to the transfer is to continue in operation and may only be altered if the self-same procedures used to establish the model in the first place are reiterated. However the directive does not address what happens in the case of a transfer where the member state has already restricted the choice of models that can be applied on its territory.

The ECS is also the template for separate legislation on the formation of European Associations, European Cooperative Societies, and European Mutual Societies (see *OJ* C99 of 21.4.92). In each case, and like the ECS, one part of the legislation takes the form of a regulation (based on Article 54) dealing with the company law aspects; and the other is a directive (again based on Article 100A) that establishes the rules for employee participation. Formal provision for participation is as usual the *sine qua non* of incorporation.

Unlike the ECS and its daughter regulations/directives, the final piece of legislation considered here, the draft Fifth Company Law directive, most recently amended in 1990, applies to all public limited companies and not just a self-selecting group.[21] The directive, which has a treaty basis in Article 54, provides for worker participation rights in public limited companies employing 1000 or more (the member state being permitted to set a smaller figure). It establishes four options paralleling those of the ECS. Note, however, that in this case the collectively agreed solution must result in a structure directly analogous to one of the first three options, and indeed one such option is to be imposed if the parties fail to agree within a fixed time interval. Whatever the ruling option, member states may provide that employee participation is not required in a company when a majority of the employees are opposed to it.

With respect to information, the formal requirements differ only slightly according to whether the workers are represented on company boards or in 'separate bodies.' Information includes three-monthly reports on the current operation and situation of the company and the provision of reports/documents. Interestingly, the rights to information in the 1990 draft are expressed in more general terms than hitherto.

With respect to consultation, rather more significant changes have occurred. The 1983 legislation gave clear rights to either non-executive directors or supervisory board members to authorize certain executive decisions. Specifically, closures or transfers of the undertaking, substantial curtailment or extension of its activities, major organizational changes, and the establishment/termination of long-term cooperation agreements all required prior authorization. Similarly, workers represented on separate bodies had to be consulted by the administrative or supervisory board on such matters. Under the latest draft, these authorization and consultation rights are now at the discretion of the member state.

The Commission's proposals on the involvement of workers in their companies have retreated from an initial insistence upon worker directors and obligatory two-tier board structures. And the latest drafts of the Fifth Company Law directive and the ECS proposal are apparently less detailed and prescriptive than their precursors. That being said, such matters as closures and transfers, together with management actions likely to have serious consequences for employees' interests, are of course covered either by pre-social charter legislation or by the revised collective redundancies directive and the legislation on European Works Councils. The proposals discussed here cannot be considered in isolation: they are part and parcel of a wider agenda governing worker participation (see Section 2.7).

2.5. The Treaty on European Union

The institutional machinery and 'competence' of the Community is subject to periodic review, based on the work of intergovernmental conferences. The proposals of the conference are discussed by the European Council (of heads of state) who decide on the final form of the amendments to be made to the treaties establishing the common market. Member states have then individually to ratify the decisions before they can take effect.

On 9–10 December 1991, the European Council met at Maastricht in the Netherlands following one such review and reached agreement on a Treaty on European Union (see Foreign and Commonwealth Office, 1992). The new Treaty provides an expanded menu of goals and policies for what is termed the 'European Union'. It does not replace the existing social provisions of the Treaty of Rome, as amended by the Single European Act – namely, Articles 117 to 122 (see Appendix 2). However, it extends Community competence into new areas of social law, in particular with regard to education and training (Articles 126 and 127), and economic and social cohesion (including the Cohesion Fund – Article 130D).

The Treaty also gives the European Parliament (EP) new powers. Increases in the power of the EP are important because it tends to take an interventionist stance. For example, the EP has argued for a directive on minimum wages instead of a mere opinion (see item 4 of Table 2.2). In the first place, the Commission as a whole cannot take office without the EP's vote of approval. The European Parliament is also given the power to request the Commission to draw up a proposal and, if supported by 25% of its members, it can set up a commission of inquiry into 'maladministration in the implementation of Community law'.

A further power for the EP arises out of the new 'codecision' procedure for deciding on Community legislation (Article 189B). The codecision procedure builds on the 'cooperation' procedure introduced by the Single European Act for social measures under Article 118A. Under the cooperation procedure (now Article 189C), the Council adopts a 'common position' on a proposal by qualified majority which the EP can amend at a 'second reading'. There is a penalty for Council if it does not accept the EP amendments, since then it may only accept the proposal by unanimity.[22] However, under the new codecision procedure, if the EP rejects the common position at its second reading the draft legislation must be dropped. If the EP wishes instead to amend the proposals and the Council fails to accept the amended text then a conciliation process involving a Conciliation Committee – made up 50:50 of Council members and EP representatives – is activated to agree a joint proposal. At each point in this third stage the EP in effect has a veto right. This increase in the power of the EP to oppose is a radical new departure. That said, the codecision procedure is currently limited to less controversial issues: education and training (Articles 126 and 127), movement of workers (Article 49), recognition of qualifications (Article 57), and measures having as their object the establishment and functioning of the common market (Article 100A).

In addition to increasing the power of the EP, the new Treaty also has appended to it the Protocol on Social Policy, containing the famous Agreement on Social Policy. The Protocol, which is signed by all 12 (now 15) member states, notes the intention of 11 (now 14) of their number to 'continue along the path laid down in the December 1989 Social Charter', and authorizes them to use the machinery of the Community to implement the Agreement on Social Policy. It is the Agreement on Social Policy which is commonly referred to as the 'social chapter'. This is reproduced in Appendix 4.

The term 'social chapter' was initially applied to the amendments proposed by the intergovernmental conference by way of replacing the social provisions (Articles 117–122) of the Treaty of Rome. However, the UK refused to countenance the major extension of Community competence that such amendments implied. To save the Treaty, the existing social provisions were retained but at the same time the amendments were annexed to the Protocol on Social Policy.

The effect of the social chapter is that there are now two sets of rules governing social policy. First, there is what we may describe as the traditional route, whereby proposed measures are brought before all 12 (now 15) member states using the unchanged social provisions of the Treaty of Rome as amended by the Single European Act. Second, there is the alternative procedure, the social chapter route, which can be followed by 11 (now 14) of the member states according to the Agreement on Social Policy. This route specifically excludes the UK from the decision-making process – but not from its effects, as we shall see.

The social chapter makes two fundamental changes to facilitate the passage of social legislation. First, it accords the 'social dialogue' an enhanced role in the formulation of social policy. This aspect is covered in the next section. Second, it increases the number of areas in which qualified majority voting is permitted. Qualified majority voting (44 (now 52) out of 66 (now 77) votes in the reduced Council of 11 (now 14) member states) will now be followed in five areas: improvements in the working environment to protect workers' health and safety; working conditions; information and consultation rights of workers; gender equality; and, the integration of persons excluded from the labour market. Hitherto, as we have seen, passage of such measures typically required unanimity – with the notable exception of health and safety under Article 118A. The Commission was thus forced to be 'creative' in its use of Article 118A.

The effect of introducing majority voting in these five areas is that controversial social charter measures such as the proposal on European Works Councils (item 25 in Table 2.1) need no longer be subject to veto from any single member state. Indeed, the Commission initiated the new procedure immediately following ratification of the Treaty on European Union on 1 November 1993. Having consulted with the social partners (see below), a draft directive on the subject of transnational works councils was submitted to an 11 member state Council (i.e. excluding the UK), and after a further iteration was adopted in September.

Under the social chapter unanimity will continue to apply in five defined areas, including matters of employee representation and codetermination, social security, and dismissals protection. (Nevertheless, with the exclusion of the British, such unanimity will be easier to attain. Even if the past positions of the member states are not a reliable guide to the future – in the sense that other governments were in the past able to hide behind a British veto (Lange, 1992) – there is undoubtedly closer institutional uniformity (see Wells, 1993) and ideological alignment among the 11/14.) Note, however, that the social chapter specifically excludes legislation on pay, the right to strike or lockout, and the right of association – these matters will have to continue to be processed via the traditional route.

2.6. Social Dialogue

The 'social dialogue' at European level consists of organised consultations between the Commission and recognized representatives of workers and employers, the 'social partners'. The role of such a social dialogue in formulating labour policy has developed over the years, culminating in the quasi-legislative role envisaged for the social partners in the social chapter. We now consider these developments.

The original chapter dealing with social provisions in the Treaty of Rome provided for the Commission to 'arrange consultations' when pursuing matters relating to labour law and working conditions (see Appendix 1). The consultative body set up in the Treaty was the Economic and Social Committee (ESC). This body is made up from 'representatives of producers, farmers, carriers, workers, dealers, craftsmen, professional occupations, and representatives of the general public' (Article 193). Its members are appointed by the Council from lists submitted by the member states. The members are required to be independent, and cannot be bound by mandatory instructions. This requirement has prevented the ESC from becoming the forum for organized lobby groups.

Over time, however, a more corporatist form of consultation, with organized lobby groups representing business and trade union interests – the 'social partners' – has gained in prominence. The main representative organizations involved here have been the Union of Industrial and Employers' Confederations of Europe (UNICE), the European Centre of Public Enterprises (CEEP), and the European Trade Union Confederation (ETUC). Of course, such groups have always been consulted: prior to the Treaty of Rome, there was the mixed (joint) committee for the harmonization of working conditions in the iron and steel industry, dating from December 1954 (Lemke, 1988). And similar joint committees have also long been established in the coal (1955) and agricultural sectors (1963), and for vocational training (1963). In addition, in 1971 a standing committee on employment was set up, comprising the Commission, the ministers of social affairs of the member states, and the two sides of industry.

More recently, as we have noted, the concept of an organized 'social dialogue' has been written into the Treaty of Rome. The movement to incorporate the social partners into government can be seen to date from the election of Jacques Delors as President of the Commission in January 1985. In November of that year Jacques Delors organized a summit meeting of UNICE, CEEP, and the ETUC at the Val Duchesse Château near Brussels. This meeting resulted in the establishment of joint working groups of the social partners on macroeconomics and also on new technologies. The working groups drew up joint opinions – but not collective agreements. The Val Duchesse meeting also presaged the inclusion in the Single European Act of Article 118B which committed the Commission to develop the dialogue between the two sides of industry at European level so that 'relations based on agreement' might emerge if the parties wished.

The concept of social dialogue gained a certain momentum from the social charter, which recognized that 'collective agreements' provide a means of implementing the fundamental social rights of workers (see item 27 in Appendix 3). A number of the directives subsequently issued under the aegis of the social charter duly provided the option of implementation by collective agreement rather than member state legislation.

The very number and reach of these social charter mandates, and the threat of wider Community competence in the area of social policy seem to have spurred the employer side to look more favourably on the social dialogue process, their hope being that collective agreements resulting therefrom would be less prescriptive than legislative mandates. Thus, in October 1991, UNICE, CEEP and the ETUC issued jointly agreed proposals on the future of the social dialogue to the intergovernmental conference working on the form of the new Treaty on European Union. In these proposals they agreed formally to strengthen the role of collective bargaining in the framing of social policy by (a) requiring that the Commission consult the social partners when preparing proposals in the social policy field, and (b) allowing for Community-level collective agreements to substitute for legislation.

The social partners' proposals were incorporated almost in their entirety into the Treaty on European Union as Articles 3 (consultation) and 4 (Community-level agreements) of the Agreement on Social Policy (see Appendix 4). In the words of Zygmunt Tyskiewicz, then Secretary-General of UNICE, the obligation of the Commission to consult the social partners on proposals in the social field 'is a legal guarantee'; and the social partners have the right to say to the Commission, 'stop legislating, we are going to negotiate' (*Social Europe*, 1992: 20).

The social chapter's new consultation procedures can be illustrated by the very different cases of the European Works Council (EWC) directive (item 25 of Table 2.1) and the Commission's more recent consultation on parental leave (see Table 2.4). Beginning with the former, in response to a British veto, renewed discussion on EWC-type bodies was initiated by the Commission under the social chapter procedure in November 1993. In the first stage of consultation (see Article 3(2) of the Agreement reproduced in Appendix 4), the social partners were consulted as to possible future policy in this area. In the second stage (Article 3(3)), having determined there was a need for Community action, the Commission put forward a proposal based on the pre-existing EWC directive. The social partners were unable to agree on a basis for their own European-level agreement – the ETUC arguing that a directive would be more favourable to workers' rights than a collectively bargained agreement (*EIRR*, 1994: 3). This led the Commission to proceed with draft legislation on its own. As noted in Table 2.1, the Commission's new proposals were duly adopted by Council on 22 September 1995.

Unlike the EWC proposals, the social partners (UNICE, CEEP and ETUC) were able to reach a draft framework agreement – the first of its kind – on the issue of parental leave. In February 1995, the Commission revisited its abortive 1983 proposals on parental leave, beginning the first stage of consultation with management and labour on the possible direction and scope of Community action in this area. At the second stage of consultation, the social partners announced their intention to negotiate, and requested that the legislative process be suspended. The parties arrived at a draft framework agreement in just 4 months (9 months are allowed for in the Agreement on Social Policy, unless the Commission agrees to more). The terms of the agreement are highlighted in Table 2.4 – but suffice it to say here that the agreement establishes the right to parental leave of at least 3 months until children reach a given age up to 8 years.

The framework agreement on parental leave is a far cry from the anodyne joint opinions issued by the social partners in the years following Val Duchesse, and its negotiation seems to have settled some concerns about their ability to deliver. That said, there remain concerns about the representativeness of the organizations, and already 'outsider' organizations on both the employer and union sides (respectively *EuroCommerce*, and the *Confédération Européene des Cadres*) have disputed the status of the agreement. Apart from the representativeness argument, other uncertainties concern potential contradictions in the Agreement on Social Policy – for example matters such as pay, the right of association, and the right to strike cannot be enforced by a Council Decision (see Article 4(2) of the Agreement).[23] Nevertheless, the new Treaty's requirement that the social partners be consulted by the Commission over labour matters, and the ability to implement agreements reached at European level through Council decisions will shape social policy in the Community and improve the prospects for European-level collective bargaining.

2.7. Current and Future Social Policy

As we have seen, the practical effect of the social chapter is that there are now two sets of rules governing social policy in the new European Union, a two-track social Europe as it were. In a speech before the UK Trades Union Congress in September 1993, the new social affairs Commissioner, Padraig Flynn, announced that the Commission would 'exploit to the full the possibilities offered by the social chapter of the Maastricht Treaty', attempting to do so 'with the active cooperation of all twelve member states' (*EIRR*, 1993: 2). This seems at odds with the exclusion of the UK from the social chapter. However, British employers with substantial operations in the Community will automatically be subject to legislation agreed to by the 11. Moreover, British unions have already announced their intention to incorporate the precepts of the social chapter into their collective agreements (*Financial Times*, 1991). The UK's clearly less onerous labour laws might also succumb to challenge at the hands of the European Court of Justice on the grounds that they convey an 'unfair advantage' and thereby infringe single market competition rules. Thus, to the extent that the UK will be unable to insulate its domestic procedures from rules agreed to by the other member states, one can see that the implicit threat to use the social chapter route may lead the British to accede to more far-reaching mandates than hitherto.

Subsequently it became crystal clear that, although the Community had a strong desire to proceed as 12 wherever possible, that desire could not be used as an excuse for inertia. Indeed, a statement to this effect is contained in the Commission White Paper on Social Policy of July 1994 (Commission, 1994).

The White Paper represents the Commission's blueprint for social policy for the period 1995–99, and follows on its consultative Green Paper of November 1993 (Commission, 1993d) outlining future developments now that the social charter action programme was nearing its 'natural end'. On the face of it, the White Paper is a very different animal from the social charter in that its proposals seem less founded on legislative action. This may in part be explained by the influence of an earlier White Paper on Growth, Competitiveness and Employment (Commission, 1993a) issued in December 1993, which was much preoccupied with the problems of rising European unemployment and reduced competitiveness. The White Paper on social policy thus lacks the directness of the social charter by reason of a more pressing set of economic constraints than hitherto. The document also notes that since a 'solid base' of Community legislation is now in place as a result of the social charter action programme, there was less need for comprehensive legislation. At face value, then, the emphasis seems one of consolidation.

The document does, however, offer a number of concrete proposals dealing with training, the labour market, equal opportunities, social protection, and labour standards. In the latter area it proposes to examine unadopted proposals on employee participation in the light of the EWC directive, measures on posted workers and atypical work in the event of non-adoption of the existing draft directives, a new directive on working time in those sectors excluded from the 1993 working time directive, and a set of key features of the scheduled fourth health and safety action programme.

This brings us finally to the Community's new medium-term social action programme (Commission, 1995) pursuant to the White Paper on social policy. The programme echoes the White Paper in emphasizing the role of the Commission as a catalyst to promote concerted action on a transnational basis, and makes great play of (new) analysis and research functions to facilitate the capacity to address social issues. The programme identifies 'the further development of a common framework of minimum social standards' as a priority, and contains several potential legislative initiatives, almost all of which are based on consultation with the social partners (and hence to be processed via the Agreement on Social Policy). At the same time, the Action Programme withdraws the long-standing Vredeling proposals on procedures for informing and consulting workers, the atypical worker directive(s), and of course the original EWC proposal now superseded by the framework agreement between the social partners.

An interesting feature of the programme is the emphasis on application of Community law. In particular, not only will all future directives require implementation reports by member states, but the latter will also have to impose meaningful sanctions against malfeasance. Existing Community law for its part will have to be systematized, and specific examples of measures to be consolidated and updated are provided.

Progress has already been made on a number of potential legislative proposals, two of which – covering atypical workers and worker participation – are identified in Table 2.4. The table also contains information on the content and status of several

Table 2.4. Current Labour Policy Initiatives

Initiative	Content	Status
Agreement for a binding instrument on parental leave and leave for family reasons.	The agreement aims to assist men and women in meeting their family and occupational obligations. Special mention is made of encouraging men to take parental leave so as to assume an equal share of family responsibilities Parental leave is 3 months, to be taken until a given age up to 8 years to be defined by member states and/or social partners. It is not to be transferable between spouses. Job rights to be maintained intact during the leave period. Qualifying length of service is not to be longer than 1 year. The agreement makes no specific reference to income during parental leave, which is to be decided at national level. Once the Council Decision is made, member states will have 2 years to bring in the necessary laws, or to ensure that the social partners establish the necessary measures by way of collective agreement.	Initial proposal dates from November 1983. It has now been processed via the Agreement on Social Policy, with final agreement between social partners in December 1995. It is to be enforced by a binding Council Decision.
Proposal for a directive amending the 1977 directive on worker rights in transfer of undertakings (*OJ* C274 of 1.10.94).	The proposal stems in part from the social charter which targeted the need for information, consultation and participation with respect to restructuring operations affecting employment. The aim is to update the 1977 'acquired rights' directive in the light of ECJ case law, so as to clarify the concept of a transfer, and to ensure that the measure does not prejudice the survival of insolvent undertakings. The aim is to ensure that the transferer retains obligations up to the date of the transfer, after which they become the transferee's responsibility. Also, the transferee has to continue to respect any collective agreement, and dismissals are to be permitted only for economic and technical reasons. Representatives of employees have to be informed and consulted. Undertakings employing less than 50 can be excluded.	The proposal was submitted by the Commission in September 1994, and is currently under discussion in Council.
Proposal for a Council directive amending directive 86/378/EEC on the implementation of the principle of equal treatment for men and women in occupational social security schemes (*OJ* C218 of 23.8.95).	The proposal is based on Articles 119 (equal treatment) and 100 (approximation of laws), and arises out of the *Barber* judgement that pensions also constitute pay. The proposed amendment means that any company pension schemes must respect the principle of equal treatment for men and women as from 17 May 1990 (the date of the *Barber* ruling).	Submitted to Council June 1995, and under discussion.

Table 2.4. *(continued)*

Initiative	Content	Status
Consultation on reversal of the burden of proof in equality cases.	Initial (1988) draft directive sought to modify the burden of proof in sex discrimination cases by providing for a presumption of discrimination. That is, once the plaintiff shows a series of facts which would, if not rebutted, amount to direct or indirect discrimination, the burden of proof switches to the respondent. (Indirect discrimination is said to exist where a practice simply has disproportionate effects on a particular group; motive is irrelevant.)	The initial proposal for a directive dates from May 1988. It is now being processed via the Agreement on Social Policy: the first stage of consultation began in July 1995.
Consultation on atypical workers (see items 23 and 24 of Table 2.1).	The proposed directives here have been withdrawn and replaced by a Commission initiative on flexibility in working time and security for workers. This is to be processed via the Agreement on Social Policy.	First stage consultations with the social partners commenced in September 1995
Communication on worker information and consultation (see *EIRR*, 1995).	The Commission states that it is committed to the need to ensure adequate safeguards at European level for the information and consultation of employees. The Commission is in favour of using the European Works Councils directive as a model for national information and consultation rules. All countries would have to adopt this approach, so the UK opt-out would be anomalous and give it an 'unfair advantage' (*EIRR*, 1995: 19). The participation provisions for the European Company Statute and the European Associations, Cooperatives and Mutual Societies would be dropped so these proposals could go forward (but an European Company could not be set up in the UK). The participation provisions of Vredeling and the Fifth Company Statute would also be withdrawn, the goal being to deliver a framework for national-level information and consultation of employees.	Communication published 15 November 1995, and sent to the social partners perhaps as the first stage of formal consultation in terms of Article 3(2) of the Agreement on Social Policy.

more immediate measures dealing with transfer of undertakings, equal treatment of men and women in occupational pensions, the reversal of the burden of proof in equality cases, and a Community decision formalizing the parental leave agreement reached by the social partners.

Of the proposals listed in Table 2.4, only those on occupational pensions, and on worker rights in transfer of undertakings are being processed via the traditional route involving all member states, and hence will impact on the UK directly. The directive on transfer of undertakings has already been particularly troublesome for the UK, since both this directive and that on redundancies (see item 4 of Table 2.1) require consultation with worker representatives. The UK has had to bring in a law to provide for the election of such representatives.[24]

From Table 2.4 it is clear that there is considerable scope for draft legislation in 1996, and this is underscored by the upcoming European Forum on social policy that will examine the potential for extending the social charter. In addition, the Commission is to issue a White Paper on working time that covers the sectors excluded from the 1993 directive on working hours (item 3 of Table 2.1), as well as a Green Paper on illegal work, and is to begin consultations with the social partners on individual dismissals.

In short, it would be premature to conclude either from the lull in legislative activity since the end of the social charter or the rather discursive tone of the new medium-term social action programme that the trend towards regulation has been abandoned or even substantially modified. The current medium-term social action programme is a 'rolling' action plan specifically designed to be added to as circumstances change and to meet emerging needs. The Commission has maximized its degrees of freedom precisely at the time when the issue of Community competence is again under active review with the deliberations of the 1996 intergovernmental conference on changes to the treaties establishing the Community. Qualitative differences between the current action programme and its 1989 precursor do include greater consultation and a seemingly elevated role for benefit–cost concepts in formulating policy, but – to repeat – there are few signs to suggest a sea change in the Commission's attitude, or that of its constituencies, to labour market regulation. The scene thus seems set for an active but less transparent social policy in the remaining years of the current medium-term social action programme.

2.8. Summary

We have seen that the pursuit of an active social policy at Community level is not a phenomenon dating from the late 1980s and the social charter. Rather, its lineage extends back more than two decades. The basis of the social charter itself is clearly traceable to the Commission's 1973 Social Action Plan. Now that the social charter is virtually a *fait accompli*, the second stage of social policy may be said to have come to an end. Its protracted nature is testimony to the Commission's persistence in the face of adversity; in particular, the absence of a clear treaty basis for most of its initiatives, and a trenchant opponent in the form of an equally determined but ultimately shorter-lived Thatcher administration.

Once the Commission secured a firmer treaty basis for its measures under the social chapter of the new Treaty on European Union, it could be expected to push ahead with its long-standing social agenda. The self-exclusion of the UK has removed one impediment in this regard. We have seen that after a relative lull in Community initiatives, the Commission is indeed now pressing ahead with its new 'rolling' action programme.

Notes

1 See, respectively, Council Directive of 17 February 1975 on the approximation of the laws of the member states relating to collective redundancies, 75/129/EEC (*OJ* L48 of 22.2.75);

Council Directive of 14 February 1977 on the approximation of the laws of the member states relating to the safeguarding of employees' rights in the event of transfer, of undertakings, businesses or parts of businesses, 77/187/EEC (*OJ* L61 of 5.3.77); Council Directive of 20 October 1980 on the approximation of the laws of the member states relating to the protection of employees in the event of the insolvency of their employer, 80/987/EEC (*OJ* L283 of 28.10.80). On the extent of the departure of these instruments from existing practice, see Teague (1989: 60) and Hepple (1982).

2 See Council Directive of 10 February 1975 on the approximation of laws of the member states relating to the application of the principle of equal pay for men and women, 75/117/EEC (*OJ* L45 of 19.2.75).

3 See Council Directive of 9 February 1976 on the implementation of the principle of equal treatment for men and women as regards access to employment, vocational training and promotion, and working conditions, 76/207/EEC (*OJ* L39 of 14.2.76).

4 See Council Directive of 19 December 1978 on the progressive implementation of the principle of equal treatment for men and women in matters of social security, 79/7/EEC (*OJ* L6 of 10.1.79).

5 Council Directive of 27 November 1980 on the protection of workers from the risks related to chemical, physical and biological agents at work, 80/1107/EEC (*OJ* L327 of 3.12.80).

6 See Council Directive of 12 June 1989 on the introduction of measures to encourage improvements in the safety and health of workers at work, 89/391/EEC (*OJ* L160 of 26.6.90).

7 See Proposal for a Council Directive on procedures for informing and consulting employees of undertakings with complex structures, in particular transnational undertakings, COM (80) 423 final, Brussels : Commission of the European Communities (CEC), 1980.

8 See Amended proposal for a Council Directive on procedures for informing and consulting employees, COM (83) 292 final/2, Brussels, CEC, 1983.

9 See Proposal for a Council Regulation embodying a statute for a European Company (*OJ* C124 of 10.10.70).

10 See Amended proposal for a Fifth Directive founded on Article 54(3)(g) of the EEC Treaty concerning the structure of public limited companies and the power and obligations of their organs (*OJ* C240 of 9.9.83). On the initial worker–director-only draft, see *OJ* C7 of 28.1.72.

11 See Proposal for a Council Directive on voluntary part-time work (*OJ* C62 of 12.3.82); Amended proposal for a Council Directive on voluntary part-time work (*OJ* C18 of 22.1.83).

12 See Proposal for a Council Directive concerning the supply of workers by temporary employment business and fixed duration contracts of employment (*OJ* C128 of 19.5.82); Amendments to the proposal for a Council Directive concerning the supply of workers by temporary employment business and fixed duration contracts of employment (*OJ* C133 of 21.5.84).

13 Proposal for Council Directive on parental leave and leave for family reasons (*OJ* C353 of 9.12.83); Amended proposal for a Council Directive on parental leave and leave for family reasons (*OJ* C316 of 27.11.84).

14 The European Social Charter (ESC), which is not to be confused with its Community counterpart, is an international agreement drawn up by the Council of Europe in 1965. All 15 Member States of the EC plus eight other European nations are members of the Council of Europe. The ECS complements the European Convention of Human Rights but does not have the same legally binding status; parties to the ESC have only to accept a minimum number of its commitments.

15 Of these, 23 were binding instruments in the form of regulations, decisions, and directives. Of the remaining initiatives there were five recommendations, five communications, five unspecified instruments and nine miscellaneous measures.

16 Admittedly Article 100A of the Single European Act (see Appendix 2), covering measures that have as their object 'the establishment and functioning of the internal market', also

permits majority voting. But this article specifically excludes measures relating to the 'rights and interests of employed persons', which would explain why just one measure – item 24 on atypical workers – was advanced under this Treaty basis.

17 As for private sector provision of childcare, only 3% of UK firms (but 9% of local authorities) in the Institute of Manpower Studies Survey provide creche facilities (Metcalfe, 1990: 33). This is similar to the US figure of 2% (*Employment in Europe*, 1990: 98).

18 In 1992 the structural funds were spending about ECU 15 billion annually, and Community initiative programmes are given in the budget as costing about ECU 0.5 billion (*Official Journal*, 1993: 622–23, 658), or about 3% of structural fund spending.

19 On the separate issue of monitoring member states' training efforts and the vexed question of 'additionality', see Addison and Siebert (1994b).

20 Amended proposal for a Council Regulation on the statute for a European company (*OJ* C176 of 8.7.91); Amended proposal for a Council Directive complementing the statute for a European company with regard to the involvement of employees in the European company (*OJ* C138 of 29.5.91).

21 The latest draft of the proposed legislation – amended proposal for a Fifth Directive founded on Article 54(3)(g) of the EEC Treaty concerning the structure of public limited companies and the powers and obligations of their organs – is contained in Department of Trade and Industry (1990).

22 At the second reading the EP has three options:
    (1) to approve the Council position, in which case the Council adopts the act;
    (2) to reject the position by a majority, in which case the Council can only act by unanimity;
    (3) to accept the position by a majority, in which case there are four options for Council which can: (i) adopt the original Commission proposal by a qualified majority; (ii) adopt EP amendments not approved by the Commission by unanimity; (iii) amend the proposal by unanimity; (iv) fail to act.

23 For an elaboration of the arguments on the interpretation of the Agreement, see Hepple (1993: 24).

24 The ECJ has stated that the UK infringes these directives because it has no system of worker representation outside unionized firms. The UK has had to introduce the Collective Redundancies and Transfer of Undertakings (Protection of Employment) (Amendment) Regulations of 1995 to comply with this ruling. Companies must now institute elections for worker representatives, and consult them if more than 20 redundancies are declared – though there is no provision for permanent worker representatives (see *EIRR*, 1996).

References

Addison, J. T. and Siebert, W. S. (1991). 'The Social Charter of the European Community: Evolution and Controversies'. *Industrial and Labor Relations Review*, 44 (July): 597–625.

Addison, J. T. and Siebert, W. S. (1994a). 'Recent Developments in Social Policy in the New European Union'. *Industrial and Labor Relations Review*, 48 (October): 5–27.

Addison, J. T. and Siebert, W. S. (1994b). 'Vocational Training and the European Community'. *Oxford Economic Papers*, 46 (October): 696–724.

BMDF (1993). *The Maastricht Treaty in Perspective: Consolidated Treaty on European Union*. Stroud, Gloucs: British Management Data Foundation.

Commission (1974). 'Social Action Programme'. *Bulletin of the European Communities*, Supplement 2/74: 11–36. Brussels: Commission of the European Communities (CEC).

Commission (1987a). *Report of the Fellow to the Council Resolution of 22 December on an Action Programme for Employment Growth*. COM (87) 229 final. Brussels: CEC.

Commission (1987b). *Report on Social Developments*. Brussels: CEC.

Commission (1989a). *Community Charter of the Fundamental Social Rights of Worker*. COM (89) 471 final. Brussels: CEC.

Commission (1989b). *Communication from the Commission Concerning Its Action Programme Relating to the Implementation of the Community Charter of Basic Social Rights for Workers*. COM (89) 568 final. Brussels: CEC.

Commission (1990). *Explanatory Memorandum on the Proposal for Directives Concerning Certain Employment Relationships*. COM (90) 228 final. Brussels: CEC.

Commission (1991). *Childcare Recommendation. Explanatory Memorandum*. Mimeo. Brussels: CEC, 27 May.

Commission (1992a). *From the Single Act to Maastricht and Beyond – The Means to Match Our Ambitions*. COM (92) 2000 final. Brussels: CEC, 11 February.

Commission (1992b). *The Community's Finances Between Now and 1997*. Communication from the Commission. COM (92) 2001 final. Brussels: CEC, 10 March.

Commission (1992c). *Amended Proposal for a Council Recommendation Concerning the Promotion of Employee Participation in Profits and Enterprise Results*. COM (92) 193 final of 5.5.92. Brussels: CEC.

Commission (1992d). *Community Structural Policies – Assessment and Outlook*. Communication from the Commission. COM (92) 84 final. Brussels: CEC, 18 March.

Commission (1993a). *Growth, Competitiveness, Employment – The Challenges and Ways Forward into the 21st Century*. COM (93) 700 final. Brussels: CEC.

Commission (1993b). *The Community's Structural Fund Operations 1994–99*. COM (93) 67 final-SYN 455. Brussels: CEC, 10 March.

Commission (1993c). *The Future of Community Initiatives Under the Structural Funds*. COM (93) 282 final. Brussels: CEC, 16 June.

Commission (1993d). *European Social Policy: Options for the Union*. COM (93) 551 of 17.11.93. Brussels: CEC.

Commission (1994a). *European Social Policy: A Way Forward for the Union*. COM (94) 333. Brussels: CEC, 27 July.

Commission (1995). *Medium Term Social Action Programme 1995–1997*. COM (95) 134 of 21.4.95. Brussels: CEC.

Dahrendorf, R., Aubry, M., Fraser, D., Isaac, J., Johansson, L., Kobayashi, Y. and O'Sullivan, H. (1986). *Labour Market Flexibility*. Paris: Organisation for Economic Co-operation and Development.

Department of Trade and Industry (1990). *Amended Proposal for a Fifth Directive on the Harmonization of Company Law in the Community*. London: DTI, January.

EIRR (1989a). 'Time Off for Family Reasons: Part One, Maternity/Paternity Leave'. *European Industrial Relations Review* **186** (August): 13–19.

EIRR (1989b). 'Time Off for Family Responsibilities: Part Two'. *European Industrial Relations Review*, **189** (October): 17–22.

EIRR (1990). 'Community Law: Current State of Play'. *European Industrial Relations Review*, **201** (October): 24–30.

EIRR (1993). 'Commission: Community-Wide Social Pact?' *European Industrial Relations Review*, **237** (October): 2.

EIRR (1994). 'Social Partners: Information and Consultation Talks Fail'. *European Industrial Relations Review*, **243** (April): 3.

EIRR (1995). 'Commission Relaunches Debate on Information and Consultation', *European Industrial Relations Review*, **263** (December): 18–20.

EIRR (1996). 'New Consultation Rights for Employee Representatives'. *European Industrial Relations Review*, **264** (January): 28–31.

Emerson, M. 1987. 'Regulation or Deregulation of the Labour Market: Policy Regimes for the Recruitment and Dismissal of Employees in the Industrialised Countries'. *Internal Paper No. 55*. Brussels: CEC.

Employment in Europe (1990). Brussels: CEC.

Financial Times (1991). 'Astonishing Compromise Threatens to Create a Brussels Benefit for the Legal Fraternity'. London: *Financial Times*, 12 December.

Financial Times (1996). 'European Court Rejects Working Week Challenge'. London: *Financial Times*, 13 March.

Foreign and Commonwealth Office (1972). *Treaty Establishing the European Economic Community*. London: HMSO, Cmnd 4864.

Foreign and Commonwealth Office (1988). *Single European Act*. London: HMSO, Cm 372.

Foreign and Commonwealth Office (1992). *Treaty on European Union*. London: HMSO, Cm 1934.

Hepple, B. (1982). 'The Transfer of Undertakings (Protection of Employment) Regulations'. *Industrial Law Journal*, **11** (March): 29–40.

Hepple, B. (1993). *European Social Dialogue – Alibi or Opportunity?* London: Institute for Employment Rights.

IDS (1993a). 'Equitable Wages and Minimum Pay Setting'. *Incomes Data Services European Report*, No. 383, November: 9–16.

IDS (1993b). 'European Summit'. *Incomes Data Services European Report*, No. 373, January, 3–4.

Industrial Relations Services (1990a). *Non-standard Forms of Employment in Europe. EIRR* Report No. 3. London: Eclipse Publications.

Industrial Relations Services (1990b) .*Employee Participation in Europe. EIRR* Report No. 4. London: Eclipse Publications.

Lange, P. (1992). 'Maastricht and the Social Protocol: Why Did They Do It?' *Politics and Society*, **21** (March): 5–36.

Lemke, H. (1988). *Employees' Organizations and their Contribution to the Development of Vocational Training Policy in the European Community*. Berlin: CEDEFOP.

Mazey, S. (1988). 'European Community Action on Behalf of Women: The Limits of Regulation'. *Journal of Common Market Studies*, **27** (September): 63–84.

Metcalfe, H. (1990). *Retaining Women Employees*, University of Sussex IMS Report 190. Sussex: Institute of Manpower Studies.

Official Journal (1993). 'The Community's Programme in 1993 and 1994'. *OJ* C125 of 6.5.93.

Roberts, B. C. (1989). 'The Social Dimension of European Labour Markets'. In C. J. Veljanowski (ed.), *Whose Europe?* pp. 39–49. London: Institute of Economic Affairs.

Sisson, K., Waddington, J. and Whitston, C. (1991). 'Company Size in the European Community'. *Human Resources Management*, **30** (Autumn): 94–109.

Social Europe (1990). *Social Europe*, No. 1/90. Brussels: CEC.

Social Europe (1992). 'The 1991 Social Year'. *Social Europe*, No. 2/92. Brussels: CEC.

Social Europe (1995). 'Two Years of Community Social Policy: July 1993–June 1995'. *Social Europe*, No. 3/94. Brussels: CEC.

Teague, P. (1989). *The European Community: The Social Dimension – Labour Market Policies for 1992*. London: Kogan Page.

Walters, D. R. (1990). *Worker Participation in Health and Safety – A European Comparison*. London: Institute for Employment Rights.

Wells, W. (1993). 'Does the Structure of Employment Legislation Affect the Structure of Employment and Unemployment?' Unpublished paper. London: Department of Employment.

Appendix 1: The Social Policy Content of The Treaty of Rome

Chapter 1 – Social Provisions[1]

Article 117

Member States agree upon the need to promote working conditions and an improved standard of living for workers, so as to make possible their harmonization while the improvement is being maintained.

They believe that such a development will ensue not only from the functioning of the common market, which will favour the harmonization of social systems, but also from the procedures provided for in this Treaty and from the approximation of provisions laid down by law, regulation or administrative action.

Article 118

Without prejudice to the other provisions of this Treaty and in conformity with its general objectives, the Commission shall have the task of promoting close cooperation between Member States in the social field, particularly in matters relating to:

- employment
- labour law and working conditions
- basic and advanced vocational training
- social security
- prevention of occupational accidents and diseases
- occupational hygiene
- the right of association and collective bargaining between employers and workers.

To this end, the Commission shall act in close contact with Member States by making studies, delivering opinions and arranging consultations both on problems arising at national level and on those of concern to international organizations.

Before delivering the opinions provided for in this Article, the Commission shall consult the Economic and Social Committee.

Article 119

Each Member State shall during the first stage ensure and subsequently maintain the application of the principle that men and women should receive equal pay for equal work.

For the purpose of this Article, 'pay' means the ordinary basic or minimum wage or salary and any other consideration, whether in cash or in kind, which the worker receives, directly or indirectly, in respect of his employment from his employer.

Equal pay without discrimination based on sex means:

(a) that pay for the same work at piece rates shall be calculated on the basis of the same unit of measurement;
(b) that pay for work at time rates shall be the same for the same job.

---

[1] Note that Chapter 2 of the Treaty (Articles 123–130), dealing with the European Social Fund (ESF) and the European Investment Bank, is also a component of social policy. In particular, the ESF has the task of 'rendering the employment of workers easier'. A convenient source for the Treaty of Rome is Foreign and Commonwealth Office (1972).

Article 120
Member States shall endeavour to maintain the existing equivalence between paid holiday schemes.

Article 121
The Council may, acting unanimously and after consulting the Economic and Social Committee, assign to the Commission tasks in connection with the supplementation of common measures, particularly as regard social security for the migrant workers referred to in Articles 48 to 51.

Article 122
The Commission shall include a separate chapter on social developments within the Community in its annual report to the Assembly [i.e. European Parliament].
The Assembly may invite the Commission to draw up reports on any particular problems concerning social conditions.

Appendix 2: Amended Social Policy Content of the Treaty Establishing the Common Market, Single European Act 1986 (Effective 1 July 1987)[1]

Article 18
The EEC Treaty shall be supplemented by the following provisions:

Article 100A
1. By way of derogation from Article 100 [approximation of laws] and save where otherwise provided in this Treaty, the following provisions shall apply for the achievement of the objectives set out in Article 8A [measures with the aim of progressively establishing the internal market over a period expiring on 31 December, 1992]. The Council shall, acting by a qualified majority on a proposal from the Commission in cooperation with the European Parliament and after consulting the Economic and Social Committee, adopt the measures for the approximation of the provisions laid down by law, regulation or administrative action in Member States which have as their objective the establishing and functioning of the internal market.
2. Paragraph 1 shall not apply to fiscal provisions, to those relating to the free movement of persons nor to those relating to the rights and interests of employed persons.
3. The Commission, in its proposals envisaged in paragraph 1 concerning health, safety, environmental protection and consumer protection, will take as a base a high level of protection.

[...]

---

[1] The SEA also contains a new sub-section IV on Economic and Social Cohesion (Articles 130A through 130E), the aim of which is to reduce disparities between the various regions. Full documentation is contained in Foreign and Commonwealth Office (1988).

Sub-Section III – Social Policy

Article 118A
1. Member States shall pay particular attention to encouraging improvements, especially in the working environment, as regards the health and safety of workers, and shall set as their objective the harmonization of conditions in this area, while maintaining the improvements made.
2. In order to help achieve the objectives laid down in the first paragraph, the Council, acting by a qualified majority on a proposal from the Commissions, in co-operation with the European Parliament and after consulting the Economic and Social Committee shall adopt by means of directives, minimum requirements for gradual implementation, having regard to the conditions and technical rules obtaining in each of the Member States.
Such directives shall avoid imposing administrative, financial and legal constraints in a way which would hold back the creation and development of small and medium-sized undertakings.
3. The provisions adopted pursuant to this Article shall not prevent any Member State from maintaining or introducing more stringent measures for the protection of working conditions compatible with this Treaty.

Article 22
The EEC Treaty shall be supplemented by the following provision:

Article 118B
The Commission shall endeavour to develop the dialogue between management and labour at European level which could, if the two sides consider it desirable, lead to relations based on agreement.

Appendix 3: Titles I and II of the Community Charter of the Fundamental Social Rights of Workers

Title I

Fundamental Social Rights of Workers

Freedom of movement
1. Every worker of the European Community shall have the right to freedom of movement throughout the territory of the Community, subject to restrictions justified on grounds of public order, public safety or public health.
2. The right to freedom of movement shall enable any worker to engage in any occupation or profession in the Community in accordance with the principles of equal treatment as regards access to employment, working conditions and social protection in the host country.
3. The right of freedom of movement shall also imply:

  – harmonization of conditions of residence in all Member States, particularly those concerning family reunification;

- elimination of obstacles arising from the non-recognition of diplomas or equivalent occupational qualifications;
- improvement of the living and working conditions of frontier workers.

Employment and remuneration
4. Every individual shall be free to choose and engage in an occupation according to the regulations governing each occupation.
5. All employment shall be fairly remunerated.
To this effect, in accordance with arrangements applying in each country:

- workers shall be assured of an equitable wage, i.e. a wage sufficient to enable them to have a decent standard of living;
- workers subject to terms of employment other than an open-ended full-time contract shall receive an equitable reference wage;

6. Every individual must be able to have access to public placement services free of charge.

Improvement of living and working conditions
7. The completion of the internal market must lead to an improvement in the living and working conditions of workers in the European Community. This process must result from an approximation of these conditions while the improvement is being maintained, as regards in particular the duration and organization of working time and forms of employment other than open-ended contracts, such as fixed-term contracts, part-time working, temporary work and seasonal work.
The improvement must cover, where necessary, the development of certain aspects of employment regulations such as procedures for collective redundancies and those regarding bankruptcies.
8. Every worker of the European Community shall have a right to a weekly rest period and to annual paid leave, the duration of which must be harmonized in accordance with national practices while the improvement is being maintained.
9. The conditions of employment of every worker of the European Community shall be stipulated in laws, in a collective agreement or in a contract of employment, according to arrangements applying in each country.

Social protection
According to the arrangements applying in each country:
10. Every worker of the European Community shall have a right to adequate social protection and shall, whatever his status and whatever the size of the undertaking in which he is employed, enjoy an adequate level of social security benefits.
Persons who have been unable either to enter or re-enter the labour market and have no means of subsistence must be able to receive sufficient resources and social assistance in keeping with their particular situation.

Freedom of association and collective bargaining
11. Employers and workers of the European Community shall have the right of association in order to constitute professional organizations or trade unions of their choice for the defence of their economic social interests.
Every employer and every worker shall have the freedom to join or not to join such

organizations without any personal or occupational damage being thereby suffered by him.

12. Employers or employers' organizations, on the one hand, and workers' organizations, on the other, shall have the right to negotiate and conclude collective agreements under the conditions laid down by national legislation and practice.

The dialogue between the two sides of industry at European level which must be developed, may, if the parties deem it desirable, result in contractual relations, in particular at inter-occupational and sectoral level.

13. The right to resort to collective action in the event of a conflict of interests shall include the right to strike, subject to the obligations arising under national regulations and collective agreements.

In order to facilitate the settlement of industrial disputes the establishment and utilization at the appropriate levels of conciliation, mediation and arbitration procedures should be encouraged in accordance with national practice.

14. The internal legal order of the Member States shall determine under which conditions and to what extent the rights provided for in Articles 11 to 13 apply to the armed forces, the police and the civil service.

Vocational training

15. Every worker of the European Community must be able to have access to vocational training and to receive such training throughout his working life. In the conditions governing access to such training there may be no discrimination on grounds of nationality.

The competent public authorities, undertakings or the two sides of industry, each within their own sphere of competence, should set up continuing and permanent systems enabling every person to undergo retraining, more especially through leave for training purposes, to improve his skills or to acquire new skills, particularly in the light of technical developments.

Equal treatment for men and women

16. Equal treatment for men and women must be assured. Equal opportunities for men and women must be developed.

To this end, action should be intensified wherever necessary to ensure the implementation of the principle of equality between men and women as regards in particular access to employment, remuneration, working conditions, social protection, education, vocational training and career development.

Measures should also be developed enabling men and women to reconcile their occupational and family obligations.

Information, consultation and participation for workers

17. Information, consultation and participation for workers must be developed along appropriate lines, taking account of the practices in force in the various Member States.

This shall apply especially in companies or groups of companies having establishments or companies in several Member States of the European Community.

18. Such information, consultation and participation must be implemented in due time, particularly in the following cases:

  — when technological changes which, from the point of view or working conditions and work organization, have major implications for the work force are introduced into undertakings;

- in connection with restructuring operations in undertakings or in cases of mergers having an impact on the employment of workers;
- in cases of collective redundancy procedures;
- when transfrontier workers in particular are affected by employment policies pursued by the undertaking where they are employed.

Health protection and safety at the workplace
19. Every worker must enjoy satisfactory health and safety conditions in his working environment. Appropriate measures must be taken in order to achieve further harmonization of conditions in this area while maintaining the improvements made.
The measures shall take account, in particular, of the need for the training, information, consultation and balanced participation of workers as regards the risks incurred and the steps taken to eliminate or reduce them.
The provisions regarding implementation of the internal market shall help to ensure such protection.

Protection of children and adolescents
20. Without prejudice to such rules as may be more favourable to young people, in particular those ensuring their preparation for work through vocational training, and subject to derogations limited to certain light work, the minimum employment age must be lower than the minimum school-leaving age and, in any case, not lower than 15 years.
21. Young people who are in gainful employment must receive equitable remuneration in accordance with national practice.
22. Appropriate measures must be taken to adjust labour regulations applicable to young workers so that their specific needs regarding development, vocational training and access to employment are met.
The duration of work must, in particular, be limited – without it being possible to circumvent this limitation through recourse to overtime – and night work prohibited in the case of workers of under 18 years of age save in the case of certain jobs laid down in national legislation or regulations.
23. Following the end of compulsory education, young people must be entitled to receive initial vocational training of a sufficient duration to enable them to adapt to the requirements of their future working life; for young workers, such training should take place during working hours.

Elderly persons
According to the arrangements applying in each country:
24. Every worker of the European Community must, at the time of retirement, be able to enjoy resources affording him or her a decent standard of living.
25. Every person who has reached retirement age but who is not entitled to a pension or who does not have other means of subsistence, must be entitled to sufficient resources and to medical and social assistance specifically suited to his needs.

Disabled persons
26. All disabled persons, whatever the origin and nature of their disablement, must be entitled to additional concrete measures aimed at improving their social and professional integration.
These measures must concern, in particular, according to the capacities of the

beneficiaries, vocational training, ergonomics, accessibility, mobility, means of transport and housing.

Title II

Implementation of the Charter

27. It is more particularly the responsibility of the Member States, in accordance with the national practices, notably through legislative measures or collective agreements, to guarantee the fundamental social rights in this Charter and to implement the social measures indispensable to the smooth operation of the internal market as part of a strategy of economic and social cohesion.

28. The European Council invites the Commission to submit as soon as possible initiatives which fall within its powers, as provided for in the Treaties, with a view to the adoption of legal instruments for the effective implementation, as and when the internal market is completed, of those rights which come within the Community's area of competence.

29. The Commission shall establish each year, during the last three months, a report on the application of the Charter by the Member States and by the European Community.

30. The report of the Commission shall be forwarded to the European Council, the European Parliament and the Economic and Social Committee.

Appendix 4: Agreement on Social Policy Concluded Between the Member States of the European Community with the Exception of the United Kingdom of Great Britain and Northern Ireland[1]

The undersigned eleven HIGH CONTRACTING PARTIES, that is to say the Kingdom of Belgium, the Kingdom of Denmark, the Federal Republic of Germany, the Hellenic Republic, the Kingdom of Spain, the French Republic, Ireland, the Italian Republic, the Grand Duchy of Luxembourg, the Kingdom of the Netherlands and the Portuguese Republic (hereinafter referred to as 'The Member States'),

WISHING to implement the 1989 Social Charter on the basis of 'acquis communautaire',
CONSIDERING the Protocol on social policy,
HAVE AGREED as follows:

Article 1
The Community and the Member States shall have as their objective the promotion of employment, improved living and working conditions, proper social protection, dialogue between management and labour, the development of human resources with a view to lasting high employment and the combatting of exclusion. To this

---

[1] See Foreign and Commonwealth Office (1992). The Consolidated Treaty of Rome, as amended by the Single European Act and Treaty on European Union is available in BMDF (1993).

end the Community and the Member States shall implement measures which take account of the diverse forms of national practices, in particular in the field of contractual relations, and the need to maintain the competitiveness of the Community economy.

Article 2

1. With a view to achieving the objectives of Article 1, the Community shall support and complement the activities of the Member States in the following fields:

- improvement in particular of the working environment to protect workers' health and safety;
- working conditions;
- the information and consultation of workers;
- equality between men and women with regard to labour market opportunities and treatment at work;
- the integration of persons excluded from the labour market, without prejudice to Article 127 of the Treaty establishing the European Community (hereinafter referred to as 'the Treaty').

2. To this end, the Council may adopt, by means of directives, minimum requirements for gradual implementation, having regard to the conditions and technical rules obtaining in each of the Member States.
Such directives shall avoid imposing administrative, financial and legal constraints in a way which would hold back the creation and development of small and medium-sized undertakings.
The Council shall act in accordance with the procedure referred to in Article 189c of the Treaty after consulting the Economic and Social Committee.
3. However, the Council shall act unanimously on a proposal from the Commission, after consulting the European Parliament and the Economic and Social Committee, in the following areas:

- social security and social protection of workers;
- protection of workers where their employment contract is terminated;
- representation and collective defence of the interests of workers and employers, including co-determination, subject to paragraph 6;
- conditions of employment for third-country nationals legally residing in Community territory;
- financial contributions for promotion of employment and job-creation, without prejudice to the provisions relating to the Social Fund.

4. A Member State may entrust management and labour, at their joint request with the implementation of directives adopted pursuant to paragraphs 2 and 3.
In this case, it shall ensure that, no later than the date on which a directive must be transposed in accordance with Article 189, management and labour have introduced the necessary measures by agreement, the Member State concerned being required to take any necessary measure enabling it at any time to be in a position to guarantee the results imposed by that directive.
5. The provisions adopted pursuant to this Article shall not prevent any Member State from maintaining or introducing more stringent protective measures compatible with the Treaty.

6. The provisions of this Article shall not apply to pay, the right of association, the right to strike or the right to impose lock-outs.

Article 3
1. The Commission shall have the task of promoting the consultation of management and labour at Community level and shall take any relevant measure to facilitate their dialogue by ensuring balanced support for the parties.
2. To this end, before submitting proposals in the social policy field, the Commission shall consult management and labour on the possible direction of Community action.
3. If, after such consultation, the Commission considers Community action advisable, it shall consult management and labour on the content of the envisaged proposal. Management and labour shall forward to the Commission an opinion or, where appropriate, a recommendation.
4. On the occasion of such consultation, management and labour may inform the Commission of their wish to initiate the process provided for in Article 4. The duration of the procedure shall not exceed nine months, unless the management and labour concerned and the Commission decide jointly to extend it.

Article 4
1. Should management and labour so desire, the dialogue between them at Community level may lead to contractual relations, including agreements.
2. Agreements concluded at Community level shall be implemented either in accordance with the procedures and practices specific to management and labour and the Member States, or in matters covered by Article 2, at the joint request of the signatory parties, by a Council decision on a proposal from the Commission.
The Council shall act by qualified majority, except where the agreement in question contains one or more provisions relating to one of the areas referred to in Article 2(3), in which case it shall act unanimously.

Article 5
With a view to achieving the objectives of Article 1 and without prejudice to the other provisions of the Treaty, the Commission shall encourage cooperation between the Member States and facilitate the coordination of their action in all social policy fields under this Agreement.

Article 6
1. Each Member State shall ensure that the principle of equal pay for male and female workers for equal work is applied.
2. For the purpose of this Article, 'pay' means the ordinary basic or minimum wage or salary and any other consideration, whether in case or in kind, which the worker receives directly or indirectly, in respect of his employment, from his employer.
Equal pay without discrimination based on sex means:

   (a) that pay for the same work at piece rates shall be calculated on the basis of the same unit of measurement;
   (b) that pay for work at time rates shall be the same for the same job.

3. This Article shall not prevent any Member State from maintaining or adopting measures providing for specific advantages in order to make it easier for women to pursue a vocational activity or to prevent or compensate for disadvantages in their professional careers.

Article 7
The Commission shall draw up a report each year on progress in achieving the objectives of Article 1, including the demographic situation in the Community. It shall forward the report to the European Parliament, the Council and the Economic and Social Committee.

The European Parliament may invite the Commission to draw up reports on particular problems concerning the social situation.

Declarations

1. Declaration on Article 2(2)
The eleven High Contracting Parties note that in the discussions on Article 2(2) of the Agreement it was agreed that the Community does not intend, in laying down minimum requirements for the protection of the safety and health of employees, to discriminate in a manner unjustified by the circumstances against employees in small and medium-sized undertakings.

2. Declaration on Article 4(2)
The eleven High Contracting Parties declare that the first of the arrangements for application of the agreements between management and labour at Community level – referred to in Article 4(2) – will consist in developing, by collective bargaining according to the rules of each Member State, the content of the agreements, and that consequently this arrangement implies no obligation on the Member States to apply the agreements directly or to work out rules for their transposition, nor any obligation to amend national legislation in force to facilitate their implementation.

3

The Economics of Labour Market Regulation

John T. Addison, C. R. Barrett and W. Stanley Siebert

3.1. Introduction

In this chapter we examine the cases for and against labour market regulation, and then try to assess the possible consequences of the measures proposed by the Commission by examining the impact of job protection regulations already in existence in member states of the Community and other countries.

We begin by outlining the standard competitive model, and then broaden the approach to accommodate the notion of market failure. In the latter context, our main (but not exclusive) focus will be on the role of asymmetric information, a concept increasingly invoked today to justify a variety of mandates. Our discussion of mandates will include equity as well as efficiency considerations, and distinguish in the latter case between actual and potential Pareto improvements. We note parenthetically that the Commission has nowhere presented a systematic theoretical basis for its measures. The arguments that might have been deployed by the Commission in seeking to justify its proposals are presented here.

Having examined the theoretical issues, our attention shifts to the practicalities of mandates. Optimally, of course, we would like to work with direct estimates of the effects of the regulations documented in Chapter 2. Given the vintage of the measures, however, and the limited guidance offered by the Commission's own inquiries into the possible impact of its proposals – its so-called *'fiches d'impact'* – our approach will of necessity be largely indirect. That is, we shall examine cross-national and individual country studies of the employment and other consequences of labour market regulations analogous to those proposed by the Commission.

3.2. Theoretical Observations

The Competitive Model

The standard competitive model views labour markets as not fundamentally different in kind from commodity markets. To be sure, labour markets are more complex:

the wage is just one component of a payment 'bundle' that also includes fringes and a variety of characteristics that come with the job. The characteristics comprise work effort, job security, physical risks, and potential for advancement including training opportunities. Some of these components carry negative compensating wage differentials (for example, job security), others positive (physical risks). Even if, for given worker productivity, the overall size of the package (the 'full wage') cannot exceed a specified amount, the components of the payment bundle are flexible. Thus, the parties can operate on a number of margins. Tradeoffs are available between the various components of the payment package, for example, between wages and risk of injury.

The costs of varying these components differ between firms, causing the tradeoffs to differ. Thus, there is variation in the observed job characteristics offered by firms, with each adapting the characteristics of its payment bundle to secure labour at least at cost. By the same token, workers in maximizing their utility, cannot be expected to value the characteristics of a job equally. The many margins for negotiation referred to above also accommodate worker preferences, with workers choosing among the variety of packages offered by the population of firms.

The market coordinates the worker's demand for job characteristics with the firm's need to obtain the services of labour. Given the heterogeneity of firm costs and worker tastes, a matching or sorting process takes place. For example, workers with risk aversion will gravitate towards firms that can provide stable jobs most cheaply. Wages will still rise with the risk of employment instability, but the gradient is less steep than in the absence of a matching process which extracts the maximum of worker utility from each unit of labour cost.

If we now intrude into this model a mandate that decrees a fixed or minimum level of a given benefit, it follows unambiguously that welfare (as measured by the sum of firms' and workers' surpluses) cannot be increased. Given that firms fulfil an arbitraging function for which they are rewarded by lower costs, the mandate cannot cause the value of payment bundles as evaluated by workers to rise. Firms will already have taken care of any opportunities to improve the value of these packages to their workers.

Matters are different when we broaden the model to accommodate market failure. Mandates may now have beneficial effects on welfare. In investigating this possibility, the concept of a *Pareto improvement* is useful. A Pareto-improving policy is a policy which helps at least one individual while leaving other individuals no worse off. Maintaining freedom of trade, for example, is, in principle, Pareto-improving; voluntary exchange transactions make all participants better off. Most policies, however, have losers as well as gainers, and for such cases an extension of the Pareto criterion to encompass a *potential Pareto improvement* may be used. A potential Pareto improvement is a change which satisfies the 'compensation test', that is, the winners are able fully to compensate the losers and still come out ahead. As a case in point, the removal of a monopolistic restriction is a potential Pareto improvement. The profits of the monopolistic firm fall, but consumers benefit from lower prices, and in the sense indicated the gains of the consumers outweigh the losses of the firm.

Although both actual and potential Pareto improvements increase the total surplus, only actual Pareto improvements will be taken up in private negotiations; the parties concerned are hardly likely to negotiate losses for themselves. Accordingly, the achievement of a potential Pareto improvement requires an external agency, and we would normally expect the losers involved to attempt to block any attempt by the agency to impose a potential Pareto improvement – a 'dog-in-

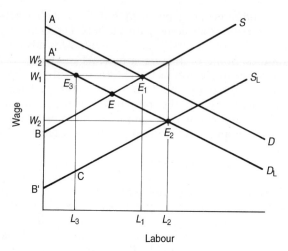

Figure 3.1. The effects of mandates, I.

the-manger' effect. Such dog-in-the-manger effects arising in the context of potential Pareto improvements may provide an obstacle to government mandates.

The impact of a mandate is illustrated in Figure 3.1. Let us suppose that the mandate gives workers the right to a period of paid maternity leave. The equilibrium without the mandate is shown as E_1 in the diagram, with L_1 workers employed at wage W_1. Once the mandate is imposed, this will have costs for firms so that the demand curve will shift downwards from D to D_L. The supply curve will also shift downwards, from S to S_L, by the amount that the workers value the benefit conferred by the mandate. If the workers value the benefit more than it costs firms, the supply curve will shift down more than the demand curve, and the new equilibrium will be at E_2, as illustrated. At E_2, employment is higher (at L_2), the pecuniary wage is lower (W_2) and the full wage (including the workers' valuation of the maternity benefit) is higher (W_2'). Note that had the government imposed a mandate which workers did not value as much as it cost firms, equilibrium employment would fall; in the extreme, where the mandate had no benefits, only costs, equilibrium will be at point E in the diagram.

As Figure 3.1 shows, if the workers value the benefit more than it costs the firm, and wages are flexible, not only does employment and national income increase, but so too does the sum of firms' and workers' surpluses. The initial sum of surpluses triangle is AE_1B. The new triangle is $A'E_2B'$. This is an example of an actual Pareto improvement – everyone is made better off.

If wages are inflexible, the mandate will not be Pareto-improving. Equilibrium with the mandate will be at point E_3 if the wage does not fall. The resulting employment will then be L_3. In this situation, even though those remaining in employment are better off (they have valuable maternity benefits), this is at the expense of the disemployment of marginal workers. The surplus area $A'E_3CB'$ as drawn is now clearly smaller than the original triangle AE_1B, so the mandate serves to reduce overall welfare in the case where wages are inflexible.

Returning to the case of flexible wages, if the mandate increases the sum of firms' and workers' surpluses, the question arises as to why the two sides did not voluntarily negotiate such a contract in the first place. If maternity leave were valued by

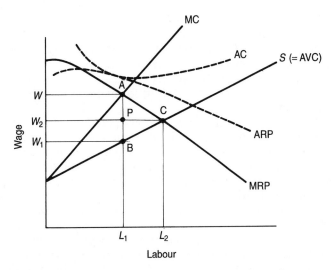

Figure 3.2. Monopsony.

workers at more than the cost to firms, then in the absence of market failure the parties would (eventually) have realized this and acted accordingly, without government help. In order for a mandate to increase the surplus triangle, we have therefore to postulate some obstacle in the way of firms and workers negotiating the surplus-maximizing contract by themselves.

The efficiency or surplus-maximizing case for mandates is that they overcome obstacles preventing firms and workers from reaching their own efficient contracts. Apart from dog-in-the-manger effects, associated with policy changes that have distributional consequences, there are two obvious obstacles to efficient voluntary exchange. First, there may be some externality associated with a particular term of the contract, possibly the poaching of trained workers by other firms that leads to suboptimal training investments. Second, there are obstacles which derive from imperfect information, such as when components of labour contracts relate to insurance against particular events (for example, ill health or pregnancy). Just as in regular insurance markets, adverse selection due to imperfect information can prevent insurance being offered in the labour market. In all these cases, further considered below, government intervention may be warranted.

Monopsony

Monopsony power arises in the labour market where workers' employment prospects are limited to a single firm or group of firms. The more limited are worker choices, the greater the monopsony power. The familiar monopsony diagram is given in Figure 3.2. The rising supply curve, S, indicates the restricted opportunity set of workers. Equilibrium employment is given by the intersection of the marginal cost of labour schedule, MC, with the demand or marginal revenue product of labour schedule, MRP. The wage paid is W_1 rather than W, and the gap between the two gives the degree of monopsony exploitation. By not paying the worker the value of his or her marginal product, the firm gains the rectangle $WABW_1$.

Now let us suppose that a wage of W_2 is paid. Equilibrium employment increases from L_1 to L_2. It can be seen that the firm is now worse off since it loses revenue in the amount of W_2PBW_1, which is transferred to workers, and gains only ACP. The worker side gains W_2PBW_1 plus PCB. This represents a potential Pareto improvement, since the gains to the workers outweigh the losses to the firm. Because it is not practicable for workers to compensate the firm for higher wages, the move to W_2 requires an external agency.

However, in determining that there is scope for a potential Pareto improvement, we are assuming that the firm remains solvent. In practice, this may not be a safe assumption. In a more general context, where the move to W_2 applies to all or most firms in the industry, the adverse effect on the firm's profits will be cushioned by an increase in prices. Nevertheless, there is a likelihood that some firms are made bankrupt. In the extreme case in which there is no effect on prices, because the move to W_2 only affects a few firms, the firm needs to be earning rent from its monopsony power (rather than just breaking even) in order to remain solvent. The hypothetical average cost and average revenue schedules given in Figure 3.2 represent a break-even situation prior to the imposition of a minimum wage. Here there is no scope for increased employment; on the contrary, employment will shrink as the firm will exit.

Monopsony is thus a case where the market may fail, in the sense that freedom of contract does not maximize the parties' joint surplus. This points to a need for government intervention. Assuming the firm remains solvent, by choosing the right wage the government can increase the size of the joint surplus and increase employment.

Before proposing minimum wage legislation, however, several questions have to be answered. In the first place, how prevalent is monopsony, and, relatedly, how strong is the monopsony power where it exists? In practice, monopsony power is difficult to define, because it will be greater in the short run than the long. In the short run all firms have some monopsony power because workers cannot move immediately if wages change; by the same token, workers also have dynamic monopoly power since they cannot be immediately replaced. Long-run monopsony power will be greatest for those groups with fewest alternatives. Married women with children are a case in point, since family commitments reduce their mobility to some extent. An investigation by Machin *et al.* (1993) of 475 residential care homes for the elderly – a low wage labour market employing mainly female workers – indeed finds evidence of exploitation, with the rate of exploitation averaging 15% $((W-W_1)/W_1$ in Figure 3.2). However, these are precisely the sort of organizations which might fail if a minimum wage were imposed because many of the homes depend on low wages for their survival.

Heterogeneity of firms calls into question the application of a single minimum wage as a means of bringing about potential Pareto improvements. The problem is that the optimum minimum wage (W_2 in Figure 3.2) varies across firms. A set of minimum wages could in principle overcome this objection, but the difficulty here is that not enough is known about individual firms, or supply and demand conditions in individual labour markets, to make this option feasible. In any case, even if a set of wage minima were drawn up, differentiated by occupation and area, there is the danger that wage differentials would then ossify. The cure might thus be worse than the disease.

At the same time, it must be admitted that the presence of some degree of monopsony power will reduce the adverse employment effects of minimum wages.

Monopsony power offers a possible explanation for the findings that (small) increases in minimum wages may have only minor adverse employment effects (see Card and Krueger, 1995). But it should also be remembered that when minimum wages are increased, other adverse changes are likely to be made to labour contracts; for example, training opportunities may be reduced, or supervision increased, as the parties try to lessen the impact of the minimum wage. While these adaptations permit more workers to be retained, they do represent real disadvantages of minimum wage laws, and should be factored into any cost-benefit analysis.

Externalities

An external economy arises when, as a byproduct of some economic activity, an individual is provided with a service for which he or she does not pay; analogously, an external diseconomy results when an individual suffers some disadvantage for which he or she is not compensated (see Pigou, 1920: 183). Since the service/disservice is not the product of a free contractual transaction (that is, there is a 'missing market'), non-market mechanisms can usefully encourage activities with positive externalities, and discourage those with negative externalities.

External economies cause marginal social benefit to be higher than marginal private benefit. In the competitive model, marginal private benefit is equated to marginal private cost. Thus, the inclusion in the model of external economies causes the social benefits of an activity to be higher than its private costs, at the margin. This is another source of market failure. Some element in the worker's compensation package is missing or under-provided, because its beneficial external effects are necessarily ignored in private calculations. In these circumstances, a mandate to force inclusion of the missing element may increase the welfare of society as a whole.

Suppose, for example, that company redundancy or severance pay schemes reduce burdens on an (imperfectly experience-rated) unemployment insurance system, either by making firms less willing to contemplate redundancies or by cushioning the effect of such redundancies. It might be argued that a certain minimum level of severance pay (and/or advance notice of layoff) might therefore be mandated to capture this externality. The position is illustrated in Figure 3.3. The initial equilibrium is at point E, which we assume for simplicity to be privately optimal, so that the private joint surplus triangle, AEB, is as large as possible.

The introduction of a mandate requiring extra contractual redundancy pay shifts down the demand for labour curve from D to D_R, reflecting the costs to the firm of making the payments. The supply curve shifts down also, from S to S_R, reflecting the value to the workers of the increased security. Since the private benefits are less than the costs of the mandate (by our assumption of private efficiency), the new equilibrium will be to the left of E at E_1, with employment L_1. The direct effect of the mandate is that the industry is in a sense paying a tax of amount FG $\times$ L_1 into a redundancy fund, this fund revenue being smaller than the sacrificed worker and firm surpluses by the amount of the deadweight loss triangle, FEG. The direct effect of the mandate is not, therefore, potentially Pareto improving; the transfer into the redundancy scheme falls short of the losses of workers and firms.

However, if redundancy pay schemes have external benefits – in the form of lower demands on the welfare system that lead to lower deadweight losses from general taxation – the mandate could have beneficial total effects. The lower demands on the welfare system, while they may be hard to measure, could more than offset FEG.

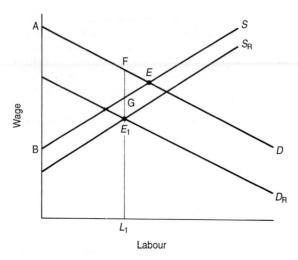

Figure 3.3. The effects of mandates, II.

Another item of the compensation package that is said to offer external economies is company health insurance (see Summers, 1989). Mandated health insurance is a topical issue in the US because of its potential role in reducing the number of indigents (individuals dependent on the state for health care). A similar case can be made for mandated pensions and employment protection.

External effects may also arise in the context of maternity benefits and company crèches. It might be argued that care of the children of working mothers leads to healthier adults who are also better citizens. Indeed, Pigou (1920: 187) gave as 'the crowning illustration' of the case of (negative) external effects

> the work done by women in factories, particularly during the periods immediately pre-ceding and succeeding confinement; for there can be no doubt that this work often carries with it, besides the earnings of the women themselves, grave injury to the health of their children.

Interestingly, however, he simply recommended prohibition of such work, accom-panied by welfare assistance where necessary, rather than any other sort of govern-ment intervention. He was not in favour of subsidised crèches because this 'ignores the fact that a woman's work has a special personal value in respect of her own chil-dren' (1920: 188). The same argument, moreover, can be used against mandated maternity benefits, since these also encourage market work by mothers. Thus, even if we are prepared to accept that women's work has significant negative externalities in the form of reduced care for children, it is not obvious that the remedy is to encourage greater provision of crèches or to mandate maternity benefits.

A 'soft' external economy concerns the benefits which the members of society derive in intangible form from the kind of society in which they live. Thus, most, if not all, individuals may prefer to live in a society in which it is mandated that a worker cannot be dismissed without just cause, or in which workers have other intrinsic rights.

In fact, there may be better arguments for mandates than their putative external economies. The difficulty with the externalities argument is not simply that the externalities themselves are often opaque, but also that a fall in employment may result. If private contracting is efficient (so that AEB in Figure 3.3 gives the largest possible surplus), mandates will tend to cause disemployment (unless this effect is overridden by the externality captured by the mandate). More interesting are those instances where the outcome of private contracting does *not* maximize the private surplus – that is, cases where there is private inefficiency. Here, a mandate seems more likely to be potentially Pareto improving. An important cause of such private inefficiency is asymmetric information, to which we now turn.

Asymmetric Information

Asymmetric information is present when one of the parties to a contract has private information, that is, information not available to the other party. The informed party may not wish to communicate this information to the uninformed party. Alternatively, direct communication of the information may be ruled out for the reason that it will not be perceived to be credible. Given such asymmetric information in labour markets, it is possible to show that government intervention may yield potential Pareto improvements.

Where firms are not sure of the characteristics of the workers they are hiring, certain insurance-type components of the labour contract may be underprovided, or not offered at all, even though both parties could be made better off with the insurance. Uncertainty about worker characteristics is presumably quite wide-spread. For example, despite tests and interviews, firms will not be in possession of full information about their employees' health, their maternity plans, or their work habits. The consequence of such uncertainty may be that a firm offers a high wage/no insurance contract in order to 'cream off' low-risk workers. High-risk workers go elsewhere for contracts with an insurance component. Alternatively, the firm may not offer insurance because low-risk workers would find it costly in terms of reduced wages, and seek employment elsewhere. Equally, high-risk workers would find the programme attractive, leading to an adverse mix of workers for the firm. If all firms were required to offer an insurance programme, however, such adverse selection would not occur. In these circumstances, it can be shown that there are grounds for expecting mandates for certain insurance-type schemes to be potentially Pareto-improving.

To be more formal, suppose that a contract is between two parties, one of which is of known type, and the other is of two possible types: 'high risk', H, with probability θ, and 'low risk', L, with probability $1-\theta$. In our model, the uninformed party (of known type) is the firm, and the informed party is the worker. We analyse the case where the uninformed party, the firm, makes an offer that the informed worker can only accept or reject, and where it is assumed that contracts which turn out to be unprofitable are withdrawn, as might be expected to happen in a competitive world. (It seems realistic to suppose that it is firms, rather than workers, that make take-it-or-leave-it offers.)

The contract between the two parties is that the firm pays a wage, w, to the worker in the good state, and a benefit, b, in the bad state. The benefit b corresponds to the insurance-type payments that are a component of many labour contracts, for example sickness, maternity and severance payments. (The case where $b=w$ then corresponds to 'full insurance'.) In the good state, a firm receives a fixed revenue $S-w$ per worker, and in the bad state $F-b$, where $0 \leq F < S$. S corresponds to 'success'

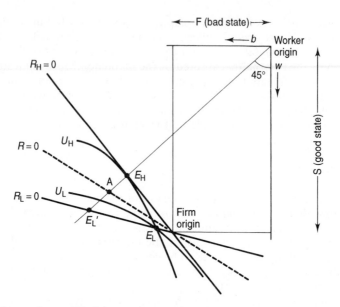

Figure 3.4. Separating equilibrium.

and F to 'failure'. In other words, S is revenue available if the worker succeeds, F if he/she fails. The high-risk type workers are the more likely to fail. For example, in the case of maternity risks, S could correspond to the value of output from 12 months' work, F to 6 months' work, where the high-risk types are those who are the more likely to become pregnant. The low-risk worker has a lower probability of failure, P_L, than that of the high-risk worker, P_H. Workers are risk averse, and for simplicity we assume that firms are risk neutral.

The basic model is illustrated in Figure 3.4, with the worker at the top right-hand origin of the Edgeworth box, and the firm at the opposite origin. The dimensions of the box are S×F. The high-risk type's utility curves, U_H, are steeper than the low-risk type's, U_L. This is because the high-risk type is more likely to fail and receive b. Thus, as b decreases, to keep utility constant, w must increase more for the high-risk than the low-risk type. Similarly, since $P_H > P_L$, the firm has steeper isoprofit lines for the worker it perceives to be high-risk. The firm's zero-profit lines for the low-risk and high-risk workers are labelled $R_L = 0$ and $R_H = 0$, respectively, in the figure. Between these lines is drawn a dashed 'pooling line', $R = 0$, giving contracts for which the expected value of the firm's profits when it draws a worker randomly is zero. The position of this line will be determined by the proportion of low-risk types, θ, in the population; the higher θ, the closer $R = 0$ will be to $R_L = 0$. Since these are zero-profit lines, they start at the firm's origin (where b=F, w=S, and profits are zero).

To start with, let us consider the case where worker types are known, the 'full information' equilibrium. In this equilibrium, low-risk types receive the contract E_L', and high-risk types receive E_H. These contracts give the maximum utility the workers can obtain when the firm is fully informed as to their type. Notice how both E_L' and E_H leave the worker with just as much utility when he/she fails as when he/she succeeds. The workers are fully insured against failure (the firm bearing the risk of failure), since the firm is assumed to be risk neutral. If the firm were risk

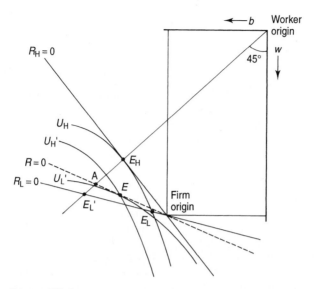

Figure 3.5.   Pooling equilibrium.

averse, so that its isoprofit curves were convex to the origin, then E_L' and E_H would have to leave the worker with less when he/she fails – a form of coinsurance. Risks of failure would then be shared by the firm and the worker.

In the more interesting and perhaps more relevant case, the firm does not know what type the worker is, and the full information contract is not attainable. We can then have either a *separating* or a *pooling* equilibrium. The significance of the distinction, as will be seen, is that a mandate amounts to enforced pooling. A separating equilibrium is shown in Figure 3.4. Here, the low-risk type of worker would prefer to be at E_L', but if the firm offered this contract there would be mimicking by the high-risk types who would be better off at E_L'. The firm would then end up making a loss since it cannot accept both low-risk and high-risk workers on E_L' terms. The firm, knowing this, will not make offers of contracts such as E_L'. In the situation illustrated, the best the firm can do is screen out the high-risk types by offering two contracts, E_H and E_L, which associate high benefits with low wages. The high-risk type will no longer have the incentive to mimic, since he/she is as well off at E_H as at E_L. Thus, the workers separate themselves: low-risk types accept E_L and high-risk types are screened out with the offer of E_H.

But separation is not always the outcome. The pooling equilibrium case is illustrated in Figure 3.5, which differs from Figure 3.4 only in that the proportion, θ, of low-risk types is higher. This difference pulls the pooling line, $R=0$, towards the zero profit line $R_L=0$, so that the low-risk type's indifference curve through E_L now cuts the pooling line. In this new situation, a better position is open to all parties: the pooling equilibrium at E. If both high-risk and low-risk workers are offered E, they can both move to higher indifference curves (U_H' and U_L'). The firm would be no worse off since E is on its pooling line, and it continues to meet its reservation profit constraint.

The pooling equilibrium, E, is also the outcome we would expect were workers unionized (Aghion and Hermalin, 1990: 402–403). Here, the contractual outcome must lie on the pooling line, assuming the union does not allow different contracts to be offered to different members. When low-risk workers outnumber high-risk workers, the median voter will be a low-risk type, and contract E will be the outcome under the median voter rule.

In summary, we have two possible solutions to the model. In the case of a separating equilibrium, low-risk types are identified by their choice of contract, namely, a high wage/low benefit contract. This is an example of screening. Screening benefits low-risk types, but they face a cost in foregoing insurance. In the case of a pooling equilibrium, high-risk types, by mimicking the behaviour of low-risk types, gain in comparison with their full information contract, E_H. High-risk types gain by pooling. We now examine the scope for government intervention in these two situations.

In Section 3.1, we distinguished between actual and potential Pareto improvements. It turns out that there is no scope in our framework for achieving *actual* Pareto improvements via a mandate. Accordingly, a mandate requiring company health insurance, for example, will make healthy types worse off – even though it benefits the unhealthy types. Both types cannot be made better off. The conclusion is no different if we relax the assumption of competitive firms. When a single, monopolistic firm makes offers to one or more workers – who constitute the informed party – only the *details* of the analysis change. The conclusion does not (see Aghion and Hermalin, 1990: 399).

By contrast, the achievement of a *potential* Pareto improvement can be demonstrated in both the separating and pooling cases. Take for example the case of an initial separating equilibrium, and suppose that the government mandates 'full insurance'. Since separation is now ruled out, both high and low-risk types must now have the same pooling contract, and this is only compatible with the zero profit constraint if point A on the pooling line in Figure 3.4 is chosen. The wage paid at A (wages equal benefits at A, so we do not need to distinguish between the two) is in fact the weighted average of wages paid at $E_L{'}$ and E_H, the weights depending on θ, the proportion of low-risk types.

If the mandate leads to A, this engineers a potential Pareto improvement *vis-à-vis* (E_L, E_H). The reasoning is that the wage at A is equal to the average wage payable under $(E_L{'}, E_H)$, and so $(E_L{'}, E_H)$ is attainable from A through a redistribution from high-risk to low-risk workers. Also, $(E_L{'}, E_H)$ is an actual Pareto improvement upon (E_L, E_H), as can be seen from Figure 3.4 (the high-risk types are indifferent, and the low-risk types are better off). This makes A a potential Pareto improvement over (E_L, E_H). (A similar argument can also be made where there is initially a pooling equilibrium at E, as in Figure 3.5; the government mandating full insurance at A will also bring about a potential Pareto improvement.) In other words, the gains of the high-risk types resulting from moving to A outweigh the losses of the low-risk types. The movement to A would give the high-risk types enough extra money for them to be able to compensate the low-risk types for their losses, and still come out ahead.

In the above instances of potential Pareto improvement, the redistributive element is from low-risk types to high-risk types. Thus, as indicated in Section 3.1, it seems that whenever high-risk types are also the less advantaged workers the policy implications are striking. However, a problem arises that indicates a need for caution.

Enforced pooling via a mandate may lead to the misallocation of workers. If we allow for heterogeneity of firms, it may be that high-risk workers cause greater difficulties for some firms than for others. For example, maternity absence could be more disruptive in small than in large firms. Extending our model, this means that small firms have elongated '(F,S) boxes', and large firms have squarer (F,S) boxes. It is then efficient for low-risk workers to allocate themselves only to small firms, or high-risk workers only to large firms (see Addison *et al.*, 1995a). In other words, small firms need to be able to offer 'no frills' contracts so as to achieve separation.

If an appropriate allocation of worker types is achieved through separation, enforced pooling must adversely affect the allocation of workers. This means that a government mandate which enforces pooling leads to loss of output, reduces the average wage payable to workers, and is no longer guaranteed to provide a potential Pareto improvement. The design of a mandate has therefore to be concerned with differences between small and large firms, and indeed other pertinent distinctions that might tend to misallocation. Mandates may need to be closely targeted rather than global in reach. The situation is different where market forces have already resulted in pooling. Workers are then randomly allocated in any case, and designers of mandates do not have this type of misallocation to worry about.

The situation is also different when instead of a mandate the government provides the benefits directly. Direct government provision can be chosen to retain worker separation, may convert pooling into separation, and, abstracting from the distortions caused by the need for funding, may even achieve actual Pareto improvements (see Addison *et al.*, 1995a).

A standard problem that needs to be mentioned, and which affects both a mandate and direct government provision, is the issue of moral hazard. This arises when the higher the benefit paid in the bad state, the less careful beneficiaries are to avoid this state. Raising benefits could result in a greater probability of failure, so reducing output. Firms and workers can be presumed to take account of moral hazard in their private arrangements, but this is less certain when the government intervenes.

Turning to applications, in the case of medical insurance, market forces are likely to result in a pooling equilibrium, so that evaluation of the mandate is not complicated by the misallocation issues raised when free markets give rise to separation. Pooling is likely to occur because firms will presumably only be willing to attract unhealthy workers at a very low wage, and at such a wage separation becomes impossible. According to our earlier discussion, mandating firms to provide increased medical benefits can bring about a potential Pareto improvement, and it appears that the potential Pareto improvement is progressive in this case. The redistribution is from more advantaged, healthy workers to less advantaged, unhealthy workers. A medical insurance mandate could thus satisfy both the efficiency and equity criteria.

The model can also be applied to maternity benefits, where maternity is the 'bad' state. Let α be some given duration for maternity leave, measured as a fraction of a year. In the good state, revenue per worker is S per year, and the worker is paid w per year. In the bad state, revenue per worker is $F=(1-\alpha)S$ and the worker receives $b=(1-\alpha)w+b_0$. (Here b_0 is the maternity benefit paid for the worker's unproductive time.) The model now concerns firms' offers of the form (w,α,b_0), namely, a combination of a wage, maternity leave, and maternity pay. In a separating equilibrium, low-risk types are now identified by their willingness to accept either a short maternity leave or low maternity pay, or some combination of the two. The essential theory is the same for maternity benefits as for medical insurance.

But in the case of maternity benefits, unlike medical insurance, market forces may be expected to give rise to separating contracts (Figure 3.4), and this raises difficulties for mandates that enforce pooling. One reason for separation is that firms will not have to offer high maternity-risk types very low wages in order to break even, unlike unhealthy workers. Separation is therefore possible and, given the high proportion of high-risk types in the relevant population, is to be expected. To repeat, where market forces bring about separation, the enforced pooling caused by mandates is likely to cause misallocation.

Moreover, it should be noted that maternity benefits are group specific benefits – they apply only to younger women. If wages are flexible, then mandating higher maternity benefits must mean a lower wage for this group. Where the wages of younger women are linked to the wages of other groups by fair wage laws, mandated maternity benefits will cause disemployment among the target group.

To summarize, the asymmetric information model shows that there may be scope for government labour market mandates to improve efficiency in the sense of achieving potential Pareto improvements. In one case our logic supports such potential Pareto improvements: medical insurance. In the case of maternity benefits, however, potential Pareto improvements are not guaranteed. In general, it appears that the more diverse are free market contracts, separating the various worker types, the less likely are mandates to be potentially Pareto-improving.

Of course, we cannot consider efficiency alone, and neglect issues of equity. Potential Pareto improvements involve the redistribution of income. In some cases, such as medical insurance, it is reasonably easy to see whether this redistribution is equitable. In other cases, such as redundancy pay, it is less obvious. Even more difficult is the maternity benefits case, which does not satisfy the potential Pareto improvement test (because average wages fall), but where the redistribution is arguably towards the disadvantaged. Here we have to balance efficiency against equity.

Public Goods

Some benefits, concerning for example health and safety at work, or the level of heating in workplaces, have 'public goods' characteristics. Necessarily in these cases, the same level of benefit is provided for all workers in the firm. If workers are unionized, this level is likely to be determined in negotiations between the firm and a union. In the previous section, we suggested that the median voter rule might apply to such negotiations. In non-union firms, by contrast, working conditions are determined by the actions of the marginal worker.

Consider health and safety at work as an example – other workplace public goods have similar characteristics. In this example, workers are diverse in the risks they face and in their degree of risk aversion, and firms are diverse in their need for low-risk workers (workers that handle risks well) and in their costs of providing any given level of benefit. With this variety of attributes among firms and workers, an important function of labour markets is appropriately to match workers to firms.

The issue is whether workers require some collective mechanism – be it unions or government mandates – to more adequately reflect their preferences. In the competitive scenario such a collective mechanism is not required because workers simply move into firms whose conditions they prefer. Arguments favouring collective mechanisms are firstly that workers are subject to some degree of monopsony power, due to factors such as training and job-specific skills which underlie internal labour markets (Viscusi, 1979: 169–73; see also Freeman, 1976). In this case it can be shown that safety will be below the socially optimal amount (that is, the amount maximizing the sum of worker and firm surpluses) when the marginal worker places a lower valuation on safety than does the average worker. This will tend to be the case if we assume the marginal worker is young and risk-loving, while the average worker is older and more careful. However, at issue here is the extent and direction of the divergence between the marginal and the average worker. It is not obvious that the marginal worker is more risk-loving than the average worker; the marginal worker might be more risk-averse since he/she is not so well matched to the job.

A second argument favouring collective action is asymmetric information, as discussed above. Given asymmetric information, firms that require low-risk workers will screen out other worker types, by offering 'no-frills' contracts – high wages but low safety expenditures. This means that health and safety at work will be underprovided for low-risk types, and as a consequence there is a possible case for a government mandate tailored to the particular industry. However, any such mandate, by forcing pooling, is likely to have an adverse effect on the role of the market in the sorting of workers among firms. Moreover, it is not clear that workers who are high-risk or highly risk-averse, and would therefore benefit from the mandate, are also disadvantaged. There is no obvious equity argument for the mandate.

The Prisoner's Dilemma

The 'prisoner's dilemma', which originates in game theory, is a special case of externalities. It concerns a situation in which individually rational behaviour is inefficient because it leads to an outcome that is less preferred by all the parties to another available outcome (see Luce and Raiffa, 1957: 94 *et seq.*). In this situation, it is sometimes possible to argue that a government mandate, by restricting the parties' choice of strategies, can shepherd them to a preferred position. The prisoner's dilemma involves a particular configuration of a 'payoff matrix', that is, the payoffs to the various parties consequent upon their adopting particular strategies. We will build up an example of this matrix in the context of an 'employment protection' mandate.

Suppose that firms have two possible strategies. One strategy is to have a 'participative' structure in which workers are actively involved in decision-making. The other is to follow a more traditional approach in which workers are motivated by the threat of dismissal. Suppose that the participative firm is more productive because it receives information that the worker side possesses. The workers are more willing to disclose this information in the participative firm, both because of group cohesiveness and also because of the protection against dismissals which such firms offer. Yet, as a strategy, the participative option will only be successful if all firms adopt it. Otherwise, we may argue, the participative firms will suffer from various forms of external diseconomy deriving from the behaviour of the traditional firm.

Such external diseconomies could include forms of adverse selection; that is, the participative firm may attract the less motivated workers who wish to take advantage of dismissals protection. There may be an even worse problem: Levine and Tyson (1990: 218) argue that the participative environment needs a compressed wage structure to build up group cohesiveness, but that such a wage structure will allow 'traditional' firms to bid away the participative firm's 'stars'. In other words, the large wage differentials offered by traditional firms provide an external diseconomy for participative firms. The remedy is to force all firms to be participative.

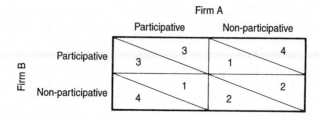

Figure 3.6. Prisoner's dilemma.

A payoff matrix that illustrates the above situation is given in Figure 3.6. The top-right cell, for example, has the following meaning: If Firm B is participative and Firm A is the opposite, then Firm A is assumed to have a payoff of 4 while Firm B only has 1, due to the negative externalities it suffers. If both firms are forced by a mandate to be participative (the top-left cell), then both receive a payoff of 3. However, with freedom of contract, the equilibrium in dominating strategies is the bottom-right cell, yielding a payoff of only 2 each.

We should note, however, that the payoff matrix set out in Figure 3.6 only demonstrates the logic of the argument, an argument which is in no sense incontrovertible. In particular, there is no strong evidence that participative firms are more productive than non-participative firms – or that the latter rely much on the dismissals threat to motivate. (Of course, Levine and Tyson could argue that this is because the participative firms are operating in the shadow of traditional firms – an empirical test of their argument would then require a comparison of two regimes, one participative, and the other not, though it would be difficult to keep other things equal.) If, when all firms adopt the strategy, the participative firms are less profitable, then we have to reverse the position of the top-left and bottom-right cells. In this case, the non-participative outcome is superior. Nor is there reason to believe that the informational asymmetry assumption underlying the role of adverse selection (that the employer cannot detect the motivation of the employees he hires, or promotes) is necessarily true. However, the point is that without a prisoner's dilemma situation, the efficiency case for mandated participation fails. We then have to rely on equity arguments to justify the ensuing second-best position.

It is sometimes argued that training is a classic case of prisoner's dilemma. All firms would be better off if they trained their workforces, so the argument runs, but any single firm providing training will suffer from poaching of its trained workers by other firms. The often cited remedy is to force all firms to provide a certain amount of training. It should be noted, however, that this argument depends on imperfect Capital markets, in which case workers cannot borrow against future earnings. Otherwise, trainees could accept lower wages, finance their (general) training investments, and the externality would disappear.

Equity

If the position prior to a mandate is efficient, that is, joint surplus maximizing, then a mandate cannot raise output, and is at best simply redistributive. (In this case it can be likened to a combination of lump-sum taxes and benefits.) Some groups will lose and others gain, but now the gainers will not be able to compensate the losers and still come out ahead (as they could if there was a potential Pareto improvement). In these circumstances, we would then have to argue that the gainers are more deserving than the losers, that is, make an 'equity' case for the redistribution.

Two major questions arise under the equity heading. The first is definitional. We might take an increase in equity to mean some movement towards equality of incomes and/or earnings and/or opportunities. There are, however, possible conflicts between these objectives. Particularly important is the fact that earnings and income equality may conflict. For example, mandatory safety expenditures will even up *earnings* by removing risk premia for dangerous jobs. However, if disemployment results, *incomes* will become less equal as some individuals receive only welfare benefits. Similarly, minimum wage laws, or collective agreements, may reduce earnings disparities while widening income disparities, if unemployment ensues. The income distribution is presumably what we should be concentrating on, but data on incomes are scarcer and harder to interpret than those on earnings.

The second question is how much equity/equality is desirable? A related question is how best to promote equity/equality. Assuming we reject objections to redistribution in principle (for example, those of Nozick, 1974), these questions are only relevant for those policies that reduce both average income (efficiency) and inequality, that is, where there is a tradeoff between average income and equality of incomes. A policy that is often said to exhibit such a tradeoff is progressive taxation, which is redistributive but has disincentive effects. A redistributive mandate – if it is inefficient – will also result in lower average earnings. For example, mandated maternity benefits might result in the misallocation of workers (small firms might want to screen out high pregnancy-risk workers, but be unable to do so if all contracts are required to be the same). As a result of such a maternity mandate, there could be redistribution from low-risk to high-risk young women, which might be equity-promoting (so long as unemployment does not ensue). However, it could also cause a reduction in average earnings by reason of the misallocation. If increasing equality means reducing efficiency, then we often have a difficult choice to make.

Some policies could result in the worst of both worlds, with both lower average earnings/incomes, and more inequality. An extreme example is the case of a dictator ruining a country in the interest of his or her ruling clique. Such policies would presumably be rejected out of hand. Other policies might provide the best of both worlds. Mandatory company health insurance, for example, redistributes from unhealthy to healthy, and we have argued that it is not likely to lower average wages. Having found such a policy there need be no debate about putting it into effect.

We can draw up a matrix, as in Figure 3.7. The four boxes allow us to classify policies as inequality-reducing or inequality-increasing, and as efficient or inefficient. Tentative illustrations of the four different types of policy are also given. The box in the bottom-left corner should identify policies which are definitely good, the box in the top-right those which are bad, and on the main diagonal are the two boxes containing policies considered to involve a tradeoff between equity and efficiency.

In practice, just as many hard questions arise over how to judge the redistributive consequences of mandates, as in assessing their efficiency properties. The appropriate box in which to classify a policy is thus controversial. The European Commission has argued that 'In order to have sustained growth we do need social consensus' (House of Commons, 1989: 1). The implication is that 'social justice' and efficiency are not alternatives, and in particular that the mandates of the social charter can simply be put in the 'good' box in the bottom-left corner of Figure 3.7.

		Inequality	
		Reducing	**Increasing**
Efficiency	**Reducing**	Redistributive taxes Some mandates such as maternity pay?	Fraud in government Mandates such as hours regulation?
	Increasing	Company health insurance Advance notice of redundancy?	Mandates such as employment protection?

Figure 3.7.   The equality and efficiency properties of mandates.

But the matter is not as easy as this, if only because in many cases the distributional consequences of mandates are arguably adverse.

For example, the IPM study of minimum wages states that 'As the groups affected (by a minimum wage) are the least powerful...they ought to be safeguarded' (IPM, 1991: 53). This is said to be the 'social justice' case for mandates. However, minimum wage legislation can result in unemployment and/or lower full wages for certain groups – in which case their interests will not be safeguarded, and their incomes will fall. Indeed, even if minimum wage legislation does not cause unemployment, it can reduce the incomes of low income households where such households do not have low-wage earners (pensioner households, for example) but nevertheless have to face the increased prices that accompany the minimum wage (see Johnson and Browning, 1983). Addison and Blackburn (1995), using US data, find that increases in state minimum wages are if anything associated with increased family income inequality among those groups most likely to be affected by minimum wage increases. If this is true, and if minimum wage legislation causes unemployment and is therefore inefficient, then this policy should be placed in the top right-hand 'bad' box of Figure 3.7.

The possible adverse distributional consequences of many mandates result from the fact that placing 'floors' under working conditions disadvantages the least skilled workers. There are several reasons for this. In the first place, the unskilled have less flexible wages, because their wages are closer to the unemployment bene-fits 'floor'. Thus, the fall in the full wage (from W_1 to W_2 in Figure 3.1), required to prevent unemployment, is less likely. Second, personnel departments will tend to be more careful in their hiring when faced with mandates (given that fixed employment costs have risen, or that workers are more difficult to fire). Accordingly, mandates will favour the more educated and experienced. Third, it is the unskilled who tend to work in the jobs with the less favourable conditions. Unskilled workers command low wage rates, and they often prefer to accept longer hours (and more dangerous jobs) so as to increase their take-home pay. Regulating working conditions thus shifts the main burden of adjustment onto these workers.

Finally, regulation of working conditions hits small firms hardest. Small firms have been shown to experience the highest workplace accident rates (Wei and Siebert, 1994), so that stricter safety regulation will have more of an effect on these firms. Large firms use unskilled labour less intensively than small firms. Small firms are more willing to 'experiment' with less qualified workers – perhaps because the boss in the small firm can more easily monitor his/her workers, so that there is not the 'arm's length' relationship found in large firms (see Siebert and Addison, 1991). Regulations which impinge more on small firms can therefore be expected to reduce job growth for the unskilled, which is inequality-increasing.

Mandates might therefore be inequality-increasing. The Commission denies such a possibility: 'Non-interference in the economic system tends to result in a distribution of income which is highly, and unacceptably, inequitable. Moves away from such a 'natural' order have been largely the result of positive government actions' (*Employment in Europe*, 1992: 4). However, the case that mandates might be inequality-increasing needs to be answered. Of course, 'positive government actions' need not only involve mandates, but could involve the many cash and in-kind transfers of the welfare state, to which we now turn.

Alternatives

Given the problems alluded to earlier, are there perhaps better ways of improving the prospects of unskilled workers (and poor families in general) than imposing mandates on working conditions? The alternatives comprise direct state transfers, either in cash or in kind. Let us consider these briefly. (For a survey of the UK position, see Barr, 1987.)

Cash Transfers   Transfers in cash include unemployment insurance, and basic income support schemes including housing subsidies. One difficulty with this type of (means-tested) transfer is that it tends to result in poverty traps. The incentive to work is reduced since untaxed income out of work tends to equal taxed income in work, at least for unskilled workers who can command only low earnings.

Unemployment is generally believed to have adverse effects on the welfare of the individual and the individual's family, distinct from any income effects (Phelps, 1994b: 11). Yet the idea that these effects, though real, are also serious may lack wide acceptability in an age of reduced emphasis on the work ethic. There is then a case for arguing that the very low skilled should not in fact do much work. Beyond some point, work will involve disutility for the individual worker, and it may be that this point is typically reached at quite a low level of activity, say 15 hours per week. It follows that, at least in theory, income maintenance directed at workers who are unable to contribute very much to total output can enhance social welfare. (For this insight we are indebted to some informal comments of James Mirrlees.)

Redistributive transfers require funding, however, and as noted above the taxes that finance these transfers will reduce the incentive to work. They will also tend to reduce incentives to save (even though long-term savings are often sheltered). Income can thus be double- , and on occasion even triple-taxed, as when bequests made out of savings are taxed. Both reduced labour supply and reduced savings will tend to lower per capita national income.

The extent to which the 'welfare state' and its associated taxes lower per capita national income is of course controversial, but empirical work by Newell and Symons (1993) suggests that there is a significant tradeoff. In the authors' cross-country analysis, using data for 1978–87, those countries with higher increases in marginal income tax, and employee social security tax rates, had lower growth in

GDP per capita, and lower labour force participation rates. Persson and Tabellini (1994: Table 8) also find that those countries with the largest transfers have lowest growth of GDP per capita. In like vein, Phelps (1994a: 54) claims that payroll taxes are a determinant of the natural unemployment rate, and Newell and Symons' empirical work also uncovers signs of this effect.

The advantage of the policy of cash transfers, such as unemployment support, is presumably that it is inequality-reducing. However, since the accompanying taxes cause inefficiencies due to incentive effects, the policy falls in the top-left box of Figure 3.7. This puts a limit on the amount of redistribution that is tolerable. The question also arises of whether there are ways of helping the unemployed at lower tax cost.

An alternative form of cash transfer is the low-wage job subsidy. This measure has been advocated by Phelps (1994a, b). For example, the Family Credit scheme in the UK provides a subsidy to a family whose breadwinner works at least 16 hours per week, who is responsible for at least one child, and whose family income is below a certain amount.[1] The earned-income tax credit scheme in the USA provides analogous benefits for low-income wage earners.

Transfer schemes such as these essentially pay low-wage earners to work. Part of the subsidy will go to the firms employing these workers since the supply curve will shift downwards. Take-home pay will now be made up in part by wages (which will fall) and in part by the subsidy. Take-home pay will rise, because of the subsidy, as will employment. The exchequer costs of the subsidy will be cushioned by savings in unemployment payments, by the extra output of the newly employed, and by reduced moral and social problems. A possible objection to the policy is that, by raising take-home pay in unskilled jobs (and reducing it in skilled jobs), the incentive to become skilled is reduced (see Layard *et al.,* 1991: 319). But if labour supply to skilled and unskilled jobs is not very responsive to the subsidy, as is plausible, this objection loses weight.

It is sometimes also argued that a switch towards indirect taxes such as VAT would be beneficial for employment. The argument is that VAT taxes all forms of income, including capital income, while income tax and national insurance charges tend to fall most heavily on labour income, encouraging unemployment. But it is not obvious that income from capital is currently lightly taxed. We have already noted how some savings are heavily taxed. Corporation tax also constitutes a form of double taxation. Hence, raising more finance through VAT and less via income and corporation tax (as is the case in Denmark, for example), might conceivably imply more rather than less of a burden on labour.

Transfers in kind   Transfers in kind include state-provided health care, education/training, and housing. The efficiency arguments for such transfers include failure of health insurance markets, and, in the case of education and training, imperfect markets for human capital (workers cannot easily borrow to finance human capital which is not good loan collateral). We have seen that in the case of training this might induce a prisoner's dilemma.

A basic problem with public education and health programmes is that they seem to be underutilized by the poor. They might well be inequality-increasing; whether they are or not depends on the alternatives. Thus, Le Grand (1982: 3) has concluded that 'Almost all public expenditure on the social services in Britain benefits the better-off to a greater extent than the poor'. He shows how mortality differences between the social classes were narrower in the 1930s than the 1970s (1982: 38), and how the proportion attending university has gone up more over the last 50 years for the higher socioeconomic groups (1982: 61). Phelps (1994b: 14) also points out that social insurance programmes have to be designed to bring median voters into a coalition to achieve the necessary majority of votes. It is therefore not surprising to find that such programmes are not targeting the most needy groups.

Furthermore, although subsidization of education and training is an apparently attractive way to benefit poorer groups, there is the problem that such programmes take a long time to bear fruit. What is to be done in the short term? In addition, there is the issue of the content of training programmes. Training-on-the-job is likely to be the best way of picking up work-related skills. In practice, state training programmes for adults do not seem to have been very successful in increasing the outflows from unemployment (for studies of Germany and the UK, see Disney *et al.*, 1992: 143, 237). These findings again raise serious questions as to the extent to which the measures have helped the poor in practice.

In sum, we find limited scope for mandates on equity grounds. Some mandates, for example company health insurance, help some disadvantaged groups, but other mandates such as maternity pay carry the danger of disemployment if wages are not flexible enough. More conventional welfare state policies, involving cash and in-kind transfers, tend to be captured by the middle-income groups, and are therefore not as redistributive as they might be. Transfers also have tax costs and disincentive effects. A key criterion is the availability of jobs for unskilled workers. These can be promoted by lower taxes, including subsidies for low wage jobs.

3.3. Empirical Evidence on Job Protection

It is obviously too soon to gauge the effect of Community-level mandates on labour market outcomes. But since these seek to build on an existing body of member state legislation, it is pertinent to review material on the effects of such arrangements. If the evidence at member state level suggests that labour market regulation is associated with unfavourable outcomes in the form of, say, lower employment and higher unemployment, then the case for harmonization is considerably weakened (see also Chapter 10 for further comparative material on the member states).

Cross-National Studies

Investigation of the effects of job protection on labour market outcomes was stimulated by Emerson's (1988) suggestive remarks on the unintended costs of well-meaning job protection legislation, based on a mix of theoretical conjectures (see above) and the facts he presented on employer perceptions as to the intrusiveness of these mandates. Three such 'reputational surveys' are widely cited in the literature.

The first survey was conducted by the International Organization of Employers (IOE) (1985) via a questionnaire distributed to 18 European and two non-European employer federations. It sought to evaluate the strength of obstacles to terminating employment and the severity of constraints on the management of working time in the use of part-time work, fixed-term contracts, and temporary work. Obstacles to terminating employment, including severance pay, were seen by IOE respondents to be 'fundamental' in six countries (France, Germany, Italy, the Netherlands,

Table 3.1. Perceived constraints on the management of working time, central employer organization responses, eight countries

Strength of constraints	Measure/Country		
	Part-time work	Fixed-term contracts	Temporary work
Fundamental	Belgium[a]	Belgium	Belgium
	France[a]	Italy	Italy
	Italy[a]	Netherlands	Spain
	Netherlands[a]		
Serious		France	France
		Germany	Germany
		Luxembourg	Netherlands
		Sweden	Sweden

Source: International Organisation of Employers (1985), pp. 33–35.
Note: [a] Survey does not distinguish between 'fundamental' and 'serious' for these countries.

Portugal, and Spain), 'serious' in eight countries (Austria, Belgium, Canada, Ireland, Luxembourg, Malta, Norway, and Sweden), and 'minor' in five countries (Cyprus, Denmark, Finland, New Zealand, and the UK).

Table 3.1 summarizes the findings with respect to perceived constraints on the management of working time, distinguishing between part-time work, fixed-term contracts, and temporary work. As shown in the table, four countries judge constraints on the employment of part-timers to be serious or fundamental. Interestingly, the source of the problem appears to be restrictions on the possibility of resorting to part-time work in France and Italy, whereas the difficulties stem from social security charges in Belgium and the Netherlands.

Countries facing significant constraints in the use of fixed-term contracts are broadly those which also face major difficulties in deploying temporary work contracts. In the case of fixed-term contracts, the constraint may be with respect to duration (direct limitations in Germany and France plus limitations on the renewal of such contracts in Belgium, Italy, Luxembourg, and the Netherlands) or recourse to such contracts (France, Italy, and Sweden). There appear to be three principal constraints on the use of temporary work: general or partial prohibition (Sweden and Italy), absence of an adequate legal basis (in Belgium and Spain), and what is perceived as an over-restrictive legal framework (France, Germany, and the Netherlands). Interestingly, the IOE notes that these constraints on the utilization of working time do not stem exclusively from regulations, but 'are equally, and sometimes even to a greater extent, to be attributed to social mentality and behaviour' (IOE: 38).

The two other and perhaps better known surveys were conducted by the Commission of the European Communities in 1985 and 1989 (Commission, 1986, 1991). They cover 8000 industrial firms in the case of the 1985 survey and 25 000 firms for the 1989 survey. The surveys were undertaken against the backdrop of the deregulation debate in the 1980s. Survey respondents were asked why they were not employing more people at that time. Current and expected levels of demand were cited as the major reason, followed by inadequate price competitiveness and then by non-wage labour costs. Interestingly, the next most important reason was 'insufficient flexibility in hiring and shedding labour', which ranked ahead of a variety of

Table 3.2. Employer survey rankings of countries by the stringency of their job protection practices

| | Study | | | |
| | Mosley and Kruppe | | | |
Ranking	1985	1989	Bertola	Grubb and Wells
1	Italy (151)[a]	Italy (123)	Italy	Portugal
2	France (129)	Neths. (115)	Belgium	Greece
3	Belgium (113)	Spain (103)	France	Spain
4	Greece (112)	France (94)	Sweden	Italy
5	Ireland (109)	Belgium (86)	Germany	Germany
6	Spain (103)	Germany (84)	Japan	France
7	Portugal (83)	Portugal (83)	UK	Belgium
8	Germany (79)	Greece (82)	Neths.	Neths.
9	Neths. (70)	Ireland (79)	Denmark	Ireland
10	Denmark (52)	Denmark (66)	USA	Denmark
11	UK (33)	UK (53)		UK

Sources: Mosley and Kruppe (1993: Figure 3); Bertola (1990: Table 1); Grubb and Wells (1993: Table 9).
Note: [a] Figures in parenthesis are index scores, as described in the text.

other constraints such as rationalization and/or the introduction of new technologies, direct wage costs, shortages of skilled labour, and insufficient production capacity. The ranking of these four most important reasons for not hiring more employees was unchanged as between the two surveys.[2]

Answers to the insufficient flexibility in hiring and shedding labour question were coded as 'very important', 'important', and 'not (so) important'. In terms of weighted responses, the 1985 survey indicates the lack of flexibility to be especially serious in Italy, France, Belgium, Greece, and Ireland, but of minimal importance in the UK. However, a change in country rankings is recorded in the 1989 survey, most notably in the case of the Netherlands which rises to the second highest ranking after Italy despite there being no major change in legislation in that country.

The first two columns of Table 3.2 contain an index of the perceived severity of employment protection by assigning one point for the percentage of all employers responding 'important' and two points for the percentage responding 'very important'. The data are taken from Mosley (1994), who imputes data for Portugal and Spain which had not yet joined the Community at the time of the 1985 survey. Also, since Denmark participated in neither survey, Mosley assigns that country a score that is equidistant between the UK score and that of the next lowest ranking country – on the grounds that the IOE survey, referred to earlier, ranked that nation lower than all Community countries other than the UK in the severity of its employment protection (see also Mosley and Kruppe, 1993).

The penultimate column of Table 3.2 adds the rankings used by Bertola (1990), constructed from Emerson (1988). The final column includes the rankings constructed by Grubb and Wells (1993) for a more comprehensive measure of employment security averaged over dismissals protection, restrictions on fixed-term contracts, and limitations on overtime, weekend and night work. Overall, it is apparent that there are some marked disparities in the rankings.

Bertola (1990) correlates his ranking of the stringency of job security provisions in his 10 country sample with corresponding rankings for a number of aggregate labour market indicators, 1962–86. He reports that the variability of the growth rate in employment is lower in high ranking job protection countries, as is the responsiveness of the unemployment rate to output changes. Similar stabilizing effects of heightened job security are also found for changes in employment and output between 1972 and 1975 – respectively 'good' and 'bad' years. Bertola also argues that his data do not point to any statistically significant relation between the degree of job security and average unemployment or even long-term unemployment over the sample period. Since Bertola's separate analysis of wage setting does not indicate that job security provisions bias wage determination toward higher wages, he interprets the balance of the above evidence as not unfavourable to job protection. (See also Bentolila and Bertola, 1990, and the criticism of the underlying model provided by Saint-Paul, 1995.)

This relatively optimistic evaluation is not readily apparent in the simple correlations provided by Mosley and Kruppe (1993), who use the reputational index given in the second column of Table 3.2 in conjunction with a set of 'outcome' indicators derived from the European Labour Force Surveys. First, there is evidence of a trade-off between dismissals and fixed-term contract terminations in the composition of national patterns. Second, there is a significantly negative association between the reputational index and dismissals as a percentage of employment ($r=-0.628$, excluding the UK). Third, there is a positive relation between the reputational index and average long-term unemployment rates ($r=0.461$). Fourth, there is a strong negative relation between the index and monthly outflows from unemployment as a percentage of the stock of the unemployed ($r=-0.742$). Fifth, the relative incidence of youth unemployment is weakly higher ($r=0.407$), and dismissal rates among older workers weakly lower ($r=-0.455$) in countries with more stringent job protection.

Finally, Grubb and Wells (1993) report that the employment–population ratio is negatively correlated with their measure of the overall regulatory climate. Interestingly, in the light of what follows, it is also indicated that the incidence of part-time work is negatively related to that index. Temporary work on the other hand is increasing in the restrictions placed on the dismissal of regular workers, even if the major explanation pertains to direct regulation of the temporary work contract itself. We will comment below on some other results obtained by Grubb and Wells. (Chapter 10 gives further correlations.)

Correlation exercises of this type are at best suggestive. The balance of the literature attempts to control for the presence of other variables that may be expected to mediate the effects of job protection. The best-known econometric study is that of Lazear (1990), who examines the impact of statutory dismissals protection on employment and unemployment in 22 developed countries over the sample period 1956–84. Four outcome indicators are identified: the employment–population ratio, the unemployment–labour force ratio, the labour force participation rate, and average hours worked per week by production workers. Lazear measures the severity of job protection legislation on the basis of the amount of severance pay and notice statutorily to be provided workers in cases of individual (as opposed to collective) dismissals. In each case the levels of protection, measured in terms of months, are those applying to blue-collar workers with 10 years service, separated for economic reasons unconnected with the performance of the worker (i.e. no-fault individual dismissals).

Lazear first regresses each outcome indicator on severance pay and linear and quadratic terms in time. Significantly negative coefficient estimates are obtained for the severance pay covariate in all but the unemployment regression where a signifi-

Table 3.3. Lazear's estimates of the effects of severance pay (combined cross-section time-series estimates)

| | | Outcome Indicator | |
	EMPPOP	UNRATE	LFPR
SEV	−0.0037	0.0011	−0.0034
	(0.0005)	(0.0003)	(0.0005)
R²	0.17	0.35	0.18
n	455	455	455

Source: Lazear (1990, Table VIII).
Notes: Standard errors in parentheses. the regressions also control for time and its square, the growth rate of per capita GDP interacted with severance,, and the proportion of the population aged 25 to 65 years.
SEV: Number of months pay given to blue-collar worker as severance pay upon no-fault dismissal after 10 years service.
EMPPOP: Employment/population.
UNRATE: Unemployment/labour force.
LFPR: Labour force/population.

cantly positive coefficient is obtained. The negative coefficient on severance pay in the hours equation will be commented on below, but Lazear rationalizes his result on the grounds that job protection is not extended to part-timers, leading employers to substitute them for full-timers and causing average hours worked to fall as a result. (We note that when notice is also included as a regressor its coefficient estimates are of the same sign as severance pay and are larger in absolute magnitude in some instances. Moreover, severance pay now loses significance in the unemployment rate equation. Lazear subsequently omits the notice variable from the balance of his analysis.)

To gauge the effects of within-country variation in dismissals protection, the indicators are next regressed on severance pay and country dummies. The results of this (preferable) fixed effects procedure are weaker: the coefficient estimates for severance pay are now only statistically significant in the unemployment and hours equations. Both coefficients are of the same sign as before: positive for unemployment and negative for hours.

Table 3.3 contains summary results from a combined cross-section time-series specification that controls for the growth in output (interacted with severance pay) and the proportion of the workforce aged between 25 and 65 years. These are Lazear's preferred results. It can be seen that higher severance pay is associated with reductions in employment and labour force participation and increased unemployment. The interlocking nature of these results – namely disemployment, lower participation and higher unemployment – present a fairly pessimistic picture of the effects of mandates on the labour market.

It can be seen that Table 3.3 omits Lazear's hours results, which we find unconvincing for a number of reasons. First, and most obviously, there are coding errors in Lazear's hours worked variable. Replication of his analysis using a corrected hours variable yields a significant positive coefficient estimate for severance pay, not the negative estimate reported by Lazear (Addison and Grosso, 1996). This finding is of course consistent with a fixed cost interpretation of severance pay, leading employers to substitute hours for men. Second, and relatedly, there is the empirical suggestion that in most countries part-timers are indeed covered by the same dismissals legislation as full-timers (Grubb and Wells, 1993: 25–26). Third, hours are also governed by distinctively different legislation from dismissals. We have in mind legislative arrangements that place restrictions on overtime work, maximum hours, and the flexible organization of hours (see Chapter 10). No such subtleties are admitted in Lazear's fitted equations. Grubb and Wells (1993: 27–28) have found that normal or usual hours are strongly related to regulatory maxima for hours if not to restrictions on overtime working, and that the proportion of workers at a modal level of weekly hours increases with restrictions on the flexible distribution of working hours.

Lazear's main results have occasioned no small controversy since they point to a strong depressing effect of just one measure of job protection on the outcome indicators. For example, the model in Table 3.3 appears to explain 59% of the growth in French unemployment between 1956/59 and 1981/84 and 206% of the rise in Italian unemployment![3] Criticisms have centred on his alleged misclassification of countries, the unidimensional nature of the job protection measure, and the failure to consider the compensating impact of other institutions such as the Italian wage supplement fund – or *Cassa Integrazione Guadagni*. It remains to be seen whether Lazear's findings will survive the incorporation of additional arguments such as the generosity of a country's unemployment insurance system. Our own research suggests that the disemployment effects will show greater staying power than the unemployment results (Addison and Grosso, 1996). But the charge of naivety is unfair at least in the context of extant comparative studies; for example, we note that Lazear addresses the issue of reverse causality, *inter alia*.

In the interim, the thrust of Lazear's analysis has received some support from a recent OECD (1993) econometric study of the impact of dismissals protection on the incidence and rate of long-term unemployment (i.e. that lasting more than 12 months) in 19 countries over the sample period 1979–91. Like Lazear, the OECD measures dismissals protection in terms of the length of a legislated standard, though on this occasion separate values are specified for white and blue-collar workers. Furthermore, each measure is constructed from the sum of severance pay and notice interval for a worker with 15 years of service. Additional regressors are the maximum duration of unemployment insurance (UI) benefits and the ratio of expenditures on 'active' labour market programmes to total expenditures on unemployment benefits, where the latter is viewed as a 'passive' labour market programme. The variables in this study are expressed as averages over the sample period so that each regression has just 19 observations. The Lazear study, by contrast, employs annual data and hence each regression has well over 400 observations.

The results of this exercise are reproduced in Table 3.4. Most important, it can be seen that each of the job protection measures is associated with higher long-term unemployment. The contribution of job security to the long-term unemployment rate is particularly strong in Southern European countries (Portugal, Italy, and Spain) and Ireland. As expected, UI serves significantly to extend jobless duration. Greater expenditures on active labour market policies seem to reduce long-term joblessness, which is of course not surprising if participation in programmes automatically removes such groups from the unemployment count.

If there is little in the above to encourage a sanguine view to be taken of job protection, that part of the econometric literature dealing with the speed of adjustment of employment and hours in response to exogenous changes in output portrays at face value a somewhat more optimistic picture. Thus, a series of studies by Abraham

Table 3.4. OECD estimates of the determinants of long-term unemployment, 1979–91[a]

Variable	Long-term unemployment rate[b]		Long-term unemployment incidence[c]	
	(1)	(2)	(1)	(2)
Dismissals protection[d] (white-collar)	0.36 (4.9)		2.89 (5.1)	
Dismissals protection[d] (blue-collar)		0.41 (5.2)		3.01 (4.4)
Maximum duration of UI benefits	0.02 (2.3)	0.03 (3.9)	0.15 (2.6)	0.23 (3.9)
Active labour market programme expenditures/unemp. benefit expenditures	−1.45 (1.8)	−2.00 (2.4)	−3.32 (0.05)	6.47 (0.09)
R^2	0.75	0.76	0.82	0.78
n	19	19	19	19

Source: OECD (1993: Table 3.12).
Notes:
($|t|$ statistics in parentheses)
[a] All variables are averages for the period 1979–91.
[b] Long-term unemployed as a percentage of labour force.
[c] Long-term unemployed as a percentage of unemployed.
[d] Composite of the sum of months of severance pay and notice for a worker with 15 years service.

and Houseman (1992, 1994) and Houseman and Abraham (1994) have concluded that strong job security may be compatible with flexibility in working hours.

Abraham and Houseman (1994) use a standard Koyck model of dynamic demand (where the speed of adjustment is indexed by the coefficient on the lagged dependent variable) to compare the adjustment of manufacturing employment and hours in Belgium, France, and Germany with that of the USA. The authors estimate their model using quarterly data for the sample period 1973–90. They report that employment adjustment in the former group of countries is much slower than in the USA: the median lag in adjustment of employment to changes in output – the time required for half of the adjustment to be completed – is three quarters in Germany/Belgium and 10 quarters in France, but only one current quarter in the USA. However, these marked disparities are not found with respect to the speed of hours adjustment, especially in the case of Belgium where the coefficient estimates are often insignificantly different from the USA – and, even where significant differences are reported in favour of the USA, the implied mean lag is never more than one quarter longer than that in the USA. (The German case is marginally less clear cut and no hours data are available for France.)

Why should European employment adjust less rapidly than in the USA but total hours adjust almost equally rapidly? Abraham and Houseman attribute the latter phenomenon to short-time working. They compute the contribution of short-time working to hours adjustment for Germany and Belgium (and inferentially to employment adjustment in the French case). The method is to add short-time hours to production hours and rerun the hours adjustment equation to obtain a speed of

ithout short-time working. The coefficient estimate for lagged
ly larger than before, implying much slower adjustment in the
ne working. In sum, short-time hours appear to make a signifi-
the adjustment of labour input.

and Houseman analyse the impact on adjustment speeds of
cally, the 1985 Employment Promotion Act in Germany (which
liberalized the use of fixed-term contracts, and also raised the thresholds concerning the number of employees who could be laid off without having to negotiate a
social plan), and analogous legislation in France in 1987 and in Belgium in 1985.
The coefficient estimate for the dummy variable corresponding to the timing of
these laws should be negative for a loosening of legislation if such changes improved
responsiveness. For Germany, the coefficients are positive but insignificant at the
most aggregative level; at lower levels of aggregation they are of mixed sign but with
one exception are always insignificant. For France negative coefficient estimates are
encountered for manufacturing as a whole and for five out of seven manufacturing
industries (significant in three of these cases). For Belgium, however, a pattern of
largely positive and often significant coefficient estimates is obtained for both types
of reforms. So these results do not give much support to the notion that relaxing job
protection laws improves responsiveness.

In a treatment comparing Germany with the USA, covering the same sample
period (1973–90), Houseman and Abraham (1994) use a dynamic demand model in
which factor demand is interrelated (i.e. hours enter the employment equation and
vice versa). Parameter estimates from the employment and hours equations are used
to simulate the dynamic effects of a one-unit permanent output shock. The results
of this exercise at the level of aggregate manufacturing confirm the earlier finding
that German employment adjusts more slowly but average hours adjust more
rapidly. But the greater average hours adjustment does not fully compensate for the
smaller employment adjustment. In other words, at this level of aggregation it seems
that total hours adjustment in Germany is significantly smaller than in the USA –
up to four quarters after the shock. However, this aggregate result is only replicated
in two out of 11 industry disaggregations. Indeed, total hours adjustment is actually greater in one German industry (printing) than in its US counterpart; for the
rest, there are either no significant differences in employment, average hours, and
total hours, or the greater average hours adjustment seems sufficient to compensate
for the smaller employment adjustment.[4]

The authors conclude from the overall evidence that strong labour market regulation is compatible with flexibility since in practice employers have developed alternative strategies enabling them to adjust their labour input to changes in output.
They argue that the principal alternative strategy of hours adjustment is facilitated
by state-subsidized short-time working, on which more below.

But we should remember that these speed of adjustment studies do not address
the issue of the overall effect of job protection on employment. If the per period
cost of labour rises then employment will fall. Moreover, it can also be argued that
the way in which total labour hours adjust does matter in the sense that if adjustment principally takes the form of changes in hours the ability of new workers to
gain employment is circumscribed, further sharpening the distinction between
insiders and outsiders. Thus, the notion that short-time working is more equitable
than layoffs because it spreads the costs of adjustment more evenly across members
of the workforce (than layoffs) has to be qualified.

Even if recourse to short-time working may be easier in a number of European countries than in the USA, however, it should be noted that the evidence supplied by Abraham and Houseman on the effect of changes in legislation on the process of adjustment is very mixed. Using a vector autoregression approach to study the relation between employment and output and hours and output, Hamermesh (1988) obtains some, albeit weak, evidence that more stringent labour protection legislation was associated with increased lags in the adjustment of employment to output. Hamermesh looks for changes in lag structures across a sample of 11 OECD countries between the two periods 1961–1973 and 1973–1985. The break point is chosen to coincide with the first oil-price shock, after which many of these countries adopted policies to slow the adjustment of employment to output shocks. In eight out of 11 countries the average lag of employment adjustment lengthened (although there is no suggestion that the duration of the adjustment lag in hours shortened). This evidence is consistent with job protection policies operating in the hypothesized manner, but, as Hamermesh cautions, such evidence is no more than a starting point for an investigation that should focus on individual policies in particular countries and industries.

The issue of short-time working is also taken up by Van Audenrode (1994), whose theoretical model properly focuses on the degree of subsidization offered by national compensation schemes for short-time working rather than the existence of such arrangements. In his empirical analysis, the author uses a simple error correction mechanism fitted to employment and total hours worked to compare the speed of labour adjustment in manufacturing industry among 10 countries, 1969–88. Van Audenrode's results for employment adjustment confirm the now familiar finding that the USA responds faster than any other nation. For total hours worked, however, Belgium, Denmark, Italy, and Sweden react about as quickly as the USA, despite their slower adjustment along the employment dimension. These four countries are distinguished by the relative generosity of their short-time compensation schemes; furthermore, each is also adjudged to have either 'some' or 'extensive' dismissals protection. Adjustments in working time in the other countries – Canada, France, Japan, the UK and Germany – are not sufficiently rapid to compensate for their slower adjustment in employment. (None of the latter group of countries is classified by the author as having generous short-time compensation schemes.)

These findings qualify those of Abraham and Houseman – most notably in the case of Germany, although there is common agreement on the flexible Belgian case – in that all hinges on the details of the short-time compensation schemes. Given strong restrictions on dismissals, generous subsidization of working time is required to generate sufficient flexibility in working time so as to achieve efficient levels of employment and working hours.

The notion that employment protection schemes interact with other policies, such as compensation for short-time working, is a sensible qualification, but one that has not been much exploited in the empirical literature – beyond the use of an aggregative 'active' labour market policy regressor in the OECD study reviewed earlier. One example might be the existence of early retirement schemes (i.e. one variant of an active labour market policy), while the discretion offered by the availability of various market escape routes would be another. Mosley and Kruppe (1993) have examined the early retirement issue, again using their subjective reputational index (see Table 3.2). Correlating this index with early retirement rates from the ELFS for 11 member states of the Community in 1989, they obtain a simple correlation coefficient of $r=0.409$. Expanding the definition of early retirement to include retirements for health reasons, in addition to those for economic reasons, the association strengthens to $r=0.741$. Such schemes may then offer an extra degree of freedom to employers in highly regulated labour markets.

National Studies

There is a growing literature at the country level on the impact of job protection, though much is descriptive rather than analytical. So as to illustrate some of the more important issues thrown up by the country studies, we draw eclectically on evidence from just three countries – the UK, France, and Germany – and conclude with some recent findings from the USA, often considered to be the examplar of a hands-off, *laissez faire* regime. The reader will not be surprised to learn that the evidence is again mixed.

Although the UK is among the least regulated member states of the Community (see Tables 3.1 and 3.2; see also Chapter 10), its job protection rules have perhaps received the greatest analytical scrutiny. In an early study of monthly employment and hours data for UK manufacturing, 1954–76, Nickell (1979) reports significant changes in the speed of adjustment of employment and hours between the two sub-periods delineated by the introduction of job protection legislation in 1966[5]. For the employment regression, the coefficient on the lagged dependent variable rose between the two intervals, indicating greater persistence, and conversely for the hours equation. In short, firms appear to have reduced their dependence on employment adjustment and increased that on hours adjustment, at a time when the fixed costs of employment may be expected to have increased because of the legislation.

The main thrust of Nickell's study, however, had to do with the level of employment demand rather than its cyclicality. He used a model in which the flows into unemployment were directly reduced by the increased costs of dismissal. Since the latter also have the effect of making employers more selective about whom they hire, Nickell further sought to model the effect of job protection on the duration of unemployment. This greater selectivity would reduce the proportion of vacancies filled, thereby offsetting the reduced dependence of the firm on employment adjustment, and increasing equilibrium unemployment. His analysis thus had a basis in two equations: one explaining inflows into unemployment, and the other explaining the proportion of vacancies filled. The effect of legislation was simply proxied by a time trend. For the inflow regression, the time trend indicated a secular inflow reduction of 0.18% per quarter. For the vacancy regression, the time trend suggested that the probability of an individual receiving (and accepting) a job offer on visiting a vacancy had declined secularly at the rate of 1.1% a quarter. These values imply that the equilibrium level of unemployment rose by approximately 23% over 1970–76, offset by a reduction of some 3% from the reduced inflows into unemployment. Nickell does of course argue that the net increase of 20% is due other than in part to job protection because of the crudeness of the time trends approach and the imprecision of the estimates (see also Andrews and Nickell, 1982; Layard and Nickell, 1986).

However, in a separate analysis of monthly UK data for 1967–77 – using two flow equations into and out of employment, with a more obvious equilibrium interpretation – Nickell (1982) reached an opposite conclusion. On net, he reported that the legislation (now proxied by the number of unfair dismissal cases rather than a trend variable) reduced the growth in (male) unemployment by −0.97 percentage points.

Since unemployment rose by 3.77 percentage points over the sample period, estimate might suggest that job protection has substantial benefits after all, if it assumed that the long-run level of employment remains unaffected by slower (short-run) adjustment. Stronger results are reported by Burgess (1988), using a dynamic model of labour demand fitted to UK quarterly manufacturing data for 1963–82 and proxying adjustment costs by the average size of unfair dismissal and redundancy payments. He concludes, among other things, that had unfair dismissal payments been eliminated, the annual fall in employment between 1975 and 1982 would have been 6.15% rather than the observed 4.2% a year. However, in a subsequent (comparative) analysis, Burgess (1994) accepts that the slower adjustment speed translates into losses in national income by retarding the reallocation of labour from declining to growing sectors of the economy.

These studies all pertain to increased regulation. There are no UK studies of the impact of reduced job protection (i.e. deregulation). For these, we have to turn to evidence from other countries. Here, perhaps the most interesting case is that of France. Deregulation in France over 1985 and 1986 took the form of eliminating the requirement that all dismissals for economic reasons receive prior authorization by the Labour Inspectorate, and liberalizing the rules pertaining to the use of fixed-term contracts and temporary (i.e. agency) workers. In the latter context, employers no longer had to give reasons for using fixed-term contracts or agency workers, and the maximum duration of either type of arrangement was generally increased to 24 months. (Such changes would of course escape identification in studies such as that of Lazear, but could be captured in a reputational index.) These changes followed on a marked tightening in legislation in 1982, which laid down the precise circumstances in which temporary work could be used, set a limit of 6 months on fixed-term and temporary contracts and required that they were not to be used to fill permanent positions, and established equality between regular and atypical work in terms of wages, fringes, and working conditions. (The social rights of atypical workers have not been affected by deregulation.)

Some peculiarities of the French system indicate the difficulties that arise in cross-country comparisons. For example, the majority of young workers in 'alternance training' are on fixed-term contracts, so that any attempt to gauge the effect of, say, deregulation should either net out such contracts, which are extensive, or in some way accommodate this aspect of policy. (A similar type of cross-country comparison problem arises with subsidies, such as the Italian wage supplement fund, failure to take account of which may obscure identification of the impact of the job protection apparatus.) Cross-country analyses can easily miss such subtleties. By the same token, many of the individual country studies are caught up in descriptive minutiae and do not offer a true *ceteris paribus* treatment.

The French data seem to suggest, firstly, that there was an increase in dismissals for economic reasons following the abolition of third party notification as might be expected (Maurau, 1993). Yet by the same token the rapid growth in both fixed-term and temporary contracts observed in that country seems to have preceded the liberalization of 1985/86. Given the peculiarities of the data on fixed-term contracts, referred to above, and the absence of a reliable time series for these contracts, statistical analysis has focused on the employment of temporary workers. A recent study by Charraud (1993) seeks to model the determinants of temporary worker employment by taking explicit account of the different reasons for hiring temporary workers, namely, to replace absentees, to meet exceptional work loads, and to assist in restructuring enterprises. Each reason is proxied in his regression model of the

ary employment using quarterly data for the period 1975–89.
riables are used to chart the effects of the legislative changes in
86. Charraud reports strongly negative effects of the 1982 legisla-
reduction in agency work of about one third – but the coefficient
wo phases of liberalization are not statistically significant, and at
y modest stimulating effect. Given that the restrictive legislation
of 1982 did not ultimately stop the growth in temporary employment – there was a
surge in such work from 1984 onward – he speculates that the liberalization of
1985/86 was designed 'to enable legislation to catch up with what had already been
happening and perhaps to give a nudge in the right direction' (Charraud, 1993: 381).

Turning next to German deregulation, we consider results on the effect of the
1985 Employment Promotion Act. Like the French legislation of 1985/86, this
measure also liberalized the use of fixed-term and temporary work contracts: the
former could now be deployed without the employer having to meet the pre-existing
set of so-called 'legitimate reasons', and could have a maximum duration of 18
months (24 months in the case of newly established small firms); the duration of the
latter was raised from 3 to 6 months. In addition, as was noted earlier, the Act freed
newly established small firms from the obligation to conclude 'social plans' in the
event of collective redundancies.

Both descriptive analysis and econometric work fail to detect any substantive
effect of this admittedly rather modest piece of legislation. Büchtemann's (1993)
examination of the use of fixed-term contracts in the wake of the legislation seeks
to quantify those incremental fixed-term hires stemming from intensified use by
traditional user firms plus first-time contracts (i.e. those generated in firms that had
not hitherto used fixed-term contracts). There were only 110 000 'genuine'
Employment Promotion Act contracts of this type, accounting for just 7% of all
fixed-term contracts concluded between 1985 and 1987. Of these, only one fifth were
classified by the firms in question as additional hires in the sense that they would
probably not have come into being without the Act. In short, additional hires are
estimated to represent no more than 1.5% of all fixed-term contracts – and 0.5% of
all new hires. Büchtemann further concludes that the large majority of the balance
of the genuine contracts probably substituted for permanent or open-ended contracts, at least in the short term.

The conclusion that the Employment Promotion Act seems to have had at best a
negligible effect is supported at a higher level of generality in Kraft's (1993) error-
adjustment model of employment determination, estimated using data on 21 manufacturing industries for the sample period 1970–87. The familiar objective is to
discover whether the speed of adjustment of employment rose in the wake of the
German legislation. In fact, Kraft reports that the coefficient estimate for the
dummy variable tracking the legislation is of perverse sign and significant, pointing
to a reduction in the speed of adjustment. This result is perhaps more indicative of
the level of aggregation of the study and the limited reach of the legislation than of
anything else. Note that the Act was intended to lead to a substitution of workers
for (overtime) hours, a possible outcome which is not tested.

The limited impact of the German Employment Promotion Act is also corrobo-
rated in an employment-adjustment study by Hunt (1994), using the same data as
Abraham and Houseman (1994), but this time without smoothing the monthly data
into quarterly data. Hunt's more sophisticated random coefficients model allows the
speed of adjustment to be different as between (seasonal) upturns and downturns.
This is in addition to examining the effects of the legislation – captured by a dummy

(BEFORE) for the interval preceding the implementation of the legislation in May 1985 – on lagged employment (expected to be positive) and lagged sales (this variable is a proxy for shocks to labour demand so that the effect of legislation is expected to be negative). Hunt's principal findings are as follows. First, consonant with the extant literature, she reports that hours adjustment is more rapid than employment adjustment, the new wrinkle being that both are slower in the upswing than the downswing, at least for blue-collar workers. Second, the coefficient estimates of the BEFORE dummy interacted with lagged employment are generally insignificant, although where significant suggest reduced flexibility after 1985. However, in the case of hours the results are rather different: there are now signs that hours flexibility was less prior to the legislation. Unfortunately, the nature of the legislative changes in question would not lead one to expect any such differential effect. Third, distinguishing between industries with high and low variability in sales provides some evidence of greater flexibility post-1985 among the former group for blue-collar workers. Finally, when closer attention is paid to the timing of particular changes in flexibility, where observed, it emerges that these do not readily correspond to the periodicity of the legislation.

These mixed results are perhaps more indicative of a failure of this and other studies to employ a direct measure of firing costs, and a reliance on simple dummies allied to the timing of legislation. Also, as Hunt notes, the general lack of impact of the 1985 legislation could reflect a variety of factors other than there being no effect on firing costs; for example, restrictions on renewing fixed-term contracts may have limited the usefulness of their wider availability, while workplace representatives may have forced employers to convert more fixed-term contracts into permanent contracts than they would have chosen if not so constrained.

Finally, we turn to the US experience. Despite the prevalence of the 'hire-at-will' principle in that country, this common law doctrine has been breached through time at the hands of state judiciaries, which have in varying degree recognized exceptions to hire-at-will. Three legal bases, in ascending order of their potential reach, have been used to establish wrongful dismissal: the public policy exception, the implied contract exception, and the covenant of fair dealing and good faith exception. By the early 1990s some 45 states had adopted one, two, or even all three of these legal attenuations of hire-at-will, although only Montana had a wrongful dismissal statute. As a result of these legal incursions, the number of wrongful dismissal suits has mushroomed. Successful settlements have been well publicized – surveys of average rewards granted in unjust dismissal cases point to substantial (and positively skewed) settlements; in successful cases the initial median award approximates to $180 000, reduced of course by post-trial actions. Although the total legal costs to employers appear to amount to less than 0.1% of the total wage bill (Dertouzos *et al.*, 1988), employers, as we shall see, appear to be reacting as if the costs of being sued are very much higher. But we note that one cannot directly infer the effects of the legal system based on total award and legal costs, because high awards and an unfavourable court climate will deter business from dismissing workers without clear-cut cause, thus lowering the total number of cases and awards.

The consequences of this back-door regulation for the aggregate level of employment (and the speed of adjustment of employment to its determinants) have been analysed by Dertouzos and Karoly (1992, 1993), using state-level data for 1980–87. States are distinguished according to which of the three (hybrid) wrongful dismissal doctrines their courts have embraced, and whether or not remedies are contractual or tort based. (Tort remedies allow punitive damages for pain and suffering, in addition to compensation for foregone earnings.) The authors estimate a fixed-effects model of employment in which the regressors include gross state product, the growth in gross state product, year dummies, and presence of one or other of the three legal doctrines and type of remedy. The latter are instrumented to account for the non-random distribution of state doctrines/remedies. This is thus the only study of which we are aware that attempts to control for the endogeneity of regulation, hinted at in some of the other country studies (in particular, Charraud, 1993).

The authors report that aggregate employment is on average 2.9% (1.8%) lower in the years following a state's recognition of tort (contractual) damages. Regressions run for other combinations of doctrine and remedy suggest that it is the availability of tort remedies rather than type of exception that drives the disemployment result. (Mixed results are reported as to the effect of the erosion of hire-at-will on employment adjustment – see Hamermesh, 1993.)

Interestingly, the powerful US results have been interpreted not so much as to warn of the potentially harmful effects of regulation as to support the case for statutory intervention in the form of new and purportedly low-cost administrative law procedures analogous to those employed in Europe! That is to say, it has been noted (Büchtemann, 1993: 43) that the uncertainties created by legal incursions into the hire-at-will common law principle in the USA are destabilizing and that a framework of just-cause legislation at the state (if not the federal) level might provide a cheaper and clearer framework. Even Dertouzos and Karoly argue that the benefits (via a reduction in uncertainty) may be worth the employment sacrifice. There are of course historical parallels: the US system of workers' compensation, which is a form of no-fault, limited liability legislation obtaining in most states, grew out of an agreement between both sides of industry that it offered an improvement – lower transaction costs and greater certainty – on the pre-existing system of judicial remedies. Analogously, it may be argued that employers will support the adoption of state legislation on unjust dismissal so as to limit their liability if it is cost-effective. That they have thus far not done so on any significant scale would suggest that the incursions of the courts have not yet swung the balance of advantage in that direction.

This partial review of the empirical evidence on the consequences of job security measures has revealed a mixed pattern of results. The claims of industry that job regulation costs jobs are not always fully reflected in the data. Thus, there is disagreement over the effects of job protection on unemployment and employment. Lazear's analysis, if correct, suggests that employment is reduced and unemployment increased by dismissals protection. The OECD also reports that long-term unemployment is increased by the same rules examined by Lazear. But these results have not gone unchallenged. For example, we have noted that other studies examining the flows into and out of unemployment have not reached a consensus on the net effect of employment protection rules on unemployment. Moreover, empirical analyses of the speed-of-adjustment type have suggested that reduced employment flexibility may be offset by greater hours flexibility, such that the constraints on firm behaviour (and hence the implied increase in labour costs because of inefficient levels of employment and working time) may have been exaggerated. Such studies have also failed to uncover evidence of any significant benefits of deregulation in this regard.

In all of this it is not clear whether the failure to detect consistent effects of job protection is a function of the theoretical ambiguity of the measures or inadequate modelling on the part of the investigator. It is notoriously difficult to quantify the costs of the various measures. Some investigators have simply used dummy variables to characterize the onset of changes in legislation and looked for corresponding temporal changes in the outcome measures under consideration. Those who have sought to tackle the costs issue using months of severance pay and notice have been confronted by the complexities of the legal rules, the unobserved role of collective bargaining, and the ever-present problems of causality. Yet other observers have deployed some reputational index, fashioned out of employer responses, to proxy the stringency of legislation. Unfortunately, this composite index glosses over the often very different sources of the constraints placed upon employers in the various countries. And irrespective of the precise manner in which legislation is calibrated, there are the problems of accounting for other variables that influence the outcome indicators. Very little attention has been paid to wage and non-wage labour costs in the economist's parsimonious reduced-form specifications. What we do know of course is that much of the variance in the relevant outcome indicators is unexplained by employment protection and that two countries with very different systems of employment protection may record similar levels of unemployment. Nevertheless, although the data are noisy, legislation and other rules do often seem to pick up distinct and adverse effects of employment protection on the labour market.

Given the pressing need properly to parameterize individual rules, it is likely that cross-country analysis will now have to give way to national studies. This focus should also allow us to obtain greater insights into the wider system in which particular rules are embedded, and hence how the tradeoffs might differ. Here, too, one would anticipate being better able to establish a closer link between study method and the theoretical arguments encountered earlier in this chapter. We have been unable to identify much progress in this regard.

One of the things we need to know more about is the effect of job regulation on atypical work. One obvious issue has to do with the possible stimulus to temporary, part-time, and fixed-term contract work caused by regulation. Surprisingly, there is as yet little evidence to suggest that regulation is systematically associated with a growth in 'precarious work' of this nature, which result in part reflects the fact that countries differentially regulate the various forms of the employment relation. But the recent liberalization in the use of fixed-term contracts in countries such as Spain, which have onerous job protection laws in respect of open-ended contracts, has been accompanied by a massive growth of such contracts (see Chapter 8). The Spanish case in particular would appear to offer a near ideal environment for studying the impact of deregulation on labour market adjustment processes and average employment, as well as allowing detailed investigation of the nature of precarious work.

Even if the impact on atypical work is unclear, the relationship between the stringency of job protection and the growth in long-term unemployment observed in a number of studies does give rise to concern, especially since the studies seem to point to a disproportionate burden being borne by younger workers. Evidently, a smaller share of employed workers seem to be enjoying greater job security – the insider–outsider problem. This suggestion of blockages in the labour market, allied to employment protection and the marginalization of certain groups, needs urgent study. Policy to regulate atypical work is, as ever, moving in advance of any such analysis, and hence without regard to the inequality-increasing potential of job protection.

Finally, it follows that only with difficulty can a case be made for harmonization on these results. This conclusion is underwritten by the fact that systems of employment protection are not a datum but instead seem to evolve through time, even if we are not yet clear as to the identity of the forces making for change.

3.4.   Evidence on Other Mandates

Other mandates described in Chapter 2 also have potentially significant resource implications. Inevitably, there has been comparatively little research into the effects of these mandates. Below we assemble some material from the available studies, including estimates made by the UK Department of Employment and Department of Social Security on the 'compliance cost' of various mandates.

Taking first the issue of mandatory admission of part-time and temporary (agency) workers to occupational pension schemes and to sick pay and holiday schemes (see items 23 and 24 in Table 2.1), the Department of Employment (1992) has estimated that this would confer benefits on workers worth some £1 billion a year as of 1990, or some 5% of the 'atypical' worker wage bill.[6] This is not to say that the extra benefits would inflate firms' costs by this figure, since we do not know to what extent part-time and temporary worker wages would fall to accommodate the measure. However, as noted in the discussion of Figure 3.1 above, if wages do not fall (in this case by about 5%) employment must decline. In fact, as will be seen below in connection with the extension of maternity rights in the USA, the pay of groups affected by a mandate might be quite flexible downwards (Gruber, 1994), so employment need not be much affected.

Turning next to mandates that place restrictions on working time, estimates by the Department of Employment (1992) again give us some idea as to the magnitude of the adjustments involved. The Department has calculated that 3.0% of hours worked in 1991 would have contravened the 48 hours maximum working week originally proposed (see item 3 in Table 2.1). Also, 0.4% of working time would have contravened the minimum rest periods (11 hours a day and 24 hours a week). In addition, extension of the right to 20 days' paid vacation to all workers is estimated to confer a benefit equal to roughly 0.5% of the wage bill.

Restrictions on working hours are sometimes given a health and safety rationale (as in the Community Directive), and sometimes a work-sharing rationale as well. The two rationales are linked. If workers need protection on health and safety grounds, then the argument must be either that they do not know what is good for them or that they are being coerced to work in unsafe conditions (i.e. lack choice). If this is true, workers should be willing to accept a lower weekly wage (an unchanged hourly wage, multiplied by fewer hours worked per week) when weekly hours are reduced. Abstracting from fixed employment costs and assuming that the cut in working hours shifts the labour demand curve outwards, employment should rise. In other words, a successful programme of work-sharing requires income-sharing, namely, a fall in weekly income proportional to the fall in hours. On the other hand, if the reduction in weekly hours is accompanied by higher hourly pay in the effort to maintain weekly incomes, then employment and output can be expected to fall, other things being equal.

Houpis (1993) reviews the evidence on whether workers are prepared to income-share; specifically, on the link between weekly hours and the hourly wage. The evidence seems mixed. Some studies report that hourly wages increase when weekly hours decline, though Houpis himself can find no significant negative relation using postwar UK data. Layard *et al.* (1991: 504) have questioned on theoretical grounds the idea that work-sharing can leave output unaffected. Using cross-country data for 1975–88 they note the tendency for nations experiencing the largest decline in working hours to have experienced the largest increase in unemployment.

In addition to efficiency issues, we should also remember that hours restrictions are likely to be inequality-increasing. This is because it is only hourly-paid workers whose hours are to be restricted; in other words, it is only they who will be called upon to 'income-share'. Workers with 'autonomous decision-making powers', that is, the higher earners, are explicitly excluded from the Directive. (In any case, the hours of professional and managerial workers are difficult if not impossible to monitor.) All in all, it is hard to resist the conclusion that policies restricting hours are likely candidates for the upper-right 'bad' box of Figure 3.7.

Estimates have also been made of the value of benefits mandated by the original version of the pregnant workers directive (item 5 in Table 2.1). Specifically, the Department of Employment (1991) has calculated that 14 weeks' leave at full pay, as called for in earlier drafts of the directive, would other things being equal give workers new benefits worth about £400 million a year. The current law, in the form of the Trade Union Reform and Employment Rights Act of 1993 (effective October 1994), is estimated to have an annual compliance cost of between £100 and £250 million, as regards the extension to all women of the right to 14 weeks' maternity leave regardless of length of service (Department of Employment, 1994). The cost figure depends on an estimate of the 'cost of leaving a job open', which is difficult to pin down. As for the increase in maternity pay,[7] this is costed at about £210 per worker, or only £55 million a year in total (Department of Social Security, 1994).

If freely negotiated contracts underprovide maternity pay due to asymmetric information, then mandates will increase employment – provided that wages of women of child-bearing age also fall (see Figure 3.1). A problem is that anti-discrimination laws, or the need to preserve horizontal equity in the workplace, might prevent such a fall in relative wages from occurring. Gruber (1994) has studied this issue in the context of US Federal and state laws mandating the inclusion of maternity coverage in company health insurance policies. The cost of adding maternity benefits to the insurance package is said to be approximately 1 to 5% of weekly earnings.

Gruber finds that the wages of married women aged between 20 and 40 fell by approximately 4 to 5% in states that passed a law relative to those states that did not (Gruber, 1994: 630, 631), suggesting full shifting of the costs of the mandate. It appears also that weekly hours worked rose by 5% for the affected group, and numbers employed fell by 2% (Gruber, 1994: 633). These findings imply that the mandate is valued by the target group, but that it disadvantages part-time labour, in part perhaps because pregnancy insurance is a fixed cost which is a higher proportion of the pay of employees working fewer hours. It is evident from this study that even where wages are flexible, mandates can have disemployment effects for the poorer workers.

Turning next to the cost implications of health and safety directives (see items 6–13 of Table 2.1), the UK Health and Safety Commission (1991: 18) has provided some indicative estimates of individual safety directives issued under the pre-social charter 'framework' safety and health directive. For example, the directive pertaining to the use of visual display units, which requires that firms provide free eye tests and eyeglasses to operators, is costed at only £30 to £40 million a year. Such a low perceived cost, together with the UK's relatively advanced level of safety regulation, presumably explains why these measures have so easily negotiated the legislative hurdles, at least up to the present. It is probably for the poorer countries that advanced safety regulations pose most problems.

The poorer Community states – Greece, Ireland, Portugal and Spain – will have the most ground to make up in complying with Community safety mandates. While these countries have strict health and safety laws (Commission, 1992: 114), enforcement of safety laws seems to be uneven. An OECD study (1989: Chart 4.4) provides estimates of annual workplace injury rates of between 20 and 30 per thousand employees in Sweden and the UK, about 40 per thousand in the USA, but no less than 70 per thousand in Spain and 90 per thousand in Portugal. This is presumably partly because of the large family worker and 'underground' sector in Greece, Portugal and Spain which is naturally difficult to regulate. Regulation is also likely to be slacker because of an income effect: in a poorer region, inspectors are likely to be more lenient on firms for fear of jeopardizing jobs and/or lowering incomes (for a model, see Fenn and Veljanovski, 1988). Poorer countries can less afford to be choosy.

While we have no evidence on whether health and safety (and other) mandates will be employment-reducing for poorer member states, such an outcome is implied by the large subsidies these states have been receiving. As noted in Chapter 2, there has been a major redistribution in favour of the poorer member states via the Structural Funds. If social charter mandates imply increased production costs and hence an erosion of the poorer states' competitive wage advantage, as orthodox economic analysis implies, then the subsidies we observe are evidence of these effects. Furthermore, it is possible that the further doubling of subsidies that has been agreed for 1994–99 (see Table 2.3), is required to offset the effects of the more ambitious mandates that may result from the extension of majority voting within the new European Union.

Finally, let us briefly consider mandates enforcing worker participation via company works councils (e.g. item 25 of Table 2.1). As noted earlier, mandated works councils could be efficient if there is market failure due to the 'externalities' imposed by non-participative firms on their participative counterparts. A further argument might be that management would veto works councils even if they were efficient because councils, while raising value-added, might nonetheless reduce profitability (Freeman and Lazear, 1995).

Both at the level of theory and measurement the link between participation in its various guises and productivity is unclear (see the essays contained in Blinder, 1990). The effects of the German works council, the examplar of direct worker participation, are reviewed in Addison *et al.* (1995b) and Addison *et al.* (1996). The authors report few indications of any positive effect on productivity – indeed, the balance of the evidence is to the contrary – although there is little indication that the uniformly negative effect on firm profitability carries over to investment. Broader evidence on worker attitudes to formal participation is also less favourable than might be thought (see Black, 1994: 108).

Mandated worker participation could be inequality-increasing or reducing. The arguments seem to rest primarily on the effects of mandated participation on small firms. In the UK, according to the 1990 Workplace Industrial Relations Survey, although 37% of unionized workplaces had joint consultative committees, just 19% of non-union workplaces had them. Thus, on the positive side, a participation mandate can be regarded as spreading the benefits of participation beyond those firms recognizing unions – and especially into small firms. However, the current European Works Council (EWC) directive applies only to large (predominantly unionized) firms – so this positive aspect cannot come into play. By widening participation only for workers in the larger firms, the EWC directive could be regarded as inequality-increasing. Still, it is perhaps as well that small firms are left out, because there is the possibility that they may be less able to cope with the costs of formal participation and slower decision making. Research in the USA indicates that environmental and safety regulation has impacted adversely on employment in small firms (Bartél and Thomas, 1987). An analogous effect might arguably operate in the case of participation rules. In addition, as mentioned in our discussion of asymmetric information, mandated participation might be regarded as redistributing from the 'more industrious' to the 'less industrious'.

In sum, both the efficiency and equity aspects of mandated participation are problematic. It is not certain that the degree of participation that firms freely negotiate with their workforces need be overridden in the interests of efficiency. As for equity, if a mandate is selectively imposed only on large firms, this could be inequitable because such firms tend already to be well unionized. If the mandate is extended to small firms, this carries the risk of disemployment for the least skilled workers.

3.5. Conclusions

Government regulation of labour markets amounts to the setting of minimum working conditions. The issues encountered are therefore similar to those raised in analysis of the setting of minimum wages. Mandates relating to working conditions are more varied than those relating to minimum wages of course, so many interesting differences of detail arise. But the basic question of disemployment effects remains. In fact, laws setting both minimum wages and minimum conditions, by removing degrees of freedom in adjusting the components of the compensation package, should in combination pose a greater risk of inducing unemployment.

In this chapter we have considered an array of mandates. We have also considered arguments relating to the efficiency of these mandates, and to their possible effects on the earnings and income distributions. A definite conclusion we can reach is that there has been less research into the distributional consequences of mandates than into their efficiency effects. This is an important gap, since we would normally be prepared to trade off efficiency for equity, as the categorization of policies illustrated in Figure 3.7 suggests. A worrying aspect of several mandates is that their distributional effects could well be adverse. Mandated hours restrictions stand out in this respect, since it is mainly the poorer workers whose hours would be restricted.

Table 3.5 summarizes the main arguments we have considered in the chapter. Taking the misallocation argument first, Freeman (1993: 404) notes that the Harberger welfare triangles in practice seem small, perhaps because mandates are not enforced strictly in bad times when the survival of firms is at stake. When tough mandates are enforced, as in the case of minimum wages in Puerto Rico, the welfare triangles can be large. As for the slower adjustment argument in row 2, this is relevant particularly to employment protection mandates. Our summary of the main

Table 3.5. Labour market regulation: the cases for and against

Case Against	Reply
1. Mandates cause misallocation	Welfare triangles associated with misallocation seem generally small
2. Slower workforce adjustment	Parties can 'contract around' mandates, thereby limiting efficiency effects
3. Redistribution is in favour of those in work and/or unionized	Unemployment effects are minor; mandates make up for lack of unionization

Case For	Reply
4. Asymmetric information	Appears to be relevant only in a limited number of cases
5. Prisoner's dilemmas require cooperation	These are only relevant if 'traditional' firms are shown to have lower labour productivity – more research needed
6. Monopoly/ monopsony power	How widespread is such power, and in any case are super-normal profits being made?

recent studies failed to present a clear pattern of results, perhaps because parties can costlessly 'contract around' the mandate; for example, by substituting hours adjustment for labour force adjustment. A more plausible explanation for the mixed results, however, probably lies in the difficulties of modelling the legislation and accounting for its effect on employment. We certainly cannot yet come to the conclusion that job protection has few adverse employment effects. Indeed, our reading of the balance of the evidence is to the contrary.

The issue of the redistributive effects of mandates needs much more research, as we have already noted. To the argument in row 3, that mandates are deficient because they redistribute only to those in work, and amongst these to the unionized 'haves', the safest answer at the moment would be that the jury is still out.

Turning to the case for mandates, we have considered the main efficiency-based arguments (asymmetric information, prisoner's dilemma and monopsony) in some detail. These arguments have considerable power, as we have noted, but they should not be carried too far. For example, the asymmetric information model applies most obviously to insurance-type mandates such as health insurance, or pregnancy risk, and can only be used to justify other mandates with difficulty, if at all. Notice, as well, the importance of wage flexibility if the mandate is not to generate unemployment. Empirical studies in the USA have in fact detected such a wage decline in the case of married women of child-bearing age consequent upon the mandatory extension of insurance for pregnancy risks. Whether such a fall in the relative wage of protected groups would be forthcoming in the much less flexible economies of the European Union is an open question. Similarly, while monopsony power (row 6) may be more widespread than is often thought, such power needs to be combined with supernormal profits if it is to act as a platform enabling minimum wages or conditions to be set without adverse employment effects.

Notes

1 The maximum weekly subsidy, as of April 1994, was about £45 for an adul
  £30 per child (depending on age). This subsidy was reduced in the amount of 7
  £1 earned above £72 per week. About 500 000 families benefit from an aver   ..cekly
  subsidy of £40.
2 Results of the latest ad hoc survey are provided in Commission (1995).
3 These are overestimates not least because Lazear inadvertently uses the coefficient estimates for severance pay from his employment-population ratio equation (first column of
  Table 3.3) rather than that for the unemployment- rate equation (second column of Table
  3.3).
4 The authors also check whether German employers have greater recourse to inventories
  of finished goods, as might be expected if their adjustment costs were higher. No support
  for this differential buffer stock argument is found.
5 In the UK the concept of 'unfair dismissal' was introduced under the 1971 Industrial
  Relations Act, and coverage extended under the 1975 Employment Protection Act.
  Earlier legislation in terms of the Redundancy Payments Act of 1965 established the principle of obligatory severance compensation. Subsequently, as is well known, a deregulatory thrust was imparted, the most important aspect of which was extension of the
  qualifying service period for unfair dismissals coverage from 26 to 52 weeks in 1979, and
  then up 105 weeks in 1985, and a gradual reduction in the rebates to employers making
  redundancy payments. The rebates were eliminated in 1986 for all firms employing 10 or
  more workers, and then for all firms in 1990.
6 With respect to the pension issue, which is the largest single item, available evidence indicates that only 15% of part-timers and no temporary workers currently participate in
  occupational pension schemes. The Department calculates that if, for example, the
  Community directive were to result in a 40% take-up of pensions for both groups, an extra
  premium of £0.4 billion would be required.
7 Maternity pay is paid for the first 6 weeks of maternity at 90% of earnings, the subsequent
  12 weeks being at statutory sick pay levels of about £50 a week. This entitlement is available for all workers with over 26 weeks service. Previously, only workers with over 2 years
  service had the first 6 weeks paid at the 90% rate, others having all 18 weeks remunerated
  at the lower rate. Of the extra pay, 92% (104% in the case of small firms paying under
  £20 000 a year in NI contributions) will be refunded to firms by their being able to deduct
  it from PAYE and NI contributions.

References

Abraham, K. G. and Houseman, S. N. (1992). 'Employment Security and Labor Adjustment:
  A Comparison of West Germany and the United States'. University of Maryland
  Working Paper.
Abraham, K. G. and Houseman, S. M. (1994). 'Does Employment Protection Inhibit Labor
  Market Flexibility?' In R. M. Blank (ed.), *Social Protection Versus Economic Flexibility:
  Is There a Tradeoff?* pp. 59–93. Chicago, Illinois: University of Chicago Press.
Addison, J. T. and Blackburn, M. L. (1995). 'Mindestlöhne und Verteilung des
  Familieneinkommens'. In V. Steiner and L. Bellman (eds.), *Mikroökonomik des
  Arbeitmarktes*, pp. 209–24. Nürnberg: Bundesanstalt für Arbeit.
Addison, J. T. and Grosso, J-L. (1996). 'Job Security Provisions and Employment: Revised
  Estimates'. *Industrial Relations, 25* (October): 585–603.
Addison, J. T., Barrett, R. and Siebert, W. S. (1995a). 'Mandated Benefits, Welfare and
  Heterogeneous Firms'. Department of Economics Discussion Paper, 95–33. The
  University of Birmingham.
Addison, J. T., Schnabel, C. and Wagner, J. (1995b). 'German Industrial Relations: An
  Elusive Examplar'. *Industrielle Beziehungen, 2* (March): 24–45.

Addison, J. T., Schnabel, C. and Wagner, J. (1996). German Works Councils and Firm Performance: Evidence from the First Wave of the Hannover Firm Panel' *Kyklos,* **49** (November): 555–82.

Aghion, P. and Hermalin, B. (1990). 'Legal Restrictions on Private Contracts Can Enhance Efficiency'. *Journal of Law, Economics and Organization,* **6** (Fall): 381–409.

Andrews, M. and Nickell, S. J. (1982). 'Unemployment in the United Kingdom Since the War'. *Review of Economic Studies,* **49** (Special Issue): 731–59.

Barr, N. (1987). *The Economics of the Welfare State.* London: Weidenfeld and Nicholson.

Bartél, A. P. and Thomas, L. G. (1987). 'Predation through Regulation: The Wage and Profit Effects of the Occupational Safety and Health Administration and the Environmental Protection Agency'. *Journal of Law and Economics,* **30** (October): 239–64.

Bertola, G. (1990). 'Job Security, Employment and Wages'. *European Economic Review* **34** (June): 851–79.

Bentolila, S. and Bertola, G. (1990). 'Firing Costs and Labour Demand: How Bad is Eurosclerosis?' *Review of Economic Studies,* **57** (July): 381–402.

Black, B. (1994). 'Labour Market Incentive Structures and Employee Performance'. *British Journal of Industrial Relations,* **32** (March): 99–111.

Blinder, A. S. (1990). *Paying for Productivity – A Look at the Evidence.* Washington, DC: The Brookings Institution.

Büchtemann, C. F. (1993). 'Employment Security and Deregulation: The West German Experience'. In Christoph F. Büchtemann (ed.), *Employment Security and Labor Market Behavior – Interdisciplinary Approaches and International Evidence,* pp. 272–96. Ithaca, New York: ILR Press.

Burgess, S. M. (1988). 'Employment Adjustment in UK Manufacturing.' *Economic Journal,* **98** (March): 81–103.

Burgess, S. M. (1994). 'The Reallocation of Employment and the Role of Employment Protection Legislation'. *Centre for Economic Performance Discussion Paper* 194, London School of Economics.

Card, D. and Krueger, A. B. (1995). *Myth and Measurement: The New Economics of the Minimum Wage.* Princeton, NJ: Princeton University Press.

Charraud, A. (1993). 'The Impact of Temporary Work Legislation in France, 1980–1989'. In Christoph F. Büchtemann (ed.), *Employment Security and Labor Market Behavior – Interdisciplinary Approaches and International Evidence,* pp. 374–82. Ithaca, New York: ILR Press.

Commission (1986). 'Employment Problems: Views of Businessmen and the Workforce'. *European Economy,* **27** (March): 5–110.

Commission (1991). 'Developments on the Labour Market in the Community: Results of a Survey Covering Employers and Employees'. *European Economy,* **47** (March): 7–162.

Commission (1992). 'The Regulation of Working Conditions in the Member States of the European Community'. *Social Europe,* Supplement 4/92.

Commission (1995). 'Performance of the European Union Labour Market – Results of an Ad Hoc Labour Market Survey Covering Employers and Employees'. *European Economy Studies and Reports No.* **3**.

Department of Employment (1991). *People and Jobs.* London: DE.

Department of Employment (1992). 'Note on the Costings Exercise for the EC Social Action Programme'. Unpublished Paper. London: DE.

Department of Employment (1994). 'Compliance Cost Assessment: Directive on the Entitlement to Maternity Leave and Dismissal Protection of Pregnant Workers and Workers Who Have Recently Given Birth'. Unpublished Paper. London: DE.

Department of Social Security (1994). *Changes to Statutory Maternity Pay: Compliance Cost Assessment.* London: DSS.

Dertouzos, J. N. and Karoly, L. A. (1992). 'Labor-Market Responses to Employer Liability'. Report No. R-3989–ICJ. Santa Monica, California: The Rand Corporation.

Dertouzos, J. N. and Karoly, L. A. (1993). 'Employment Effects of Worker Protection: Evidence from the United States'. In Christoph F. Büchtemann (ed.), *Employment*

Security and Labor Market Behavior – Interdisciplinary Approaches and International Evidence, pp. 215–27. Ithaca, New York: ILR Press, pp. 215–27.

Dertouzous, J. N., Holland, E. and Ebener, P. (1988). 'The Legal and Economic Consequences of Wrongful Termination'. Report No. R-3602–ICJ. Santa Monica, California: The Rand Corporation.

Disney, R., Bellman, L., Carruth, A., Franz, W., Jackman, R., Layard, R., Lehmann, H. and Philpott, J. (1992). *Helping the Unemployed*. London: Anglo-German Foundation.

Emerson, M. (1988). 'Regulation or Deregulation of the Labour Market – Policy Regimes for the Recruitment and Dismissal of Employees in the Industrialised Countries'. *European Economic Review,* **32** (April): 775–817.

Employment in Europe (1989). Brussels: Commission of the European Communities.

Employment in Europe (1992). Brussels: Commission of the European Communities.

Fenn, Paul, and Veljanovski, C. (1988). 'A Positive Theory of Regulatory Enforcement'. *Economic Journal,* **88** (December): 1055–70.

Freeman, R. (1976) 'Individual Mobility and Union Voice in the Labor Market'. *American Economic Review,* **66** (May): 361–8.

Freeman, R. (1993). 'Labor Markets and Institutions in Economic Development'. *American Economic Review,* **83** (May): 403–8.

Freeman, R. and Lazear, E. (1995). 'An Economic Analysis of Works Councils'. In Joel Rogers and Wolfgang Streeck (eds.), *Works Councils – Consultation, Representation and Cooperation in Industrial Relations*, pp. 27–50. Chicago: University of Chicago Press.

Grubb, D. and Wells, W. (1993). 'Employment Regulation and Patterns of Work in EC Countries'. *OECD Economic Studies,* **21** (Winter): 7–58.

Gruber, J. (1994). 'The Incidence of Mandated Maternity Benefits'. *American Economic Review,* **84** (June): 622–41.

Hamermesh, D. S. (1988). 'The Demand for Workers and Hours and the Effects of Job Security Policies: Theory and Evidence'. In R. A. Hart (ed.), *Employment, Unemployment and Labor Utilization*, pp. 9–32. London and Boston: Unwin Hyman.

Hamermesh, D. S. (1993). 'Employment Protection: Theoretical Implications and Some US Evidence'. In C. F. Büchtemann (ed.), *Employment Security and Labor Market Behavior – Interdisciplinary Approaches and International Evidence*, pp. 126–43. Ithaca, New York: ILR Press.

Health and Safety Commission (1991). *Consultative Document – Proposals for Health and Safety (General Provisions) Regulations and Approved Code of Practice*. London: HSC.

Houpis, G. (1993). 'The Effect of Lower Hours of Work on Wages and Employment'. *Centre for Economic Performance Discussion Paper* 131, London School of Economics.

Houseman, S. M. and Abraham, K. G. (1994). 'Labor Adjustment under Different Institutional Structures – A Case Study of Germany and the United States'. Staff Working Paper, W. E. Upjohn Institute for Employment Research.

House of Commons (1989). *Draft Community Charter of Fundamental Social Rights – Minutes of Evidence of EC Commission*. HC Employment Committee, Session 1988–89. London: HMSO.

Hunt, J. (1994). 'Firing Costs, Employment Fluctuations and Average Employment: An Examination of Germany'. Working Paper No. 4825, National Bureau of Economic Research.

International Organisation of Employers (1985). *Adapting the Labour Market*. Geneva: IOE.

IPM (1991). *Minimum Wages: An Analysis of the Issues*. London: Institute of Personnel Management.

Johnson, W. R. and Browning, E. K. (1983). 'The Distributional and Efficiency Effects of Increasing the Minimum Wage: A Simulation'. *American Economic Review,* **73** (March): 204–11.

Kraft, K. (1993). 'Eurosclerosis Reconsidered: Employment Protection and Work Force Adjustment in West Germany'. In Christoph F. Büchtemann (ed.), *Employment Security and Labor Market Behavior – Interdisciplinary Approaches and International Evidence*, pp. 297–301. Ithaca, New York: ILR Press.

Layard, R. and Nickell, S. J. (1986). 'Unemployment in Britain'. *Economica,* **53** (Supplement 1986): S121–S170.

Layard, R., Nickell, S. and Jackman, R. (1991). *Unemployment: Macroeconomic Performance and the Labour Market.* Oxford: Oxford University Press.

Lazear, E. P. (1990). 'Job Security Provisions and Employment'. *Quarterly Journal of Economics,* **105** (August): 699–726.

Le Grand, J. (1982). *The Strategy of Equality.* London: George Allen and Unwin.

Levine, D. and Tyson, L. D. (1990). 'Participation, Productivity and the Firm's Environment'. In Alan S. Blinder (ed.), *Paying for Productivity – A Look at the Evidence,* pp. 183–237. Washington, D.C.: The Brookings Institution.

Luce, R. D. and Raiffa, H. (1957). *Games and Decisions.* New York: Wiley.

Machin, S., Manning, A. and Woodland, S. (1993). 'Are Workers Paid Their Marginal Product? Evidence from a Low Wage Labour Market'. Discussion Paper, **158**, London School of Economics.

Maurau, G. (1993). 'Regulation, Deregulation, and Labor Market Dynamics'. In Christoph F. Büchtemann (ed.), *Employment Security and Labor Market Behaviour – Interdisciplinary Approaches and International Evidence,* pp. 358–373. Ithaca, New York: ILR Press.

Mosley, H. (1994). 'Employment Protection and Labor Force Adjustment in EC Countries'. In Günther Schmid (ed.), *Labor Market Institutions in Europe: A Socio-Economic Evaluation.* Armonk, New York: M.E. Sharpe.

Mosley, H. and Kruppe, T. (1993). 'Employment Protection and Labor Force Adjustment – A Comparative Evaluation'. Social Science Research Centre Discussion Paper, Berlin (April).

Newell, A. and Symons, J. (1993). 'Macroeconomic Consequences of Taxation in the 1980's'. Discussion Paper, **134**, London School of Economics.

Nickell, S. J. (1979). 'Unemployment and the Structure of Labor Costs'. *Carnegie-Rochester Conference Series on Public Policy,* **11**: 187–222.

Nickell, S. J. (1982). 'The Determinants of Equilibrium Unemployment in Britain'. *Economic Journal,* **92** (September): 555–75.

Nozick, R. (1974). *Anarchy, State and Utopia.* New York: Basic Books.

Organisation for Economic Co-operation and Development (1989). 'Occupational Accidents in OECD Countries'. *Employment Outlook* (July): 133–59.

Organisation for Economic Co-operation and Development (1993). 'Long-Term Unemployment: Selected Causes and Remedies'. *Employment Outlook* (July): 83–117.

Persson, T. and Tabellini, G. (1994). 'Is Inequality Harmful for Growth?'. *American Economic Review,* **84** (June): 600–22.

Phelps, E. S. (1994a). 'Low-Wage Employment Subsidies Versus the Welfare State'. *American Economic Review,* **84** (May): 54–8.

Phelps, E. S. (1994b). 'On the Damaging Side Effects of the Welfare System: How, Why and What to Do'. Working Paper No. 58, Russell Sage Foundation, New York.

Pigou, A. C. (1920). *The Economics of Welfare.* London: Macmillan.

Saint-Paul, G. (1995). 'The High Unemployment Trap'. *Quarterly Journal of Economics,* **110** (May): 527–50.

Siebert, W. S. and Addison, J. T. (1991). 'Internal Labour Markets: Causes and Consequences'. *Oxford Review of Economic Policy,* **7** (Spring): 76–92.

Summers, L. H. (1989). 'Some Simple Economics of Mandated Benefits'. *American Economic Review,* **79** (May): 177–83.

Van Audenrode, M. A. (1994). 'Short-Time Compensation, Job Security, and Employment Contracts: Evidence from Selected OECD Countries'. *Journal of Political Economy,* **102** (February): 76–102.

Viscusi, W. K. (1979). Employment Hazards: An Investigation of Market Performance. Cambridge, MA, and London, England: Harvard University Press.

Wei, X. and Siebert, W. S. (1994). 'The Determinants of Workplace Accidents'. Unpublished Paper, The University of Birmingham.

4

Does Europe's Common Market Need a 'Social Dimension'? Some Academic Thoughts on a Popular Theme

Karl-Heinz Paqué[1]

This chapter discusses the economic, moral and political rationale of the efforts to supplement the common market by a social dimension. It does so in a very brief and general way – focusing on the main questions involved and leaving aside all institutional details that are not relevant to the core of the matter. The chapter is divided in four sections. In Section 4.1, we briefly present a workable definition of the two terms 'common market' and 'social dimension'. In Section 4.2, we evaluate whether welfare economics provides a case for a social dimension of the common market on the grounds of market failure. In Section 4.3, we examine the major ethical arguments for the social dimension, which are based above all on the idea of preventing unfair competition or so-called social dumping. In Section 4.4, we take up the main political rationale for the social dimension as an instrument to speed up the gradual merging of the EC member states in a federalist Europe.

4.1. Some Definitions

Let us first of all develop tentative definitions of the two relevant terms of 'economic integration' and 'social dimension'. By economic integration we mean all steps towards a common market, namely, (i) the removal of all tariff and non-tariff barriers to the free trade in goods and services, and (ii) the abolition of all impediments to the free movement of labour, capital and technology. By social dimension we mean all steps towards a state of (full) international social integration, that is, a state in which (i) national welfare systems and labour market regulations are adjusted to a common model, and (ii) a system of international redistribution is established and run by all countries involved.

The specific elements of a social integration may depend on the particular historical circumstances. For the social dimension of the Community, the following matters are presently on the agenda or may move onto it in due course:[2]

- all regulations of individual labour contracts, and in particular legal restrictions on dismissal, safety standards of worker protection, and the determination of wages and working conditions through collective bargaining;
- the legal framework of a company statute, which may prescribe a specific form of labour participation in the management and/or the control of the company (codetermination);
- a tax-financed system of aid to the poor and needy;
- a basically contribution-financed system of more or less compulsory insurance for old age, unemployment, sickness and invalidity;
- a system of interregional redistribution to equalize living standards.

Note that our definition of the social dimension is narrower than that underlying many statements and publications of the Community. For example, in an early working document the Commission (1988) interprets a cooperative growth strategy to fight unemployment (as was actually proposed by the Commission in 1985!) as a genuine part of the social dimension. In our view, this is a most unfortunate use of language: a growth strategy, whether internationally coordinated or not, is just another variant of macro- or microeconomic policy, which may be good or bad in its own right, and which may have important social and regional repercussions. In any case, it clearly does not belong to the realm of the welfare state, of labour market regulations and of company statutes. If one subsumes any such economic policy initiative under the heading of a social dimension, the term becomes useless for analytical purposes. Therefore, we will make a conceptually sharp distinction between economic and social policy and, for that matter, between an economic and a social dimension.

The question whether a social dimension is a necessary or desirable condition for economic integration may be interpreted in three different ways:

(1) Does economic integration without a social dimension lead to results which are not acceptable from the welfare economics standpoint of efficiency? (the social dimension as a means of correcting market failure)
(2) Does economic integration without a social dimension lead to results which are unacceptable from an ethical standpoint of fairness? (the social dimension as a moral judgement)
(3) Does economic integration without a social dimension lead to results which contain the germ for serious political conflicts in Europe? (the social dimension as a political requirement)

These three modes of interpretation are often confused in actual political practice. We shall keep them strictly separate in the following discussion of the matter.

4.2.   The Economic Perspective: Correcting a Market Failure

Steps towards a common market lead to two kinds of resource reallocations.[3] First, free trade in goods and services allows for specialization according to comparative cost advantages, which can be traced back to international differences in factor endowments, technologies and/or demand structures. Second, the free movement of labour, capital and technical knowledge gives all factors of production the opportunity to settle in those places where their value productivity and thus, under free market conditions, their price is highest. The standard theory of international economics tells us that, under a set of reasonable assumptions, both free trade and the free movement of factors promote economic efficiency. Theory also tells us that both forces tend to bring about an international equalization of factor prices, at least insofar as these prices are determined in free markets and thereby adequately reflect relative scarcities. For example, an international difference in the rates of return on capital in a two-country world may be reduced either directly through the migration of capital from the capital-rich to the capital-poor country or indirectly through a change of the pattern of specialization in the capital-rich country towards the production of relatively capital-intensive goods.[4]

This is the basic welfare economics case for a common market, which rests on straight economic efficiency grounds. In its own right, it delivers a powerful and widely accepted argument for economic integration.[5, 6] However, it has *per se* no bearing on the issue of the social dimension because it abstracts from any international differences in the welfare state, labour legislation, and company statutes, etc. Therefore, we extend the scope of the theory by assuming that, in a common market of two countries (call them A and B), country A decides to introduce a welfare state, which encompasses the elements mentioned above; most notably, a system of social aid, social insurance, worker protection, codetermination and interregional fiscal equalization.[7] Within the common market, the introduction of the welfare state in country A induces a reallocation of resources whenever (i) the structure of comparative cost advantages of both countries changes, and (ii) pecuniary incentives for international factor movements emerge. If nothing of this kind happens, the introduction of the welfare state is allocationally neutral – no doubt an odd special case. Realistically, allocational effects are to be expected as a direct consequence of what may be called the benefits and the costs of the welfare state.

If the welfare state in country A produces benefits in the form of, say, greater 'social peace', the risks for investment will be reduced and labour productivity will rise; factors will then move from country B to country A, as both labour and capital are attracted by the locational advantage of an improved social atmosphere. To the extent that the ratio of marginal factor productivities changes, the structure of comparative cost advantages will be altered and so will the international division of labour. Empirical guesses about the likely magnitude of these effects are very difficult, because social peace is hardly a quantifiable variable and its influence on factor productivities necessarily remains open to speculation. In turn, the allocational impact of the costs of the welfare state in the form of taxes, social security contributions and regulatory constraints are somewhat easier to grasp since they are mostly linked to the input of the factor labour.[8] They do not increase labour costs if wage claims in collective or individual bargaining are correspondingly modified so as to neutralize the welfare cost push. If this happens, firms face a mere substitution of labour cost components, from take-home pay to non-pecuniary compensation of whatever kind. Of course, this is very unlikely to happen because workers do not regard their future private benefits of the extension in the welfare state to be perfect substitutes for cash payments. Insofar as workers are not ready to carry the welfare cost burden by reducing their wage claims, the introduction of the welfare state leads to a rise in the price of labour (the 'producer wage').[9] In our example, there will then be a factor reallocation which takes account of the higher labour costs in country A: the production of labour-intensive goods will shift from country A to country B; capital will move in the same direction because country B (due to the lower cost of the complementary factor labour) has a relatively high rate of return on capital and thus an international locational advantage. With a sufficient degree of wage rigidity, there may also be a rise in unemployment in country A as a final consequence of the welfare state.

Given these scenarios, can we still speak of an efficient endstate, or is it necessary to propose an *ex ante* harmonization between the two countries to a common welfare state level so as to avoid all induced reallocations in the first place? Our example shows that, in a common market, the welfare state is none other than an additional component of a country's competitive position as a supplier of goods and services and as a location for production. It is part of the bundle of locational factors such as infrastructure, education and skills of the workforce, quality of the environment, availability of raw materials, and the level of real wages and real interest rates which quite naturally determine the relative position of a country as a producer of internationally tradeable goods and services. By choosing a certain supply of tax-, contribution- or credit-financed public services and a particular mix of labour market regulations, any country or even any region fixes a package of conditions, which has then to stand up to international or interregional competition. By definition, free trade and the free movement of factors are just those limiting cases in which there is no opportunity to scoop protectionist rents by raising barriers to trade and factor movements. Thus, the benefits and costs of the entire 'welfare state apparatus' social aid and insurance, labour market regulations, and company statutes are exposed. In this sense, a common market yields the best possible test of efficiency for the national welfare states as locational factors. To prevent such a test by cutting back on the common market project would amount to open protectionism, and no serious political voice seems to go that far. Yet the seemingly non-protectionist alternative to limit the scope of the test through steps towards a harmonization of social systems is very hard to defend on purely economic grounds. Why should some parameters of international competition be removed through *ex ante* harmonization while others such as infrastructure, education and skills of the workforce, and environmental quality continue to determine the structure of the international division of labour? A convincing economic argument for special treatment of the welfare state could only be made if there were technological externalities which directly influence the well-being of people and/or the physical productivity of factors of production in other countries. This may well be expected in the case of cross-border environmental pollution; yet for all practical purposes it is very unlikely to obtain in the case of the welfare state. Hence, there is hardly a convincing economic efficiency argument for not treating the welfare state just like any other locational factor.

On theoretical grounds, one may be tempted to argue against this line of reasoning on the grounds that pecuniary externalities (not just technological externalities) also matter. But this view is flawed: if pecuniary externalities are correctly defined in our context as the cross-border effects of introducing or extending a national welfare state on the terms-of-trade of market participants in other countries, then they simply (re-)describe the working of the welfare state on locational conditions, thus adding nothing to the conceptual framework above. In fact, transmitting and internalizing pecuniary externalities in this sense is the very essence of a market system, as is locational competition.

Not only normative theory but also positive historical experience shows that the process of economic integration need not be accompanied by a harmonization of national welfare states. Thus, for example, the dramatic upswing of transatlantic trade between western Europe and the United States, as participation of Japan and most recently the East Asian NIC sion of labour, are all very successful examples of integ harmonization of the various, and varied, social systems. Als. trade and factor movements within the EC itself came about w.. stantial harmonization of national welfare states, and is nevertheless just, ered as a major step towards a more efficient intra-European division of labo.. Why the last step towards a common market should involve a qualitatively different state of affairs, and a so far unknown problem of efficiency, remains an analytical mystery.

Hidden in the historical experience of economic integration, there is also a very important aspect of 'system dynamics': international competition in the field of the welfare state serves as a kind of process of discovery to identify which welfare state package – for whatever reason – turns out to be economically viable in practice.[10] For many years a huge welfare state, heavily regulated labour market, and high degree of union power did not lead to a lack of internationally competitive companies or to chronic unemployment in a country like Sweden. More recently the pressure on the formerly celebrated 'Swedish model' has increased dramatically, and the government of that country is presently being forced to carry out substantial reforms to slim down the welfare state. Nevertheless, it is highly unlikely that Sweden will ultimately settle on American standards of 'free capitalism'. On the other hand, Switzerland was economically quite successful with just the opposite characteristics to the Swedish model. Apparently, the cultural space of Europe provides enough leeway for a broad social search process which may lead to very different results, depending on the mentality of the population and the particular local conditions. These results cannot simply be discarded a priori as economically good or bad. It is all the more important that the decentralized experimentation with different social systems and labour relations is given enough degrees of freedom without the 'straitjacket' of Community-wide harmonization.

4.3. The Moral Perspective: Unfair Competition

In any event, discussion of the social dimension is clearly dominated by arguments based on criteria of social ethics, not those of economic efficiency. For example, German unions and employers' associations like to emphasize that a process of economic integration without a social harmonization would provoke social dumping by producers in those countries which have a comparatively cheap welfare state and more market-type labour relations. In the long run, competition would thus lead to a dismantling of social achievements in those other countries with expensive welfare programmes and extensive labour market regulations; this is why it would be immoral to focus on economic integration alone.

To avoid any misunderstanding, it is important to note at the outset that an international competition of welfare states as locational factors hardly involves 'dumping' in the standard economic sense of the term, that is, a market supply at a price which is lower than the price at which the identical or a similar product is sold by the same producers on the exporting country's domestic market.[11] Obviously, the so-called social dumping has nothing to do with this kind of discriminatory practice since the costs and benefits of the welfare state apply no matter whether the ant products are exported or not. Hence the word 'dumping' in this context is ,emantic misfit, even when the explanatory attribute 'social' is added. It may, ,owever, make sense to speak of unfair competition which violates some generally accepted ethical norms without any genuine element of dumping.

In this case, the question then arises: what are these norms which could be violated by taking advantage of specific locational conditions due to the absence or the relatively small size of the welfare state, lax labour market regulations, or, more generally, low labour costs? Or more bluntly: what is the yardstick for speaking of unfair competition? As an absolute yardstick, only human and civic rights as they are set down in some generally accepted human rights charter or national constitution could be at stake. However, it is assuredly uncontroversial that Community nations with relatively low labour costs such as Greece, Ireland, Portugal, Spain and also the UK are in the top league of countries in the world as regards the observation of human rights. Hence the claim that the competitive advantages of these countries are based on a kind of violation of human rights would only make sense if one were to postulate a human right to a broad provision of social aid, of worker protection, of labour participation and of living standards along northern and central European lines. Then, however, not only southern European countries but also the United States and even Switzerland, with their relatively slim welfare states, their low levels of labour market regulation, and their weak unions would have to be classified as pursuing unfair competition. The absurdity of this claim makes it clear that an absolute ethical yardstick for the extent of the welfare state fails badly. The reason is simple: it ignores internationally different traditions of the welfare state which are usually based on a broad consensus of the population in the respective countries.

So one is left with a more modest relative ethical yardstick. The main criterion for judging a national welfare state – be it large or small – becomes one of whether it is supported by a democratically legitimized consensus in the respective countries. If this support exists, however, any international 'compromise model' will almost certainly have to be classified as inferior. Naturally, an external observer cannot easily decide whether and to what extent there is such a consensus. Nevertheless, at least one crude indicator for a judgement of this kind is available: the standard of living. 'Rich' countries with a high per capita income such as Denmark, West Germany and the Netherlands typically have extensive welfare states, heavily regulated labour markets, and a strong union influence while the opposite is true at least in a de facto sense of 'poor' countries like Greece or Portugal. Apparently, the demand for social cushioning (and also for worker protection and participation) has in the past been a function of the income level, with a relatively high income elasticity of demand. As long as the income differentials within the Community remain wide,[12] the demand for the services of a welfare state will perhaps vary substantially between the European nations. To enforce a harmonized and relatively high level of social provision throughout the Community would thus run counter to the interests of consumers, workers and taxpayers in the poorer countries since, at their present levels of per capita income, they are apparently not willing to finance a costly welfare and participative state, even if one takes account of a prospective gain in social peace which this might entail. Only after a long process of economic catchup that leads to an approximate equalization of per capita income between the countries of the Community might harmonization of welfare states be desirable. However, this harmonization would then come about as the natural result of a political process in which the call for a larger welfare system and more extensive labour market regulation would become ever louder and more powerful in the parliaments of the countries. Yet, such a combined process of economic and social convergence can only proceed fast enough if the poorer countries fully use their locational advantages, including their temporarily lower costs of the welfare state in the broadest sense. Social harmonization is then not the moral precondition of economic integration, but its final consequence.

Of course, the process of income convergence by no means wipes out all welfare state differences, because they are in part deeply engrained in different legal, social and cultural traditions. For example, the labour market in the UK today displays a degree of deregulation and differentiation in wages and working conditions that makes it much closer to the American model than to the continental European counterpart, despite the fact that, in terms of geographical proximity and level of per capita income, the UK belongs to the European mainstream.[13] However, it is also obvious that these differences can hardly be indicted on ethical grounds either.

4.4. The Political Perspective: The Vision of Federalism

From our preceding analysis, it can be concluded that the economic and moral rationales for a social dimension are very weak. If there is a 'need' for a social dimension in any meaningful sense, it is instead to be found in the realm of politics. In fact, much of what has happened in the Community in the aftermath of the Single European Act – culminating in the Maastricht treaty on European Union and the ill-defined social dimension – can be understood as a politically motivated rush into federalism and an attempt to rationalize this by postulating some economic and moral justification for harmonization. The political backing for this rush came from a powerful implicit coalition of three groups of countries: France, which sought to 'lock in' a supposedly overmighty united Germany in a close network of European institutions; a unified Germany, trying to calm fears abroad about its newly found political weight and to hide its new political responsibilities behind a European facade; and the southern rim-countries (plus Ireland), who anticipated a further dose of transfers from the centre to the periphery in the wake of the Maastricht deal.

It is very difficult to evaluate the political notion of federalism that underlies the Community's efforts to produce social integration, both for practical and for more fundamental theoretical reasons. On a practical level, the concept has so far not been elaborated by either its proponents or opponents beyond the stage of vague generality. If anything, the long-term vision of federalism is taken to resemble the model of the United States or the Federal Republic of Germany – somewhat more the latter than the former, since Germany has the European trappings of a welfare state, corporatist labour markets with a strong reliance on a 'social partnership' between labour and capital, and a system of fiscal equilibration between regions. After the cooling of popular support for European integration, the federalist vision was significantly tuned down by the Commission so as to contain strong elements of subsidiarity – meaning, roughly defined, the principle that the Community should only engage in legislative activity in whatever field if there was a genuine need for supranational legislation, thus reversing the 'burden of proof' in favour of national or even regional decision units.[14] However, as long as subsidiarity remains ill-defined legally, it will be virtually impossible to clarify the underlying vision of federalism.

At a more theoretical level, it is difficult to offer a normative evaluation of a political concept that lacks a firm economic and ethical rationale simply because political thinking *per se* does not provide much guidance with respect to the legitimacy of particular aims. Of course, in a positive sense, the emergence of political conceptions may well be explained by the working of pressure groups which steer governments towards policies that benefit particular sectional interests. In the case of the social dimension, these interests can be identified above all in the power of organized labour and business in those countries where labour costs are high.[15] In a normative sense, however, political objectives are usually derived aims, that is, they receive their ultimate justification not from politics itself, but rather from some underlying economic or ethical principle. For example, free trade may seem to be a distinct political objective, yet it is justified in the end by the non-political aim of providing as much consumer satisfaction as possible to the population of a given geographical entity. Similarly, internal and external security may appear to be political objectives, but ultimately they are no more than the means to secure economic and ethical aims – namely, the preservation of a legal order conducive to economic efficiency and growth and the protection of human rights in their many guises. Given these restrictions, a judgment on the political need for a social dimension can only be based on an evaluation of whether a tighter federalist structure – including the social dimension – is apt to raise or to lower the likelihood of potential political conflicts among the member states as well as between the Community and the rest of the world (essentially the countries of central and eastern Europe). By its very nature, such an evaluation must remain not only modest in scope but also highly speculative.

In this sense, a social dimension may be interpreted as a tool to delimit the political damage done by unfettered locational competition within the Community. An indication of this damage is the resistance with which large-scale relocations of business activity are usually met by the local population that loses jobs. If this resistance develops into a major political issue, then the whole venture of a common market might become quite unpopular in those relatively rich core regions of the Community – notably, France and western Germany – that were once the driving forces behind the political and economic integration of Europe. This, in turn, could jeopardize the whole project of a peacefully united Europe.

That a relocation of industry following the establishment of a common market with its free movement of capital might lead to political turmoil was demonstrated in almost showcase fashion in early 1993 when an American domestic appliance maker (Hoover) decided to concentrate its production activity in Scotland and to close down a plant in Dijon. The company stated publicly that the major motive for its decision was the much lower labour costs (especially, the low non-wage costs) in the Scottish location. This business decision aroused a storm of protest in France. Virtually the whole political establishment denounced the economically rational decision as a case of social dumping.[16] With an accelerated consolidation of many business activities in fewer locations than used to be the case in a more fragmented market, it can be anticipated that there will be permanent pressure group squealing and possibly even a genuine political uproar, especially in times of recession.

So much for the core of the political argument in favour of a social dimension, which is often couched rather loosely in terms of giving labour its due share in the common market venture to soothe workers' fears about heightened competitive pressures. Prima facie, the argument appears to be quite plausible, at least if it is narrowly interpreted as a mere case for political prudence rather than as upholding some moral principle. On closer inspection, however, it has serious shortcomings because it is confined to a rather narrow short-term view of the economic, and thus also the political, consequences of the social dimension. Taking a somewhat longer-run perspective, there may be strong countervailing forces that work in the opposite direction of more political conflict potential.

As noted in Section 4.2, most elements of the welfare state lead to an increase in labour costs, because collective bargains are unlikely to fully trade off wages for social benefits. Hence social harmonization on a relatively high level is most likely to narrow the gap in wage costs between the centre of the Community and its periphery (Ireland, Scotland, southern Italy, southern Spain, Portugal, and Greece), and to widen unemployment rates. Only in a perverse sense would this contribute to an equalization of living conditions: the interregional structure of wages would be more 'equal', yet the structure of unemployment more 'unequal'. The political consequences are easy to figure out: the call for Community-financed regional policy measures (e.g. another boost in the structural and cohesion funds) would become louder and fuel political conflicts which would further hinder smooth integration.

To put it more generally: by giving up or restricting the use of an important economic parameter of locational competition, poorer countries will be driven into lobbying for indirect fiscal compensation via the political process. Hence the political price the rich countries will have to pay for soothing workers' fears in the short run by establishing a harmonization of social standards is very likely to be a higher level of transfers to the poorer countries. The political validity of the social dimension will thus crucially depend on the readiness of the population in rich countries to support the poorer parts of the Community, probably much more so than in the past under standard regional aid programmes. Thus, the final political verdict about the social dimension depends on whether and to what extent there is a social consensus in the Community that could provide a firm basis for an extensive redistributive system.

In theoretical terms, the question may be formulated as follows: to be politically viable and stable, any redistributive system in a given geographical entity must be backed up by an 'extent of morals' that covers the whole of the respective entity.[17] In philosophical terms, one may conceive of this extent of morals as the readiness of any individual taxpayer picked at random to imagine himself behind a Rawlsian veil of ignorance with respect to his geographical position in the relevant entity.[18] If this readiness cannot be realistically expected, then it is highly unlikely that any massive redistribution across regions will in the last resort receive a consensual support of the population, at least on a constitutional level. Is there such a consensus at European level, or is it likely to emerge in the near future?

Although this question is very hard to answer with any degree of precision, there are good reasons to lean to the sceptical side, simply because the predominant element in all major systems of social legislation and redistribution is a feeling of national or regional identity. A few examples may clarify this. In Germany, for example, one may roughly say that taxpayers in the rich southern city of Munich do not grumble too loudly about transfers going to the relatively underdeveloped northern coastal region; of course, they do complain, but not to such an extent as to question the system, which is still based on something like a 'national' consensus on the scope of redistribution. But would the same people stand ready to transfer anything close to the same amount to Sicily, Andalusia, Portugal, or Greece? Similarly, would the people of Madrid be ready to transfer the same amount in 'fiscal equilibration' to the west coast of Ireland as they do to Andalusia? Or would they be ready to devote the same amount as a percentage of GDP to rebuilding the wrecked economy of post-communist eastern Germany as the Germans themselves do? By and large, one can readily agree that they would not, and one should face up to the important message behind this reluctance to pay: a tribal identity based on a common history, culture, language, and so on plays an extremely important role in laying the ground for the extent of morals and thus for a stable and viable redistributive system. Only if this ground is intuitively accepted by the vast majority of the population in a given geographical entity, can a 'welfare state' in the broadest sense be maintained. Whether one likes it or not, the most important unit of reference for this tribal identity is still the nation state, or even parts of the nation state in countries with particularly strong regional traditions such as Germany, Italy and Spain. Compared with this deep-rooted identity, the feeling of Europeanness seems too feeble to build anything like a large-scale redistributive system and a common welfare state on it.[19]

Any such consensus may be further eroded by the past experience with what may be called 'intergovernmental long-distance redistributive systems', the most important of which are the bilateral and multilateral networks of development aid. As the record of past decades shows, such aid tends to suffer in its effectiveness from the fact that it is channelled through large and often rather inefficient public administrations of the relevant recipient countries that use the funds to further their own political or bureaucratic aims, with little regard to strict criteria of economic efficiency.[20] Although the corresponding Community control systems may be more efficient than is the case for most schemes of intercontinental development aid, they are still likely to remain substantially weaker than redistributive systems at the national level – where there is at least a longstanding tradition and 'culture' of centralized administration, and where the more egregious cases of fraud and corruption are subject to prosecution under a common jurisdiction. Until a fully integrated legal system with facilities and powers comparable to those at national level is established, any large-scale redistribution project will necessarily remain to some extent uncontrollable when implemented. This, in turn, would make major redistributive efforts all the more unpopular in the richer countries and further undermine any nascent consensus.

Even if the requisite consensus did exist to a high degree, however, it would support a system of 'fiscal equilibration' only within rather narrow limits – limits that fall well short of existing differences in per capita income, in the degree of industrialization, and in the level of unemployment between the centre and the periphery of the Community. A United Germany provides a nice example – almost a laboratory experiment – of how 'fiscal equilibration' works and at what point it virtually breaks down. Before German unification, West Germany had a persistent 'regional problem', that is, an imbalance of per capita income between different regions. The 'problem' was tackled by transfers and special programmes, which by and large helped a little bit, but not all that much. At any rate, the system itself – a mixture of 'fiscal equilibration' via redistributing tax receipts between states and regional policy initiatives – remained sustainable for decades. To be sure, the disparities in income it had to tackle were rather minimal by international standards, with most regions remaining above the 90 %-threshold of the average income level. With unification, this changed dramatically: there is now a huge disparity between the two parts of the country, West and East, with even the most advanced regions in the East having income levels far below and unemployment levels far above those of the poorest regions in the West. Now that the system of fiscal equilibration confronts real disparities, it is widely perceived that it cannot survive in its present shape. The lesson from this is simple: the celebrated German system of fiscal equilibration – often floated in Brussels as the model case of federalism to be followed – is not designed for handling a persistently wide gap in incomes. In essence, it is a fair weather system: viable but not very important in sunny times, potentially important but not viable on rainy days. Assuredly, any federalist system of this kind is likely to share the same fate: it works as long as it is hardly needed – that is, when income differentials are minimal – and is simply swamped when income differentials become substantial. Note that this is also the point at which the social consensus begins to break down. Whatever his or her thoughts on historical obligations and German cultural identity, the taxpayer in the western half of Germany is now beginning to refuse to bear the burden of the social dimension now being implemented in the eastern part of the newly united country.

A final reason to quarrel with this federalist vision of the new European Union lies in the political and economic reshaping of the rest of the continent, which contains a huge potential for external political conflicts in the future. In the 1990s and beyond, the Community will be increasingly confronted with an uneasy choice between deepening its institutional and social integration and widening its scope by allowing new potential members to enter the club – to begin with the EFTA countries and then at some later date the Central and Eastern European nations of Poland, the Czech Republic, and Hungary, possibly to be followed by the Baltic states plus Slovakia and Slovenia among others.[21] Despite many assertions to the contrary, the former development would raise political and economic barriers to entry, at least for the relatively poor Eastern countries who would also have to become part of the 'social space of Europe'. Resistance to their admission would increase, especially from competing aid-recipient countries at the southern rim of the Community. Naturally, this would make it much harder for them to be integrated into the European division of labour, which is so vital for their future economic prospects. Hence, in the longer run, a slower pace of social integration should help to keep the political doors open to the East, which is an essential precondition for these countries to overcome the political and economic heritage of their communist past.

To sum up, processes of integration are first and foremost long-term social and cultural developments, which entail the necessarily slow growth of a common value system and the gradual overcoming of parochialism and nationalism. After all, it took nationalism decades or even centuries to conquer the world so why should one expect it to disappear overnight? In this sense, a social dimension may be the final result of a gradual evolution of a European identity, which at present is rudimentary at best.

Notes

1 Thanks are due to the editors, John Addison and Stanley Siebert, for most valuable comments on an earlier draft of this chapter.
2 For a concise account of the manifold institutional details of the Community social dimension, see Chapter 2 of this volume.
3 In the following paragraphs we ignore any allocational effects on economies outside the European Union (e.g. trade diversion). For our purposes, these effects are not relevant.

4 *Mutatis mutandis*, this applies also to international wage differentials. The argument is based on the factor price equalization theorem of neoclassical trade theory.

5 Theoretical arguments against free trade and free factor movements are ignored here, since there is a general consensus within the Community on the economic gains of the common market.

6 In recent years, a new strand of growth theory has given the case for free trade an additional, dynamic dimension (see, most importantly, Grossman and Helpman, 1991). This strand, though extremely important in its own right, is not very fertile for the analysis of the trade effects of the welfare state and is omitted here. For a survey of the policy implications of this dynamic theory, see Paqué (1993).

7 In the following paragraphs, we use the term 'welfare state' in this very broad sense, that is, we do not explicitly distinguish the different elements enumerated in the text.

8 Examples include direct costs such as social security contributions and indirect costs such the monetary equivalent of the constraints imposed by dismissal protection, safety standards, and codetermination statutes.

9 In fact, there are strong theoretical reasons why labour cost neutrality of the introduction of the welfare state in the above sense is implausible. If workers were prepared to fully trade off wages against benefits, they would have done so voluntarily before the introduction of the welfare state. If they have not done so, this would indicate that the benefits are not perfect substitutes for money wages which in turn means that wage flexibility will not be neutral. Only if there were a (still unexplained) market failure in the first place (which prevents workers from voluntarily substituting benefits for money wages) could one expect wages to be perfectly flexible.

10 The idea of competition as a process of discovery goes back to Hayek (1984: 254–265).

11 This corresponds to the definition of dumping according to Article 6, Section (1) of the General Agreement of Tariffs and Trade (GATT), which is also the definition used in economics in general. See, *inter alia*, Corden (1974: 235).

12 In the 1980s, per capita income in the two richest EC countries, Denmark and West Germany, was more than 30% above the EC-average; per capita income in the three poorest EC-countries, Spain, Greece and Portugal, was more than 40% (and in the case of Portugal even 70%) below that average.

13 On the welfare state and labour market regulations in the United Kingdom, the United States and continental Europe, see Emerson (1988); on wage differentiation in the respective countries, see OECD (1993).

14 On the post-Maastricht terminology of subsidiarity, see the *Economist* (1992a, b, c).

15 The analysis of the interplay of these interests lies in the realm of public choice theory or the political economy of social harmonization, which is covered in a number of other chapters in this volume.

16 For a narrative, see the *Economist* (1993a).

17 The term 'extent of morals' goes back to Buchanan (1978).

18 For a similar line of reasoning as to community size, see Mueller (1974). And on the veil of ignorance, see Rawls (1971).

19 The recent troubles in assigning structural aid to different regions in need gives a vivid example of the political problems involved. See the *Economist* (1993c).

20 For a classical and still valid critique of development aid along these lines, see Bauer (1976).

21 On which, see the *Economist* (1993b).

References

Bauer, P. T. (1976). *Dissent or Development* (revised edition). Cambridge, Mass: Harvard University Press.

Buchanan, J. M. (1978). 'Markets, States, and the Extent of Morals'. *American Economic Review,* **68** (May): 364–68.

Commission (1988). *The Social Dimension of the Common Market*, SEC (88) 1148. Brussels: Commission of the European Communities, 14 September.

Corden, W. M. (1974). *Trade Policy and Economic Welfare*. Oxford: Oxford University Press.

Economist (1992a). 'Trial by Subsidiarity'. London: *Economist*, 4 July, p. 15.

Economist (1992b). 'Into the Void. Survey of the European Community'. London: *Economist*, 11 July, p. 54ff.

Economist (1992c). 'Scapegoat Passes Buck'. London: *Economist*, 3 October, p. 27.

Economist (1993a). 'Europe's Single Market: Labour Pains'. London: *Economist*, 6 February, p. 67

Economist (1993b). 'A Rude Awakening. Survey of the European Community'. London: *Economist*, 3 July, after p. 52.

Economist (1993c). 'European Community: Poorer Than Thou'. London: *Economist*, 10 July, pp. 21, 24.

Emerson, M. (1988). *What Model for Europe?* Cambridge, Mass.: MIT Press.

Grossman, G. M. and Helpman, E. (1991). *Innovation and Growth in the Global Economy*. Cambridge, England: Cambridge University Press.

Hayek, F. A. (1984). 'Competition as a Discovery Procedure'. In C. Nishiyama and K. R. Leube (eds), *The Essence of Hayek*, pp. 254–65. Palo Alto, California: Hoover Institution Press.

Mueller, D. C. (1974). 'Achieving the Just Polity'. *American Economic Review*, **64** (May): 147–52.

OECD (1993). *Employment Outlook*. Paris: Organisation for Economic Co-operation and Development.

Paqué, K-H. (1993). 'A Recipe for Prosperity? Policy Implications of the New Growth Theories'. In H. Siebert (ed.), *Economic Growth in the World Economy*, pp. 273–87. Tübingen: Siebeck/Mohr.

Rawls, J. (1971). *A Theory of Justice*. Cambridge, Mass.: Harvard University Press.

5

Integration through Law? The Law and Economics of European Social Policy

Simon Deakin

5.1. Introduction

An enormous amount of critical attention has been devoted to the 'social dimension' since the adoption of the Social Charter and Action Programme in 1989 and a vigorous case has been made for it being irrelevant at best and most likely harmful to prospects for economic growth and job creation within the internal market (Addison and Siebert, 1991, 1992, this volume). It is perhaps paradoxical, in the light of this discussion, to note that social policy remains largely peripheral to the aims and objectives of the European Community and that its legal basis is somewhat precarious. This is both a reflection of a long-standing lack of political consensus on the value of social policy interventions at Community level and a factor in the weak and partial nature of those measures which make up the body of existing Community labour and social law, features which the implementation of many of the Action Programme proposals has not fundamentally altered.

The legal and institutional framework within which social policy measures are formulated has an important bearing on the wider debate over the likely impact of the social dimension. 'Harmonization' is not a straightforward concept; a number of different legal instruments operate at transnational level, most of which do not require the automatic convergence of standards or legal mechanisms at state level. The general limits to the jurisdictional competence of Community organs need to be taken into account together with more specific matters such as the issue of the 'treaty base' which determines whether a particular measure is one requiring unanimity or a 'qualified majority' of the votes cast by the member states in the Council (Wedderburn, 1990). The operation of Community law at state level rests in large part on the successive rulings of the European Court of Justice which have developed the doctrines of the *supremacy* of Community law and its *direct effect* within the legal systems of member states. In some instances, as a result of these doctrines, European Community law will take precedence over laws passed by national legislatures. But this does not necessarily imply greater uniformity in the labour and social security laws of member states. As explained below, many issues concerning the precise nature of the relationship between domestic and European legislation and the scope of the doctrine of 'subsidiarity' have yet to be clearly resolved.

If the social dimension is regarded sceptically by those who question its economic legitimacy, a quite different but in some ways equally sceptical perspective on its impact is offered by those writers who see it as having made a minimal contribution (at least so far) to the advancement of social protection as a goal in its own right. From this point of view, linking European social policy to the goal of market integration has been detrimental to the prospects for extending and deepening the social dimension. Notions such as 'social dumping' provide an unsteady foundation for the social dimension precisely because they have no clear meaning and may be nothing more than disguised protectionism in favour of the more developed northern European economies (Davies, 1992: 346).

For the goal of social protection to be given greater priority in its own right there would have to be changes of a fundamental kind in Community law, going well beyond what was achieved at Maastricht. Such developments are, nevertheless, once again on the agenda for reform, and will constitute an important part of the work of the Intergovernmental Conference which was inaugurated at Turin in 1996 and which will pave the way for the next round of treaty revisions. Whether, on this occasion, the Community will make any clearer progress on social policy matters than it did at Maastricht remains to be seen. In any event, the limited legal competence of the Community in the social field means that, at least for the foreseeable future, European social policy continues to be linked to the search for an economic rationale for social legislation. But in some ways this is no bad thing. If the social dimension were just protectionism in disguise, as its critics suggest, it would hardly deserve to be supported, whether or not a clearer legal base could be found for social policy interventions. The future development of social policy will be stalled, at both national and transnational level, if convincing answers are not given to the critical questions posed by deregulatory analyses.

This chapter addresses these questions by examining, firstly, the debates over legal competence and the 'treaty base' which importantly structure the capacity of the Community to act in the social policy area. The roles of the Commission, the Council and the Parliament within the legislative process are explained, and the extensive influence of the Court in the development of social policy is also considered (see also Deakin and Morris, 1995). The second half of the chapter addresses the broader themes of how far there exist potential arguments in support of transnational labour standards, and to what extent they are reflected in the current body of Community law and practice. It will be suggested that there is a powerful case in favour of labour standards both as part of a 'floor of rights' but also as guarantors of economic participation and development, and that this is becoming increasingly important as a basis for Community initiatives in the social policy field.

5.2. The Legal Bases of European Social Policy

Legal Competence and the Treaty Base

The European Community was founded as a customs union and internal free trade area within western Europe, initially in the form of the European Coal and Steel Community of the Treaty of Paris of 1951 and then the European Economic Community of the Treaty of Rome of 1957. The Treaty of Rome did not place a strong priority on social policy. In the Preamble to the Treaty, the 'constant improvement of the living and working conditions of the peoples of the Community' was stated to be its 'essential objective', but it was envisaged that this would be achieved principally through the liberalization of trade and economic mobility – through the establishment of the 'four freedoms' of freedom of movement for labour, capital and goods and freedom of establishment for employers – and not through the harmonization of social legislation. The 'Spaak Report' of Foreign Ministers (Spaak, 1956) which preceded the Treaty argued that convergence of social and labour standards would be the *result* of the common market in goods and services rather than the means of bringing it about. The Report contended, on the one hand that:

> competition does not necessarily require a complete harmonisation of the different elements in costs; indeed, it is only on the basis of certain differences – such as wage differences due to productivity – that trade and competition can develop. (Spaak, 1956: 233)

The dynamic benefits of liberalization would be lost if a single regulatory regime was imposed from the centre. On the other hand, the free movement of labour and capital could be expected to lead, in and of themselves, to a levelling-up of wages and living standards, rather than to any deterioration:

> wage and interest rates tend to level up in a common market – a process which is hastened by the free circulation of the factors of production. This is a consequence rather than a condition of the common market's operation. (Spaak, 1956: 233)

This point of view was reflected in the list of the Community's activities set out in Article 3 – which made no reference to social harmonization and only two references to social policy in the broad sense of that term, one to the principle of free movement of labour and the other to the establishment of the European Social Fund – and in the ambiguous terms of Article 117:

> The Member States agree upon the need to promote improved working conditions and an improved standard of living for workers, so as to make possible their harmonisation while the improvement is being maintained.
>
> They believe that such a development will ensue not only from the functioning of the common market, which will favour the harmonisation of social systems, but also from the procedures provided for in this Treaty and from the approximation of provisions laid down by law, regulation or administrative action.

This provision did not create any jurisdiction to implement Community social policy through legislation in the form of either directives or regulations. Similarly, under Article 118 the Commission was confined to promoting cooperation between the member states on a number of matters relating to social policy (including working conditions, social security, occupational health and safety, the right of association and collective bargaining) while under Article 122 it simply had an obligation to make annual reports on social policy to the Parliament.

Articles 119 and 120 alone placed specific obligations on member states in relation to social policy. Article 119 laid down the celebrated principle of equal pay for equal work between men and women which was to form the basis for many of the later interventions of the European Court of Justice; Article 120, which required the member states to 'endeavour to maintain the existing equivalence between paid holiday schemes', by contrast proved to be completely insignificant. These two Articles were included on the insistence of the French government which anticipated more recent debates over 'social dumping' by raising the threat of unfair competition from states with less extensive legal protections. The line that harmonization of labour standards was required to counter unfair competition on the basis of inter-country differences in pay and conditions had been rejected, for most purposes, in a report commissioned prior to the Treaty of Rome from the International Labour Office (ILO), the 'Ohlin Report'. The ILO experts took the view that differences in real wage levels between member states were most likely to be the outcome of different levels of productivity in those states and that any 'distortion' of international competition could be avoided, where necessary, by adjustments to states' exchange rates. They made an exception, however, for a situation in which employers in one member state were able to take advantage of wages and social charges which were not only lower than those elsewhere in the Community but were also out of line with the *general* level of costs in that state. Low pay of such a kind was seen as an artificial subsidy to employers:

> a certain distortion of competition arises from differences in the extent to which the principle of equal pay for men and women applies in different countries. Countries in which there are large wage differentials by sex will pay relatively low wages in industries employing a large proportion of female labour and these industries will enjoy what might be considered a special advantage over the competitors abroad where differentials according to sex are smaller or non-existent. (ILO, 1956: 107)

This was the rather fragile rationale for the inclusion of Article 119 in the Treaty; but even then no provision was made for the Community to adopt more precise legislation for the implementation of equal pay. Overall, then, 'the social provisions of the Treaty . . . turned out to be pretty meagre' (Davies, 1992: 325).

The period of the implementation of the first phase of the common market up to the late 1960s was one of 'benign neglect' as far as social policy was concerned (Mosley, 1990). A series of measures were adopted in relation to free movement of labour; most of these took the form of requiring member states to loosen national restrictions on free entry, employment and residence on the part of the citizens of other member states. A number of directives and regulations were adopted with the aim of improving the social security rights of migrant workers.[1] These were based not on the concept of harmonization, however, but on the more limited concept of 'coordination'; this did not necessarily imply the creation of common minimum standards but rather a process of mutual recognition between different legal systems for the benefit of those acquiring social security rights in more than one country. Coordination, indeed, presupposed that national legal systems would retain their separate forms of provision and would not move closer together to provide a common framework of rights. Two forms of coordination were adopted: the aggregation of qualifying periods and contribution records which determined eligibility for benefits and their amounts; and the principle of deterritoriality in the payment of benefits, whereby benefits acquired in one state could become payable in another. Even then the degree of mutual recognition involved was extremely limited, in particular with regard to unemployment benefit, the rules for which were more restrictive than many of the bilateral treaties which the member states had had with each other before the Treaty of Rome came into force (Wikeley, 1989). During this period the Social Fund, established by Articles 123–128 of the Treaty, was also used to support a number of labour market programmes designed to facilitate the process of implementing the common market; but there were not initiatives in the field of social legislation as such.

The enlargement of the Community to nine states in 1971 provided the occasion for a new emphasis on social policy, with the governments of the member states pledging to give it equal priority with industrial and financial integration and the Commission adopting its first Social Action Programme of 1974 (for details see Hepple, 1987; Davies, 1992). This led eventually to the adoption by the Council of Ministers of a series of directives relating to equal pay and equality of treatment between the sexes in relation to employment and social security.[2] Less extensive but nevertheless significant measures were also adopted in relation to employment protection, with directives laying down minimum standards of redundancy consultation and protection of employee rights in the event of business transfers and the insolvency of companies.[3] The adoption of these measures did not involve the amendment of the Treaty; general provisions empowering the Council of Ministers to adopt measures for the implementation of the common market and related purposes were used as a jurisdiction base (Articles 100 and 235 of the Treaty respectively). The difficulty was that these provisions required the Council to be unanimous. From the early 1980s onwards it proved all but impossible to achieve unanimity, ostensibly because of the veto wielded on numerous occasions by the UK. During this period draft directives to strengthen the employment rights of part-time and temporary workers and to compel multinational companies to observe minimum standards of worker consultation and participation (the 'Vredeling' proposals), amongst others, failed to gain the Council's approval (see generally Chapter 2, above).

The Single European Act of 1986 was intended to break the logjam on social policy by clarifying the Community's competence to adopt social legislation and by extending to social policy the principle, applicable in some other areas, of qualified majority voting in the Council, the broad effect of which is to nullify the veto of a single member state. A new Article 118a was inserted into the Treaty of Rome, according to which 'Member States shall pay particular attention to encouraging improvements, especially in the working environment, as regards the health and safety of workers, and shall set as their objective the harmonisation of conditions in this area, while maintaining the improvements made'. The Council was empowered to adopt directives laying down 'minimum requirements for gradual implementation, having regard to the conditions and technical rules obtaining in each of the Member States' and in particular avoiding 'imposing administrative, financial and legal constraints in a way which would hold back the creation and development of small and medium-sized undertakings'. This led to the formulation of a group of health and safety Directives, the most important being the Framework Directive of 1989 (Directive 89/391), none of which was vetoed in the Council. Article 118a was the only concession to qualified majority voting, however; as far other matters concerning 'the rights and interests of employed persons' were concerned, it would remain necessary to obtain unanimity in the Council (Article 100a(2)).

The so-called Social Charter adopted by 11 of the 12 member states at the Strasbourg summit in November 1989 (the UK was the exception) did not mark a significant legal advance.[4] The Social Charter is not binding in international law even upon the states which signed it; it is intended simply to be a declaration of principle, and at best is just one factor to be taken into account by the courts as an aid to the interpretation of Community legislation which makes reference to it and in the interpretation of powers under the Agreement on Social Policy made at the Maastricht summit (Wedderburn, 1990; Bercusson, 1990; Hepple, 1990, 1993). In terms of its substantive content, it does little more than summarize certain of the main principles of international labour law as derived from the Conventions of the International Labour Organisation and the Council of Europe's Social Charter of 1961. In some respects, such as employees' collective rights of freedom of association, the EC charter is significantly *weaker* than the parallel instruments of the ILO and Council of Europe.[5]

It was left to the Commission to devise a further Social Action Programme containing the 47 proposals put before the Council between 1990 and 1994 (see Chapter 2). Because this had to be done within the existing legal framework of the Treaty of Rome and Single Act, a number of strategies were adopted as part of the 'treaty base game'. The Commission has the responsibility of proposing legislation and so has the option of framing measures with a particular treaty base in mind. The governments of the member states, acting through the Council, can respond either by challenging the legal base chosen by the Commission or by raising objections to the substance of a proposal. Some of the strategies adopted by the Commission have proved to be more successful than others. Article 118a, which provides for qualified majority voting and therefore makes it less likely that a single member state will attempt to mount a veto, has been used to enact numerous Directives in the field of health and safety and, more contentiously, in the areas of pregnancy and maternity rights (Directive 92/85) and working time. The UK government mounted a challenge to the validity of Directive 93/104 on working time, on the grounds that it is not principally concerned with health and safety matters as required by Article 118a[6], but the Court ruled that the directive was valid with the exception of one provision relating to Sunday working.

Other Treaty bases involving qualified majority voting which the Commission has invoked include Articles 57(2) and 66 concerning self-employment and the provision of services respectively (in the context of the draft Directive on the Posting of Workers) and Article 54(3) (in the context of the proposal for the European Company Statute: Wedderburn, 1990: 52–53). In relation to the contentious question of the protection of part-time and fixed-term contract workers, the Commission advanced three different draft directives on related areas, each one derived from a different treaty 'base'. One of these, relating to health and safety aspects of fixed-term employment, was put forward under the qualified majority voting procedure of Article 118a and was eventually agreed by the Council as Directive 91/383. The other two were put forward under Articles 100 and 100a respectively. Article 100 requires unanimity; this has not been forthcoming and there appears to be no immediate prospect of the proposal advanced under this Article being accepted. Article 100a, which was inserted by the Single European Act, envisages the use of qualified majority voting for the purposes of implementing the single market; but as we saw above, it reverts to unanimity in relation to any matter relating to the 'rights and interests of employed persons' (Article 100a(2)). It has been suggested that this derogation would have no application in a case which was concerned to a significant degree with *both* employee rights *and* with the distortion of competition; in such a case, therefore, the qualified majority could operate (Bercusson, 1990; Vogel Polsky, 1990). This view is based, however, on a somewhat ambitious reading of the legal text. The matter has not come before the European Court of Justice and may never do so, since the member states themselves appear to have taken the view that Article 100a(2) clearly requires unanimity in employment matters whether or not distortion of competition is also at stake, and have accordingly rejected the treaty base used by the Commission in this case. The failure of these two proposals on 'flexible' employment relationships is the biggest single blow so far to the progress of the Social Action Programme; and it is worth stressing that had they been adopted, they would still have provided for inferior protection to that envisaged in the failed proposals of the mid-1980s (Hepple, 1990b).

The continuing dissatisfaction with the lack of progress on social policy led to a number of Treaty amendments being proposed as part of the Intergovernmental Conference on economic union leading up to the Maastricht summit in November 1991. Treaty amendments require unanimity, and the UK duly used its veto to block what would have been the 'Social Chapter' of the new Treaty, intended as a series of amendments to Articles 117–120.[7] Under a last-minute political compromise, the other 11 member states agreed to a procedure for the implementation of the social dimension separately from the UK, contained in a separate Protocol and Agreement on Social Policy. Those countries joining the Community after 1992 – Austria, Finland and Sweden – also acceded to the Protocol and Agreement on Social Policy. These instruments in addition bind certain EFTA countries which, although parties to the Treaty for the European Economic Area of 14 February 1992, have subsequently stayed outside the EC (Norway and Iceland). Signatories to the EEA Treaty undertake to observe at least the minimum content of Community labour law forming part of the *acquis communautaire* (or general principles of Community law), which the Commission takes to include the Protocol and Agreement on Social Policy (Blanpain and Engels, 1993: 47).

The Agreement on Social Policy, concluded by the 11 and now binding on 14 member states, indicates their wish to 'implement the 1989 Social Charter on the basis of the *acquis communautaire*', that is to say on the basis of the general principles of Community law including, where relevant, the jurisprudence of the Court of Justice. The reference to the Social Charter is important in this context since it suggests that the Charter – which is otherwise a document of little or no legal consequence – should now be used as a guide to the formulation of proposals under the Agreement and to their subsequent interpretation by the courts. The Agreement has three main purposes: to confirm and clarify once and for all the legal competence of the Community in regard to social policy; to extend qualified majority voting in the social area; and to give greater institutional priority to the social dialogue between management and labour at transational level (for further details, see Appendix 4 in Chapter 2). The Agreement provides for greater qualified majority voting among the 14 on matters including health and safety, working conditions, information and consultation of workers, equality between the sexes and integration of excluded groups. Unanimity is required for matters which include social security, protection of workers in relation to the termination of employment, 'representation and collective defence' of workers, including codetermination, rights of third-country nationals and financial measures for the promotion of employment. Finally, some matters are excluded completely: these are 'pay, the right of association, the right to strike [and] the right to impose lock-outs'. These blanket exclusions make it clearer than ever that there is no intention to develop a Community-wide framework of collective bargaining rights, and that pay determination is to be left, at best, to general guidance of the kind found in the Commission Opinion on the Equitable Wage of 1992. However, it is slightly odd that rights which are contained in the Social Charter of 1989 – and which, presumptively, the Agreement is intended to implement – should be placed completely outside the jurisdiction created by the Agreement. This inconsistency seems to be the result of the last-minute political compromises which accompanied the final drafting of the Agreement.

In seeking to promote social dialogue at Community level, the Agreement broadly follows the pre-Maastricht agreement between the transnational federations of ETUC, UNICE and CEEP (see Chapter 2). It calls on the Commission to promote social dialogue at Community level and requires it to consult management and labour before putting forward social policy proposals. The social partners then have the option of concluding a Community-wide agreement on the relevant matter, which may be implemented either according to the procedures and practices of each member state or by way of a Council 'decision'. If the social partners do not act within a period of nine months, the way is clear for the Commission to bring a proposal of its own before the Council.

The legal status and effects of the Agreement on Social Policy are far from clear (see Barnard, 1992; Bercusson, 1992, 1994; Fitzpatrick, 1992; Whiteford, 1993; Hepple, 1993). The Agreement is annexed to the Protocol on Social Policy which, in turn, is attached to the EC Treaty. A Protocol such as this is deemed to be part of the Treaty by Article 239. The Protocol authorizes the 14 member states 'to have recourse to the institutions, procedures and mechanisms of the Treaty for the purposes of taking among themselves and applying so far as they are concerned the acts and decisions required for giving effect' to the Agreement; the UK is not to take part in the deliberation and adoption of measures put forward by the Commission under the Protocol and Agreement. However, a crucial point here is that the Protocol is *agreed by all 15 Member States including the UK.* The UK is therefore a party to the Protocol as it is to the rest of the Treaty, and has consented to the procedure it lays down; what is not clear from the text is exactly what that procedure entails.

One possible interpretation of the Protocol is that directives agreed by the 14 should have the same status in Community law as other forms of Community legislation, subject only to the UK's exemption from their scope. The European Works Councils Directive was the first to be agreed under the special procedure laid down by the Agreement (see Chapter 2). Is this measure a treaty, simply binding on the 14 in international law, or is it an instrument capable of giving rise to Community law obligations, forming part of the national legal order of the 11 member states and so potentially conferring rights directly on the citizens of those states which could be asserted in their national courts?[8]

Much depends on how the UK's exemption is viewed. What is meant by the 14 'taking among themselves and applying as far as they are concerned' acts and decisions implementing the Agreement? This could mean that directives adopted by the 14 would have no effect within the territory of the UK. However, UK companies and employees located on the territory of other member states could be bound. This partial territorial effect could pose a threat to the Agreement's legal validity: by exempting the UK from its effects, the Agreement could be seen as contravening the principle of the unity of the Community legal order as well as creating distortions of competition within the internal market. It is perhaps difficult to envisage the Court of Justice provoking a clash with the member states by striking down the Agreement altogether (Fitzpatrick, 1992). But it would probably regard itself as having the power to do so, and the outcome of any reference would not be beyond doubt. Instead of declaring the Agreement to be repugnant to the Treaty, the Court could decide that it is valid as such but merely creates inter-governmental obligations between the 14 and cannot be used to produce directives and regulations with the full effect of Community law, a view currently taken by the UK government but opposed by the Commission, on the grounds that the Protocol and Agreement are part of the *acquis communautaire*.

A further odd result of the last-minute compromise agreed at the Maastricht summit is that the old social policy provisions of the Treaty of Rome remain in place as Articles 117–122 of the new, amended Treaty. The Protocol and Agreement are stated to be 'without prejudice to the provisions of [the] Treaty', which on one view means that the 14 may use the Agreement only after attempting to invoke the procedures laid down in Article 118a and the other more general law-making powers. The UK will participate in the discussion of any proposals put forward under the main body of the Treaty and (with the exception of measures under Article 118a) will be able to exercise its veto at this point; but if this happens the 14 may then invoke the procedure under the Agreement, from which the UK is excluded. If this continues to happen the UK may well come under pressure to compromise on social policy proposals, given that it will be powerless to influence the course taken by the 14 under the Agreement:

> no one supposes ... that in the long term, and perhaps not even in the short term, the UK can remain part of the European project and stay aloof from the social elements of the emerging social structure. (Davies, 1992: 348)

But it is also entirely possible that:

> [s]tripped of the predictable objections of the UK, it may become clearer that is it not just the UK which has a problem with many of the Community initiatives in the social sphere. (Whiteford, 1993: 211)

Even if the Agreement is either found or assumed to be valid, numerous legal and practical uncertainties remain, above all with regard to its social dialogue procedures (Hepple, 1993). It is not clear at precisely which stage the Commission is entitled to intervene to put its own proposal to the Council under Article 3(4), following the failure of the social partners to agree; nor what legal form is envisaged by the reference in Article 4(1) to 'contractual relations, including agreements', possibly collective agreements, between the federations of labour and management at EC level; nor what would be the effects of a Council 'decision' implementing such agreements under Article 4(2), since it is not completely clear whether the reference here is to a 'decision' in the sense meant by Article 189 of the Treaty (a determination 'binding in its entirety on those to whom it is addressed') or to some other form of legal instrument; nor what level of obligation is imposed on the signatory member states with regard to the implementation of transnational collective agreements, particularly in the light of the Declaration of the 11 (now the 14) which states that Article 4(2):

> implies no obligation on the part of the member states to apply the agreements directly or to work out rules for their transposition, nor any obligation to amend national legislation in force to facilitate their implementation.

Social dialogue, it seems, must be clearly distinguished from collective bargaining: 'collective bargaining at transnational level is still little less than a dream' (Wedderburn, 1991: 3). If framework agreements of some kind are to emerge from the dialogue, difficulties concerning the lack of representativeness of the existing transnational federations, ETUC, UNICE and CEEP will have to be resolved. Dialogue is perhaps best seen as an additional means of maintaining the pressure on the member states to take social policy seriously and as a mechanism for monitoring and enforcing Community-wide standards. It should also be borne in mind that the process of social dialogue long pre-dates Maastricht and that numerous joint opinions have already been arrived at by the transnational federations and in the work of the industry-based joint committees (Hepple, 1993).

At the end of the day, then, the Treaty on European Union left the future of social policy as uncertain as ever. What has been achieved to date in the social policy field unquestionably constitutes a substantial body of regulation, but it can hardly be said to constitute a coherent and systemic code of labour regulation, since large areas of concern are simply not yet addressed. For the immediate future, the failure to agree on the inclusion of the social chapter in the main body of the Treaty on European Union has left the resulting Protocol and Agreement under a legal cloud. With the exception of the health and safety directives of 1998–92, those measures which were adopted as part of the Action Programme either have no legal force, such as the Opinion on the Equitable Wage; were watered down in negotiations to the point where much of their potential impact was dissipated, as in the case of the Directives on Pregnancy and Working Time; or were relatively unambitious from the start, such as the Directive on Information concerning the Employment Relationship. In contrast to the unity of purpose which can be found in the case of other areas of Community law, such as competition and the law governing free movement within the single market, Community social legislation remains fragmented and marginalized.

The Role of the European Court of Justice

So far we have said little about the role of the European Court of Justice in the implementation of social policy; but this should not be taken to mean that the Court's role is negligible. On the contrary, there is a case for regarding the Court as having been far more instrumental in the application of social policy than either the Council or the Commission. It is largely thanks to the Court that certain provisions of the Treaty and of Directives are capable of taking *direct effect* in national law without the approval of national legislatures, thereby requiring member states to pay more than close attention to the contents of Community law. The effect of Community law in national law is of course not simply a function of the Court's rulings. As far as the UK is concerned, membership of the Community is reconciled with the traditional constitutional theory of Parliamentary sovereignty by the European Communities Act 1972, which incorporates Community law into the UK legal order in a particularly effective and far-reaching way.[9] However, Community law today, and in particular the nature of its relationship with national law, are not what they were in 1972; and this *is* very largely due to the judicial activism of the Court.

Of the legal instruments created by the Treaty of Rome, only *regulations* are deemed by the Treaty itself to be 'directly applicable' in the laws of member states without the need for them to be transposed into national legislation (Article 189). *Directives*, by contrast, are in effect instructions to member states to adapt their laws to certain Community-wide standards; they impose an obligation upon the member states to act but envisage that national legislation or, in some cases, collective bargaining will be used to bring them into effect. In most cases an implementation period of several years is also envisaged. The principal sanction for the non-implementation of a directive is the initiation of *enforcement proceedings* against a recalcitrant member state, normally by the Commission but possibly by another state, whereupon the Court, if it finds against the member state, has the power to declare it in breach of its obligations under the Treaty (Articles 169 and 170). This route to enforcement has had a substantial impact on British employment law, leading for example to the 1983 amendments to the Equal Pay Act which introduced into UK law the principle of equal pay for work of equal value or 'comparable worth', and to further changes to equality law in the Sex Discrimination Act 1986. The repeal by the Employment Act 1989 of certain restrictions on women's employment (such as the prohibition of women working underground in mines and quarries) was also prompted by Commission insistence that the UK (and other member states) should implement certain provisions of Directive 76/207 on Equal Treatment (Deakin, 1990).

Enforcement proceedings can be lengthy and their outcome uncertain. It is not unknown for the Commission to have to initiate more than one set of proceedings against a member state in order to obtain compliance, as in the case of Italy's refusal to observe the provisions of Directive 75/129 on Collective Redundancies. Partly because of such difficulties, the Treaty of European Union supplied a new power which could lead to a member state being fined for its failure to observe a ruling of the Court to the effect that it had not acted in compliance with Community law (now Article 171(2) of the EC Treaty). However, it is not specified what powers the Court can exercise if the member state in question then refuses to pay the fine, and it seems unlikely that the Commission will seek to use this method of enforcement very frequently. A similar power to fine which was contained in Article 88 of the Treaty establishing the European Coal and Steel Community was never invoked.

The doctrine of *direct effect* is likely to be a far more effective route to the imposition of Community norms, since it allows those norms to be applied as part of the legal order of the member state whether or not there is national legislation in place and, if there is, whether or not that legislation is adequate to the task of implementing the directive. A provision which has direct effect is one which 'grants individuals rights which must be upheld by the national courts' of the member state (Hartley, 1988: 183). The doctrine is not to be found in the Treaty; it was developed by the Court of Justice in decisions dating from the early 1960s. It was first used to give direct effect to provisions of the Treaty itself concerning free movement of goods.[10] The Court held that it could use its power to issue preliminary rulings on questions of Community law under Article 177 – a power which essentially confines it to advising national courts and which does not grant it any original jurisdiction to hear individuals' complaints – as the occasion to clarify the meaning and effect of Community norms. A provision is capable of having direct effect if it is clear and unambiguous, unconditional, and in no need of further action by either the state or the Community to come into force (other than implementation by the member state). Moreover, in the event of conflict with a competing norm of the domestic law of the member state, the Community provision will prevail thanks to the principle of the *supremacy* of Community over national law.[11] In most cases a national court or tribunal will be required not just to recognize the overriding effect of Community law but to grant a remedy, whether damages or injunction, which will adequately protect the applicant's Community law rights. It is only if the remedy needed is completely unprovided for within the laws of that state that the national court may avoid giving effect to it. This meant, for example, that the UK courts were required to grant the plaintiffs in the *Factortame* case[12] an injunction to prevent the application against them of an Act of Parliament, the Merchant Shipping Act 1988, which the Court of Justice had found was in breach of the freedom of establishment provisions of the Treaty of Rome. The rights in question had direct effect, and it was irrelevant that up to that point the UK courts had not recognized the possibility of granting an injunction against the Crown. The remedy existed, and its extension to cover the Crown was required by the principle of the supremacy of European law.

A Treaty provision, if it has direct effect, will apply both *horizontally* and *vertically*, that is to say it will confer rights upon individuals both against other private citizens and against the state.[13] A provision in a directive may only have vertical direct effect, that is to say it will apply only against an organ of the state. The same applies to a decision under Article 189.[14] The concept of an organ of the state has been flexibly interpreted; it will cover not just the Crown but also such institutions as a regional health authority,[15] a state-owned industry such as British Gas or British Coal prior to privatization[16] and a privatized, regulated utility such as South West Water.[17] This distinction in the effects of Treaty provisions and directives reflects the more fundamental nature of the rights guaranteed by the Treaty. Directives, being instructions to the member states, may impose obligations upon state organs through the notions of direct effect, but may not impose obligations directly on private citizens to whom they are not addressed except through the medium of domestic legislation.[18] No provision of a directive may have direct effect until the period laid down for its implementation by the member states has elapsed.[19]

The most important use of direct effect in the field of social policy has been in relation to the principle of equal pay for equal work between men and women. In *Defrenne* v. *SABENA (No. 2)*[20] the Court held that Article 119, which had lain dormant and in some countries unimplemented throughout the 1960s, possessed both horizontal and vertical direct effect despite a certain lack of clarity as to its precise scope. A series of later decisions has clarified both the scope of Article 119, extending it to cover the prohibition of indirect or 'adverse impact' discrimination, and the nature of its relationship to Directive 75/117 on Equal Pay and Directive 86/378 on Equality in Occupational Social Security.[21] Particularly controversial was the Court's 1990 ruling in *Barber*[22] to the effect that occupational pension benefits constituted 'pay' within Article 119. By bringing occupational pension benefits within the scope of Article 119, the Court overrode an express derogation from the principle of equality made in the 1986 Directive, which had purported to allow occupational schemes to maintain unequal pensionable ages for men and women. *Barber* decided, in effect, that the Directive operated on a false premise: the matter was already resolved by the terms of Article 119 which, as a Treaty provision, automatically took priority. The Court then attempted to limit the effects of its judgment to *prospective* or future pension benefits, in order not to upset the financial balance of occupational schemes which had been constructed on the assumption that Article 119 was of no relevance to them. However, so unclear was the ruling that several further references were needed to sort out what it meant; and by the time this process was complete, after several years of financial and administrative uncertainty, very little of the initial ruling remained.[23] This episode has not shown the Court in a good light.

An example of the direct effect of a directive is the Court's application of Directive 76/207 in the *Marshall* case.[24] Here it held that British legislation which allowed employers to dismiss women at a retirement age of 60 and men at 65 contravened the principle of equal treatment in employment. Because the right was derived from a Directive and not from the Treaty, this decision only applied to employers qualifying as 'organs of the state' until Parliament enacted the Sex

Discrimination Act 1986, which among other things made it unlawful for an employer to operate a policy of differential retirement ages.

Certain Treaty provisions are not capable of having direct effect, because of their uncertainty or ambiguity. One such example is Article 117 of the Treaty, considered above.[25] The same is also true of many provisions in directives; it is, on the whole, exceptional for a provision to be given direct effect. This does not mean, however, that provisions without direct effect are of no value to individuals asserting rights before national courts. *All* provisions of directives may be used to give a purposive interpretion to national legislation; they will then bind public and private employers alike under the terms of the relevant national law. This principle, sometimes referred to as *indirect effect*, has been applied by the British courts to avoid literal interpretations of the Equal Pay (Amendment) Regulations 1983[26] and and the Transfer of Undertakings (Protection of Employment) Regulations 1981[27] which would plainly have contradicted the aims of the directives from which these statutory instruments were ultimately derived. The principle of indirect effect may operate to require a purposive interpretation not just of a statute passed with the aim of implementing a directive but also one which *preceded* the relevant Community measure.[28] This last possibility is not easily reconcilable with normal principles of statutory interpretation in English law, and marks a further inroad into the autonomy of domestic law.

Where, finally, there is no flexibility in interpretation and the member state's legislation openly conflicts with the requirements of a directive, and the relevant provision of the directive does not have direct effect because, for example, it fails the test of precision, as a matter of last resort the claimant can sue the government of the member state for damages for its failure to implement the directive properly. This doctrine was elaborated by the Court in the *Francovich*[29] case which arose out of the Italian republic's failure to observe the terms of Directive 80/987 on Protection of Employee Rights in Insolvency.

While many of these developments have been dramatic and far-reaching from a constitutional point of view, some words of caution are needed. National courts retain a high degree of autonomy, not least because, in the end, they have substantial *de facto* discretion whether or not to refer a question of Community law to the Court of Justice. It may be stressed again that the Court of Justice has no original jurisdiction to hear claims arising from the implementation of social policy and cannot be petitioned directly by an individual; it can only pronounce on a point of Community law once the national court makes a reference to it under Article 177. The highest court of the member state is required, in principle, to refer a matter which is unclear, but it is the national court which decides whether the matter is sufficiently uncertain or not.[30] The jurisprudence of the Court also recognizes that the application of Community law frequently involves questions of interpretation which are matters for the national court to decide.

Nor has the Court sought to promote the aims of a transnational social policy as such. It is more concerned with preserving and developing the constitutional framework of the Community and with the promotion of market integration. At best, social policy and market integration may go hand in hand, as the Court suggested in *Defrenne* v. *SABENA (No. 2)*[31] in the context of Article 119. At no point has the Court articulated social and employment protection as a goal of Community action *in its own right*, though. The Court's refusal to grant direct effect to any part of Article 117 is a sign of a general reluctance to give the core of social policy an expansionist interpretation. Whereas the rights articulated in Article 119 have been recognized to be of a fundamental kind, requiring a substantial degree of uniformity in the approach taken by national courts to their interpretation in the same way as those contained in the law relating to the free movement of goods and persons, the same is not true of most of the rights contained in the Employment Protection Directives, which the Court has treated as 'measures of partial harmonisation' only (Hepple, 1990b: 649). This leaves national courts a very wide discretion to mould them to local circumstances.

The effect of this is observable in the context of the 1977 Acquired Rights Directive (77/187), which the Court has interpreted to encompass, potentially, many cases of the contracting-out or privatization of public services.[32] Under the Directive and the UK Transfer of Undertakings Regulations (TUPE), in the case of any relevant transfer the existing pay and conditions of the in-house workforce are preserved, together with their right to continuing employment with the 'transferee' who takes over the management of the work in question. The Court's rulings have a potentially devastating impact on the programme of market testing being promoted by the UK government, since they would deny contractors the right to undercut the terms and conditions of employment maintained by public-sector employers prior to the transfer taking place; moreover, thanks to the *Francovich* ruling (discussed above), the government's failure to implement the Directive properly in the early 1980s could open up claims for compensation against it by workers who lost employment or had their pay reduced as a consequence of contracting out. But because the Court's rulings do not mean that contracting-out procedures *must* come under the protective scope of the Directive, but only that they *may* do so under certain circumstances, in practice the matter is far from clear. This is partly because the central test of whether the process of contracting out involves the transfer of an 'undertaking' is for national courts to apply, with only loose guidance from the Court on the meaning of the relevant expressions in the Acquired Rights Directive. Different courts and tribunals in the UK have accordingly reached various different conclusions on the applicability of TUPE to cases which have come before them (Napier, 1993). In general, the rights of employees are far less clear cut in this area than they are under Article 119 and the Equal Pay and Equal Treatment Directives.

The Doctrine of Subsidiarity

The doctrine of subsidiarity, which is referred to in the Social Charter of 1989 and, most significantly, in the Treaty on European Union itself, has been held out as a means of preserving the autonomy of the national legal systems. In practice, any centralizing tendency is much more likely to be restrained by the lack of an adequate treaty base for social policy, as explained above. Both the Social Charter of 1989 and the accompanying Social Action Programme make frequent mention of the need to apply general standards with reference the practices of individual member states. According to the Preamble to the Social Charter, 'by virtue of the principle of subsidiarity, responsibility for the initiatives to be taken with regard to the implementation of [the] social rights lies with the member states or their constituent parts and, within the limits of its powers, with the European Community'; the Action Programme, with a slightly different emphasis, refers to the Community acting 'when the set objectives can be reached more effectively at its level than at that of the member states' (paragraph 3). As Hepple comments, these references to effectiveness 'add nothing of substance to the well-established legal bases of competence in the social field. . . . The so-called "principle of subsidiarity" in the context of the Charter is of political rather than legal significance' (1990b:647). Subsidiarity in this *political* sense is reflected, for example, in the failure of the Social Action Programme to propose Community-wide standards in the area of pay determination, other than the non-binding Opinion on the Equitable Wage, on the grounds that 'in matters of employment and remuneration, responsibility and, therefore, initiative lie mainly with the member states and the two sides of industry according to national practices, legislation and agreements' (Action Programme Chapter 2, introduction).

The only definition of subsidiarity of any great legal relevance is that now contained in Article 3b of the Treaty, as inserted at Maastricht; according to this,

> [i]n the areas which do not fall within its exclusive competence, the Community shall take action, in accordance with the principle of subsidiarity, only if and in so far as the objectives of the proposed action cannot be sufficiently achieved by the member states and can therefore, by reason of the scale and effects of the proposed action, be better achieved by the Community.

It is perhaps open to the Court to develop a broader set of principles against which, conceivably, future directives and regulations could be judged and potentially struck down on the grounds of excess of powers. At present this prospect seems unlikely, and it is too early to say what criteria, if any, the Court would adopt for judging when a certain measure cannot be 'sufficiently achieved by the member states'. In particular, it is completely premature to speak of member states using the doctrine of subsidiarity to earn exemption from *existing* social policy directives, such as those on equal pay or employment protection. For derogations of this kind to be permitted there would have to be a revolutionary change in conceptions of the Community legal order. It is more likely that the principle of subsidiarity will be interpreted to imply a greater role for the process of social dialogue and collective bargaining at national and transnational level, supplementing the Commission's role in the law-making process (Bercusson, 1994: 15).

5.3.   The Economics of Transnational Labour Standards

We now turn to a closer evaluation of the policy debate over transnational labour standards. The first section analyses the potential meanings of 'harmonization' and the second is concerned with more general arguments about the efficiency implications of labour regulation. Reference is made both to the general discussions and debates in this area and to the specific justifications advanced by the Commission for its policies in important documents of the past few years, including the Social Action Programme of 1989, the Green Paper on Social Policy of 1993 and the White Paper on Social Policy of 1994.

The Forms and Functions of Labour Standards

As Sengenberger notes (1994a: 3), 'the term "labour standard" has two distinct meanings. The first refers to the actual terms of employment, quality of work and the well-being of workers at a particular location and point in time'. The second meaning 'is a normative or prescriptive one. . . . They specify rights, such as the right to form associations of workers and employers, and the right to bargain collectively; they stipulate normative rules such as minimum wages, or maximum hours per week, or rules of conduct and dispute resolution'. As far as normative standards are concerned, it is normal to draw a further distinction between substantive and procedural regulation (Mückenberger and Deakin, 1989: 157 ff.).

Substantive regulation consists of the insertion of particular levels of minimum protection into the employment relationship, directly displacing individual bargaining. Norms may be either compulsory or 'inderogable' (Wedderburn, 1992), in which case contracting out is legally ineffective, as in the case of most minimum wage legislation; or, less usually, optional or facilitative, in which case some limited exception or 'derogation' is allowed below the floor of rights, as is the case with most forms of statutory control of working time. The latter form is inherently flexible, in the sense that the implementation of the standard can be varied according to local circumstances.

Procedural regulation, by contrast, is concerned with the establishment of norms governing the process of bargaining, and does not imply the setting of any particular level of remuneration or protection. Examples here include laws promoting collective as opposed to individual bargaining, which range from protection for the right to strike and freedom of association to the concept of the employer's 'duty to bargain' at collective level which some systems recognize.

Elements of both substantive and procedural regulation are to be found in the important case of 'controlled derogation', where limited exceptions from substantive norms are allowed on condition that they are agreed and monitored collectively, through a trade union or other representative bargaining agent, or by the labour inspectorate (Wedderburn and Sciarra, 1988; for a now repealed UK example, see Deakin, 1990: 3, 17).

A third form is that of *promotional standards*, designed to channel economic activity through the provision of public support services or subsidies, as happens in the case of vocational training and worker placement (Sengenberger, 1994b). The balance between these three forms varies considerably between different European systems; for example, British labour law has tended historically to rely on voluntary standard-setting through the collective bargaining system, with only a minimal role for direct legal intervention in the contract of employment, in contrast to the more heavily state-regulated systems of mainland Europe. But in any one system, 'it is the notion of complementarity which accords standards their "strategic" significance when intervening in the processes of growth and modernisation, strategy being understood as an overriding orientation for coordinating and integrating a set of policies' (Sengenberger, 1994b: 45); by extension it is equally important that the process of transnational standard setting should not address isolated aspects of the question (as the body of Community labour law currently does). It will be of little use to set normative standards which provide for a high and legally inderogable level of protection for individual workers, if adequate collective or procedural means for their implementation do not exist.

It is evident that labour standards, in each of these ways, control competition in the labour market, although the scope for flexibility in their application is considerable. Moreover, the regulation of competition is not synonymous with uniformity of practice. Harmonization of standards in the second sense identified by Sengenberger – standards as norms – does not *necessarily* imply the achievement of uniformity of standards in the first sense, that is the actual level of protection achieved in a particular country.

The debate about the social dimension has suffered from a failure to draw this distinction. It is a complete exaggeration, for example, to describe the social dimension as requiring *uniformity* or 'steps towards a state of (full) international social integration, i.e. a state in which national welfare systems and labour market regulations are adjusted to a common model' (Paqué, Chapter 4, this volume); nor is it necessarily appropriate to talk of ossification (Addison and Siebert, Chapter 2, this volume). Not only does harmonization not necessitate uniformity within a common model, as will be seen; nobody other than a few critics is currently suggesting that this is what the social dimension of the Community is designed to achieve.

Instead a number of more limited objectives have been advanced. One possibility is that harmonization in social policy is needed to achieve a *level playing field* between member states, in particular by establishing *parity of costs* imposed by the regulatory systems of member states. At first sight, this view has a certain plausibility: following the establishment of the single market in goods and services, differences in the cost structure of member states brought about by variations in relative burdens of taxation and regulation will produce 'distortions of competition'. Companies in low-cost countries will be placed at what some might consider an 'artificial' competitive advantage compared to those located elsewhere in the single market. This is what the Court seems to have had in mind when, in its judgments in the enforcement proceedings brought against the UK in respect of the Collective Redundancies and Acquired Rights Directives, it stated that 'the Community legislature intended both to ensure comparable protection for workers' rights in the different member states and to harmonise the costs which such protective rules entail for Community undertakings.'[33]

In its explanatory memorandum of 1990 concerning the proposals for directives on part-time and fixed-term employment ('certain employment relationships'), the Commission nevertheless rejected this argument in the context of differentials in wage costs:

> Wage levels, non-wage labour costs and rules on working conditions vary considerably between member states. Broadly speaking, however, these differences do not hamper the operation of healthy competition in the Community. The differences in productivity levels attenuate these differences in unit labour costs to a considerable degree. Moreover, other production cost components tend to be higher in the less-developed member states where nominal labour costs are lowest. (Commission, 1990: para. 22)

The Commission used this as the justification for declining to make any provision in the proposals for part-time and fixed-term workers to receive pro-rata rights to equal pay with those employed on a full-time basis. Oddly enough, the argument thereby rejected was the very argument which had succeeded in relation to equal pay between men and women at the time of the drafting of the Treaty of Rome, and which led to the adoption of Article 119, namely that the availability of a source of cheap (or undervalued) labour within a particular country could give companies located there an artificial competitive advantage. The Commission's line is even odder when it is remembered that the discriminatory treatment of part-time workers has been held to give rise to questions of indirect sex discrimination under Article 119, given that married women make up the vast number of part-time employees in most member states;[34]

> looked at through the lens of part-time work, the analysis now offered in 1990 by the Commission denies protection on pay through proportionality with full-time workers

as that is not required to avoid distortions to competition, [but] if they are looked at through the other optic of sex discrimination, these same workers may receive just that protection which they cannot acquire from the 1990 proposals. (Wedderburn, 1991: 22)

Whether a convincing argument can be put forward for regulating the pay and conditions of part-time workers with reference to their full-time equivalents is a matter considered in more detail elsewhere (Deakin and Wilkinson, 1991). For present purposes it is relevant to note that having rejected arguments for the harmonization of regulations concerning relative pay in the 1990 explanatory memorandum, the Commission then accepted the same arguments in relation to differences arising from indirect wage costs (such as dismissal protection) and from social charges (social security contributions and other forms of taxation):

Other cost differences are not offset by factors such as differences in productivity and do not help to improve the Community's economic and social cohesion. This is so in particular as regards the relative cost differences resulting from different kinds of rules on different types of employment relationships, which may provide comparative advantages which constitute veritable distortions of competition. Clearly, if a member state can produce with lower labour costs than the other member states – yet that difference does not result from factors such as those mentioned above, but is due to segmented labour markets having different costs for the same type of work, attributable solely to the different rules applicable to the different types of employment relationships – it will have a comparative advantage which cannot be considered permanent and runs counter to common interests. (Commission, 1990: para. 25)

The distinction thereby drawn between direct and indirect wage costs and charges is open to criticism. Since regulations in some countries, such as France and Germany, impose on employers the obligation to treat part-time and fixed-term contract workers equally with those employed full-time – an obligation which requires them to pay pro-rata wages and benefits – and other countries, such as the UK, do not have such regulation (Deakin, 1991), it is difficult to see how inter-country differences in the cost-structure of flexible employment *necessarily* result from productivity differences in the sense implied by the Commission. The Commission also ignored a wealth of evidence showing that differentials in terms and conditions between full-time and 'flexible' or 'atypical' workers are only weakly correlated with comparative productivity, suggesting that there is a high degree of labour market segmentation and an implicit subsidy to employers in the use of 'atypical' labour separately from the impact of rules concerning dismissal procedures and social charges (see Craig *et al.*, 1982, 1985; Mückenberger and Deakin, 1989: 184–86).

But the most important objection is to the Commission's entire approach in arguing for harmonization on the basis of 'relationships between cost levels and the relative weight carried by the different factors of production' (Commission, 1990: para. 24). This may have been done in an attempt to justify the decision to bring forward one of the three draft directives under the qualified voting procedure provided for in Article 100a of the Treaty; it was thought at that time that the derogation in Article 100a(2), requiring unanimity, would not apply to a case in which it could be shown that a substantial issue of the distortion of competition could be made out (Vogel-Polsky, 1990). Since then it has become clear that the member states will not acquiesce in this use of Article 100a, and that, for the time being at least, this provision cannot be used to support a directive concerned with the 'rights and interests of employed persons' whether or not it is also concerned to prevent distortions of competition. In seeking to comply with the perceived needs of the Treaty base game, however, the Commission advanced a basis for harmonization which is questionable in principle and impossible to operate in practice.

The notion that a static parity of costs must be established by harmonization for intra-Community competition to be 'fair' is dubious from almost any of the rival points of view on the merits of transnational standards. Those who would argue for a minimalist (or non-existent) Community social policy from the viewpoint of neo-classical economic theory would not normally argue for the imposition of a single standard, even if it were a low one. They would be more likely to consider that the removal of barriers to trade and factor mobility would be enough to subject welfare state regimes to competition on the basis of comparative costs (see Paqué, Chapter 4). The lower costs of lower-wage countries would enable them to attract additional investment which, over time, would bid up demand for labour in those countries, and would allow for a gradual convergence with the higher-wage systems. A central standard, not being based on a process of market discovery of this kind, would fore-stall this process and lead to an overall welfare loss. In the same way, it is argued to be undesirable for the federal courts in the United States to impose a common norm governing state takeover statutes, even if that norm were to be an apparently deregulationary one (Easterbrook and Fischel, 1991).

Those, by contrast, who would argue for a variety of reasons for the pursuit of social policy as a goal in its own right would also have reason to be sceptical of the Commission's approach. This is because the explanatory memorandum says nothing about the level at which any common norm is to be set, nor about harmon-izing 'upwards' as such. Using the arguments advanced by the Commission it would be perfectly possible to set a low standard as long as it was a common one, which is in fact a plausible interpretation of what actually happened in this case: the three proposals, taken together, suffer from serious gaps and do not attempt to approach the more rigorous standards envisaged by proposals in the same area of the middle 1980s (Hepple, 1990a).

The imposition through the Community of a 'level playing field' of costs would, of course, involve an enormous degree of disruption to existing labour law systems, even if it were possible to isolate the question of wage levels from that of social pro-tection regimes. But it is also worth stressing that other, central features of Community law and in particular the law on the free movement of goods has rec-ognized the right of states to set high and, by definition, differential standards in social legislation, even where these could be seen as potentially creating a 'distor-tion of competition' which would be harmful to employers located within such states. Article 30, which prohibits member states from imposing quantitative restrictions on imports, also restricts them imposing 'measures having equivalent effect'. This extremely broad concept includes 'all trading rules enacted by member states, which are capable of hindering, directly or indirectly, actually or potentially, intra-Community trade,'[35] and could, on the face of it, cover protective legislation such as health and safety regulations, working time laws and legislation such as Sunday trading controls. However, not only is this qualified by Article 36 which provides, by way of derogation, that restrictions may be 'justified on grounds of public morality, public policy or public security [and] the protection of health and life of humans', but the Court itself has added to this list a number of legitimate 'mandatory requirements' which includes legislation for the improvement of working conditions.

For this reason the Court held in *Oebel*[36] that German legislation regulating nightwork in bakeries was capable of complying with Article 30 while in *Webb*[37] it held that legislation could be upheld on the grounds that it promoted 'good relations on the labour market' and the 'lawful interests of the workforce concerned'. The Court has recently stressed that it is legitimate for states to enact legislation limiting Sunday employment and Sunday opening of shops,[38] and has rejected an analysis which would require such measures to be submitted to a 'proportionality' test, or rule of reason,[39] thereby limiting the use of Article 30 as a basis for a wide-ranging inquiries into the economic effects of social legislation (Barnard, 1994; Barnard and Deakin, 1996). This is probably the best view to take, in the absence of clear criteria which might guide the Court and the danger of competition-based arguments being advanced to undermine social legislation by a side assault.

A similar problem is posed by the potential clash between the norms of free movement of labour and freedom of establishment for companies, and the principle of the territorial effect of national labour laws, which is common to all labour law systems within the Community. According to the principle of territoriality, all workers employed in the territory of the country in question, and not just those who are nationals of the state in question, are covered by that state's protective legislation; any other solution would provide a straightforward means of evading regulatory controls. In the *Rush Portuguesa*[40] case the Court confirmed that the compulsory application of French labour legislation to workers who were themselves nationals of another member state and who were employed in France by an employer of another member state, did not contravene the employer's rights to supply services under Article 59, even though the application of the stricter French laws could from one point of view be seen as discouraging freedom of movement for both labour and capital. *Rush Portuguesa* confirms that states are entitled to apply their own, differential labour standards even where these create something less than a completely level playing field for both firms and workers. The proposed Directive on the Temporary Posting of Workers would further confirm this by requiring overseas workers employed by contractors to given the benefit both of compulsory social legislation of the state in which they work – this in itself does not add much to national territoriality, except to entrench it at Community level – and of collective agreements applicable *erga omnes*, that is to say, to all employers and employees in the relevant sector, industry or region. The inclusion of collective agreements here is particularly important as these will not necessarily have compulsory *legal effect* under the principle of national territoriality, depending on the rules which operate in each member state.

These decisions and instruments indicate that the goal of market integration within the common or internal market is not seen by Community law as requiring either uniformity of social provision, or the static parity of costs which seems to underly the Commission's analysis in the 1990 Explanatory Memorandum on employment relationships. On the contrary, diversity of social provision (and hence, indirectly, differences in costs) has long been defended by the European Court in its rulings in these areas, and has been reflected in the terms of directives and regulations.[41]

Rather than viewing harmonization in terms of a static end-point in which member states provide parallel forms and levels of protection, it is potentially much more useful to see it as a *dynamic process* in which transnational labour standards interact with the economic integration to produce a continuous upwards movement in social provision. The standards set by the norms themselves and those which operated in practice (standards in the dual sense identifed above) would gradually rise. This version of harmonization does not imply uniformity of provision; what it does require is that states do not regress to a lower level of provision by engaging in destructive competition over nominal labour costs. Insofar as the notoriously obscure notion of 'social dumping' has any meaning, it should be taken to refer neither to capital flight nor to the practice of underpricing goods for export to higher cost countries, but to the practice of states competing with each other to retain or attract capital by dismantling protective legislation. A legitimate aim of transnational standards is to set a minimum *floor of rights* designed to forestall resort to strategies of this kind. Convergence as such is only necessary to the extent that a particularly large *divergence* in costs may heighten the chance of social dumping in the sense explained above.

The floor of rights character of Community law is stressed in directives adopted both before and after the Single Act of 1986. The employment protection directives of the late-1970s specified that they 'shall not affect the right of member states to apply or introduce laws, regulations and administrative provisions which are more favourable to employees'.[42] Article 118a of the EC Treaty, inserted by the Single Act, refers to the adoption of directives laying down '*minimum* requirements' in the field of the working environment (emphasis added). Directive 89/391, the Framework Directive on Health and Safety, states that 'this Directive shall be without prejudice to existing or future national and Community provisions which are more favourable to protection of the safety and health of workers at work' (Article 1(3)), while Directive 92/56, amending the 1975 Collective Redundancies Directive, specifies that that Directive 'shall not affect the right of member states to ... promote or allow the application of collective agreements more favourable to workers'.[43] The 1993 Directive on Working Time provides that 'this Directive shall not have the effect of reducing the general level of protection of workers in comparison with the situation existing in each member state at the time of its adoption',[44] and Directive 92/85 on Protection of the Health and Safety of Pregnant Workers contains a broadly analogous provision. The legal significance of the difference in wording in each case is not completely clear; whereas the Framework Directive and the amendment to the Redundancies Directive clearly envisage future improvements, the other two are more cautious in ruling out *downwards* harmonization as a result of their adoption. But it is clear in each case that parity of costs, at a low or high level, is not as such the goal, and that a reduction in protection to achieve parity of costs is not required by the directives. This may be contrasted with certain instruments in the field of consumer protection and product safety, which require parallel provisions in the member states and which are open to an interpretation which would prevent states improving on the standards they lay down; the notion of social policy harmonization has diverged from the meaning of harmonization in other areas of Community law.[45]

The conjunction of economic and social goals in the concept of the floor of rights is also found in the case law of the European Court interpreting Article 119. In *Defrenne* v. *SABENA (No. 2)* it stated that:

> in the light of the different stages of the development of social legislation in the various member states, the aim of Article 119 is to avoid a situation in which undertakings established in member states which have actually implemented the principle of equal pay suffer a competitive disadvantage in intra-Community competition as compared with undertakings established in states which have not yet eliminated discrimination as regards pay.

At the same time it regarded social policy as not completely subsumed into an economic integrationist rationale: the Community is 'not merely an economic union,

but is at the same time intended, by common action, to ensure social prog
seek the constant improvement of the living and working conditions of
peoples, as is emphasised by Preamble to the Treaty.' In its later rulings on Art.
119, the Court stressed that the implementation of the principle of equality implied
a 'levelling up' between the sexes.

More recently, the Commission's 1993 Green Paper, *European Social Policy
Objectives for the Union* expressed the concept of the transnational floor of rights
in the following way:

> Whilst a common labour market policy at the level of the Union is neither feasible nor
> desirable, it would be dangerous if under the pressures to change, the conditions in
> national labour markets began to diverge excessively. A commitment to high social
> standards and to the promotion of social progress forms an integral part of the new
> Treaty. A 'negative' competitiveness between member states would lead to social
> dumping, to the undermining of the consensus-making process identified in the
> Maastricht Social Agreement, and to danger for the acceptability of the Union. This
> is why the attempt to reach agreement on certain common minimum labour standards
> should be pursued and why cooperation between the member states ... should be
> strengthened. (Commission, 1993: 46)

How far does this imply a social policy which is independent of the goal of market
integration? The Green Paper refers to the need to cope with the particular stresses
caused by the process of economic integration. This can be seen as a justification for
the emphasis on protection of health and safety under Article 118a and for the regulation of economic restructuring under the employment protection directives of the
1970s, a justification which has if anything strengthened with the advent of the
single market. In a broader sense, the Green Paper implies that social progress is
itself a mechanism for achieving greater economic cohesion. A dual purpose is
ascribed to the 'social ground rules' of market integration: 'on the one hand a defensive mechanism to ensure that there is a minimum floor below which social standards should not fall in certain key areas and on the other hand a more pro-active
concept aimed at ensuring convergence through social progress', ideas which the
Green Paper claims are enshrined in Article 118a, the Social Charter and the
Agreement on Social Policy. While this still ties social policy to economic integration, it also provides a much more plausible basis for extensive Community action
in the social field than the arguments advanced in the 1990 explanatory memorandum. It also provides a potential basis for the elaboration of the doctrine of subsidiarity in the social field. Although the Community may only act under Article 3b
of the Treaty 'if and in so far as the proposed action cannot be sufficiently achieved
by the member states', it is plain that the member states cannot *in principle* achieve
alone the establishment of common 'social ground rules' in the sense described
above. While the precise meaning in practice of this distinction is yet to be worked
out, the broad outlines of a division of labour in the social field between the
Community and the member states are beginning to be discernible.

Standards as Guarantors of Economic Development and Participation

Are these arguments, as some have suggested, simply an expression of collective
action by entrenched groups attempting to preserve protectionist rents (Paqué,
Chapter 4)? This point of view is, of course, closely linked to the general neoclassical

al legislation and the welfare state which has been so influ-
ndation for deregulatory policies in many industrialized
970s. Some of the arguments put against the social dimen-
bout transnational harmonization at all, but are related to
eneral lines of the neoclassical economic argument against
een the subject of extensive discussion elsewhere and will
here (see Chapter 3 above; and for a critical review of neo-
enberger and Deakin, 1989). In broad terms, the neo-
classical critique sees regulation as an exogenous interference with market relations,
doubts whether such intervention can be justified on market-failure grounds and
tends instead to view state action as the outcome of rent-seeking activity by organized labour and other self-interested groups such as state bureaucracies (Heldman
et al., 1981). This has led to calls for deregulation in the sense of a return to the
common law of the contract of employment as the basis for labour relations
(Epstein, 1983, 1984).

It has long been recognized that the critique of regulation rests on rather fragile
methodological grounds, disputed even within mainstream economics, and that its
contentions are not easily susceptible of proof either way. A major theoretical challenge has been posed by the growing 'new institutional' literature which sees economic institutions as a potential response to the high transaction costs inherent in
a system of decentralized exchange. Labour markets are seen as less than fully competitive, as a consequence of limited information and 'asset specificity' or the presence of relation-specific investments within the employment relationship (Solow,
1990). Practices associated with 'internal labour markets' – job guarantees of
varying degrees of explicitness, the linking of salaries and pensions to seniority, and
the provision of in-firm training and career development – have been explained in
economic terms as providing the basis for the maintenance of cooperation based on
'trust' within long-term employment relationships (Williamson, *et al.*, 1975), while
efficiency wage theories have sought to show that similar factors prevent firms from
responding to external changes in market conditions by immediately cutting pay
and benefits, so providing an explanation for the stability and continuity over time
of many employee welfare arrangements (Bulow and Summers, 1986).

If it is one thing to demonstrate the efficiency properties of long-term economic
relationships, it is another matter to show that they should be imposed on employers through regulation. Liberal job-dismissal regimes, such as that in the USA where
the employment at-will rule still prevails in most states, may be compatible with a
very high degree of job stability and with continuity in the employment relationship
over time (Addison and Castro, 1987), although this is still less than in the more
highly regulated European systems such as those of France and Germany. However,
both transaction cost and game theoretical approaches have been shown to have
useful insights into the beneficial welfare effects of regulation in overcoming
externalities and other instances of market failure arising from the limits of collective action (Büchtemann, 1993; Grahl and Teague, 1992; Aghion and Hermalin,
1990). Regulation may be needed to enable the parties to private contracts to capture
rents from cooperation which will not be attainable in a regime of pure market
competition (Deakin and Wilkinson, 1996). Where this is the case, regulation will
be neither ineffective nor counterproductive, in the sense of causing unemployment,
as Addison and Siebert suggest it necessarily must be (1992: 511).

These perspectives call into question the effectiveness of policies designed
to make labour markets more competitive or contestable through a policy of

wholesale deregulation, which is the preferred solution of some (Addison and Siebert, 1992: 510). At the very least, an institutional perspective cautions against attempts to dismantle job security regimes for the 'core' workforce; if there is to be deregulation it should be partial in nature, designed to encourage the integration of excluded groups through the selective removal of dismissal protection for certain part-time and fixed-term hirings (Emerson, 1988). But even this view is open to the challenge that 'atypical' jobs of this kind form 'traps' rather than 'bridges' back to stable employment (Büchtemann and Quack, 1989), and what little empirical evidence there is to date confirms that limited deregulatory measures of this kind have had little or no positive impact on job creation in the countries where they have been adopted (Evans *et al.*, 1985; Büchtemann, 1990).

Much has been made of the superior job creation record of the US economy in the 1980s, and the comparatively low employment rate of the EC member states during the same period. However, the link between job creation and regulatory systems is still to be satisfactorily explained. The principal cause of job creation in the USA in the 1980s was population growth (Houseman, 1995). In the USA, there was a large increase in the working-age population, which the US economy was able to absorb, leading to dramatic headline increases in jobs and a less dramatic but still significant growth in employment participation rates. The converse of the United States' superior jobs record, however, was its poor record on wage growth and on productivity. In the USA, labour productivity grew more slowly than in the main EC economies, working hours were extended and average wages fell in real terms. Also, GDP per head declined relative to the main EC economies (Deakin and Wilkinson, 1994). In one sense, 'maybe the United States "paid" for employment creation through low or declining wages, while Europe "paid" for high or rising wages with sluggish growth of employment' (Freeman, 1994: 14). But the downside for the US economy is not simply its reduced capacity to generate or preserve 'good' jobs: it is also felt in terms of reduced efficiency in the use of labour. There is recent evidence to suggest that effective employment protection and legal support for collective institutions in the EC systems is linked to their superior economic performance in terms of higher wage levels and labour productivity (Buchele and Christiansen, 1995). In this vein, a debate has began around the idea that social policy systems should be judged not solely by reference to the immediate costs which they impose, in terms of social charges or regulatory costs, but also in terms of their capacity to promote wider economic benefits such as encouraging improvements in labour quality, ensuring non-inflationary economic activity by promoting the full and effective use of resources, encouraging fair competition and promoting innovation by supporting economic relationships based on cooperation. In addition to enhancing competitiveness by these means, it is also suggested that social policy interventions may bring broader benefits, or reductions in costs in terms of enhanced social cohesion. This idea of 'social policy as a productive factor' has been taken up by the Commission President Jacques Santer.[46]

Not only are there concerns about the poor quality of the most of the 'new' jobs created in the US economy in the 1980s (Loveman and Tilly, 1988); within the EC it is not the case that the UK has an obviously better job creation record than other countries (Cosh *et al.*, 1993), despite its much stronger commitment to the deregulation of labour and social legislation and the relative absence of mandatory employment benefits which goes back to the period before the present wave of deregulation began. The role of macroeconomic policy and in particular the restrictive effects of monetary policy in the attempt to implement the goal of currency union must also be taken into account in any account of European unemployment in the early 1990s (Michie and Wilkinson, 1994). No doubt the jury is still out on the effects of employment protection laws, and further empirical research is needed for firmer comparative conclusions to be drawn. But it is also clear that no consensus has been reached on the strident allegations of the disemployment effects of protective legislation made by neoliberal and neoconservative critics.

A more specific critique of transnational harmonization is that it will unduly hamper the operation of competition between different regulatory regimes which is one aspect of the single market; as Paqué argues,

> why should some parameters of international competition be removed through *ex ante* harmonization while others such as infrastructure, education and skills of the work-force, and environmental quality continue to determine the structure of the international division of labour? (Chapter 4: 108)

In particular, it is arguable that the convergence of standards between systems at different stages of economic development will remove an obvious source of comparative advantage for those states with lower labour and social costs. From their point of view, harmonization may indeed be nothing more than a form of protectionism imposed by the stronger economic systems for their own benefit. At its core this argument is, again, based on strong assumptions about the operation of competitive forces and their effects upon the evolution of institutions. It is being suggested that a process of natural selection will operate with regard to institutional forms, once they are thrown into competition with each other in the integrated trading system of the internal market; just as the common law is said to have evolved through the selection or rules from among a 'capital stock' of legal precedents (Posner, 1993), or as state systems in the USA evolve in response to competitive pressures posed by the free interstate commerce guaranteed by the federal constitution (Fischel, 1984). A 'race to the bottom' in social standards is most likely ruled out by the pressure on states to adapt those measures which are best suited to the needs of a productive economy; or, if there is a race to the bottom, that may simply imply a readjustment of welfare state systems to the demands of efficiency as expressed through the full force of transnational competitive forces.

Many will find this a somewhat Panglossian view; and an historical perspective on economic development would indeed indicate that while

> there will be *some* tendency for inefficient institutions to be selected against evolutionarily . . . the process of change is subject to complicating features [which] open up possibilities of there being differences between countries and sectors and periods in the effects of institutional change, including retrogression sometimes. (Matthews, 1986: 912–13)

The thesis of 'path dependency', using transaction cost reasoning, suggests that national systems can become locked into particular arrangements, on account of sunk costs, long after it has become obvious that they are not the most efficient form available; the costs of starting anew with new institutional forms are too large, or too difficult to estimate *ex ante*, as not to make it worthwhile for the change to take place without some form of state intervention or centralized coordination. Limited information and bounded rationality play their part in the market for institutional forms as in other markets (North, 1990). This implies that some form of transnational coordination of welfare state systems is not, in itself, illegitimate. There can be no assumption that an optimal set of norms will naturally emerge from a process of market integration; on the contrary, obstacles to mobility of resources and information are if anything greater in a single market where specific national customs and practices prevail and are likely to do so for the foreseeable future. Under these circumstances 'there is a clear danger that Community labour markets may face what could be called a *coordination deficit*; that is, they may be exposed to demands for change and adaptation which outrun their actual capacity to adjust' (Grahl and Teague, 1992: 525).

Scepticism of the neoclassical view that convergence will come about as the natural result of free trade provides a more than adequate basis for a theory of transnational labour standards which would stress their *universality*, or common application to developed and less well-developed systems alike. As Sengenberger suggests, the economic benefits to be gained from normative standards, in terms of inducing cooperation between economic agents and foreclosing the option of destructive downwards competition, mean that they should be regarded as an input or ingredient to balanced and sustainable development, and not as the output of that development (Sengenberger, 1994b). Effective regulation setting common standards in such areas as wage levels, working time and job protection removes or at least limits the implicit subsidy which low pay offers to firms which cannot effectively compete on the basis of managerial or technological innovation. The same goes for national systems: systems whose comparative advantage lies mainly or exclusively in lower nominal labour costs will only be able to compete by continuously depressing the actual level of labour and welfare standards enjoyed by their populations, at the cost of a longer term loss of productive efficiency and job quality. This general point is particularly relevant to the debate over the future of social policy in eastern Europe. Over time it may well be, as the Green Paper on social policy suggests, that 'management practice which does not take into account co-operative rather than hierarchical organisation structures, development of employee skills and initiatives and the establishment of client-orientated marketing practice will be punished in the market-place' (Commission, 1993: 46). But so far as states are concerned, market sanctions will be neither immediate nor necessarily effective to penalize one country's determination to engage in wholesale deregulation.

If normative standards can be seen as guarantors of economic development, they also have a role in extending participation in the broad sense of that term to include both political and industrial democracy. It is significant, then, that recent initiatives in social policy have tended to emphasize procedural regulation at least as much as substantive controls; the European Works Council Directive of 1995 and the attempt to formalize the European-level social dialogue in the Maastricht Agreement on Social Policy are perhaps the two most prominent examples, but also important is the renewed stress on collective bargaining as a means of implementing social policy goals which is to be found in some parts of the Social Action Programme (Wedderburn, 1992: 251–8). Measures of this kind which aim to strengthen the role of representative organizations have the merit of not seeking to impose heavy direct costs on firms, in the form of social charges or mandated benefits.

Equally, the Commission has accepted that there is a role for employment policy interventions which are designed to provide routes back to regular employment for groups excluded from employment, and that, in this context, a policy of using labour standards to promote high-wage, high-productivity employment may not be enough. The 1994 Commission White Paper on Social Policy proposed that 'as well as supporting high productivity jobs, the Union maximises its ability to generate and sustain jobs at other levels, particularly in the unskilled, semi-skilled and personal and local services fields' (Commission, 1994: 10). This is a recognition that the same labour standards which induce employers to invest in labour resources may also slow down flows into and out of employment, reducing opportunities for integration of youth, the longer-term unemployed and other groups excluded from the labour market. At the same time, such a policy is not without its difficulties. With increasing pressures on organizations in both the private and the public sector to improve efficiency, it seems doubtful that there are many areas left in which truly low productivity jobs can be created, without cost to the overall efficiency of the economy. Moreover, the evidence from the USA, where low productivity jobs are more widely available, is that they may be of limited value as a means of promoting employment opportunities, at least for certain groups: 'less skilled and low-paid American men [still] had relatively poor employment prospects despite falling real wages' (Card and Freeman, 1994: 233).

Other measures which have been put on the agenda for the 1996–97 Intergovernmental Conference include a more positive role for macroeconomic policy. The Edinburgh summit of the European Council in 1992 agreed to increase the Community's resources from 1.20% of Community-wide GDP to 1.27% by 1999, and called on member states to take a number of steps to promote employment including the use of public spending to combat unemployment. Community-level action in the field of vocational training for the long-term unemployed, persons under 25 and those excluded from the labour market has also been identified as an area in which the European Social Fund has a role to play (Commission, 1994: 18–20). However, for the time being the prospects for the coordination of state-level macroeconomic measures aimed to boosting employment seem limited.

A debate has also begun, parallel with the Intergovernmental Conference, about amendments to the 'convergence criteria' laid down at Maastricht as preconditions for participation by member states in the process of currency union which is meant to lead to the adoption of the single currency. These criteria currently require member states to meet limits on public debt, budget deficits and inflation rates,[47] but make no mention of convergence on unemployment or employment rates or on indices of earnings or income equality. The introduction of 'social convergence criteria' has been strongly supported in the Nordic member states, but has so far been resisted by the Commission on the grounds that to impose additional preconditions for the single currency could unravel the whole process of currency union.[48]

5.4. Conclusion

This chapter has shown that the present state of Community labour and social legislation is inadequate and its legal base uncertain; that its future progress, for reasons related to the inadequacy of the legal base, is tied up with the debates over the role of regulation in the process of economic integration; and that a viable economic case can be made for social policy harmonization as a central part of the process of economic integration, not in terms of the imposition of uniformity nor with parity of costs in mind, but as a floor of labour standards whose goals include the promotion of labour as a productive resource. This does not mean that integration will be 'law-directed' but it does imply a certain role for transnational regulation in channelling economic activity in the direction of productive efficiency and social cohesion.

The threat of destructive downwards competition, although real, should not be exaggerated; nor should it be supposed that labour standards offer a panacea enabling the economies of the Community to retain their capacity to compete effectively in global markets. What is being suggested is that labour standards do have a crucial role to play in ensuring that market integration and the growth of international trade proceed in an orderly and progressive fashion. It is clear that there needs to be a debate about the form of transnational standards, about the degree to which substantive regulation through law is used in preference to procedural norms and how far general guidance through recommendations and opinions is preferred to legislation through directives and regulations; the level at which norms are set and the criteria for implementation and application, the role to be played by collective bargaining at national and transnational level and by national courts within the doctrine of subsidiarity all need to be discussed. The danger of covert protectionism should be recognized together with that of excessive rigidity of regulation, as the experience of certain national systems demonstrates (Büchtemann, 1993: 60). But this debate will not be advanced very far as long as exaggerated and speculative claims continue to be made about the illegitimacy of regulation *as such*.

The intense debate over European social policy has coincided with a broader reassessment of the welfare state and in particular of mechanisms for employment protection and income redistribution. The future development of national systems will be affected to some degree by the establishment of the integrated internal market. It is inevitable that welfare state systems will to some extent be thrown into competition with one another, although how far or how quickly this will happen is difficult to judge. Nor is it clear that those systems which outwardly appear to be more rigid, or more intensively regulated, would lose out in such a process. There can be no doubt, however, of the potentially destabilizing effects which 'social devaluations' might have on the wider project of economic integration. In these circumstances it will be vital for the Community to evolve principles for transnational intervention which do not just amount to defending the pre-existing welfare state but articulate the case for *re-regulation* 'in the sense of a European social order which increases the requirements of equality, individual freedom and welfare within a network of collective security and participation' (Mückenberger and Deakin, 1989: 197). The further elaboration and implementation of this programme should form the next phase in the development of Community social policy; but that is another story.

Notes

1 Directive 64/221 on freedom of movement; Directive 68/360 on residence rights; Regulation 1612/68 on freedom of movement; Regulation 1251/70 on rights of residence.
2 Directive 75/117 on Equal Pay; Directive 77/207 on Equal Treatment in Employment; Directive 79/7 on Equal Treatment in Social Security; Directive 86/378 on Equal Treatment in Occupational Social Security.
3 Directive 75/129 on Collective Redundancies; Directive 77/187 on Acquired Rights on Transfers of Undertakings; Directive 80/987 on Protection of Employee Rights in the event of Insolvency.

4 The Social Charter acquired added significance *later*, as a consequence of the Agreement on Social Policy of 1992, which makes reference to it. On the Agreement on Social Policy, see below, pp.124–126.

5 The Council of Europe is a wider body than the European Community, covering as it does most of the democratically constituted states of western and eastern Europe. Conventions of the ILO, the European Convention of Human Rights of 1950 and the Social Charter of 1961 are in each case treaties which bind their signatories in international law. However, few member states of the ILO have a complete record of ratification of Conventions while the Council of Europe's Social Charter allows states to make derogations or exceptions from particular provisions. In neither case is there an effective enforcement mechanism, beyond the periodic reports of Committees of Experts.

6 At the time of writing, this case has not yet been reported.

7 The Maastricht Treaty established the wider Union as an instrument of cooperation between the member states in the fields of defence and foreign policy and justice and home affairs, while retaining, in a modified form, the legal entity of the European Community as the basis of economic integration through the internal market. The amended Treaty of Rome is now known as the 'Treaty establishing the European Community'. Community law, as a body of rules and principles which is capable of operating not just to govern relations between states but also within the legal systems of those states, relates only to the activities of the Community in this sense and not to the matters of cooperation between the member states which are the subject of the Union alone. It therefore remains accurate to refer, in this regard, to both the 'European Community' and to 'Community law', although as a matter of practice the term 'European Union' is being used as an all-purpose term.

8 See below on the European Court of Justice.

9 Under section 2(1) of the European Communities Act, 'all such rights, powers, liabilities, obligations and restrictions from time to time created or arising by or under the Treaties, and all such remedies and procedures from time to time provided for by or under the Treaties, as in accordance with the Treaties are without further enactment to be given legal effect or used in the UK'. For the effects of this provision, see generally Collins (1990).

10 The first such decision, Case 26/62 *Van Gend en Loos* [1963] ECR 1, concerned Article 12 of the Treaty of Rome prohibiting the introduction of new customs duties between member states.

11 Most notably elucidated in Case 106/77 *Simmenthal* [1978] ECR 629.

12 Case 221/89 [1991] ECR I-745.

13 Case 152/84 *Marshall* v. *Southampton and South-West Hampshire AHA* [1986] IRLR 140; Case C-91/92 *Faccini Dori* v. *Recreb* [1995] 1 CMLR 665.

14 Under Article 189, a decision is binding only on the person to whom it is addressed. This will normally be the member state. Although the Court has held that a decision can have direct effect (Case 9/70 *Grade* [1970] ECR 825), the same restrictions apply as in the case of directives, so that a decision addressed to a member state could not have horizontal direct effect between private persons (Hartley, 1988: 212). A *recommendation* is a form of 'soft law' which is not directly binding on anybody, but which should be taken into account by courts when resolving issues of interpretation or ambiguities in relation to other legal instruments and provisions: Case C-322/88 *Grimaldi* v. *Fonds des Maladies Professionels* [1990] IRLR 400.

15 Case 152/84 *Marshall* v. *Southampton and South West Hampshire AHA* [1986] IRLR 140.

16 Case C-188/89 *Foster* v. *British Gas* [1990] IRLR 833; *R.* v. *British Coal Corporation, ex parte Vardy* [1993] IRLR 104.

17 *Griffin* v. *South-West Water Services Ltd.* [1995] IRLR 15.

18 See the discussion of the Advocate General and of the Court in Case C-262/88 *Barber* v. *Guardian Royal Exchange Assurance Group* [1990] IRLR 240.

19 Case 148/78 *Ratti* [1979] ECR 1629. Complex rules also govern the question of time limits in relation to the doctrine of direct effect. In principle, time cannot begin to run against

the applicant under the procedural laws of his or her member state until the point at which that member state takes steps to implement the directive: Case C-208/90 *Emmott* v. *Secretary of State for Social Security* [1991] ECR I-4269. However, this principle may be limited by the need to maintain the administrative effectiveness and financial equilibrium of, for example, social security and occupational welfare schemes: Case C-338/91 *Steenhorst-Neerings* [1994] IRLR 244; Barnard, 1995: 36.

20 Case 43/75 [1976] ECR 455.

21 See Nielson and Szyszczak (1993: Chapter 3).

22 [1990] IRLR 240, above.

23 The Court's ruling in Case C-109/91 *Ten Oever* exactly aligned its interpretation of Article 119 with the so-called *Barber* protocol attached by the member states to the Treaty of European Union in 1992. See generally Fitzpatrick (1994). The Court later ruled that employers could implement the principle of equality by, for example, raising the pensionable age of women employees to 65, as opposed to cutting men's pensionable age to 60: Case C-408/92 *Smith* v. *Advel Systems Ltd.* [1994] IRLR 602.

24 Case 152–84 *Marshall* v. *Southampton and South-West Hampshire AHA* [1986] IRLR 140. Another instance is the judgment of the House of Lords in *R.* v. *Secretary of State for Employment, ex parte Equal Opportunities Commission* [1994] IRLR 176, in which it was held that the 16–hour weekly qualifying threshold for employment protection rights under UK legislation infringed Directive 76/207 (see Deakin, 1994).

25 Case 126/86 *Giménez Zaera* v. *Instituto Nacional de la Seguridad Social* [1989] 1 CMLR 827.

26 *Pickstone* v. *Freemans plc* [1988] IRLR 357.

27 *Litster* v. *Forth Dry Dock & Engineering Co. Ltd.* [1989] IRLR 161.

28 Case C-106/89 *Marleasing SA* v. *La Commercial Internacional de Alimentacion SA* [1990] 1 ECR 4135.

29 Cases C-6 and C-9/90 *Francovich* v. *Italian Republic* [1992] IRLR 84. See Hervey and Rostant, 1996, for a discussion of the post-Francovich case law.

30 See, for example, the decision of the House of Lords not to refer the question posed in a case related to Sunday trading, *Kirklees MBC* v. *Wickes Building Supplies Ltd.* [1993] AC 227.

31 Case 43/75, [1976] ECR 455, 472.

32 The most important judgment is Case C-209/91, *Rask* v. *ISS Kantineservice* [1993] IRLR 133.

33 Cases C-382/92 and C-383/92 *Commission* v. *UK* [1994] IRLR 392, 412, at paras 15 and 16 respectively.

34 See the ECJ decisions in Case 170/84 *Bilka-Kaufhaus* v. *Weber von Hartz* [1986] IRLR 317; Case 171/88 *Rinner-Kuhn* v. *FWW Spezial-Gebaudereinigung* [1989] IRLR 493; Case C-33/89 *Kowalska* v. *Freie und Hansestadt Hamburg* [1990] ECR I-2591; Case C-184/89 *Nimz* v. *Freie und Hansestadt Hamburg* [1991] ECR I-297; see Nielson and Szyszczak (1993: 118–19).

35 Case 8/74 *Procureur du Roi* v. *Dassonville* [1974] ECR 837 at para. 5.

36 Case 155/80 [1981] ECR 1993.

37 Case 279/80 [1981] ECR 3305.

38 Case C-312/89 *Conforama* [1991] ECR I-997; Case C-332/89 *Marchandise* [1991] ECR I-1027; Case C-169/91 *Stoke-on-Trent City Council* v. *B. & Q. plc* [1993] 2 AC 730.

39 Joined Cases C-267/91 and C-268/91 *Keck* and *Mithouard* [1993] ECR I-6097; Joined Cases C-401/92 and C-402/92 *Criminal Proceedings against Tankstation t Heukske vof and j.b.E. Boermans* [1994] ECR I-2199.

40 Case C-113/89, *Rush Portuguesa Lda.* v. *Office Nationale d'Immigration* [1990] ECR 1417; Case C-43/93 *Van de Elst* v. *Office Nationale d'Immigration* [1994] ECR-I 3803.

41 Some areas of doubt remain with regard to the application of the Treaty's provisions concerning competition policy (Articles 85–86) and state aids (Articles 90–92), in particular following the decision of the Court in Case C-179/90 *Merci Convenzionali Porto di Genova SpA* v. *Siderurgica Gabrielli SpA* [1991] ECR I-5889 in which it struck down a labour

monopoly being operated in the Genoa docks (discussed by Wedderburn, 1995: 370 *et seq.*). However, it is not obvious that the principle enunciated in this case has any application to cases other than those of state-supported monopolies which can be shown to be inefficient or unduly restrictive (see Case C-41/90 *Höfner and Elser* v. *Macrotron* [1991] ECR I-1979; Davies, 1995).

42 Directive 75/129, Article 5; Directive 77/187, Article 7; Directive 90/987, Article 9.

43 Directive 92/56, Article 1(5), amending Directive 75/129, Article 5.

44 Directive 93/104, Article 1(5).

45 See Case 278/85 *Commission* v. *Denmark* [1987] ECR 4069; Nielson and Szyszczak, 1993: 255–56.

46 See his speech to the European Social Policy Forum, 28 March 1996: '*Je plaide pour une nouvelle approche de l'emploi et du social comme facteur productif, au coeur de notre project politique*'.

47 EC Treaty, Articles 104c and 109j(1), and Protocols 5 (Excessive Deficit Procedure) and 6 (Convergence Criteria).

48 See speech of Jacques Santer, Commission President, *European Parliament Verbatim Report of Proceedings*, 28.2.96: para. 3–012.

References

Addison, J. T. and Castro A. (1987). 'The Importance of Life-time Jobs: Differences between Union and Non-union Workers'. *Industrial and Labor Relations Review*, **40** (April): 393–405.

Addison, J. T. and Siebert, W. S. (1991). 'The Social Charter of the European Community: Evolution and Controversies'. *Industrial and Labor Relations Review*, **44** (July): 597–625.

Addison, J. T. and Siebert, W. S. (1992). 'The Social Charter: Whatever next?' *British Journal of Industrial Relations*, **30** (December): 495–513.

Aghion, P. and Hermalin, B. (1990). 'Legal Restrictions on Private Contract can Enhance Efficiency'. *Journal of Law, Economics and Organisation*, **6** (Fall): 381–409.

Barnard, C. (1992). 'A Social Policy for Europe: Politicians 1, Lawyers 0'. *International Journal of Comparative Labour Law and Industrial Relations*, **8**: 15–31.

Barnard, C. (1994). 'Sunday Trading: a Drama in Five Acts'. *Modern Law Review*, **57**: 449–60.

Barnard, C. and Deakin, S. (1996). 'Social policy in search of a role: integration, cohesion, citizenship'. In A. Craiger and D. Floudas (eds.), *1996 Onwards: Lowering the Barriers Further*. Chichester: Wiley.

Bercusson, B. (1990). 'The European Community's Charter of Fundamental Social Rights'. *Modern Law Review*, **53**: 624–42.

Bercusson, B. (1992) 'Maastricht: a fundamental change in European labour law'. *Industrial Relations Journal*, **23** (Autumn): 177–191.

Bercusson, B. (1994). 'The dynamic of European labour law after Maastricht'. *Industrial Law Journal*, **23**: 1–31.

Blanpain, R. and Engels, C. (1993). *European Labour Law*. Deventer: Kluwer.

Buchele, R. and Christiansen, J. (1995). 'Productivity, real wages, and worker rights: A gross-national comparison'. *Labour*, **8**: 405–22.

Büchtemann, C. (1990). 'More jobs through less employment protection? Evidence for West Germany'. *Labour*, **3**: 23–56.

Büchtemann, C. (1993). 'Introduction: employment security and labor markets'. In C. Büchtemann (ed.), *Employment Security and Labor Market Behavior. Inter-Disciplinary Approaches and International Evidence.* Ithaca NY: Cornell University Press.

Büchtemann, C. and Quack, S. (1989). '"Bridges" or "traps"? Non-standard employment in the Federal Republic of Germany'. In G. Rodgers and J. Rodgers (eds) *Precarious Jobs in Labour Market Regulation.* Geneva: International Institute for Labour Studies.

Bulow, J. and Summers, L. (1986). 'A theory of dual labor markets with application to industrial policy, discrimination and Keynesian unemployment'. *Journal of Labor Economics*, **4** (July): 376–414.

Card, D. and Freeman, R. (1994). 'Small differences that matter: Canada vs. the United States'. In R. Freeman (ed.) *Working under Different Rules*. New York: NBER/Russell Sage Foundation.

Collins, L. (1990). *European Community Law in the UK* (4th. ed.) London: Butterworths.

Commission (1989). *Social Action Programme*. COM (89) 568 final. Brussels: Commission of the European Communities.

Commission (1990). *Explanatory Memorandum on the Proposals for Directives Concerning Certain Employment Relationships*. COM (90) 228 SYN 280. Brussels: Commission of the European Communities.

Commission (1993). *Green Paper: European Social Policy Options for the Union*. COM (93) 551 final. Brussels: Commission of the European Communities.

Commission (1994). *White Paper: European Social Policy. A Way Forward for the Union*. COM (94) 333 final. Brussels: Commission of the European Communities.

Cosh, A., Hughes, A. and Rowthorn, R. (1993). 'The competitive role of UK manufacturing industry'. In K. Hughes (ed.) *The Future of UK Competitiveness and the Role of Industrial Policy*. London: PSI.

Craig, C., Rubery, J., Tarling, R. and Wilkinson, F. (1982). *Labour Market Structure, Industrial Organisation and Low Pay*. Cambridge: CUP.

Craig, C., Rubery, J., Tarling, R. and Wilkinson, F. (1985). 'Economic, social and political factors in the operation of the labour market'. In R. Roberts, K. Finegan, and D. Gaillie (eds.) *New Approaches to Economic Life*. Manchester: MUP.

Davies, P. (1992). 'The emergence of European labour law'. In W. McCarthy (ed.) *Legal Intervention in Industrial Relations. Gains and Losses*. Oxford: Blackwell.

Davies, P. (1995). 'Market integration and social policy in the Court of Justice'. *Industrial Law Journal*, **24**: 49–77.

Deakin, S. (1990). 'Equality under a market order: the Employment Act 1989'. *Industrial Law Journal*, **19**: 1–23.

Deakin, S. (1994). 'Part-time employment, qualifying thresholds and economic justification'. *Industrial Law Journal*, **23**: 151–55.

Deakin, S. and Morris, G. (1995). *Labour Law*. London: Butterworths.

Deakin, S. and Wilkinson, F. (1991). 'Labour law, social security and economic inequality'. *Cambridge Journal of Economics*, **15** (June): 125–48.

Deakin, S. and Wilkinson, F. (1994.) 'Rights vs. efficiency? The economic case for transnational labour standards'. *Industrial Law Journal*, **23**: 289–310.

Deakin, S. and Wilkinson, F. (1996). 'Contracts, cooperation and trust: the role of the institutional framework'. In D. Campbell and P. Vincent-Jones (eds.) *Contract and Economic Organisation: Socio-Legal Initiatives*. Aldershot: Dartmouth.

Easterbrook, F. and Fischel, D. (1991). *The Economic Structure of Corporate Law*. Cambridge, Mass.: Harvard University Press.

Emerson, M. (1988). 'Regulation or deregulation of the labour market: policy regimes for the recruitment and dismissal of employees in industrialised countries'. *European Economic Review*, **32** (April): 775–817.

Epstein, R. (1983). 'A common law for labor relations: a critique of the New Deal labor legislation'. *Yale Law Journal*, **92**: 1357–408.

Epstein, R. (1984). 'In defense of the contract at will'. *University of Chicago Law Review*, **51**: 947–82.

Evans, S., Goodman, J. and Hargreaves, L. (1985). *Unfair Dismissal Law and Employment Practice in the 1980s*. Research Paper No. 53. London: Department of Employment.

Fischel, D. (1984). 'Labor markets and labor law compared with capital markets and corporate law'. *University of Chicago Law Review*, **51**: 1061–77.

Fitzpatrick, B. (1992). 'Community social law after Maastricht'. *Industrial Law Journal*, **21**: 199–213.

Fitzpatrick, B. (1994). 'Equality in occupational pension schemes: still waiting for *Coloroll*'. *Industrial Law Journal*, **23**: 155–63.

Freeman, R. (1994). 'How labor fares in advanced economies'. In R. Freeman (ed.) *Working under Different Rules*. New York: NBER/Russell Sage Foundation.

Grahl, J. and Teague, P. (1992). 'Integration theory and European labour markets'. *British Journal of Industrial Relations*, **30** (December): 515–29.

Hartley, T. (1988). *The Foundations of European Community Law* (2nd. edn). Oxford: Clarendon Press.

Heldman, D., Bennett, J. and Johnson, M. (1981). *Deregulating Labor Relations*. Dallas: Fisher Institute.

Hepple, B. (1986). 'Restructuring employment rights'. *Industrial Law Journal*, **15**: 69–89.

Hepple, B. (1987). 'The crisis in EEC Labour Law'. *Industrial Law Journal*, **16**: 77–87.

Hepple, B. (1990a). Working Time. A New Legal Framework? Employment Paper No. 3. London: Institute for Public Policy Research.

Hepple, B. (1990b). 'The implementation of the Community Charter of Fundamental Social Rights'. *Modern Law Review*, **53**: 643–54.

Hepple, B. (1992). 'The fall and rise of unfair dismissal'. In W. McCarthy (ed.) *Legal Intervention in Industrial Relations. Gains and Losses.* Oxford: Blackwell.

Hepple, B. (1993). *European Social Dialogue – Alibi or Opportunity?* London: Institute of Employment Rights.

Hervey, T. and Rostant, P. (1996). 'After Francovich: State liability and British employment law'. *Industrial Law Journal*, **25**: 259–285.

Houseman, S. (1995). 'Job growth and the quality of jobs in the US economy'. *Labour*, **8**: S93–S124.

ILO (1956). 'Social aspects of European economic cooperation'. *International Labour Review*, **74** (July): 99–123.

Loveman, G. and Tilly, C. (1988). 'Good jobs or bad jobs? Evaluating the American job creation experience'. *International Labour Review*, **127**: 593–611.

Matthews, R. (1986). 'The economics of institutions and the sources of growth'. *Economic Journal*, **96** (December): 903–18.

Michie, J. and Wilkinson, F. (1994). 'The growth of unemployment in the 1980s'. In J. Michie and J. Grieve-Smith (eds.) *Unemployment in Europe*. London: Academic Press.

Mosley, H. (1990). 'The social dimension of European integration'. *International Labour Review*, **129**: 147–63.

Mückenberger, U., and Deakin, S. (1989). 'From deregulation to a European floor of rights: labour law, flexibilisation and the European single market'. *Zeitschrift für ausländisches und internationales Arbeits- und Sozialrecht*, **3**: 157–206.

Napier, B. (1993). *CCT, Market Testing and Employment Rights. The effects of TUPE and the Acquired Rights Directive.* London: Institute of Employment Rights.

Nielsen, R. and Szyszczak, E. (1993). *The Social Dimension of the European Community*, (2nd edn). Copenhagen: Handelshojskolens Forlag.

North, D. (1990). *Institutions, Institutional Change and Economic Performance*. Cambridge: CUP.

Posner, R. (1993). *Economic Analysis of Law* (4th edn). Boston: Little Brown.

Rodgers, G. and Rodgers J. (eds.) (1989). *Precarious Jobs in Labour Market Regulation. The growth of atypical employment in Western Europe*. Geneva: International Institute for Labour Studies.

Sengenberger, W. (1994a). 'Labour standards: an institutional framework for restructuring and development'. In W. Sengenberger and D. Campbell (eds.) *Creating Economic Opportunities: The Role of Labour Standards in Industrial Restructuring*. Geneva: International Institute for Labour Studies.

Sengenberger, W. (1994b). 'Protection – participation – promotion: the systemic nature and effects of labour standards'. In W. Sengenberger and D. Campbell (eds.) *Creating Economic Opportunities: The Role of Labour Standards in Industrial Restructuring*. Geneva: International Institute for Labour Studies.

Solow, R. (1990). *The Labour Market as an Institution.* Oxford: Blackwell.

Spaak, (1956). *Rapport des chefs de délégation aux ministres des affaires étrangères.* Brussels: Comité Intergouvernmental crée par la Conférence de Messine. Reprinted in PEP, *Planning,* **405**: (1956).

Stapleton, J. (1991). 'Three problems with the new product liability'. In P. Cane and J. Stapleton (eds.) *Essays for Patrick Atiyah.* Oxford: Clarendon Press.

Vogel Polsky, E. (1990). 'What future is there for a Social Europe following the Strasbourg summit?' *Industrial Law Journal,* **19**: 65–80.

Wedderburn, Lord (1990). *The Social Charter, European Company and Employment Rights. An outline agenda.* London: Institute of Employment Rights.

Wedderburn, Lord (1991). 'European Community law and workers' rights. Fact or fake in 1992?' *University of Dublin Law Journal,* **13**: 1–33.

Wedderburn, Lord (1992). 'Inderogability, collective agreements and Community law'. *Industrial Law Journal,* **21**: 245–64.

Wedderburn, Lord (1995). *Labour Law and Freedom: Further Essays in Labour Law.* London: Lawrence & Wishart.

Wedderburn, Lord and Sciarra, S. (1988). 'Collective bargaining as agreement and as law: neo-contractualist and neo-corporative tendencies of our age'. In A. Pizzorusso (ed.) *Law in the Making.* Berlin: Springer-Verlag.

Whiteford, E. (1993). 'Social policy after Maastricht'. *European Law Review,* 202–22.

Wikeley, N. (1989). 'Migrant workers and unemployment benefit in the European Community'. *Journal of Social Welfare Law,* 300–315.

Williamson, O., Wachter, M. and Harris, J. (1975). 'Understanding the employment relation: the economics of idiosyncratic exchange'. *Bell Journal of Economics and Management Science,* **6** (Spring): 250–278.

6

The 'Social Dimension' as a Basis for the Single Market

David Marsden

6.1. Introduction

In many west European countries, postwar prosperity has been built upon cooperative industrial relations. Important contributions they have made to productivity include information sharing and flexible working. The systems of cooperative relations have taken many years to build, and their survival will be critical to the future competitiveness of Europe's industries. However, one of the major challenges posed by the creation of the Single European Market (SEM), and more generally by internationalization, is that it may destabilize the patterns of worker–employer cooperation, and so undermine future economic performance. The challenge it poses is of two kinds: that of adapting predominantly national compromises to a world in which many of the key actors are increasingly international, and that of the transition itself to the new economic system. The social dimension of the European Union's Single European Market programme, and in particular, the 'social dialogue' involving European worker and employer organizations, have a critical part to play in sustaining such cooperative relations.

This chapter starts by arguing that cooperative relations between workers and their employers can make a key contribution to achieving high levels of productivity and quality. There is now a good deal of evidence, reviewed elsewhere, that workgroup and workplace employee participation boosts productivity (eg. Levine and Tyson, 1990; Appelbaum and Batt, 1994). The chapter seeks to show that the survival of cooperative work relations over time depends upon the support of a strong representative framework both at the enterprise and at the inter-employer levels. Such frameworks have played an important part over the last few decades, but are now threatened by the economic and social upheavals of which the SEM programme is a part. It then explores how European 'social dialogue' can help sustain these relations, and concludes with an argument about the kinds of action on which such dialogue should focus.

6.2. Cooperation and Productivity: 'High Trust' and 'Cheap Talk'

Cooperative industrial relations can contribute to good economic performance at both the macro, micro and intermediate levels. At the micro level, they can help reduce X-inefficiency, and contribute to flexible utilization of labour and effective information sharing, and so help a firm's productivity levels, and ability to respond to new technology and new markets. At the macro level, taking account of the macroeconomic consequences of pay settlements on employment and economic growth can boost the scope for investment. They can also be important at the intermediate level, above that of individual firms, in affecting the quality of cooperation among firms on such issues as training for transferable skills, and maintaining inter-firm labour markets.

In this chapter, we are defining 'cooperative relations' more in relation to the kind of behavioural outcomes that can be achieved than to what might be called 'atmosphere'. The argument will then focus on how the social charter might contribute to these outcomes. They will be distinguished from 'live and let live' relations in which groups refrain from overt conflict because of its potential costs but in which cooperative exchange is limited. The former might be styled as 'active' cooperation and the latter as 'passive' or 'defensive' cooperation.

Firm Level Cooperation

Cooperation in the workplace between workers and management, and among groups of workers can generate gains in productivity and quality, particularly when focused on sustaining flexible working patterns, and sharing information concerning production and the provision of services. Faced with variable demands upon the enterprise, and the difficulties of specifying *ex ante* exactly what labour employers will need, it is easy to see that lack of flexibility will generate higher levels of under-utilization and X-inefficiency. Similarly, a free flow of information about production and service problems between the points of provision and other parts of the organization enable more effective adaptation to changing conditions, better utilization of existing resources, and when such information includes feedback from customers, it also helps adjustment to market demand. This may seem trivial, yet cooperation involving such areas is often hard to achieve because of the importance of both work flexibility and information to power relationships within organizations.

Power relations are important between management and workers, between different groups of workers, and in a three-way relationship. Although all may have a general shared interest in the overall prosperity of the firm or organization for which they are working, there are also many areas, not just distributional ones, where interests diverge. Between workers and managers, interests may diverge as new investment programmes lead to redundancies, lower earnings, or fewer career opportunities. Between groups of workers, a wider diffusion of skills may diminish the status of a skilled élite, or new graduate entry streams may cut short upgrading opportunities for blue collar workers, and so on. In a three-way relationship, one group's cooperation with management may undermine the position of another group.

The problem of cooperation aimed at better productivity or quality is that often the first steps in this direction expose the parties concerned to possible exploitation by other groups in the same set of power relations. For example, between workers and management, sharing information which enables the job to be done better or more quickly may deprive workers of opportunities to enhance their own earnings, or to have more control over their work rhythm (Mottez, 1966). It may also reveal possibilities of reorganizing work to the disadvantage of the workers concerned, or even for scrapping certain jobs altogether. The information may also have enabled a particular work group to bargain more effectively with first-line management. Equally, allowing more flexible working methods could deprive the work groups concerned from negotiating a change in work practices in exchange for management agreeing to no redundancies in the event of work reorganization. In many instances, such small group power relations are the means by which workers oblige management to share the gains arising from greater productivity.

Similar problems can arise between work groups in their relations with management. If, for example, management wants semi-skilled workers to undertake some routine preventive maintenance, skilled workers will most likely have to share some of their own expertise with the semi-skilled. This could lead to reduced job openings for skilled workers in the future. Crozier's (1963) examples of the way skilled maintenance workers withheld such information from semi-skilled operatives in a very weakly unionized environment illustrates that such practices are not necessarily the result of union action. Sharing the information would have made management less dependent upon the maintenance workers, and so greatly reduced their power within the organization.

On its side too, management can boost its power *vis-à-vis* the work groups by withholding, or partially releasing, information about the state of the enterprise, and about its future plans.

In many respects, the problem of cooperative action in the workplace is analogous to that of the 'prisoner's dilemma' (see Chapter 3). All parties could gain from cooperation, but equally, if party A adopts a cooperative stance, and makes concessions by sharing information or by starting to work flexibly, B could use the resulting surrender of A's small group power in order to take a larger share of the resulting gains of cooperation. The fear, or expectation, that party B will exploit the resulting weakness of A and not reciprocate then causes A to be reluctant to cooperate in the first place. Party B reasons in the same way, and the result is that neither cooperate, and the potential gains of cooperation are lost.

It has been argued that this simple version of the prisoner's dilemma is inappropriate because it presumes a once-only exchange whereas in enterprise-based transactions all the parties are engaged in repeated exchanges. Hence, party A could hope that B would reciprocate cooperation because it knows that in the next round it could retaliate. However, it can be shown that such 'tit-for-tat' strategies do not guarantee mutual cooperation except in infinitely long games. In any finite number of exchanges, each party has an incentive to exploit in the final one, and as a result, the whole process of cooperation may unravel.[1] In practice, most exchanges are of indefinite number, irregularly spaced in time, and each occasion could be the last, so the difficulty of sustaining cooperation is considerable. Indeed, it can be shown that provided one party expects the other to behave non-cooperatively, cooperation is hard to achieve and to sustain over time unless there is some additional support, in the form of trust (a mutual expectation of cooperation), or some institutional or external normative support (Lorenz, 1988; Williams, 1988).[2]

Before developing the latter points, two main objections to the argument must be dealt with: that unilateral management control may avoid the necessity for cooperative relations if a suitable organization structure can be found; and that in practice, often what passes for cooperative industrial relations is really a form of 'live and let live' relationship, or else supported by a degree of rent-sharing.

It might be argued that unilateral management control combined with narrowly defined jobs, as under Taylorist patterns of work organization, would minimize the need for cooperative work relations. However, Crozier's (1963) analysis of the 'vicious circle of bureaucracy' highlights many of the shortcomings of such an approach. In an uncertain environment, management cannot predict enough likely eventualities to adapt narrowly defined jobs to changing demands. As a result, bottlenecks develop within the organization, and these create opportunities for small group bargaining power. Within the logic of the system, management may respond by issuing new or more rules to cater for the new circumstances, but these have the effect of increasing the organization's rigidity. A paradox of such organizational systems is that by placing workers in such a relation, management is in effect depriving itself of necessary information on how to react to emerging problems. Workers in narrow jobs have little incentive to pass on information, even if their job gives them a broad enough view to understand where coordination is breaking down, and groups whose power arises from bottlenecks have every incentive to withhold information from management.

A second paradox of such organizational forms which are intended to dispense with the need for much cooperation is that management's narrow instructions define what a worker's job is. If that job is to change, then new instructions are needed. Since it is difficult for management to obtain the information needed, it is hard to be sure that the new instructions meet the new needs.

In recent years, the limitations of Taylorist patterns of organization have been challenged both from the point of view of the difficulty of motivating workers under such conditions, and from the emergence of 'lean production' and similar practices which have demonstrated their ability to achieve better quality and productivity levels (Womack *et al.*, 1990). Lean production, by greatly reducing or eliminating buffer stocks, achieves high productivity by revealing organizational weaknesses in production (or in services) much more rapidly, and so forces management to remedy them. Because the workforce has much of the information needed, and because low levels of buffer stocks give discontented workers much greater powers of disruption, management chooses a more participative style of management.

Thus even if Taylorism provided a sound basis for unilateral management control in the past, which in fact it rarely did for the very reasons Crozier discussed, it is now even less likely to do so given the achievements of lean production.

The second objection is that what often passes for cooperative industrial relations is peaceful only because management have decided to abstain from any productivity enhancing measures which would upset the workforce. Management knows workers have a large power of disruption, and the worker representatives know that management will leave them in peace provided enough performance is available from the workforce. Peaceful labour relations coexist with low productivity growth because of a 'live and let live' relationship.[3] Particularly where management enjoys the protection of a localized monopoly, it can afford to continue such a relationship for a considerable time.

This kind of relationship highlights the need to distinguish between a cooperative atmosphere in workplace relations and cooperative exchange in such areas as work flexibility and information sharing. Under 'live and let live', management abstain from any action that would undermine the workforce's power, and the workforce abstains from excessive disruption. But the cooperation is passive and does not extend to the kind of exchange needed to enhance productivity and quality. Cooperative exchange may be facilitated by a cooperative atmosphere, but the atmosphere need not signal the presence of cooperative exchange.[4]

Two factors are critical to sustaining cooperative exchange: trust, and wider institutional support. In this context, trust can be defined as a mutual expectation of reciprocal cooperation. When there is such trust, neither side expects the other to take unfair advantage of its own cooperative stance. It is built on two elements: repeated demonstration of trustworthy action in the past, and some belief about the motivations of the other party (Williams, 1988). Mere repetition is not enough: as was suggested above, repeated cooperative action could be intended simply to lull the other party into a false sense of security. Beliefs about the other party's motivation may be built upon demonstration that trust is maintained even though it is costly, and on communication about each party's goals.

For example, in the realm of employment security, firms do not demonstrate their commitment just by refraining from laying people off as they might not need to, but by keeping workers on occasions when it would be much cheaper, or more convenient to lay them off. One proves one's honesty only when under temptation. Demonstrating how much a firm is prepared to spend in order to avoid eventualities such as layoffs does not necessarily prove its commitment, but it makes it more probable in the eyes of the other party.

Communication is also important because in most cases even though committed to cooperative relations, a firm may not always be able to sustain its promises. Knowing how to distinguish genuine _force majeure_ from action in bad faith cannot be done purely on the basis of past actions because each set of circumstances is unique. Some communication can be maintained within the enterprise, but institutional structures which span many firms also have an important role to play.

The role of Inter-firm Structures in Sustaining Cooperation within the Enterprise

The importance of inter-firm structures in supporting cooperative exchange within the enterprise emerges in three ways:

- the potential to call on higher levels of organization to escalate or to regulate conflict;
- the higher levels provide coordinating mechanisms and can avoid the need for 'tit-for-tat' strategies, by resolving disputes and guaranteeing reciprocity;
- and the structure of the inter-firm institutions can itself be designed so as to favour cooperative rather than combative relations.

Coalitions and escalation By forming into an alliance or a coalition with other similar groups, for example an industry union, the key actors at the enterprise level gain additional means of escalating conflict if their opposite number chooses to exploit. However, such alliances only have a power advantage over individual, enterprise level actors, and so quickly dissipate their strength if every local conflict involves escalation and direct involvement of the whole alliance. Hence, to be effective such a coalition has to develop policing powers over its own side. The main power is presumably the decision whether or not to apply collective support in local disputes.

If the other side also forms a coalition (for example, an employers' association), then the initial power advantage of the industry union is checked, and the costs of escalation are raised very considerably. Something akin to a balance of terror between two military superpowers might develop, but unlike the superpowers whose economic survival can continue on either side of an iron curtain, the production of goods and services depends upon joint activities. Thus, again, both coalitions have a strong incentive to police the activities of their members.

Coalitions and policing of grievances   To police such activities, procedures for sifting through local grievances and differences of opinion are needed. If the worker representatives in one firm or the local employer believe that cooperative action is being exploited by the other side, then they can raise it within their own coalition. Would such behaviour in other firms be regarded as exploitative or as betraying trust? Is one or other side unreasonably withholding important information in order to gain a bargaining advantage, or is one or other side deliberately blocking agreement on one item in order to gain an unfair advantage?

Such problems of interpretation may also arise at the level of the whole coalition, but at this level one is dealing with more encompassing organizations, able to take a wider view of the repercussions of their actions on the economy.

Although legal channels can also provide redress for non-fulfilment of contracts, they have a number of disadvantages in the present context. The quality of cooperation and the spirit of agreements can rarely be enforced by law because it relies upon what is explicit in the agreement, not the intention. Moreover, as mentioned earlier, the employment contract is rarely specified in great detail, so perfunctory performance is hard to penalize. As argued earlier, specification in more detail can itself lead to rigidity in work assignments.

Inter-firm organizations can provide an important means of coordination among local agreements. The central bargains consist only rarely of detailed list of rates of pay, but provide instead a framework for negotiations at lower levels. Sometimes these leave more freedom for local agreements, sometimes less. In practice, even in Sweden, which used to be famed for its 'centralized' bargaining system, it would have been more accurate to talk of 'articulated' bargaining in which the central agreement usually also defined a 'kitty' for negotiation at local level (Schager, 1993). Indeed, a single central bargain could not have worked because of the need to adapt to the circumstances of individual firms and local labour markets. The difficult task for the central bargainers is to arrive at a settlement which leaves sufficient flexibility at local level while remaining consistent with macro-economic constraints.[5]

By providing a framework for local bargains, the central bargain limits the extent to which any one individual group can press for a large increase, and it can also reassure groups wishing to opt for a moderate increase that they will not be exploited by others who choose not to. Employers will also know that if the union in their firm goes for a large increase it will not be supported by the industry or national union. They will also know what will probably be the going rate for other employers so that if they do concede a much higher increase they will probably be the only ones to do so. Thus the centrally agreed framework changes the incentives for both sides at the industry and especially at the enterprise levels. Of course, this does depend upon the industry agreement setting a range for subsequent settlements and not a floor, as sometimes occurs.

Structure of relations   Finally, the structure of relations between different levels can itself favour either cooperative or adversarial behaviour. The way joint regulation is divided between the industry, and enterprise levels, and the way the different areas of competence and the different powers are defined can affect the way they are used. In particular, a more stable framework is provided if bargaining power is confined within discrete levels for different issues, so that it cannot be cumulated across levels such that strength at one level can be used to supplement strength at another.

For example, the German system provides considerable powers to worker representatives at the industry level through collective bargaining, at the plant and enterprise level through codetermination on works councils, and on company supervisory boards. However, these different areas of joint regulation are articulated in such a way that powers exercised at one level cannot be translated to other levels. The way they are articulated favours cooperative exchange within each level and is geared against combative action (Marsden, 1978). For example, the powers of collective bargaining and the right to strike or lock-out which can be used in industry-regional negotiations cannot be harnessed to support enterprise level works council codetermination. Equally, the powers of codetermination cannot easily be harnessed to support bargaining at the industry level.[6]

A similar logic could be observed structuring relations between employers and worker representatives in large parts of British industry, dividing up areas of joint regulation in order to stabilize the distribution of power (Marsden, 1978). However, it was much less stable, and during the 1960s both industry agreements and industry-wide conciliation procedures declined in favour of a concentration of representative functions at the enterprise level, at least in the private sector. As a result, opportunistic behaviour by both workers and management became much easier, and low-trust relations more widespread.

This section has argued that high-trust cooperative relations between management and workers lead to lower levels of X-inefficiency and better sharing of information which contribute to better productivity growth. The argument is reinforced by the shift in production philosophy in many firms away from Taylorist work patterns which have been unable to provide the levels of productivity and quality provided by lean production. It has also been argued that cooperative relations between groups with divergent interests depend upon the expectation that the other party will reciprocate. This is hard to achieve at the level of individual workplaces. 'Tit-for-tat' strategies at the workplace level cannot be relied upon to avoid low-cooperation relationships. A powerful way in which expectations of reciprocity can be sustained is by means of inter-firm organizations which establish their own frameworks for policing non-cooperative behaviour. Because the inter-firm employer and worker organizations of employers and worker representatives are more encompassing, they are better able to assess the overall consequences of their actions and have more effect on overall outcomes.

Similar arguments apply in the case of pay bargaining, where systems with a lesser bias towards inflation enable governments to run their economies at higher rates of capacity utilization.

Thus, if these theoretical arguments are justified, then cooperative relations are an important ingredient of high productivity industrial relations systems, and the inter-firm organizations within these play a key role in sustaining cooperation. The case is most readily made for Germany, although there are dissenting voices,[7] and the opposite case is most easily made for the UK where adversarial industrial relations combined with managerial weaknesses and fractional bargaining over control issues have often combined to hamper productivity (eg. Batstone, [?] Willman, 1986). The French case is more awkward to interpret as adversarial union ideologies have coexisted with statutory guarantees for works councils (Lorenz, 1995). However, two important aspects of the French case have enabled French firms to achieve high productivity and more flexible work relations than in the UK. First, the unions have generally confined militant action to general demands, such as wages, and eschewed job and work organization related issues (Eyraud, 1983); and second, even the adversarial, communist-led, CGT has had a strong 'productivist' orientation favouring productivity, especially in the large firms of the state-run sector.[8]

Inter-firm Level Cooperation

There are a number of benefits that depend upon cooperation among firms, most notable among these are inter-firm labour markets for professional or occupational skills which, in many respects, are analogous to public goods.

In the case of transferable skills, it can be shown that the free market solution derived by Becker (1975) is inherently unstable, and that markets for such skills depend upon an institutional underpinning (Marsden, 1986: Chapter 8). If employers bear a significant part of the net cost of training for transferable skills, for which there are a number of theoretical reasons and a good deal of empirical evidence, then there is an incentive for some firms to cut training, and to seek to poach their skilled labour from their competitors. Since the former have not incurred training costs, they can also afford to offer higher benefits to the skilled workers. In such a market, the more severe the shortage of skilled workers, the less the incentives for individual firms to train as the probability of losing their investment to their competitors increases.[9] If they nevertheless need a certain number of skilled workers, they have every reason to seek ways of tying them to their own organization, for example, by developing internal promotion runs, and by spreading training for transferable skills over a longer period of time, and over a number of jobs. In effect, they begin to internalize what was previously an occupational labour market.

In doing so, firms stand to lose a number of important productivity enhancing benefits. If workers have transferable skills, then they are less likely to oppose layoffs, and they are more likely to cooperate in firms' restructuring. They have less human capital investment at stake in their current firm than do workers with non-transferable internal labour market skills. Occupational markets also mean that should firms need to expand output at short notice, they can expect to recruit a number of already experienced skilled workers from outside without having to incur the expense and time for internal training. Without this flexibility, firms are obliged to keep a larger number of workers available for precautionary reasons, to ensure they can meet a surge in product demand. Finally, well stocked occupational markets ease the entry of small firms into a particular market so there is a good level of product market competition.

Such benefits depend upon a large number of employers being committed to training to common standards, and to organizing work in such a way that they can use the skills concerned effectively. The collective benefit is clear, but the structure of incentives for individual firms seems to run against it. The main problem is to curb both the free-riding tendencies, and the fear that other firms will seek to free-ride.

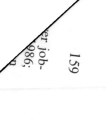

ed by peer group pressures. These can help to reassure firms
provide suitable levels of training, and also to put moral pres-
do not. One successful example is provided by the German
m, in which the chambers of industry and commerce, of which
members, provide a powerful channel for peer group pressures.
d by the chambers publishing pass rates of apprenticeships by
This exposes poor training records, and also shows potential
apprentices w.... are the best firms to join.[10]

Such inter-firm relations may include worker representatives. Marsden and Ryan
(1990) argue that a powerful aid to training for transferable skills, such as apprentices, is an adequate level of cost sharing between employers and trainees. As in the
Becker model, this involves commonly low trainee allowances during the training
period, although in practice, these have not generally been low enough to cover all
of the costs in those countries with apprenticeship schemes. Skilled adults are often
leery of low rates of pay for trainees fearing that the latter will be used by employers not for training purposes, but as cheap substitute labour. Indeed, historically, the
way apprentices repaid their employer was by working as fully skilled but not yet
fully qualified workers: hence the 7-year apprenticeships (Elbaum, 1990).

Again, the free-market solution may be difficult to apply as acceptance of low
trainee rates implies a risk for skilled adults.[11] If their fears cannot be assuaged, then
they have little incentive to share their knowledge with the trainees. Again, the
German experience is instructive, as the strong interest taken by unions, and particularly the works councils, in monitoring training creates an environment in which
skilled workers can accept low trainee pay rates, and are willing to share their knowledge.

Thus training for transferable skills involves a complex set of exchanges involving many different firms, skilled workers, and trainees. The presence of strong
collective organizations provides a framework in which each of the parties can
expose themselves in a relationship in which exploitation by one of the other parties
would be possible. Firms that train can be exploited by firms which do not. Skilled
workers may be exploited by passing on their skills to those who undercut them.
Apprentices may be exploited as cheap labour and denied the full amount of training. Other firms might provide only perfunctory training in order to get the low-
wage apprentices, and so on.

In such a complex pattern of exchanges, it is easy to see that a breakdown at one
point could very easily cause a breakdown at others, and lead to a cumulative departure from the free market equilibrium. Trust in the other parties is critical, hence the
importance of the institutions supporting such trust.

Macro-level Cooperation

Pay bargaining systems which have an inherent inflationary bias are likely to force
governments to take corrective action, and run their economies at a lower level of
output, thus depressing growth and employment. More generally, persistent and
variable inflation may encourage a short-term orientation to investment and other
economic decisions as the long-term returns are more uncertain than under stable
prices (Leigh-Pemberton, 1992).

At the macro-level, there are a number of arguments to explain why both centralized bargaining and decentralized bargaining systems can achieve a more favourable

trade-off between inflation and unemployment than partially centralized ones. The unfavourable position of intermediate type bargaining systems is the result of two countervailing tendencies: as bargaining units increase in size, their power grows; and the more they 'encompass' the great majority of interested parties, the greater the incentives to wage moderation.

In a highly decentralized system of plant bargaining, competitive pressures keep wages at the equilibrium level, and militate against 'whip-sawing', or 'leap-frogging' practices by which one group seeks to catch up with, or get ahead of, other bargaining groups. As bargaining units aggregate from plant to industry level, their bargaining power (measured by the elasticity of labour demand) increases (Calmfors and Driffill, 1988), and with this their ability to engage in competitive wage bargaining with other groups. There is also little incentive for groups to moderate their pay claims because they know that if they act alone, they will only gain a small proportion of the benefit of their sacrifice: if a typical group represents 1% of the workforce and, by taking a zero increase, causes the average rise in pay to be 1% lower than otherwise, its members will suffer a loss in real pay (Olson's 'proportionality principle': Olson (1971, 1982)). Indeed, each such group has an incentive to be the last to settle in a given negotiating round since it would then know what the others had achieved, and how big an increase in money rates would be needed to get a real pay increase for its members.

However, in a completely centralized system which encompasses all the workers in a particular economy, the bargainers know that the rate they agree upon with employers will determine the effective rate of increase for all workers. Thus encompassing groups, even though they may be as selfish as the smaller groups, are able to take account of the wider effects of their decisions, indeed, they cannot escape them.

The problem lies in the middle where bargainers have sufficient bargaining power to go above the competitive equilibrium wage, and also to engage in whip-sawing, but lack the moderating influence associated with encompassing groups. Thus, Paloheimo (1990) seeks to show that the relatively favourable inflation–unemployment performance of the USA, and of the Scandinavian countries and Austria, can be explained by the respective decentralization and centralization of their bargaining systems. The problems of France, Italy and the UK arise from the intermediate degrees of centralization of their systems. Germany, according to Soskice (1990), owes its good performance to the central control exercised by the industrial unions over plant and company level bargainers.

For the moment, three conclusions should be drawn: that encompassing bargaining units have a greater capacity for wage moderation than partially decentralized ones; that there are powerful incentives, but no logical necessity, for encompassing unions to behave in this way; and that there are good theoretical reasons, and some evidence, that the cooperative patterns associated with encompassing bargaining can help economic performance.

The one major drawback of this kind of organization is that there is an inherent bias towards reducing labour market inequalities. There is general evidence that collective bargaining reduces wage dispersion – see Blanchflower and Freeman, 1992 (USA, Australia and some European countries), Hibbs, 1990 (Sweden) and Metcalf, 1990 (UK) – which is often presumed to be the result of establishing a single rate for a particular kind of job. Additionally, however, encompassing organizations have the problem of how to maintain a broad coalition of different groups of workers. In particular, groups with greater bargaining power forego some of their potential gains of going it alone by throwing in their lot with weaker groups. Since self-restraint would

1st their immediate self interest, they presumably need some other
; the organizational importance of moral and ideological argu-
issing unions for wage solidarity and greater equality.[12] It was to
...nts of this kind that the Swedish employers eventually decided to
..w from central bargaining, and its associated institutions.

Time and Trust

Trust relations can only develop over time, and with considerable investment by the
parties involved. Institutional structures may provide guarantees, but these are
probably not sufficient on their own because although they can underwrite major
confrontations, they cannot monitor every detail of cooperation or deviation from
it. The most convincing token of cooperative behaviour is neither promises (which
may be broken), nor the mere repetition of cooperative behaviour, but acts of cooperation when it would clearly be advantageous to 'exploit'. For example, the most
effective way for a firm to demonstrate its commitment to long-term employment
for its staff is to keep people on when it would be cheaper in the short-run to lay
them off. In this respect, one might understand the extreme reluctance of large
Japanese firms to lay people off in the current very deep recession, and the very
small numbers actually laid off when compared with the behaviour of western firms.

The more frequently occasions emerge in which the parties can demonstrate their
commitment to cooperation, the easier it may be to build up the practice of cooperation. However, in many cases, such occasions may be neither frequent nor pre-
dictable. Major recessions which afford the chance to demonstrate commitment to
long-term employment, or major restructuring which provide the chance to demonstrate commitment to consultation and employee involvement also occur infre-
quently. Given the difficulty of establishing cooperation within the prisoner's
dilemma model, it is likely that a single departure from cooperation could undermine trust for a considerable time. It takes a long time to earn a reputation for
honesty, but a single lie can quickly destroy it. It takes even longer to rebuild a reputation for honesty.

To illustrate the point, the current state of cooperative exchange in the German
industrial relations system emerged only slowly during the postwar period. In their
study of West German union bargaining policy, Bergmann *et al.* (1975) identified
two rival strategies, the 'activist' or 'combative', and the 'cooperative' strategies. It
was only from the latter 1950s that one could really say that the 'cooperative' wing
had gained the upper hand over the 'activist' wing in the major unions, and notably
in IG Metall, and it was not until then that the major unions abandoned national-
ization and a radical programme of social change (Markovits, 1986). There was also
plenty of evidence in the early years that many individual workers were sceptical of
the value of workplace codetermination, one famous study finding that many
workers referred to their elected representatives as '*die da oben*' ('them up there')
(Popitz *et al.*, 1957).

An important factor behind the change was the widespread perception among
German workers and union officials that the structure of codetermination was well
geared to rewarding cooperative exchange, and was indeed providing substantial
benefits (Markovits, 1986). In more recent years, the willingness of German employers to discuss investment and location policies and their employment consequences
with their works councils stands in marked contrast to the practices of employers in

many other industrial countries (Streeck, 1984). In addition, the division between the unions and works councils, which the employers have fought hard, and consistently, to maintain, has been a significant obstacle to combative policies.[13]

Thus, time is not only important at the micro level for the development of mutual confidence and cooperation, but the German case illustrates the time scale needed in order to build up cooperative relations at the higher, and more institutionalized levels.

However, one of the major challenges posed by the creation of the SEM is that it may destabilize the patterns of worker–employer cooperation, and so undermine future economic performance.

6.3.   The Nature of the Threat posed by the Transition to Economic and Monetary Union

The establishment of the Single European Market involves a number of important economic and social adjustments which could potentially undermine the basis of cooperation between employers and workers.

Increased Competition and Large-scale Industrial Adjustment

The key to the growth forecast as a result of the Single Market is increased competition and a large amount of industrial restructuring. The Single Market is one element in the general increase in competition world-wide although of special relevance to firms in European Union countries. With it comes added pressure on costs and quality, and the ability of firms to innovate in their products and production processes. In their study of the world automobile industry, Womack *et al.* (1990) highlighted the need of most European firms to catch up with the best practice lean production methods perfected in Japan and now becoming well established among producers in the USA. In other industries too, European managers are under intense pressure to improve performance, and hence, to restructure working practices. To cope with these pressures, a number of European firms have now fixed themselves targets for annual improvements in productivity, for example Peugeot and BMW.[14]

On industrial restructuring, one of the main incentives for the lower wage regions to accept the Maastricht treaty is that they should be able to attract additional investment from the higher wage regions. Indirectly, the higher wage regions benefit by a stronger and larger domestic market, and are able to specialize more in those activities in which they have a comparative advantage. Hence, industrial restructuring is at the core of the Single Market process, and according to Vaughan-Whitehead (1992), a large number of industrial sectors should be able to take advantage of this. A similar scale of changes is to be expected in the services, and notably financial services as the removal of barriers to trade takes effect.

Internationalization of Firms

The increasing integration of firms across national borders challenges the predominantly national frameworks for cooperation that have been established during the postwar era. During the late 1980s there was a considerable acceleration of mergers and acquisitions among larger firms in the European Union, especially in the industrial sector (Commission, 1990: Chapter 3). This has three effects. National employer organizations become less encompassing, and from labour's point of view, it becomes less clear how far the employer's prosperity is tied to that of the country in which the union is based. Secondly, the increased importance of the international dimension develops an area for manoeuvre which is not open nearly to the same extent for unions. Thirdly, the location of decision-making may move out of the reach of national employee representatives.

These factors may undermine cooperative relations. First, in the past, both employers and unions could see that each had a shared interest in the overall prosperity of the country in which they were based. Thus the constituency that each group's organizations encompassed related to same economic and geographical space. This is now changing with the internationalization of companies and their management.[15] Secondly, expectations of the other party's actions are partly tied to one's judgements of the potential courses of action available. The international dimension opens up a new range of options as concerns the geographical location of the different activities undertaken by the firm, and the choice of which ones should remain within the firm's core business, and which might become peripheral.

The third problem which may undermine expectations of cooperation is the potential removal of decision centres to other national locations. Management may be making their personnel decisions on the basis of the whole organization's needs across its different geographical locations, but employee representatives will see only what relates to their own national part of the organization.

Like the other changes, it does not necessarily imply that management will seek to reduce cooperation, but the incentives within the relationship have changed. Earlier it was argued that inter-firm structures played an important part in underwriting workplace cooperation because of the potential sanctions made available should one side feel that the other had betrayed trust. If the employers begin to escape these, the equilibrium in the relationship shifts. If the employee representatives feel they can no longer enforce reciprocity if they cooperate with management, then there is a danger that cooperation will be eroded.

Monetary Strains of Adjustment

Key aspects of the monetary strains of adjustment concern the different inflationary pressures among member countries, and the differences in the weight of social charges on employers between countries.

Inflation An integral part of the SEM programme is monetary convergence and eventually union, with the consequence that divergencies in wage inflation pressures between countries will be increasingly severely punished by unemployment. During the 1980s there was considerable divergence in national inflation rates, which was absorbed partly by productivity change, but mainly by currency movements. With reduction of scope for currency realignments, and limited scope for differential changes in productivity, much will depend on each country's success in controlling inflation. Here a number of difficult problems emerge. First, inflationary expectations and behaviour differ considerably among countries, in part as a result of past experience of inflation, and in part as a result of institutional weaknesses in labour

markets. Secondly, the effect of integration on different indu
some wage structures and widen others. Thirdly, labour mar
generate new problems of pay comparability, and finally, the
expenditure will fall on public sector pay systems.

Inflationary expectations have been shaped by widely diff
during the 1970s and 1980s. During the 1980s, hourly labour co
a third in the Netherlands and Germany, more than three quarters in France and
the UK, more than doubled in Ireland, Italy, and Spain, and more than tripled in
Greece and Portugal. Among the behavioural changes that come with the experience of high inflation are that employers expect other employers to concede pay rises
in line with inflation, and expect to be able to pass on increases, and so have less
incentive to resist claims at that level. On the employees' side, people become accus-
tomed to annual pay increases irrespective of changes in productivity or performance. Indeed, the size of pay increases for inflation usually swamps any increase
for merit or promotion, or in exchange for productivity enhancing concessions, and
so reduces any incentive effect they have. Ending expectations of annual pay
increases to compensate for inflation takes time. In France, although the government announced the end of its customary indexation of public service salaries in
1982, it took the best part of the decade to change expectations (Guilhamon, 1988).
In Britain, despite the slowing of inflation over the 1980s, many firms still report
pressure from employees for increases to compensate for inflation, causing the
President of the Confederation of British Industry to warn employers strongly
against the dangers of renewed inflation in June 1994.[16]

Such pressures are likely to test weakness in bargaining systems, and place special
strain on areas where bottlenecks in labour supply provide special bargaining
advantages.

The strain of economic adjustment on wage structures may also prove explosive
(Marsden, 1992). This is because one can expect pressures for pay increases to build
up in those industries and in those regions benefiting most from restructuring. These
are likely to be the low-wage sectors in low-wage regions, and the high-wage sectors
in high-wage regions. In the low-wage regions, one can expect the high-wage sectors,
which are mostly better unionized, to seek to resist the compression of wage differentials, and so to make it very difficult for these countries to keep average pay and
average productivity in step. The problem may be less severe in high-wage countries
because their low-wage industries, which are mostly the same as those in the low-
wage countries, are generally less unionized, and so less able to defend their relative
pay levels. However, taking the European Union as a whole, the low-wage countries
have generally been those with the most severe inflation problems.

The public sector also poses severe problems because of the very large numbers
still employed there (40 million across the EU), the weakness of competitive pressures, and the general strength of employee organization. The financial pressures on
public budgets place public sector pay in the front line of governments' adjustment
policies. The strains have become visible in the unrest in the French public service
in November-December 1995, and in much harder public sector bargaining rounds
in Germany in 1994 and again in 1996.

Finally, integration of labour markets across the Union may create new contours
of pay comparability. Establishing mutual recognition of vocational qualifications
provides one basis because it is easier for workers to claim that they are doing substantially the same work, and in the many border areas between countries, it may
increase the opportunities for mobility. A more potent problem may arise with the

ration of firms across national borders. As firms seek to deploy their staff more
xibly within the firm but across national borders, inevitably comparisons of pay
and benefits are made. A recent example of such pressures occurred with the strike
by British scientists working alongside their continental colleagues but at somewhat
lower levels of pay and benefits.[17] Projects such as the Channel Tunnel pose similar
problems as British and French security and maintenance teams have to be able to
work according to the same procedures, and to collaborate closely (Pinder, 1990).

All of these influences place great pressures on pay determination systems, and
thus on the quality of relationships between employee representatives and employers. Since the parties to pay bargaining are also those which underwrite workplace
cooperation, it is clearly important that the strains on pay do not undermine firms'
scope to sustain trust and productivity. Trust relations take a long time to build, but
may be swiftly destroyed.

Labour costs and social charges Because the arrangements in each country for
financing economic risk sharing through unemployment and sickness benefits are
so different, there are differential pressures to reduce their level and extent of coverage. In some countries, social insurance systems are funded largely through
employer contributions, while in others they are funded out of direct taxation on
individuals. Employers' social contributions as a percentage of total hourly labour
costs range from around 30% in Belgium, France and Italy, to just over 10% in the
UK and 3% in Denmark (1988 Labour Cost Survey). This is perceived[18] by many
employers as a disadvantage in competing within the SEM, and has created forces
for a reduction in social charges to give a more even playing field.[19] The problem is
that with financial stringency and the albeit postponed target of monetary integration, governments cannot transfer the bill to the public purse, nor can they easily do
it by raising other taxes. There is therefore a very strong pressure to cut spending on
social insurance, and with that, to reduce the extent of sharing economic risks.

Since sharing economic risks has been part of the postwar compromise underlying European industrial relations systems, and a factor in making workplace flexibility more acceptable to individual workers, eroding such protection threatens the
whole fabric.

All of these influences on industrial relations systems arising from the adjustment
to the Single Market are both straining existing relationships, and creating forces
that encourage firms to take unilateral action in order to gain time.

6.4. Current Strains within European Industrial Relations Systems

Since the late 1980s a number of tensions have developed within national industrial
relations systems in response to wider competitive pressures, but which could undermine cooperative industrial relations. These can be illustrated at the firm, inter-firm,
and macro levels.

At the firm level, and in countries where worker and union representation does
not have legal support, de-recognition has occurred in a number of firms. Perhaps
more importantly, employers in new firms and new plants have been increasingly
unwilling to recognize unions, particularly in Britain. In France, the acrimonious
debate of early 1992 between the socialist Minister of Labour, Martine Aubry, and
the CEO of Peugeot, Jacques Calvet, highlighted the way in which the firm, despite

being profitable, was using 'social plans' agreed between the works council and management for a new purpose: as a means of pursuing programmed job reductions in order to keep productivity rising. Social plans had originally been introduced by the French parliament as a means of enabling firms to cope with major crises of restructuring. The Minister and the unions objected to Peugeot's use of social plans and shifting the cost of Peugeot's restructuring to the national unemployment and early retirement funds.[20] In Germany, IBM's impatience with the metal industry unions and employer organizations, as it struggled with its commercial crisis, precipitated its withdrawal from the industry's negotiating machinery and agreements in July 1992.[21]

The issue of 'social dumping' in the employment decisions of individual firms was highlighted by Hoover's decision, announced in January 1993, to close its French plant near Dijon and to transfer much of the work to its Cumbernauld plant in Scotland. Hoover had negotiated a favourable deal with the local engineering unions in Scotland involving a pay freeze, flexible working practices, fixed term contracts for new employees which appeared to undercut the terms of French employees, but which neither the British unions nor management were willing to make public (*EIRR*, 1993). The agreement seemed to open the way for management to play off unions in one country against those in another and so gain competitive concessions. Subsequently, details of similar moves at a number of other firms, such as Grundig, were reported.[22]

Finally, the public sector employers seem to have shifted towards a more unilateral style of management after having sought to encourage representative activities in earlier decades. In France, despite legislating to promote public service collective bargaining in 1982, the government's use of public sector pay restraint as the key instrument in incomes policy effectively undermined negotiations on several occasions. In Britain, tight pay restraint in recent years has restricted the scope for negotiation, and in Germany too, the strong line holding down public sector pay increases has considerably hardened the atmosphere in industrial relations.

At the industry level, the 1992 German pay round, under strain from the costs of reunification, reached new levels of conflict as the parties put in unusually divergent demands, prompting the former Chancellor, Helmut Schmidt, to warn of the dangers of 'class struggle' replacing 'solidarity'.[23] Facing strong adjustment pressures medium-sized and smaller firms in Germany have threatened the survival of the industry employer organizations and of industry bargaining over both working time and the rate of pay equalization between eastern Länder and the rest of Germany.[24] In the metalworking industry, bargaining was saved *in extremis* in May 1993 by an agreement that individual firms should be able to opt out of the relevant industry agreement subject to approval by the union and employers' organization (Bispinck *et al.*, 1993). The bitterness surrounding the collapse, in early 1996, of the proposed 'Alliance for Jobs', and the employer proposals to dilute industry agreements, by allowing membership without automatic participation in industry agreements, further illustrate declining employer confidence in the industry bargaining system.

In other countries too, such arrangements have come under pressure. In Sweden, the scope of industry agreements remains in a state of flux. In Italy, the new bargaining system set up by the agreement of July 1993 is still in the process of establishment. In several other countries, pressures of change have encouraged individual employers to seek their own arrangements and to detach conditions in their own firms increasingly from industry agreements.

At the macro level, in a number of countries, established patterns of joint discussions on macroeconomic questions as a framework for cooperation at lower levels have either been abandoned, or come under great strain. The most notable case has been the end of articulated bargaining in Sweden, and the winding up by the central employers' confederation of many of its structures associated with central bargaining. The government has also followed this philosophy with acceptance of the main recommendations of the Lindbeck Report (Lindbeck *et al.*, 1993). In Germany, unusually, the unions were not consulted by the Chancellor about arrangements for reunification, and in both public and private sector industry pay negotiations the government has taken a strong line. Similar precipitate action by the government can be seen in the German government's proposal that works councils in the eastern Länder should be allowed to agree rates of pay below those set in industry agreements, or the German government's proposal that sickness benefit should not be paid for the first three days. Both were widely seen as a potential threat to independent collective bargaining (*die Zeit*, 1992a; *Handelsblatt*, 1992a).

In the Netherlands, reduction of the powers of the long established tripartite Social and Economic Council has been increasingly discussed (notably, whether the government should be obliged to seek its opinion), and in Britain, the last symbol of tripartism, the National Economic Development Council, was abolished in 1992, and the Wages Councils which set sectoral minimum wages were abolished in 1993. In Italy, the abolition of indexation was pressed on the unions in conditions which were felt so humiliating that the then leader of the CGIL, Bruno Trentin, resigned once the agreement was signed in July 1992.[25]

Thus, at all three levels, firm, industry, and economy-wide, collective bargaining arrangements are under considerable strain. Clearly, not all of the strains are directly attributable to the adjustments made necessary by the Single Market programme, although many are related to similar processes of adjustment to new markets and to more international competition. Indeed, the pressures from the SEM programme are a microcosm of these more general pressures. Nevertheless, they all challenge the mechanisms of cooperation between employers and employees, and among their organizations.

6.5.   The Role of the Social Dimension

The 'social dimension' can make a central contribution to sustaining cooperative relations by providing a means for discussing the problems of adjustment; providing a forum for adapting to common European-wide problems, and supporting the institutions which sustain trust relations.

It was argued earlier that the parties' beliefs about each other's motivations are an important aspect of cooperative relations and knowing how the other side thinks is an important clue to its motivation. One of the dangers is that of a regression towards unilateral decision-making on employment issues, and away from joint regulation. The illustrations from recent experiences in a number of countries suggest that such dangers are real. It was also argued that even when the parties were committed to a certain range of policies within a trust relationship, *force majeure* was often recognized as a legitimate reason for exceptions. Yet the identification of justified '*force majeure*' circumstances in a new environment is problematic.

The European 'social dialogue' provides a means by which European unions, employers and firms may jointly analyse some of the problems arising out of European integration, and in doing so, gain a clearer perception of the nature of the pressures on each side, and also on their many different constituent members. Understanding the implications of contribution versus tax-based social insurance systems for labour costs and for the level and breadth of coverage is a critical first step to exploring ways of resolving problems of differential competitiveness and for employment. Attempting to work out a joint opinion on an equitable wage, which did not materialize, enabled the parties to clarify their mutual positions to each other. Understanding the nature of representative systems and patterns of cooperation in different countries is an important first step towards appreciating the nature of the constraints on the parties within each country. Understanding the nature of flexibility agreements and concession bargaining in one country may enable social partners in another better to judge whether a particular case represents the first step on the path to competitive reduction of labour standards ('social dumping'), or whether it is equivalent to adjustment policies adopted in other countries.

In all of these cases, intensive discussion of the issues not only provides each side with greater technical information on practices, and organization, which might theoretically be provided by an expert study, but also on political constraints and the different priorities of the parties. For example, the 1994 discussions among the social partners of the European Works Council proposals forced employer and union organizations in the different countries to reveal their objectives and priorities to the other side. It may be relatively easy for the German employers to reassure their unions that they continue to support the works council system, but they can prove this more strongly when they argue the case with employers from other countries which are more sceptical. The latter act incurs a political cost whereas the former might be 'cheap talk'. If the European employers eventually proved unable to agree to such a scheme, it is important for the unions to know whether this is because of general opposition from all countries, or because of opposition from employers in one country.

The other type of issue concerns identification of the nature of the new environment, and how this affects existing systems of employee management and industrial relations. This again arises out of the need to be able to identify whether new patterns of behaviour adapted to the new environment signal new intentions, or whether the same commitment to cooperative relations persists. Adjusting to the new more integrated economic area is affecting the constraints on firms and on the way they organize their businesses. Progress, albeit slow, towards monetary union involves movement towards a new regime in which employers' and unions' failure to master inflationary consequences of their actions will be more severely punished by loss of business and jobs than in the past. Attempts to develop more encompassing organizations on both sides could be interpreted in two ways: to gain greater control over the members of employer and labour coalitions in order to support cooperative policies; or to gain greater bargaining power over the other side. Although the motivation might be quite different in either case, the organizational consolidation itself might look remarkably similar. As Zoll (1976) argued in the case of German unions, the same organizational strength could serve either as a force for order ('*Ordnungsfaktor*') or as one of countervailing power ('*Gegenmacht*'). Regular contact can help to reveal the underlying motivations and objectives.

The third area is to prevent national level institutions which underwrite

,rom being undermined by the increasing internationalization of man-
the sense of both the increasingly international level of management
,aking, and of the framework within which the workforce is managed.

,s restructure in order to position themselves on a European rather than a
natio... market, management's decision centres are likely to move. As a result
nationally focused systems of employee relations, be they within the enterprise or at
sectoral level, find that they no longer face a management team that has the same
power of decision, or has to make decisions within new parameters. It can then
become very difficult for employee representatives to know whose intentions and
whose motivations they are dealing with, and what are the causes of the choices
management are making.

This uncertainty is increased by the other implication of restructuring, namely
that management is becoming responsible for units of a larger and more complex
scope than previously. If one considers the emotive issue of 'social dumping', it is
clearly possible that firms could seek to set workers in different plants in competition with each other by trying to get very favourable terms in areas of, say, high
unemployment. Such were the allegations in the Hoover affair, and the fears of such
action were no doubt increased by the reluctance of both the unions and management in Scotland to make public the terms of their agreement.[26] This might be contrasted with the extensive consultation with works councils and unions in some of
the German automobile firms over the setting up of new plants in the United States,
as a result of which the employee representatives accepted the need for such investment patterns (Streeck, 1984).

6.6.   Important Issues for the Social Dimension

In considering some of the most important elements for the social dimension, it has
been argued that 'process' has a large role to play because of the need to understand
the motivations of each party. However, 'substance' is also important because
without it, process may degenerate into 'cheap talk', even if in nine languages.

For this reason, the social dialogue is one of the most important elements in the
Single Market's social dimension, at least as concerns the maintenance of high productivity cooperative exchange. Although discussions in European Works Councils
or between the social partners in Brussels are far removed from workplace cooperation, and therefore unlikely to have a direct effect upon productivity, it is through
their indirect effects that they are critical. It was argued that inter-firm networks and
organizations played a critical part in helping to stabilize cooperative workplace
relations. The contribution of the social dialogue as a process lies in the support it
can give to these inter-firm relations, and in preventing them from being undermined by the transition from a predominantly national to a more international
economy.

The social dialogue can help sustain the institutional structures between firms,
just as European Works Councils may support cooperative relations which have
developed between national enterprise managements and their enterprise-based
employee representatives.

On the substantive side the social dialogue can contribute by tackling some of the
issues raised by integration which are most likely to unsettle existing patterns of
cooperation. These also serve as indicators of management's commitment to them

because they do involve at least a short-run cost. Two very imp
out: the maintenance of acquired rights, bargaining and codeter
and adult training.

The first of these is needed in order to reassure workers durin
of their enterprises, and is currently one of the most contentiou
lations set up in the mid-1970s provided for consultation be   ...ployers
and employee representatives, and the transfer of acquired rights (Blanpain,
1991).[27] At the time, the rate of restructuring and that of mergers an acquisitions
was somewhat lower than now, and often restructuring was associated with major
employment crises, rather than as a part of a more radical and more continuous
process of adaptation to fast changing markets. It also predated the reform programmes that are beginning to transform the public sector management in many
EU countries.

The transfer of undertakings rules give some protection to employees, and
provide for compulsory consultation, but there may be need for flexibility. Rigid
transfer of rights to a new undertaking of a different economic nature may cause a
loss of efficiency. Incorporation of the substantive content of such rights into law
can be very restrictive. But without some protection, it is hard to imagine how
employees will be willing to forego the very real small group power that can be a
major block on change. A more flexible solution, where employees are sufficiently
organized, is to submit the issue to joint regulation. Agreements can be more rapidly
changed than can laws, and they are altered by those most closely affected.

Another major issue that goes to the heart of the economic adjustments fostered
by the Single Market is the redeployment of workers displaced by firms' restructuring. Here adult training and retraining, and labour market placement policies
have a critical role. They greatly facilitated the restructuring of the Swedish
economy during the 1960s and 1970s, and did much to reduce its social cost. Since
many workers stand to lose their jobs in the process, it is important that they have
some prospect of gaining skilled employment elsewhere. Although government
action can be important, creating the right conditions for acceptance of retrained
workers by their peer group is critical. Incumbent workers can undermine retraining policies by refusing to pass on their practical skills and by refusing to work
alongside those coming off various retraining programmes. Skilled 'dilutees' from
government training centres in Britain were never really accepted by apprentice-
trained craft workers, and so would commonly have to make way for an appren-
tice-trained person should a suitable candidate appear (Donovan, 1968: paras 345
ff). In France, vocationally qualified young workers coming out of the educational
system still have to start work in unskilled and semi-skilled positions, and wait subsequent upgrading within enterprise internal labour markets (Marsden and Germe,
1991). Thus the ability of the state or employers to impose retrained workers on
their peers is limited. Nevertheless, skilled workers have a dual interest: they may
fear substitution by those retrained, but equally, the opportunity of skilled level
employment after retraining provides some protection against layoffs and obsoles-
cence. Small group bargaining may stress the substitution fear, whereas representation by a more encompassing organization could strike a better balance between
the two.

Thus, by making the transfer of acquired rights and adult training major elements
within the social dialogue two goals are served: not only is an important substantive
component given to the social dialogue, but also the process of economic adjustment required by the Single Market programme is facilitated.

1 It is hard to demonstrate that one's past cooperation has not been designed to deceive, as is the case in espionage with double agents.
2 The close connection between cooperative exchange and trusting behaviour is highlighted in Fox's (1974: 66) account where he defines the latter as 'consisting of actions that (a) increase one's vulnerability, (b) to another whose behaviour cannot be controlled'.
3 According to Ashworth (1980) such a relationship prevailed in the less active trenches during the 1914–18 war. Each side had the power to inflict a great deal of damage on the other, but also knew that aggression would be reciprocated. Ashworth describes how aggression became ritualized, despite pressure from high command, and on the 'quiet' sectors of the trenches intentionally caused relatively little damage. Dunn (1990) applied this analogy to the 'trench warfare' atmosphere of British industrial relations pre-Thatcher.
4 Indeed, cooperative exchange may well be accompanied by periodic major conflicts in order to prove that each side still has the power to inflict sanctions should cooperative exchange break down.
5 For an interesting account of how this problem was dealt with in successive wage rounds in Sweden see Gourevitch *et al.* (1984).
6 It might be thought that this separation of powers has been determined by law, but, in fact, the law has been only partially responsible. Ford for many years remained outside industry bargaining, and negotiated company agreements with its works council. It was only under the threat of enterprise bargaining with the union that, in 1963, it opted for joining the metal industry employers and industry bargaining. The latter were pleased that Ford chose to join them rather than open up the precedent of a major company engaging in direct bargaining with the metal workers' union (Delp *et al.*, 1974).
7 For example, Addison *et al.* (1995), reviewing the evidence on the effects of German works councils on economic performance, stressed its somewhat inconclusive nature, whereas one might have expected strongly positive results in Germany. However, as they point out, data problems are severe, not least because the firms without works councils tend to be small ones.
8 A good example is provided by a recent history of Electricité de France (Wieviorka and Trinh, 1995).
9 For evidence of similar problems in connection with training for general skills see Lynch (1993). She argues that underinvestment in general skills in the USA, as indicated by its high rate of return, are a consequence of 'cherry picking'. For a review, see Addison (1994).
10 I am grateful to Ingrid Drexel for this information.
11 True, in a purely competitive equilibrium with the ratio of skilled worker and apprentice employment costs equal to the ratio of their respective net marginal products there would be no incentive for firms to substitute one for the other. However, if skilled workers have negotiated a wage above their competitive market wage, or they have a fixed wage rate while the value of their marginal product fluctuates, they could indeed fear substitution.
12 Hibbs (1990: 22), on the basis of his study of the Swedish unions' wage policy, suggests that solidarity wage policies may help sustain organizational unity of unions, but he does not explain this further.
13 Unlike their British counterparts, German employers fought hard to maintain the position of works councils (Marsden, 1978). They successfully resisted attempts by the metal workers' union to substitute direct union–enterprise bargaining for works councils, the so-called '*betriebsnahe Tarifpolitik*', and by refusing to recognize shop stewards, they prevented them from eroding the councils' representational powers.
14 The nature of the pressures on European producers emerged in the debate in France between the then Minister of Labour, Martine Aubry, and the CEO of Peugeot, Jacques Calvet, over the use of successive 'social plans' for layoffs by Peugeot. Peugeot insisted that it had to cut jobs, despite being profitable, because of the slack market, and in order

to maintain its target of a 12% annual productivity growth rate (*le Monde*, 1993a). In June 1994, Herr Pieschetsrieder, CEO of BMW, announced a similar plan of cost cuts of 20–30%, and a productivity growth target of 4–5% a year on an ongoing basis at BMW (*Financial Times*, 1994a).

15 A somewhat extreme example is provided by Sweden. By the mid-1980s, nearly three quarters of the total sales of the seven largest Swedish companies were outside Sweden; and between 1965 and 1985, employment by overseas subsidiaries of Swedish companies increased from the equivalent of 18% to 43% of Swedish domestic employment (Ghauri, 1990). Against such a background it is easy to understand why major Swedish employers should lose interest in domestic corporatism.

16 See *Financial Times* (1994b).

17 The strike by British nuclear scientists working on European projects could be a forerunner of other disputes (*Financial Times*, 1992).

18 The perception may be misleading as it has been argued that in the long run the incidence of social charges is borne by employees in the form of lower wages, at least on average (e.g. Nickell and Bell, 1996). However, the perception has a great deal of influence in policy circles.

19 For the range of variation of non-wage labour costs across the European Union, and the problems that social contributions are perceived as causing employers in high contribution countries see *die Zeit* (1993).

20 *Le Monde* (1992).

21 *Handelsblatt* (1992b). IBM restructured its organization, separating its manufacturing from its software activities. Subsequently, it concluded an agreement with HBV with effect from January 1995 (*EIRR*, 1995).

22 *Le Monde* (1993b).

23 Reported in *die Zeit* (1992b).

24 *EIRR* (1992).

25 *Il Corriere della Sera* (1992). Trentin resigned after signing the agreement on incomes policy and labour costs on 31 July arguing that not to have signed would have precipitated a major political crisis, but that he had nevertheless betrayed his mandate because he had not succeeded in maintaining the freedom to bargain at enterprise level.

26 *EIRR* (1993).

27 The question is subject to two EU directives: on acquired rights (1977) and on collective redundancies (1975). Employers are obliged to consult with their workforces when planning to make more than 10 redundancies, or when transferring workers from one business to another. In the UK, these obligations were incompletely incorporated into the Transfer of Undertakings (Protection of Employment) Regulations (TUPE) in 1981, and following adverse judgments by the European Court of Justice, the British government extended TUPE to cover public sector employees (in 1993), and non-union workplaces (announced in 1994) (*Financial Times*, 1994c).

References

Addison, J. T. (1994). 'School-to-work Transitions in the United States'. Paper for the seminar on 'Transition to Work and Youth Employment', Porto, 9–10 December 1993.

Addison, J. T., Schnabel, C. and Wagner, J. (1995). 'German Industrial Relations: An Elusive Exemplar'. *Industrielle Beziehungen*, **2** (1): 25–45.

Appelbaum, E. and Batt, R. (1994). *The New American Workplace: Transforming Work Systems in the United States.* Ithaca, NY: Cornell University Press.

Ashworth, T. (1980). *Trench Warfare 1914–18: The Live and Let Live System.* London: Macmillan.

Batstone, E. (1986). 'Labour and Productivity'. *Oxford Review of Economic Policy*, **2** (3), Autumn: 32–43.

Becker, G. S. (1975). *Human Capital: A Theoretical and Empirical Analysis, with Special Reference to Education*. Chicago: University of Chicago Press.

Bergmann, J., Jacobi, O. and Müller-Jentsch, W. (1975). *Gewerkschaften in der Bundesrepublik: gewerkschaftliche Lohnpolitik zwischen Mitgliederinteressen und ökonomischen Systemzwangen*. Frankfurt: Europäische Verlagsanstalt.

Bispinck, R. and WSI-Tarifarchiv (1993). 'Der Tarifkonflikt um den Stufenplan in der ostdeutschen Metallindustrie'. *WSI Mitteilungen*, **46** (8), August: 469–80.

Blanchflower, D. and Freeman, R. (1992). 'Unionism in the US and other advanced OECD countries'. In M. Bognanno and M. Kleiner (eds), *Labor Market Institutions and the Future Role of Unions*. Cambridge Mass: Blackwell.

Blanpain, R. (1991). *Labour Law and Industrial Relations in the European Community*. Deventer: Kluwer.

Blinder, A. S. (ed.) (1990). *Paying for Productivity*. Washington DC: Brookings Institution.

Brunetta, R. and Dell'Aringa, C. (eds) (1990). *Labour Relations and Economic Performance*. London: Macmillan.

Calmfors, L. and Driffill, J. (1988). 'Centralisation of Wage Bargaining'. *Economic Policy: a European Forum*, **6**: April 14–61.

Commission (1990). *Employment in Europe 1990*. Brussels: Commission of the European Communities.

Corrriere della Sera (1992). 'Trentin si dimette, guerra nella CGIL', 2 August.

Crozier, M. (1963). *Le Phénomène Bureaucratique*. Paris: Seuil.

Dasgupta, P. (1988). 'Trust as a commodity'. In D. Gambetta (ed.), *Trust: Making and Breaking Cooperative Relations*. London: Blackwell.

Delp, V., Schmidt, L. and Wohlfahrt, K. (1974). 'Gewerkschaftliche Betriebspolitik bei Ford'. In O. Jacobi, W. Müller-Jentsch and E. Schmidt (eds), *Gewerkschaften und Klassenkampf, Kritisches Jahrbuch '74*. Frankfurt: Fischer Verlag.

Die Zeit (1992a). 'Gift für den Frieden: Karenztage und Untertarif-Löhne', 3 July.

Die Zeit (1992b). 'Klassenkampf statt Solidarität', 22 May.

Die Zeit (1993). 'Steuern statt Beiträge, 18 June.

Donovan (1968). *Royal Commission on Trade Unions and Employers' Associations 1965–68*. Cmnd 3623, London: HMSO.

Drexel, I. (1993). *Das Ende des Facharbeiteraufstiegs? Neue mittlere Bildungs- und Karrierewege in Deutschland und Frankreich: ein Vergleich*. Frankfurt: Campus Velag.

Dunn, S. (1990.) 'Root Metaphor in the Old and New Industrial Relations'. *British Journal of Industrial Relations*, **28** (1), March: 1–31.

E.I.R.R. *European Industrial Relations Review* (1992). 'Germany: Revolt of the Mittelstand – Pressures of Bargaining Reform', **221**, June: 12-14.

E.I.R.R. *European Industrial Relations Review* (1993). 'International: The Hoover Affair and Social Dumping', **230**, July: 14–20.

E.I.R.R. *European Industrial Relations Review* (1995). 'Germany: IBM Agreement Leads to Substantial Savings', **258**, July: 7–8.

Elbaum, B. (1990). 'L'évolution de l'apprentissage en Grande-Bretagne et aux États-Unis depuis le XIXème siècle'. *Formation Emploi*, **31** (July–September): 72–84.

Eyraud, F. (1983). 'The Principles of Union Action in the Engineering Industries of Britain and France: Towards a Neo-Institutionalist Analysis of Industrial Relations'. *British Journal of Industrial Relations*, **21** (November): 358–78.

Financial Times (1992). 'Strike Vote Over Pay', 1 June.

Financial Times (1994a). 'Heavy Cuts Ahead at Rover', 3 June.

Financial Times (1994b). 'CBI President Gives Strong Warning on Inflation', 10 June.

Financial Times (1994c). 'Britain Ruled in Breach of EU Employment Law: Companies Must Consult Workforces About Changes', 9 June.

Fox, A. (1974). *Beyond Contract: Work, Power and Trust Relations*. London: Faber.

Gourevitch, P., Martin A., Ross, G., Bornstein, P., Markovits, A. and Allen, C. (1984). *Unions and Economic Crisis: Britain, West Germany, and Sweden*. London: George Allen and Unwin.

Guilhamon, J. (1988). *Les Négociations Salariales dans la Fonction Publique.* Paris: Rapport au Ministre de la Fonction Publique et des Réformes Administratives.

Handelsblatt (1992a). 'Karenztage sind Eingriff in die Tarifautonomie', 2 July.

Handelsblatt (1992b). 'IBM-Flucht aus dem Arbeitgeberverband: Beispiel für andere Firmen', 3 July.

Hibbs, D. A. (1990). *Wage Compression under Solidarity Bargaining in Sweden.* Economic Research Report No. 30. Stockholm: Trade Union Institute for Economic Research (FIEF).

Leigh-Pemberton, R. (1992). The first Bank of England Lecture given at the London School of Economics, 12 November 1992.

Levine, D. I. and D'Andrea Tyson, L. (1990). 'Participation, Productivity, and the Firm's Environment'. In A. S. Blinder (ed.), *Paying for Productivity,* pp. 183–244. Washington DC: Brookings Insittution.

Lindbeck, A., Molander, P., Persson, T., Peterson, O., Sandmo, A., Swedenborg, B. and Thygesen, N. (1993). 'Options for Economic and Political Reform in Sweden'. *Economic Policy,* October: 220–63.

Lorenz, E. (1988). 'Neither Friends nor Strangers: Informal Networks of Subcontracting in French Industry. In D. Gambetta (ed.), *Trust: Making and Breaking Cooperative Relations.* Oxford: Blackwell.

Lorenz, E. (1992). 'Trust and the Flexible Firm: International Comparisons'. *Industrial Relations,* **31** (3), Fall: 455–72.

Lorenz, E. (1995). 'Promoting Workplace Participation: Lessons from Germany and France'. *Industrielle Beziehungen,* **2** (1): 46–63.

Lynch, L. (1993). 'Private Sector Training and the Earnings of Young Workers'. *American Economic Review,* **82** (March): 299–312.

Maguire, M. (ed.) (1993). 'Pay Flexibility in the Public Sector'. Paris: OECD.

Markovits, A. A. (1986). *The Politics of West German Trade Unions: Strategies of Class Interest Representation in Growth and Crisis.* Cambridge: Cambridge University Press.

Marsden, D. W. (1978). 'Industrial Democracy and Industrial Control in West Germany, France and Great Britain'. *Research Paper No. 4.* London: Department of Employment.

Marsden, D. (1986). *The End of Economic Man? Custom and Competition in Labour Markets.* Brighton: Wheatsheaf.

Marsden, D. W. (1992). 'Incomes Policy for Europe? Or Will Pay Bargaining Destroy the Single European Market?' *British Journal of Industrial Relations,* **30** (4), December: 587–604.

Marsden, D. W. and Germe, J-F. (1991). 'Young People and Entry Paths to Long-term Jobs in France and Great Britain'. In P. Ryan, P. Garonna and R. Edwards (eds.), *The Problem of Youth: The Regulation of Youth Employment and Training in Advanced Economies.* London: Macmillan.

Marsden, D. W. and Ryan, P. (1990). 'Institutional Aspects of Youth Employment and Training Policy in Britain'. *British Journal of Industrial Relations,* **28** (3), November: 351–70.

Metcalf, D. (1990). 'Trade Unions and Economic Performance: The British Evidence'. In R. Brunetta and C. Dell'Aringa (eds), *Labour Relations and Economic Performance.* London: Macmillan.

Le Monde (1992). 'L'obstination de M. Calvet', 25 April.

Le Monde (1993a). 'M. Jacques Calvet, s'attend à une année 1993 morose et aléatoire', 19 January.

Le Monde (1993b). 'Le dumping social à la mode Européenne', 28 January.

Mottez, B. (1966). *Systèmes de salaire et politiques patronales: essai sur l'évolution des pratiques et des idéologies patronales.* Paris: Centre National de la Recherche Scientifique.

Nickell, S. and Bell, B. (1996). 'Changes in the Distribution of Wages and Unemployment in OECD Countries'. *American Economic Review,* **86** (May): 302–8.

Olson, M. (1971). *The Logic of Collective Action: Public Goods and the Theory of Groups.* Cambridge, Mass.: Harvard University Press.

Olson, M. (1982). *The Rise and Decline of Nations: Economic Growth, Stagflation, and Social Rigidities*. London: New Haven.

Paloheimo, H. (1990). 'Between Liberalism and Corporatism: The Effect of Trade Unions and Governments on Economic Performance in Eighteen OECD Countries'. In R. Brunetta and C. Dell'Aringa (eds), *Labour Relations and Economic Performance*, London: Macmillan.

Pinder, M. (1990). *Personnel Management for the Single European Market*. London: Pitman.

Popitz, H., Bahrdt, H., Jüres, E. and Kesting, H. (1957). *Das Gesellschaftsbild des Arbeiters: soziologische Untersuchungen in der Hüttenindustrie*. Tübingen: J. C. B. Mohr (Paul Siebeck).

Ryan, P., Garonna, P. and Edwards, R. (1991). *The Problem of Youth: The Regulation of Youth Employment and Training in Advanced Economies*. London: Macmillan.

Schager, N-H. (1993). 'An Overview and Evaluation of Flexible Pay Policies in the Swedish Public Sector'. In Maguire (ed.), *Pay Flexibility in the Public Sector*. Paris: OECD.

Soskice, D. (1990). 'Wage Determination: the Changing Role of Institutions in Advanced Industrialised Countries'. *Oxford Review of Economic Policy*, **6** (Winter): 36–61.

Streeck, W. (1984). *Industrial Relations in West Germany: The Case of the Car Industry*. New York: St. Martin's Press.

Vaughan-Whitehead, D. (1992). 'The Internal Market and Relocation Strategies'. In D. W. Marsden (ed.), *Pay and Employment in the New Europe*. Aldershot: Edward Elgar.

Wieviorka, M. and Trinh, S. (1995). *Le modèle EDF*. Paris: Editions de la Découverte.

Williams, B. (1988). 'Formal Structures and Social Reality'. In D. Gambetta (ed.), *Trust: Making and Breaking Cooperative Relations*. Oxford: Blackwell.

Willman, P. (1986). *Technological Change, Collective Bargaining and Industrial Efficiency*. Oxford: Oxford University Press.

Womack, J., Jones, D. T. and Roos, D. (1990). *The Machine That Changed the World*. New York: Rawson Associates.

Zoll, R. (1976). *Der Doppelcharakter der Gewerkschaften: zur Aktualität der Marxschen Gewerkschaftstheorie*. Frankfurt: Suhrkamp.

7

Social Engineering in Europe: A German Perspective

Rüdiger Soltwedel

7.1. Introduction

In this paper it is argued that the long-standing tradition of strong labour unions and employers' associations in Germany and the devotion of economic policy to the regional equalization of living standards was conducive to a widespread approval of the idea of a 'social dimension' for Europe. Thus, German corporatism was supportive of an active social policy agenda to help improve cooperation between organized labour, employers and the government and to help reduce social disparities at the European level. Yet, at the same time, the consensus in Germany was that 'subsidiarity' should be the dominant principle in order to ensure that German social policy largely remained within national jurisdiction. Nevertheless, management and labour do not see eye to eye. Trade unions, anxious about their influence on labour and enterprises, seek greater protection of the high standards in Germany than do employers' associations; that is, the unions favour more binding social rights as well as minimum standards in other member countries. For the unions, then, the social charter and Maastricht Protocol are more of a starting point than the end of the road. The unions are not a uniform bloc, however, and they differ in their protectionist zeal to harmonize social standards throughout Europe. With respect to the German labour market itself, it is received wisdom in Germany that the country should not be exposed to open competition from outside; hence, the strict territorial principle is given priority.

When the 'social dimension' turns away from cheap talk and towards the commitment of resources, the subsidiarity flag is waved vigorously by all the major German social policy players. This is apparent in the virtually unanimous criticism in Germany of the European Court, whose decisions, in several instances, are perceived as securing harmonization through the backdoor.

Second thoughts about minimum standards as a promising and affordable avenue for the equalization of living conditions have arisen since the unification of Germany, because of the scale of transfer payments involved. The empty public coffers and the inertia of unemployment will further discourage German enthusiasm for swiftly working down the Maastricht social policy agenda. Therefore, the further evolution of labour law and social policy will be scrutinized more carefully, with more regard for basic economic principles than during the more prosperous times when the Maastricht Treaty was drafted.

7.2.   The Corporatist Tradition

The German labour market is subjected to a highly developed and encompassing regulatory regime. In particular, collective agreements between trade unions and employers' associations deal with almost every aspect of labour relations – most notably, wages and working conditions – within a legal and institutional framework that secures a high degree of protection for the employed. The features of the collective bargaining system and of labour market regulation have been described at length elsewhere.[1] In this context it is important to note that the rationale for collective bargaining has, since the late nineteenth century, been to avoid (i) 'wage dumping' (or 'dirty competition') and (ii) conflicts on the shop floor. The agreements between unions and employers' associations in this bilateral cartel have been tightly sheltered against competition, unorganized employers and unemployed labour.

Furthermore, German economic policy-making has been geared to the objective of regional equalization.[2] Even wage policy has largely complied with this objective, according to the maxim 'equal pay for equal work'. In several instances, such as the investment goods industries, interregional differences in the structure of negotiated minimum wages were virtually abolished by the mid-1970s.

This has fostered a kind of 'cosy corporatism'[3] in which there is a peculiar division of labour between, broadly speaking, management and labour on the one hand (promoting high wages, good working conditions and solving social problems in a cooperative manner) and the government on the other (dealing with the employment problems generated by the non-market clearing employment costs set by collective agreements). The provision of employment and income security is perceived to be more of a collective than a private good. The outcome of this tightly knit web of regulation is a spiral of intervention: non-market clearing employment costs have been encouraged; government intervention has helped enforce contractual wages as minimum wages (by declaring collective agreements compulsory for all employers in the relevant industry), thus preventing efficient underbidding by outsiders; and labour market policies and early retirement schemes have been designed to buy out labour at existing wages in order to reduce excess labour supply. In addition, rather generous income support schemes have implied considerable individual moral hazard. All this has enhanced labour market rigidity and caused a marked insider–outside segmentation, as well as a substantial drain on taxpayers' money.[4]

In a joint declaration that is unique in Europe, the German Trade Union Confederation or *Deutscher Gewerkschaftsbund* (DGB), and the Federation of German Employers or *Bundesvereinigung der Deutschen Arbeitgeberverbände* (BdA) welcomed the Community move towards a European 'social dimension' in 1989.[5] This was much in line with the official position of the federal government. In fact, the notion of the 'social dimension' goes back to the Brandt era (Erdmann, 1990), a time when the slogan 'daring more democracy' dominated the political arena in Germany.

7.3. Priority for Subsidiarity

In principle, the thrust of the Community's social engineering in the social charter and the social chapter was very much in line with what unions and employers' associations were willing to accept because it reflected the major ingredients of German corporatism: some more intervention (pushing ahead with the Action Programme) and, as a corollary, some more money for regional equalization (the Cohesion Fund). Furthermore, the German government was successful in obtaining explicit recognition of the subsidiarity principle and finding support for the notion that social convergence is a long-term catch-up process. Hence, it came closer to the position of the government and the employers' associations than to that of the unions.

The employers basically regard the Maastricht Protocol as satisfactory and do not see any need for a further extension of the social policy mandate at the European level. Their major concern is that the European Commission will try to develop a genuine European social policy. They are afraid that the principle of subsidiarity will be violated, and that there will be arbitrariness in choosing the legal basis for decisions in order to opt for majority voting instead of unanimity in the Council of the European Union. Furthermore, they question the need for regulation and note the danger of overregulation (Thüsing, 1993: 12). The unions think, and this comes as no surprise, that the European social policy agenda is incomplete, most obviously in those areas where the Treaty does not give competence to the Commission or where unanimity is required in the Council. We proceed to the main differences between management and labour, focusing on basic social rights and minimum social standards.

Basic Social Rights

One contentious issue between the employers and the unions is the question of whether there should be an explicit definition of basic social rights at the European level, especially as regards collective labour law (issues such as collective bargaining and strikes) and codetermination. It is very much an unsettled question whether or not these issues should be put into the European social basket at all. In essence, the position of the employers is 'no', whereas that of the unions is more 'yes' than 'no'.

The employers argue that the governing principles of collective labour law are too diverse in the member countries, each having followed a historical trajectory of its own, and that, ultimately, there would not be more unity but more disequilibrium and inconsistencies between the respective social structures. With respect to codetermination as well as the legal framework of collective bargaining, the German system is genuinely distinct from that obtaining in other member countries. Strict obedience of the principle of subsidiarity is the *conditio sine qua non* on these issues for the German employers. Any interference at the European level with the constitutive elements of the labour markets of member countries is perceived as counterproductive (Erdmann, 1990).[6] The employers welcome the social dialogue provided for in Articles 3 and 4 of the Agreement on Social Policy but would not go beyond this affirmation.[7] Hence, while endorsing the existence of basic social rights, the employers reject any attempt at making the Community institutions (including the European Court of Justice) responsible for defining and implementing these rights and freedoms at the Community level.

The unions strongly oppose this position. They do not want to leave these issues to the individual member countries. Enforceable rights should be defined at the European level.[8] The DGB's foremost concern is the implementation of a legally binding social charter aimed at protecting workers' rights.[9] The unions do not want 'subsidiarity' to translate into inactivity at the European level; from their point of view, subsidiarity means that the Community is obligated to use its social policy instruments to harness basic social rights in those member countries where they are deficient (Ms Engelen-Kefer, deputy chair of the DGB, *Handelsblatt*, 4 August, 1992). The principle of unanimity voting, which still governs a substantial part of social policy matters at Community level, annoys the unions: 'The need for a complete consensus has thus far been the most effective barrier to harmonization in the area of social norms' (Meyer, 1991).

Basically, the unions are anxious about enterprises 'fleeing from tough German labour law' *(Arbeitsrechtsflucht)* (see Däubler, 1989: 66) to member countries with less strict provisions.[10] Anxiety, distrust, and perceived impotence characterize the unions' attitude towards enterprises with subsidiaries in various member countries whom they suspect of effectively undermining organized labour's attempt to improve its situation via the strike threat and industrial action.[11]

In particular, unions strive for European collective bargaining not least so as to avoid 'wage dumping'. Meyer (1991), the head of the DGB, holds that without supranational collective bargaining there is no European social dimension; at any rate, argues Meyer, there is no way that a further economic integration in the Community can bypass the objective of building a supranational collective bargaining system. Their grasp of reality, though, tells the unions that European collective bargaining is a very ambitious objective that will encounter enormous difficulties and that they still have a long way to go given the diversity of union structures and the limited strength of the union movement across Europe.[12] From that perspective, the Maastricht Treaty provided real progress in involving the social dialogue in more red tape. Unions regard this as an important and absolutely necessary impulse for collective bargaining in a future European industrial relations framework. For this reason, the political clout of the unions in member countries is important. German unions look at the weak, fragmented French labour relations systems with some concern. The upgrading of the social dialogue in the Maastricht Treaty may not only strengthen the attempt of French unions to gain more political strength but also give them more leverage for a cross-border cartelization of European labour markets. This may help prevent – from the German unions' perspective – the European wage structure and wage differentials from conforming more closely to productivity differentials (Lecher, 1993). Altvater and Mahnkopf (1993: 505) even argue that with labour markets becoming more global there should be joint union activity at the European level 'to stem basic economic requirements'.

Although the social dialogue as presently constituted is totally inadequate for the German unions and although they will continue to press for a more powerful institutional arrangement for collective bargaining at the European level, they are not prepared, however, to compromise their own *Tarifautonomie*: 'The German trade unions would certainly not be willing to relinquish their autonomy in matters of collective bargaining to a European institution or to European representatives' (Engelen-Kefer, quoted in *Handelsblatt*, 4 August, 1992). This attitude – which is quite rational in itself – seems to reveal a sort of subsidiarity-cream-skimming. That is, the German trade unions are ready to accept a European mandate whenever their own position is mired at the national level and could use an additional push from a powerful outside player, while they drag their feet where the autonomy of German unions is endangered.

Minimum Social Standards

This is the hard core issue of 'social dumping'. The employers maintain that any attempt to fix minimum standards has to steer clear of the Scylla of fixing them at too low and hence meaningless a level and the Charybdis of setting them too high and jeopardizing the endogenous development potential of the poorer nations. According to an estimate by Clever (1990), adjusting standards in poorer member countries to the German level would cost about a thousand billion Deutsch marks. On the other hand, the employers endorse the kind of signalling function for the low-standard countries that minimum standards might entail because they may be conducive to social cohesion. As far as Germany is concerned, no substantial changes are expected given its above average norms in most of the areas likely to be affected by the Agreement on Social Policy. In their joint declaration with the unions, and as endorsed by the German Federal Ministry of Labour and Social Affairs, they have recommended Community-wide minimum standards in areas such as annual vacations, protection of children and youth, maternity protection, integration of the disabled, vocational counselling and labour exchanges, vacation pay, sickness pay, health protection and on-the-job safety, and temporary work (see Appendix).

Although the employers maintain that the dividing line between issues requiring majority voting and those issues restricted to unanimity voting has not been shifted substantially following the Treaty on European Union, they are annoyed that measures having to do with 'working conditions' (*Arbeitsbedingungen*) may be introduced under the former route. They are afraid that the vagueness of this term may become a broad entry gate for the Commission to make inroads into the national domain of labour law (Thüsing, 1993: 12). Hence, the employers expect that there will be substantial haggling over the legal bases with differing requirements for a quorum on which decisions will finally be made.

Again, the trade unions regard the Agreement on Social Policy as more of a stop-over than as the end of the road. Given that the high standards in Germany have clear wage-cost implications, the unions' insistence on raising minimum standards in low-standard countries may reflect doubts as to whether high German standards are really sustained by productivity and workers' preferences. Quite understandably from their point of view, unions do not really welcome the imminent threat of cross-border locational competition, especially under full monetary union.[13] Allowing unions to raise standards, and thereby raise labour costs in the poorer member countries would assuredly weaken the market test of the sustainability of regulation in a regime of monetary union.

Jointly Against the Odd Man Out

Employers and unions find common ground once again on the question of the self-exclusion of the UK from the Agreement on Social Policy. The unions maintain that social standards on the Continent will be impaired, and the competitive position of the UK improved, if the latter does not have to implement the minimum standards.

Ms Engelen-Kefer, for the DGB, argues that the UK may gain a competitive edge by not participating in the further implementation of the Action Programme as agreed upon in the Agreement on Social Policy (*Handelsblatt*, 9 March, 1992).

One such area where it is felt that the UK benefits from an 'unfair' advantage is temporary employment, which is far less restricted than elsewhere.[14] A British agency could happily continue to rent its labour, even in the Federal Republic of Germany, without being forced to comply with the prevailing minimum standards in the Social Union; thus, the UK can avail itself of the advantages of the common market but can avoid the social burden to which the other member countries have committed themselves in the Social Union. The thrust of Ms Engelen-Kefer's diagnosis is that either the UK should join the Agreement on Social Policy, or 'it should be exempted to some extent from the advantages of the free movement of goods and services'. This perceived tilted playing field also angers the employers' associations, who maintain that the segmentation that could ensue runs against the objective of creating 'homogeneous' competitive conditions within the Community (Thüsing, 1993). In these statements the legacy of collective German labour relations is immediately apparent, resting as it does on the implicit understanding that 'fair' competition means competing on the basis of the same cost level.

7.4. The Union Divide: Activists and Accommodationists

German trade unions are by no means a homogeneous group. They differ substantially in their ideology and perceived economic interests and, hence, in their attitudes to the European social dimension. Markovits and Otto (1992) have analysed four DGB unions, which typify two distinct wings that have developed inside the DGB, and which they term 'activists' and 'accommodationists'. The activist unions are always critical of Germany's political economy and they regard themselves as the major agents of social reform. Two of the leading activist unions are *IG Medien* (the media union) and *IG Metall* (the metalworkers' union). The accommodationists, on the other hand, stress the common interests of labour and capital and opt for a close and cooperative relationship, best called 'social partnership'. They see the political and economic institutions of the Federal Republic of Germany in a more positive light than do the activists. The leading unions of this wing are *IG Chemie-Papier-Keramik* (the chemical workers' union) and *Gewerkschaft Nahrung-Genuß-Gaststätten* (NGG, the food processing workers' union). These two groups differ in their position towards competition in the Internal Market in general – although their basic assessment is positive in tone and substance – and on the 'social dumping' issue in particular. Let us focus on the results of Markovits and Otto's research as regards social dumping.[15]

Although both activists and accommodationists worry that the Internal Market will create a downward levelling of workers' rights, their positions differ. The activists believe that foreign workers have a right to benefit from Germany's economic prosperity. Hence, they tolerate diverging standards to some extent and welcome German investments in Europe's backward regions even at the expense of jobs within Germany; likewise, they are positive on the inflow of foreign workers into Germany that may accompany the completion of the Internal Market. In contrast, the accommodationists tend to support the broadest possible harmonization of working conditions and worker participation in order to prevent a migration of investment and jobs to low-wage areas in southern Europe or Ireland; and they are a good deal less enthusiastic than the activists about investment abroad and an increasing inflow of foreign workers into Germany. The accommodationists have also expressed concern about the German consumer: though clearly NGG's concerns about the high German safety and quality standards and the health of the German consumer coincides with the economic interests of workers in the German food industries. The research of Markovits and Otto thus reveals a more protectionist stance in the accommodationists' position.

7.5. The German Council of Experts and the Territorial Principle: Restricting Outsider-Competition in the Labour Market

The free movement of goods from low-cost countries and, even more so, the free movement of their peoples within the common market, is seen as threatening national labour market regimes. The idea that, say, a team of Portuguese construction workers could work in Germany at Portuguese wages is chilling for unions as well as domestic construction companies. However, it is received wisdom in Germany, even sanctioned by the German Council of Experts,[16] that the strict territorial principle should apply to the movement of labour. Trade in goods has to conform to the country-of-origin principle, endorsed and enforced on several occasions by the European Court. On the other hand, the labour market is subjected to the country-of-destination principle. Competition on the basis of the home country's conditions is perceived as unlawful: German labour market conditions can only be contested indirectly, via trade or the migration of firms to low-wage member countries. This is very much in line with the rules of the cosy corporatist set-up in Germany which has briefly been sketched above. On the country of origin basis, it is argued, there would be a deluge of 'cheap' labour from low-wage member countries to rich countries.[17]

We cannot go into an in-depth analysis here of the question of whether or not Germany really would witness a downward wage adjustment if there were an inflow of labour from low-cost member countries. It seems safe, though, to conclude that the strict application of the territorial principle helps sustain the corporatist set-up of the German labour market.

The German Council of Experts argues that the principle of nondiscrimination requires that foreigners be treated on the same basis as the indigenous labour force (Sachverständigenrat, 1989: para. 465). Thus, national labour law and social policy norms are binding for foreign workers in the Federal Republic of Germany. This requirement would hold also in the case where an enterprise is conducting business in another member country: it would not offer conditions on the basis of its domestic rules on working hours, labour safety rules, norms of labour law, and social security charges, etc., but rather on the basis of the other member state's regulations.[18]

The Council of Experts does not feel quite at ease with such an orientation, and it concedes that this position could be questioned on competition policy grounds. From a competition policy perspective, cross-border movements of labour should not be treated differently from trade flows between member countries; that is, the strict country-of-origin rule should apply. By subjecting the movement of goods and the movement of people to different principles – country of origin/country of destination – the scope for competition between the systems of labour market regulation and social policy regimes will be substantially curtailed.

However, the Council of Experts sees clear-cut disadvantages in applying the country-of-origin principle to the labour market. This may foster the segmentation of labour markers, since the norms to be applied would depend upon the location of the home office of the enterprise. Such segmentation would, in its view, entail negative external effects (Sachverständigenrat, 1989: para. 465). If the norms were to differ substantially, tensions between labour in the various segments would result. Domestic labour law and social policy institutions could hardly be developed further; they would be directly contested by the inflow of labour from member countries with lower standards. Domestic firms might even consider relocating their headquarters to countries with lower levels of regulation. These effects would trigger conflicts between countries. At the end of the road, one would have to countenance a move towards a harmonization of standards, which would run counter to the competition between the various labour market and social policy regimes that the Council of Experts in principle regards as beneficial. In this dismal trade-off, the Council of Experts sides with the destination principle: the norms of that country should apply where the production actually takes place.

Although the logic of the Council of Experts is far from being really convincing, it is important to note that all major players in the economic and social policy arena endorse this view. It reflects the well-received German wisdom that for the sake of 'social peace' there should be substantial limits to outside competition in the German labour market.

7.6.   National Law, the European Court, and Subsidiarity

Social engineering in Europe is not only confined to the social charter and its Action Program and whatever results from Maastricht. Another major player is the European Court. Substantial German concerns about social policy do not arise from the developments at Maastricht but rather from the decisions of the European Court. It is argued by the German government, the unions, and the employers' associations that the Court regards itself as an 'engine of integration' and, on this basis, attempts to influence and give momentum to social policy-making in the European Union by the extension of law (*Rechtsfortbildung*) in favour of the Union's interests at the expense of national competence, thereby compromising the notion of subsidiarity.[19] The activity of the European Court is perceived as leading to harmonization via the back-door. Furthermore, given the vagueness of 'subsidiarity', Erasmy (1993: 64) is afraid that the European Court will itself define the principle and thereby shift competence in its own favour.

The allegation is that in several of its decisions the Court has not taken the systemic structure of German labour and social law into account, and has disregarded the (potential) fiscal implications of those decisions on German social policy institutions and the economy at large. A particularly conspicuous case in point dates from 1983. In the child allowance (*Kindergeld*) case, the Court decided in favour of an Italian worker in Germany who sought child allowances on the basis of (the comparatively generous) German law for his children living with his wife in Italy – even though the spouse could have applied for child allowances on the basis of Italian law (but did not do so).[20] Since the decisions of the Court are binding on all member countries and the Court bases its decisions on previous decisions, the German authorities are worried that the historical development of domestic labour and social law in Germany will be disregarded. Hence, there is the perceived risk that the national scope for introducing new social benefits, or extending existing ones, will be restricted because it may become very expensive for the national social policy institution, and, ultimately, the taxpayer. Furthermore, there is every reason to be anxious about an enforced extension of national social benefits by the European Court to persons or groups of persons who were not intended to be covered when the norms were implemented in the first place.[21]

Such problems mainly arise with benefits that are granted on the basis of solidarity, charity and need. These benefits may be regarded as a kind of 'club good' that in general is granted on the principle of some regional congruence between the contributors to and the recipients of such benefits. The question at stake is whether this principle is violated in those instances where there is a legal entitlement to benefits within the Federal Republic of Germany, which are granted on a lump sum basis, and which go to persons outside the country.

It seems reasonable to assume that any 'export' of social benefits of this kind was not intended when these benefits were first introduced. The extension to outside beneficiaries may call into question the contributors readiness to pay and may entail moral hazard (Laaser and Soltwedel, 1993). In other words, the decisions of the European Court may substantially raise the cost burden of national social policy measures. Under the subsidiarity principle it should be a matter for the Council of the European Union – and not for the Court – to give clear guidance as to whether or not, as a general rule, the territorial principle strictly applies in these cases (Engels, 1989).

7.7. Second Thoughts on Social Engineering after German Unification

The German system of labour market regulation, its 'cosy corporatism', and its sophisticated system of fiscal equalization has been put under considerable strain since the unification of Germany.[22] Economic unification has been largely dominated by the objective of equalizing living standards at the greatest possible speed. Social policy benefits and wages in eastern Germany have increased considerably, while wage development in western Germany has not moderated at the same time. Eastern Germany was, is, and will be for some time to come viable only if it continues to receive huge transfers. These transfers amounted to DM 138 billion in 1993, and about DM 130 billion in 1994 and 1995, roughly 4.5% of the former West Germany's GDP.[23] Since the end of the 1980s, public expenditures have increased at an extraordinary rate; and the budget deficit and the public debt have climbed to a level never before experienced in the postwar period, even though taxes and social security contributions have been raised quite substantially.[24] Despite harsh fiscal consolidation measures, the ratio of public expenditures to GDP is slated to increase to about 52%, about six percentage points higher than the preunification level.[25]

These indicators demonstrate that a change in policy is long overdue. The challenge is to bring the mix of wage policy, labour market policy, and social policy back into line with basic economic principles. All this boils down to the point that the 'cosy corporatist' sort of division of labour alluded to above – the employers'

nd the unions concerning themselves with wages, the government con-
with unemployment – is no longer sustainable.[26] There is already some
. this message has got through to the economic actors and that the tight
aightjacket will be loosened somewhat. Doubts remain as to whether
this w... ur to a sufficient degree and in timely enough a fashion to have significant and lasting effects on unemployment. In any event, there is a clear message for
social engineering at the European level: since any move towards harmonization will
translate into higher transfers (on top of the impressive redistribution machinery
that already exists), the German government would firmly oppose it. The empty
public coffers have at least the positive aspect that there is no more money to hand
out as a bribe to member countries with less regulation and lower social standards.
Germany simply cannot afford it. From the German perspective, there is no reason
to believe that there is a case for swiftly working down the European social policy
agenda, or even for extending it beyond the Maastricht compromise.

Notes

1 For details see Paqué (1992), Soltwedel *et al.* (1990), Soltwedel and Trapp (1988).
2 In the political arena, it is often (albeit erroneously) argued that this is an objective of the
constitution (see Soltwedel, 1987).
3 I owe this expression to Karl-Heinz Paqué.
4 For a more detailed assessment, see Soltwedel and Trapp (1988: 194–222).
5 Quoted in Bundesministerium (1991: 46). See the Appendix for the joint declaration of
DGB and BdA.
6 'Hardly any of the building blocks of German law on collective bargaining can be found
in the systems of other member countries. Likewise, the organization of collective bargaining is characterized by far-reaching differences *vis-à-vis* German conditions. ... It
would entail extremely negative consequences to pick individual segments out of these
complex systems and try to regulate them separately' (Erdmann, 1990: 29) (author's translation).
7 'The Maastricht Treaty thus opens the possibility for the employers' associations and the
unions to deal with social policy issues on their own responsibility and most probably
more appropriately than from far-away Brussels. However, this has nothing to do with
European collective bargaining! ... Since expectations are flying high, one has to move
with care. It should not be overlooked that the employers' associations and the unions
assess the issues at stake from distinctly different, even opposing, perspectives' (Thüsing,
1993: 17) (author's translation).
8 See the Joint Declaration, para. 3.
9 For a detailed review of the DGB's position, see Breit (1989) and Siebert (1989).
10 This anxiety boils down to a revelation that, *mutatis mutandis*, the economic costs of these
legal and institutional arrangements exceed the returns that they may entail.
11 In order to reduce the tensions that arise in this context and to build up confidence, several
multinational firms (such as Volkswagen) have already agreed to joint meetings at the
enterprise level with works councils of their subsidiaries in member countries. These
meetings still fall short of cross-border codetermination.
12 See, for example, the section on Europe in various issues of *Gewerkshaftsbund* (1989: **573**;
1990: **619**; 1992: **650**) and Steinkühler (1988, 1989).
13 For an economic assessment of the 'social dumping' allegation, see Chapter 4, this
volume.
14 See, for example, Carley and Suri (1993) and Mückenberger (1993).
15 Here, we closely follow Markovits and Otto (1992: 170–79).

16 For an amplification of the following, see Sachverständigenrat (1989: paras 454–70).
17 Anxieties about unrestricted immigration of cheap labour have always arisen with proposed enlargement of the Community. Hence free labour mobility (*Freizügigkeit*) upon accession was delayed for Greece (1981–88), and for Spain and Portugal (1986–93). Likewise, in the context of the British entry, the UK was anxious about immigration from low-cost southern Italy, and the Netherlands feared an inflow of Sikh and Pakistani people with a British passport. In all of these cases, the perceived deluge turned out to be a mirage rather than a realistic scenario (Böhning, 1972; Pennix and Muus, 1991).
18 Though beyond the scope of this paper, it would be quite interesting to look closely into the issue of liberalizing public procurement policies.
19 See, for example, Erasmy (1992, 1993) and Clever (1992).
20 Some of the cases in point, apart from the *Kindergeld* decision (C-191/83) mentioned above, are the following: the *Barber* (C-262/88) and the *Moroni* cases (C-110/91) involving pensions at the enterprise level (*Betriebsrenten*); the *Paletta* case (C-45/90) involving sickness pay (*Lohnfortzahlung im Krankeitsfall*); and the *Stanton-Newton* case (C-356/89) involving medical benefits in kind (*medizinische Sachleistungen*). For further cases and details, see Clever (1992).
21 This criticism is a parallel to a long-standing discussion on the economic effects of labour law in Germany which has similarly proceeded on the basis of case law (*Richterrecht*). Labour and social law have as their primary objective the goal of humanizing the world of work (and of integrating dependent labour into society). Functioning as they did as a social and humanitarian watchdog, the economic implications were lost sight of by the courts – *judex non calculat!*
22 For a detailed description and assessment of the unification process, see Siebert (1993).
23 See Boss *et al.* (1994: Table 4).
24 See Boss *et al.* (1993) and Siebert (1993: 146–76).
25 Note that his ratio was about 43% in the early 1980s and was, at that time, regarded as a severe impediment to growth and employment.
26 For an assessment of the current and future challenges for the German labour market, see Paqué and Soltwedel *et al.* (1993).

References

Altvater, E. and Mahnkopf, B. (1993). 'Tarifautonomie gegen Ökonomische Sachzwänge im vereinigten Europa'. *WSI-Mitteilungen,* August: 503–12.
Böhning, W. R. (1972). *The Migration of Workers in the United Kingdom and the European Community.* London: Oxford University Press.
Boss, A., Döpke, J., Fischer, M., Kramer, J., Langenfeldt, E. and Schatz, K-W. (1993). 'Bundesrepublik Deutschland: 1994 Konjunkturelle Erholung bei finanzpolitischem Konsolidierungskurs'. *Die Weltwirtschaft,* **3**: 282–301.
Boss, A., Döpke, J., Fischer, M., Kramer, J., Langenfeldt, E. and Schatz, K-W. (1994). 'Bundesrepublik Deutschland: Zögerliche Erholung der Konjunktur'. *Die Weltwirtschaft,* **1**: 28–53.
Breit, E. (ed.) (1989). *Für ein Soziales Europa.* Köln: Bund-Verlag.
Bundesministerium für Arbeit und Sozialordnung (1991). 'Gemeinsame Erklörup van DGB and BDA'. *Der EG-Binnenmarkt und die Sozialpolitik. Leben und Arbeiten in Europa,* **1**: Bonn.
Carley, M. and Suri, O. (1993). 'Atypische Beschäftigung in Großbritannien'. *WSI-Mitteilungen,* March: 600–10.
Clever, P. (1990). *Internationales und Europäisches Sozialrecht.* Saarbrücken: Universität des Saarlandes, Europa-Institut.
Clever, P. (1992). 'Rechtsprechung des EuGH im Sozialbereich auf dem Prüfstand'. In Bundesministerium für Arbeit (ed.), *Der EG-Binnenmarkt und die Sozialpolitik. Leben und Arbeiten in Europa,* **3**: 70–82. Bonn.

Däubler, W. (1989). 'Sozialstaat EG? Notwendigkeit und Inhalt einer Europäischen Grundrechtsakte'. In W. Däubler (ed.), *Sozialstaat EG? Die andere Dimension des Binnenmarktes.* Gütersloh: Verlag Bertelsmann-Stiftung.

Engels, W. (1989). 'Die Sozialcharta ist ein Irrweg'. *Frankfurter Allgemeine Zeitung 2,* December: 15.

Erasmy, W. (1992, 1993). 'Der EuGH konterkariert Nationales Arbeitsrecht'. *Der Arbeitgeber* nos 22/44, 24/44 (1992), no. 2/45 (1993).

Erdmann, E-G. (1990). 'Sozialpolitik in der Gemeinschaft'. Paper presented at the University of Mannheim, 26 October. *Mimeo.*

Gewerkschaftsjahrbuch: Daten – Fakten – Analysen (1988, 1990, 1992). Köln: Bund-Verlag.

Handelsblatt (1992). 'Subsidiaritätsprinzip darf nicht zu Untätigkeit führen', **4** August, 4.

Handelsblatt (1992). 'Wo Großbritannien Rechte beansprucht, dort muß es auch Pflichten Übernehmen', **9** March, 5.

Laaser, C-F. and Soltwedel, R. *et al.* (1993). *Europäische Integration und Nationale Wirtschaftspolitik.* Kieler Studien No. 255. Tübingen: Mohr.

Lecher, W. (1991). 'Konturen Europäischer Tarifpolitik'. *WSI-Mitteilungen,* March: 194–201.

Lecher, W. (1993). 'Das französische Arbeitsbeziehungssystem -und was uns das angeht'. *WSI-Mitteilungen,* July: 421–30.

Markovits, A. S. and Otto, A. (1992). 'German Labour and Europe '92'. *Comparative Politics,* **2**: 163–80.

Meyer, H.-W. (1991) 'Ohne internationale Tarifpolitik keine soziale Dimension'. *Handelsblatt,* **31** December, 6.

Mückenberger, U. (1993). 'Ist der "Sozialraum Europa" noch auf der historischen Agenda? – Neue Beschäftigungsformen und deren europäische Regulierung'. *WSI-Mitteilungen,* September: 593–600.

Paqué, K-H. (1992). 'Labour Market Contracts and Institutions: The Case of Germany'. Paper presented at the International Workshop 'Comparative Labour Market Institutions and Contracts'. NIAS, Wassenaar. *Mimeo.*

Paqué, K-H. and Soltwedel, R. *et al.* (1993). 'Challenges Ahead: Long-Term Perspectives of the German Economy'. Institute of World Economics, *Kiel Discussion Papers* 202/203, March.

Pennix, R. and Muus, P. J. (1991). 'Nach 1992 Migration ohne Grenzen? Die Lektionen der Vergangenheit und ein Ausblick auf die Zukunft'. *Zeitschrift für Bevölkerungswissenschaft,* **17**: 191–207.

Sachverständigenrat zur Begutachtung der gesamtwirtschaftlichen Entwicklung (1989). *Jahresgutachten 1989/1990.* Stuttgart: Metzler-Poeschel.

Siebert, G. (ed.) (1989). *Europa '92.* Frankfurt am Main: Nachrichten-Verlags-Gesellschaft.

Siebert, H. (1993). *Das Wagnis der Einheit. Eine wirtschaftspolitische Therapie.* Stuttgart: Deutsche-Verlags-Gesellschaft.

Soltwedel, R. (1987). 'Wettbewerb zwischen Regionen statt Zentral Koordinierter Regionalpolitik'. *Die Weltwirtschaft,* **1**: 129–45.

Soltwedel, R. (1990). 'Regulierungen auf dem Arbeitsmarkt in der Bundesrepublik'. *Kieler Studien,* no. 233. Tübingen: Mohr.

Soltwedel, R. and Trapp, P. (1988). 'Labour Market Barriers to More Employment: Causes for an Increase of the Natural Rate? The Case of West Germany'. In H. Giersch (ed.), *Macro and Micro Policies for More Growth and Employment.* Symposium 1987. Tuebingen: Mohr.

Steinkühler, F. (1988). 'Arbeitnehmer sollen für den Abbau von Sozialleistungen weichgeklopft werden'. *Handelsblatt,* **27** July, 4.

Steinkühler, F. (1989). 'Chancen innerer Zukunftsgestaltung gegen Kapitalmacht und Sozialdumping'. In F. Steinkühler (ed.), *Europa '92. Industriestandort oder Sozialer Lebensraum.* Hamburg: VSA-Verlag.

Thüsing, R. (1993). 'Europäische Sozialpolitik nach Maastricht'. *Personalführung,* **1**: 8–18.

Appendix: Joint Declaration of the DGB and the BdA[1]

The chairman of the *Deutsche Gewerkschaftsbund* (DGB), Ernst Breit, and the president of the *Bundesvereinigung der Deutschen Arbeitgeberverbände*, Klaus Murmann, issued the following statement on the social dimension of the European internal market on 26 July 1989, in Frankfurt:

1. The *Deutscher Gewerkschaftsbund* (DGB) and the *Bundesvereinigung der Deutschen Arbeitgeberverbände* (*Bundesvereinigung*) agree that the implementation of the European internal market is a step in the right direction as concerns the shaping of Europe's future. Both expect the internal market to provide additional positive stimuli for economic growth and employment and an increase in the overall welfare of the population of the member states.

2. The *Bundesvereinigung* and DGB further agree that the social dimension of implementing the European internal market is extremely important. The fusion of the 12 EC economies would be incomplete if social policy in these economies were not, in the long term, made to conform to the higher standards among these economies. But by no means does this mean social policies in Europe should be completely harmonized. The social dimension of the internal market has to take into account the different systems that have evolved in the member countries as well as their different economic situations. Nonetheless, European social policy will increase in relevance *vis-à-vis* national social policies.

3. Both the DGB and the *Bundesvereinigung* advocate the Community-wide formulation of minimum social norms, to be based on the agreements founding the EC, as far as it is essential to the creation and the functioning of the common market. The means to accomplish this must be worked out jointly. In order to safeguard these basic norms in the legal systems of the member states, recourse should be taken only to such means and instruments as are prescribed by the EC agreements and are otherwise considered suitable.

Both sides also agree on the necessity of recognizing qualitative constitutional rights and liberties such as the freedom of association, the freedom to engage in autonomous wage bargaining, and the freedom of employees to participate in the European Community. Whereas the *Bundesvereinigung* would like to leave the responsibility for such rights solely with the member states, the DGB would like to see these rights become inalienable rights that are secured in all the member states by Community law.

4. The *Bundesvereinigung* and the DGB feel that the highest possible standards of health and occupational safety must be guaranteed. Everything must be done to prevent the harmonization of standards in the EC from leading to a deterioration of attained national standards.

5. In light of the high unemployment in the European Community, the DGB and the *Bundesvereinigung* consider it extremely important for the Community to have an effective labour market policy. They emphasize the importance of existing Community-level institutions, in particular the Standing Committee for Employment, the European Institute for Vocational Training in Berlin, and the social structural funds of the Community. They also advocate the setting up in all EC countries of a public labour administration that can effectively fulfil the task of social mediation.

---

[1] Translation by Paul Kramer.

6. Increased investments in human capital are crucial for the success of the internal market. In order to improve the qualifications of employees and to increase corporate competitiveness, quality vocational training for youths should be guaranteed, the number of advanced training schemes increased, and the standard of further education improved.

Attaining these goals will require special efforts on the national as well as on the European level. The *Bundesvereinigung* and the DGB consider it part of their responsibility to help in attaining these goals. They would like to see trade unions and employers participate in employing the instruments of educational policy provided by the EC – especially the structural funds and the action programmes of the Community.

7. Employee participation and codetermination in company decisions in the Federal Republic of Germany is unique among the member states. Thus, a Europe-wide harmonization will hardly be possible. The DGB and the *Bundesvereinigung* do not feel that the completion of the European internal market necessitates changing the system of codetermination in the Federal Republic of Germany.

8. The European social dialogue has already proven to be an important arena for conducting discussions and consultations between employers' associations and trade unions in Europe. The *Bundesvereinigung* and the DGB support increasing the powers of this committee, for example, the power to promote and ascertain consensus in those sociopolitical issues that are of concern to all European employers' associations and trade unions.

8

Spain and the European Social Charter: Social Harmonization with Unemployment and High Wage Growth

Antonio Argandoña

8.1. Introduction

For decades, among those who were fighting for social, political and economic modernization in Spain, Europe was the guiding light and the example to be followed. With the advent of democracy in 1977, and Spain's subsequent entry into the European Economic Community on the 1 January 1986, the country began to pick up speed on its path towards Europeanization. The implementation in Spain of the European Social Charter (ESC) and adherence to the social chapter of the Maastricht Treaty was merely one more step along the path of alignment.

However, Spain is a country beset with serious employment problems: real wages have grown at higher rates than in other member states, the unemployment rate is currently the highest in the Community, and labour market rigidities appear to exceed the already high levels obtaining in other European nations. Is the route traced by the Community towards social harmonization the best route for Spain?

This is the subject of the present chapter. In Section 8.2 the evolution of the Spanish economy in recent years is discussed, with particular reference to the labour market, and reform of the Spanish legal framework on employment during the 1980s. The Spanish labour market's current problems are examined in Section 8.3. Finally, the relevance and likely impact of the ESC on the labour market are considered.

8.2. The Spanish Economy in Recent Years

Economic and Labour Market Developments

The postwar economic boom did not take hold in Spain until the 1960s. A vigorous stabilization plan (1959) and partial liberalization of prices, foreign investment, and

Table 8.1. Labour market indicators, Spain and EU-12 (percentage annual rates of growth)

Period[a]	Real GDP		Employment		Inflation[b]		Unit labour costs		Real wages[c]	
	Spain	EU-12	Spain	EU-12	Spain	EU-12	Spain	EU-12	Spain	EU-12
1961–73	7.2	4.8	0.7	0.3	7.2	5.2	7.6	5.3	7.0	4.4
1974–77	3.1	2.1	−0.7	−0.1	18.2	12.7	19.0	17.6	4.5	2.9
1978–84	1.1	1.9	−1.8	−0.1	14.4	10.0	12.8	10.1	1.6	1.0
1985–90	4.2	3.1	2.3	1.2	7.5	5.1	6.3	6.3	0.6	1.2
1991–93	0.6	0.6	−1.6	−0.8	6.1	4.4	5.6	4.1	1.9	1.1
1994–95	2.5	2.8	0.3	0.2	4.1	2.9	2.3	1.1	0.4	0.7

Periods[d]	Unemployment[e]	
	Spain	EU-12
1964–75	2.7	2.4
1976–77	6.5	5.0
1980–86	17.6	8.6
1987–91	18.0	8.5
1992–95	22.3	10.3

Source: *European Economy*, **60** (1995), Tables 2, 3, 10, 22, 26, 31, 32, 35
Notes:
[a] According to the main stages of the Spanish economy
[b] Deflator of private consumption
[c] Deflator of GDP
[d] Taking into account the lag in unemployment adjustment
[e] As a percentage of active population.

trade (but not the labour market) put the country on track for a high level of sustained economic growth (see Table 8.1). This growth was based on an abundant supply of cheap, relatively skilled and disciplined labour, an intense capitalization process (assisted by foreign investment), a lowering of barriers to foreign trade (exports grew at a mean real annual rate of 12.4% and imports by 16% during the period 1961–73), and an institutional environment that encouraged hard work, entrepreneurship, savings and investment. In spite of the high growth in the economically active population and the steady migration from the rural areas to the cities, unemployment was minimal (helped in part by emigration to other European countries).

The Years of crisis, 1974–85   The first oil shock (1973) caught the Spanish economy in a phase of expansion and optimism but with serious economic and political problems. The authoritarian regime was in crisis, brought on by General Franco's failing health (he died in November 1975) and by the growing social and political strife. Price increases had been high since the late 1960s, but wage increases were set considerably above the inflation rate in the hope of achieving industrial peace (Table 8.1 and Figure 8.1), but to no avail. Successive governments devoted their time and energy to the political transition and consequently valuable time was lost in designing and implementing the necessary measures of stabilization and reform.

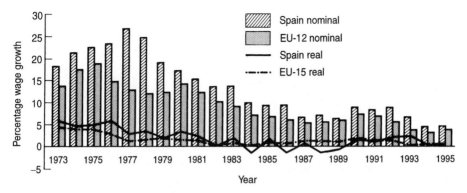

Figure 8.1. Nominal and real-wage growth, Spain and EU-12.
Source: *European Economy* (1995) **60**: Tables 31 and 32.

During this period, the structure of production underwent considerable disloca-tion. The heavy dependence on oil for energy sharpened the industrial crisis. Many companies went into liquidation, and tens of thousands of jobs were lost in spite of the laws that were designed to protect them. Employment growth turned negative (see Table 8.1). The country's traditional sources of comparative advantage – low labour costs and high rates of capital investment – deteriorated. High inflation and current account deficit added to the worrying state of the Spanish economy during the difficult period of political transition.

In 1977, the first democratic government (centre-right) implemented a stabiliza-tion plan that included a devaluation of the peseta by 20% and a tight monetary policy. The plan also included another programme aimed at reforming, liberalizing and deregulating the economy, namely, fiscal reform, deregulation of the financial system, and liberalization of markets for goods and services (but only partially for labour). One of the keystones of this programme was a set of political agreements – the so-called *Acuerdos de La Moncloa* – by which all the parties with seats in Parliament accepted the government's measures. The trade unions and employers' organizations, legalized only a few months earlier, also gave their support, and the rate of growth of wages moderated.

The harshness of the stabilization programme was compounded by the second oil shock (1979). The growth rate of real GDP fell to an average of 1% in 1978–84, unemployment increased sharply, and inflation and wage costs moderated (see Table 8.1 and Figures 8.1 and 8.2). In October 1982, a new (socialist) government with a comfortable majority in Parliament was able to give added momentum to the stabilization and reform measures. A recovery process was under way.

As for labour market developments, the Spanish economy lost 2.25 million jobs (more than 17% of total employment in 1974) between 1974 and 1985. This situa-tion marked a significant departure from the rest of Europe: employment in Community countries as a whole was stable but falling by 1.8% a year in Spain (see Table 8.1). By 1985 unemployment had risen to 21.5% of the economically active population (see Table 8.2).

Empirical studies of the fall in employment during this period point to four causes.[1] First, until well into the 1970s, high real wage growth was encouraged by the authorities in an attempt to 'buy' social content. Thus, illegal trade unions which operated within the official union structure were able to press for wage rises well

194   *Antonio Argandoña*

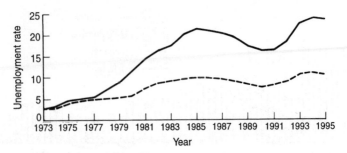

Figure 8.2. Unemployment rate, Spain and EU-12.
Unbroken line=Spain; dotted line=EU-12. Source: *European Economy* (1995) **60**: Table 3.

Table 8.2. Overview of employment and unemployment

	1976	1985	1995
Employed (as % of total)			
Women	29.7	31.7	34.4
Men	70.3	68.3	65.6
16–24	20.9	14.9	12.9
25–54	61.7	68.2	74.5
> 55	17.4	16.9	12.6
Illiterate/without schooling	17.1	13.5	7.6
Primary	63.2	49.9	30.0
Secondary	14.3	27.0	48.3
University	5.4	9.6	14.1
Wage-earners, private sector			
+ self-employed	90.6	83.0	82.5
public sector	9.4	17.0	17.5
Unemployed (rates of unemployment as % of economically active population)			
Total	4.7	21.5	22.9
16–19	13.7	54.9	50.6
20–24	8.2	42.5	39.8
25–54	3.3	15.7	20.0
> 55	1.7	8.0	11.4
Women	5.5	27.6	30.6
Men	4.4	18.5	18.2
Duration (as % of total)			
> 2 years	4.2	45.5	34.9
> 1 year	17.5	64.9	56.5
in search of first job	38.4	41.5	22.7

Source: Ministerio de Trabajo y Seguridad Social, *Encuesta de Poblacion Activa*, various issues.

above the growth of productivity. Second, increased social security contributions raised labour costs. (Contributions per employee rose from 8% of GDP in 1970 to 12% in 1986.) Third, aggregate demand fell because of the recession that followed the two oil shocks and the stabilization policies. Furthermore, investment fell for a variety of reasons, some of them related to the functioning of the labour market. Companies confronted rising wages, energy and capital costs but were unable to offload redundant labour easily, due to employment protection laws.

The growth of unemployment also reflected a fall in the number of jobs (see Table 8.3), even though the total population grew faster than in the Community as a whole. At the same time, the activity rate increased as a result of the large influx of women to the labour market. The reversal of migratory flows to the rest of Europe also modestly contributed to this increase in unemployment.

The boom, 1985–90   After 1985 the Spanish economy returned to a high growth rate. As Table 8.1 shows, employment increased at a rate of no less than 2.3% per year over the period 1985–90, and wage increases continued to moderate. Moreover, gross foreign investment flows averaged 3.0% of GDP over the period 1986–91.

The labour market reacted strongly to the recovery. Between 1985 and 1990, 1.75 million jobs were created. Unemployment only fell by 550 000, however, as employment growth was offset by an increase in the economically active population (Tables 8.2 and 8.3).

The increase in employment benefited women and young workers in particular, thanks to the increase in temporary contracts (see below). From 1985 to 1991 women's employment grew at an annual rate of 5% (as compared to 2.1% for men), and employment for those under 25 grew at an annual rate of 5.3% (2.6% in the case of those older than 25). This period was also marked by a change in the composition of the demand for labour (affecting both geographical location and skills) without this being fully matched by a change in supply, because of rigidities in vocational training and low incentives to migration.

The 1990s: recession and recovery   Beginning in 1988, the inflation rate and the external deficit worsened again amid union unrest. The implementation of restrictive monetary measures in July 1989 (immediately after the entry of the peseta in the exchange rate mechanism of the European Monetary System), the international recession, and the uncertainties created by the Gulf War signalled the end of the boom. Employment declined (−1.6% p.a. in 1990–93 as shown in Table 8.1), as did the active population, and unemployment increased.

The economy bottomed out in the second quarter of 1993 and returned to positive growth rates in 1994. Employment started to show a strong recovery in 1995 (growing at an approximate rate of 2.5%), thanks, to a large extent, to the reform of the labour market in 1994 (see below), while the macroeconomic imbalances were slowly corrected.

The structural imbalances of the Spanish labour market   The picture we have painted here broadly corresponds with that of the other Community member states, but the symptoms are more intense in Spain. In particular, unemployment rates have been anomalously high in Spain, and have responded only partially to economic growth (unemployment stood at 15.9% at the height of the boom, 1991–II, and reached a maximum of 24.6% in 1994–I).[2] The existence of a significant underground economy does not make these figures any less serious. According to a

Table 8.3. Population, employment and unemployment in Spain (end of period values, in millions)

Years[a]	Total Population	Active Population	Unemployed	Employed Total	Employed Agriculture	Employed Industry	Employed Construction	Employed Services
1974	34.5	13.5	0.35	13.1	3.1	3.6	1.3	5.1
1985	38.5	13.8	3.0	10.9	2.0	2.7	0.8	5.4
1995	39.6	15.6	3.6	12.0	1.1	2.5	1.1	7.3

Sources: National Institute of Statistics, various issues
Ministerio de Trabajo y Seguridad Social, various issues.
Note:
[a] According to the main stages of the Spanish economy.

detailed study for 1985, unemployment is only reduced by slightly more than 3.5 points when recipients of unemployment benefits working in the underground economy are deducted (see Muro *et al.*, 1986). The structural component of the unemployment rate therefore seems to be very high.[3]

Between 1985 and 1993, jobs were created only when the GDP grew at rates above 2.6%, but after the 1994 reform the growth-elasticity of employment seems to have increased considerably (but see Jimeno, 1996, for a contrary opinion). The cyclical creation and destruction of jobs within the economy as a whole must be contrasted with the steady growth of the employment in the civil service and state-owned companies, namely, from 11.8% of the employed workforce in 1978 to 17.2% in 1995–IV. Compared with other industrialized countries, the activity rate is low in Spain (49.1% of the population of working age in 1995–IV), mainly because of a low but steadily increasing rate of female labour force participation (36.5% in 1995–IV).

Long-term unemployment has been very high in Spain (see Table 8.2). Among other factors, this is caused by: generous unemployment benefits (see below); the underground economy which provides a source of informal support to the unemployed; financial support provided by the unemployed person's family (less than 25% of unemployed are the primary family breadwinners); feedback effects whereby long-term unemployment causes a loss of human capital and motivation on the part of the unemployed; and lack of labour mobility. Under this last heading, rent controls have a part to play: such controls have been in force since the 1940s, so that rented homes in Spain are scarce (18.4% in 1990), in spite of partial liberalizations in 1985 and 1994.

Wages and Collective Bargaining

Trade unions, employers' associations and collective bargaining In Spain, workers have the right to elect worker representatives, the number elected depending on firm size.[4] In firms employing more than 50 workers, worker representatives form a works council which can bargain and even call strikes. Elections for works councils take place every four years, and are organized by unions, whose members have become increasingly dominant on the councils: in the 1990 elections, only 3% of representatives were not union members (Milner and Metcalf, 1994: 58). The 'most representative' unions as determined in works council elections (see below) are permitted to negotiate legally binding sectoral wage agreements. The system of worker representative elections thus ensures a union presence on works councils, so firms cannot choose not to recognize unions.

There are two big unions, *Unión General de Trabajadores* (UGT, General Union of Workers, and *Comisiones Obreras* (CCOO Worker Commissions), plus several small unions, national or regional in scope, and a number of professional unions. The rights to organize and strike are recognized by the Constitution, the Workers' Statute Act of 1980 and the Unions' Freedom Act of 1985. A special status in collective bargaining, negotiations with the government and representation in official institutions is given to the 'most representative unions'. Such unions must have more than 10% of the total number of representatives at the national level, or 15% at the regional level. Only UGT and CCOO have this status at the national level, and they act like a duopoly with collusion. (Indeed, they have reached an agreement on the mutual distribution of representatives and public funds.)

The Worker Commissions (CCOO) had historical ties with the Communist Party, and UGT with the Socialist Party. Both have problems of organization, bureaucracy, insufficient internal democracy, high debts, scandals in the administration of their assets, and so on. Membership is very low – around 10–12% of the economically active population in 1992 (Prieto, 1993), down from 27% in 1977. Trade union incomes come partly from the state's budget, and from participation in the funds of the National Institute for Employment (INEM) devoted to training, as well as from the union dues.

Nevertheless, the Spanish trade unions are politically strong, because of their role as interlocutors of the government, the privileges granted to the 'most representative unions', and the possibility of extending to all the workers of a company or industry the agreements signed by one union (Milner and Nombela, 1995).

The main employers' association, *Confederación Española de Organizaciones Empresariales* (CEOE, Spanish Confederation of Business Organizations), conducts industry-wide collective bargaining on behalf of its members, and provides services of legal and economic advice, information, research, management training, and so on. In 1987 it claimed to represent 1 350 000 companies, employing 95% of the workforce (Pardo and Fernández, 1993). Nevertheless, it should be remembered that small and medium-sized companies are under-represented in the governing bodies of the CEOE, because of its centralized organization and its relatively high fees.

Collective bargaining in Spain is relatively centralized (García-Perea and Gómez, 1993; Milner and Metcalf, 1994). The coverage rate is high, with 68–75% of workers covered by collective bargaining agreements. Less than 15% of workers are covered by company collective agreements; the rest are mainly included in industry-wide agreements (though most of these agreements are negotiated separately for each province). In any case, until the 1994 reform, unless special permission was obtained, company agreements had to observe as a minimum the conditions stipulated at industry level. It is sometimes argued that a highly centralized negotiating system, similar to that in force in the Nordic countries, is better suited to take into account the aggregate effects of wage increases on inflation and competitiveness, at the cost of disregarding the specific needs of each sector and individual companies. The Spanish system, halfway between the two, might be said to suffer from the disadvantages of both (Jimeno, 1992), although there seems to be increasing informal bargaining at the company level (Calvera and Gómez, 1994).

In Spain questions relating to work organization and job demarcation have been regulated by the labour ordinances (*Ordenanzas Labourales*). These date back to 1960s, when jobs were classified so as to limit what workers could be ordered to do: industries had three to seven categories in general, though some had as many as 100. These categories have been outside the remit of collective bargaining, and are obviously important because they are a source of job demarcations, and limit functional flexibility. One aim of the 1994 reform was to reduce the importance of these labour ordinances by permitting collective agreements to negotiate new job classifications (though this does not seem to have happened to a great extent – see Milner *et al.*, 1995: 16, 39; Jimeno, 1996).

Wages: determinants and structure   Legal minimum wages are established every year by the government, but they are so low as to have little effect. In 1995 the minimum wage for workers aged 18 or older was only around 33% of the gross average wage of a blue-collar worker. Nevertheless, collectively agreed wage rates are higher than the legal minimum, and their extension to third parties is likely to have negative effects on employment.

There are small interregional and inter-sectoral wage differentials. Wage dispersion narrowed during the 1970s, but has widened slightly since 1985. In general, wage changes in Spain respond poorly to the state of the labour market and appear to be mainly influenced by insider power, that is, by skilled workers with indefinite employment contracts, who form the bulk of the union membership (see Andrés and García, 1993; De Lamo and Dolado, 1993; Bentolila and Dolado, 1994). Generous unemployment benefits (see below) also reduce wage sensitivity to market conditions.

8.3. Spanish Labour Legislation

The Legacy of Franco

The labour system established at the end of the Civil War (1936–39) had the following characteristics (García-Perea and Gómez, 1993; Malo de Molina, 1983; Milner *et al.*, 1995):

(1) Priority was given to public order: the rights to association, strike, demonstration, etc. were abolished or limited.
(2) The state extensively intervened in the labour market: job classification, dismissals, transfers, etc.
(3) Workers and employers were compulsory affiliated in joint, centralized organizations (*sindicatos verticales*) inserted into the political machine and controlled by the government.
(4) Wages were settled centrally, first, by the government and, since 1958, by means of collective bargaining inside the official unions and under government control. A system of compulsory arbitration was established to minimize conflicts in case of disagreement.
(5) Indefinite contracts were the rule, with few exceptions. Layoffs, both individual and collective were submitted to a long process for administrative approval, and high severance payments were required.

Surprisingly, the labour market was rather flexible in practice, because the employers were able to reduce labour costs in recessions by making good use of overtime, and the irregular economy. This is one of the reasons for the model performing rather well during the 1960s (see Table 8.1). The growth of real wages was such as to allow companies to have substantial profits, to have the incentive to invest and to innovate, and to permit workers to improve their standard of living.

The model evolved with the passage of time. New 'illegal' trade unions penetrated into the official unions, making the most of a number of free elections of representatives. They claimed higher wages, and added their voice to the clamour for political freedoms. The workers, hurt by the high inflation of the late 1960s, were also dissatisfied. And many businessmen wished for a more open and deregulated economy and labour market. The regime's answer was a timid liberalization in 1973 in the realms of collective bargaining, collective dismissals and temporary contracts.

After General Franco's death in November 1975, the labour system collapsed in the middle of recession, high inflation, and an explosion of wage claims. The labour market rigidities were exacerbated when the unions resisted the collective dismissals

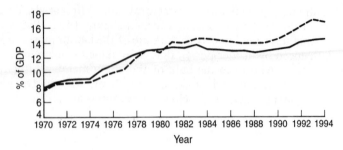

Figure 8.3.   Social security contributions and benefits.
Unbroken line=contributions; dotted line=benefits. Source: INE, *Contabilidad Nacional de España*, various issues.

that the recession made necessary, seeking instead a reduction in overtime, an increase in the fixed component of wages, and across-the-board wage increases to equalize income. At this point, the full burden of the rigid institutions of the labour market was perceived. The unemployment benefit regime was also adapted in a generous and expensive way in 1976, and was covered by increasing social security contributions as shown in Figure 8.3.

The Democratic Reforms, 1977–95

This was the situation in the summer of 1977 when the first democratic government took office. Unions and employers' associations were legalized and free collective bargaining was established. A stabilization and reform plan was put forward, and endorsed by all the political parties represented in the Parliament: the *La Moncloa* Agreements of October 1977. The main aspect of the wage agreement was full indexation of wages on the basis of expected (rather than actual) inflation.

A major task facing the new regime was to adapt the legal and institutional framework to the new Constitution approved in 1978. This was a formidable task in itself since vested interests had been created that were difficult to break. The trade unions, for example, wished to retain all the 'social conquests' from the previous regime (indefinite contracts, job stability) plus the new ones granted with the advent of democracy (increased social benefits and union rights).

The point of reference used in the process of reforming the Spanish labour system was Europe because it was the model of democracy and market economy that Spain had closest at hand and, above all, because it was the country's long-standing wish to join the European Community. The result was a system of labour law that closely matched that of the Community, but which retained a number of specifically national features from the previous regime.

The centre-piece of the new democracy's legislation was the Workers' Statute Act of 1980. This Act attempted to homogenize working conditions in different industries, and extended the effectiveness of collective agreements to the whole sector or industry. However, it left issues such as job organization to the old Labour Ordinances. The inability of the government to withstand the pressures of the unions, and build the new labour legislation on a more democratic basis – relying on freedom of contract – meant a new loss of flexibility in the labour market, only partially corrected by the new varieties of contracts (see below).

During the 1980s, a number of major changes were made to labour legislation (see Gómez and de la Calle, 1995), particularly the increased use of temporary employment contracts, mentioned previously (1984). However, the most important changes took place in 1994 (see below). These reforms went ahead after lengthy negotiations between the government, the employers and the trade unions, and in spite of the general strike called by the unions in January 1994.

The Policy of Social Dialogue

Following the onset of the democracy in 1977, industrial relations have centred on free collective bargaining. Nevertheless, governments have sought to establish some kind of corporatist 'global agreement' with the unions and the employers' associations so as to help prevent future social conflicts. This dialogue has had the aim of reaching agreements that would enhance the credibility and legitimacy of the measures taken by the government.

Five global agreements were signed between 1977 and 1984. The global agreements were set as a part of a 'strategy against inflation' based on wage growth moderation. Growth rates of wages negotiated between the employers' association and the unions were meant to be based on the expected inflation rate put forward by the government. In fact, the agreements seem to have made a positive contribution to curbing inflationary expectations, and to the recovery of business profits, hastening the end of the recession. But such wage growth moderation as was attained came about to some extent by means of market segmentation between insiders (usually adults with indefinite contracts) and outsiders (young workers and women, with temporary contracts). Wage moderation fell mainly on the latter.

The social dialogue failed during the economic bonanza period 1985–90. The unions demanded a more redistributive policy, but the government attempted to resist both wage increases (as an anti-inflationary strategy) and social expenditure (to balance the budget). The conflict led to the general strike of 14 December 1988, the outcome of which was a victory for the unions. The government met the main points of their demands, the immediate result being an increase in social security benefits (see Figure 8.3). Subsequently, an attempt was made to restore social dialogue on several occasions, particularly when the Spanish economy entered the recession, but without positive results.

Types of Contract and Termination Costs

Indefinite *vs* temporary contracts   The long recession that began in 1974 demonstrated the rigidities caused by labour contracts of indefinite duration, and restricted and expensive dismissals. Legislative changes since then have sought to increase the range of permitted contracts, thereby lowering termination costs. But there have been reversals and interruptions.

The Workers' Statute Act of 1980 confirmed the preferential role of the indefinite contracts, although it recognized the function of the temporary contracts, and extended their range. The Act 32/1984 extended the varieties of contracts permitted to promote the employment of specific groups (women, people over 45, young workers, etc.) or to promote employment creation, either by reducing termination costs or by granting financial advantages. In fact, in 1994 there were around 18 different legal categories of labour contract in Spain.

As Table 8.4 shows, temporary contracts have ended up systematically replacing indefinite contracts. At present, 35% of the country's workforce is governed by temporary contracts, compared with a Community average of 10%. The part-time proportion is low however – only 12% of the female workforce were part-time in 1992, compared to the Community average of 30% – but it has grown rapidly since 1992.

The rapid expansion in the number of temporary contracts has benefited particularly those population groups that were hit hardest by unemployment, namely, young people, women, and unskilled personnel. Equally, it has increased worker turnover. Thus, in 1994 new recruits were 51% of the workforce, compared to only 26% in 1985 (see Bentolila *et al.*, 1992; Bentolila and Saint-Paul, 1992; Bentolila and Dolado, 1993). Evidence on the effects of temporary contracts on productivity is not conclusive (see Alba, 1991; Hernando and Vallés, 1992; Jimeno and Toharia, 1992a, b).

The extensive use of temporary contracts has intensified the segmentation of the labour market which is already pronounced in Spain. In the short-term, the market power of permanent workers may have been increased due to the buffer provided by temporary workers. However, with employers stepping up the elimination of permanent jobs, and replacing them with temporary contracts, this may in future weaken the power of the insiders (see Draper, 1993).

The reform undertaken in 1994 introduced major changes in the types of contract. The temporary contract 'for job creation' disappeared and was replaced by new types of contract. Thus, a new apprenticeship contract was introduced for unskilled workers younger than 25. It has a duration of 6 months to 3 years, 15% of the working week is to be devoted to formal training, the wage is lower than the minimum wage, and there are to be low contributions to social security. New contracts have also been established for young workers, with wages lower than those approved in collective bargaining for the first 2 years.

In addition, some of the restrictions on part-time contracts have been relaxed; in particular, the limit to two-thirds of the maximum hours of work in a day. Thus, while only about 8.6% of the contracts registered in 1991 were part-time, they had risen to 16.7% of the total registered in the first 10 months of 1995.

Termination costs   The main policy alternative to the free use of temporary contracts is a reduction in termination costs. In Spain, however, termination of indefinite contracts has been minutely regulated.

Individual dismissal is restricted to disciplinary or 'objective' causes such as the incompetence of the worker. The legal severance payment for a 'fair' dismissal is 20 days of wage per year of seniority, with a maximum of 12 months of wage; for an 'unfair' dismissal the required payment is 45 days wages per year of seniority, with a maximum of 42 months. As objective causes are usually difficult to prove in litigation, employers generally resort to an 'unfair dismissal', and negotiate a generous severance payment with the employee concerned. Sanromá (1993) estimates that the mean severance payment was equivalent to 8–10 months salary, a cost which is considered to be less than that of Italy, Belgium, France and Germany but greater than that of Denmark, Holland and the UK. Severance payments in large companies in particular (more than 200 employees) have been considerable: in 1992 payments were about 43 months salary in the case of voluntary redundancies or collective layoffs.

Prior to the 1994 reform, collective layoffs were permitted only for technological

Table 8.4. Types of labour contracts (millions of contracts signed per year)

Year	Total contracts (a)	Total indefinite (b)	Total temporary (c)	Related to employment promotion				Ordinary		
				Total (d)	Indefinite (e)	Part-time (f)	Temporary (g)	Total (h)	Indefinite (i)	Temporary (j)
1986	3.4	0.1	3.1	1.4	0.1	0.2	1.1	2.0	0	2.0
1990	5.5	0.2	4.9	2.3	0	0.4	1.9	3.2	0.2	3.0
1995	7.3	0.2	5.9	1.7	0	1.2	0.5	5.6	0.2	5.4

Source: INEM, *Estadísticas de Empleo*, various issues.

Notes:
Total contracts: (a)=(b)+(c)+(f)=(d)+(h).
Total indefinite: (b)=(e)+(i).
Total temporary: (c)=(g)+(j).
Related to employment promotion – a variety of contracts devoted to the promotion of employment, with or without economic incentives:
   Total: (d)=(e)+(f)+(g).
   Temporary (g): temporary for workers older than 64, in training, etc.
   Ordinary: total (h)=(i)+(j).

or economic reasons (which labour courts had established as three years of losses) or for acts of God. The employer had to negotiate the layoff with the representatives of the workers, and also obtain official authorization. The consent of the workers' representatives was a prerequisite for securing a positive solution, but increased the cost of the layoff. The legal severance payment was the minimum referred to above for individual 'fair' dismissals, unless a higher payment had been agreed on. These requirements are more restrictive than those stipulated in the EC Directives 75/129/EEC and 92/56/EEC, which simply require consultation with the workers' representatives and notification to the authorities.

In the 1994 reform, administrative authorization for collective dismissals has been retained. However, the legally acceptable causes for a collective dismissal have been expanded to include production and organization causes; this reduces severance payments, but not necessarily legal costs. Several types of 'collective' dismissal are turned into 'individual' dismissal, especially in small and medium-sized companies – without administrative permission being required, and with lower severance payments. A study carried out by the Ministry of Finance on the application of the 1994 reform suggests that severance costs for individual dismissals have fallen (*El País*, 1995).

The Extension of the Welfare State

The system of social security was rearranged in the 1940s and 1950s, as a 'safety net' for workers and their families, including medical protection and a variety of pensions and benefits for sickness, industrial accidents, invalidity and retirement. Its financing through the contributions paid by employers and employees in a pay-as-you-go system was stable in the years of high growth of population and wages, so that the benefits improved in the 1960s. Protection for the unemployed was intended to be based on indefinite contracts and high severance payments, without a specific unemployment insurance.

But in the 1970s it became necessary to widen the social security net in response to the serious situation created by the recession. This in turn led to a marked increase in social expenditure (to cover unemployment benefits, early retirements, and pre-retirements in sectors undergoing industrial restructuring). And when economic recovery came, it seemed reasonable to increase retirement pensions, and extend the benefits to new population groups that had hitherto not paid contributions to the social security. Thus, social transfers increased from 9.3% of the GDP in 1975 to 16.7% in 1994 (see Figure 8.3). As a result, Spain now possesses a system of social security comparable to that of other advanced countries.

With the Unemployment Protection Act of 1984, the Spanish unemployment protection system became one of the most generous in the Community (Martín and Martí, 1994). It had a long duration of benefits (24 months since 1984) and the replacement rate (80% in the first 6 months, 70% in the next 6 months, and 60% in the second year) was comparable to that of the Netherlands and only less than that of Denmark (90%). Furthermore, unemployment payments were not taxable. There was also the Rural Employment Plan (*Plan de Empleo Rural*), a generous subsidy for people in regions with high seasonal rural unemployment (Andalusia and Extremadura).

There were reforms in 1992 and 1993, for example requiring contributions for at least 12 months over 6 years (instead of 6 months over 4 years), and making benefits taxable. But there are no effective measures to withdraw benefits from those unemployed workers who turn down job offers or training schemes. However, these measures have had the effect of reducing the percentage of protected unemployed workers to less than 50% in 1995, down from 67% in 1993.

Another weakness of the system is that the percentage of social security contributions paid by employers and employees is high compared with other Community countries. In 1991 social security contributions paid by the Spanish employers accounted for 8.8% of the GDP, a percentage second only to France (12.0%), Belgium (9.8%) and Italy (9.2%) (Confederación Española de Organizaciones Empresariales, 1993). Admittedly, the Spanish literature on the effects of social contributions on job creation or destruction is not conclusive (see Zabalza, 1987; Escobedo, 1992), but it seems logical that since payroll taxes are a direct tax on labour they will impede job creation.[5]

Other Institutional and Regulatory Issues

(1) *Job placement.* Before 1994, there was an obligation to contract only unemployed people registered at the National Institute of Employment (INEM), in spite of its clear ineffectiveness as an employment agency. Now private placement agencies have been authorized – but they must be non-profit-making.

(2) *Occupational mobility.* The organization of labour into rigid job categories by the Labour Ordinances (see above) is in the process of being abolished, and more flexible job categories will be implemented by collective bargaining.

(3) *Geographical mobility.* Government authorization was required for within company transfers of more than one year of duration. Moves of shorter duration were also complex and slow. In 1994 permitted reasons for company transfers were broadened, and the requirement for administrative permission eliminated.

(4) *Working hours, vacations and overtime.* The Workers' Statute Act of 1980, as amended, limited working hours (40 per week, with a maximum of 9 in a day, and no more than 80 hours overtime per year) and rest time (12 hours per period of 24 hours, and one uninterrupted day and a half each week). For full-time workers, the average Spanish working week (40.7 hours) was in fact one of the shortest in the European Community (Sanromá, 1993). Since 1994, working time will be computed annually, so it can be distributed freely through the year. The overtime premium and night shift rates is to be set by collective agreement, but the maximum of 80 overtime hours per year is retained.

(5) *Changes in working conditions.* The employer can modify the conditions of work (e.g. the working day, timetable, shift regime, and systems of remuneration and performance) only for proven reasons related to productive, technical or organizational causes – and, since the 1994 reform, also for economic reasons.

(6) *Subcontracting.* Temporary employment agencies that hire employees to other companies were approved in 1994.

8.4. The European Social Charter (ESC): A Spanish Viewpoint

The Foreseeable Impact of the ESC

Having explained the structure and problems of the Spanish employment system, we are now in a position to analyse the foreseeable effects of the application of the ESC to Spain.

(1) *Freedom of movement.* The ESC seeks to guarantee freedom of movement and a common measure of protection to workers in the member states of the Community, while at the same time preventing 'social dumping' (e.g. in public contracts). Spain would seem to be a net beneficiary of legislation on freedom of movement, in its capacity as a potential exporter of workers to other Community member states, but any input from this source must be limited because current emigration figures are very low and are not expected to increase in the future.

(2) *Employment and remuneration.* This package of measures is aimed at achieving a 'decent' standard of living for workers, and preventing 'distortions in competition' and 'social dumping' as a result of the 'improper' use of temporary and part-time contracts ('atypical' workers). In fact, Spain already complies with ESC policy on minimum remuneration.

As regards temporary and part-time contracts, we have already pointed out that they have made a contribution to job creation in Spain. They have certain flaws, which need correcting, but not along the lines proposed in the ESC, particularly considering the nature of the sectors that use these contracts more extensively, namely, tourism, agriculture, and construction.

(3) *Improvements in living and working conditions.* The ESC seeks to harmonize living and working conditions at a high level. Collective agreements and legislation (Acts 4/1983 and 11/1994) already correspond with Community provisions, often with greater restrictions. Spanish legislation is also in line with that of the Community with regard to layoffs for economic or technical reasons.

(4) *Social protection.* The ESC includes workers' rights to social protection in employment, unemployment and other circumstances. As noted above, Spanish legislation is already generous. This has been achieved at no small cost (and overprotection of the unemployed). The application of the ESC will not, then, help the Spanish laws to become more flexible.

(5) *Freedom of association and collective bargaining.* This refers to the right to union membership and collective bargaining (including the right to strike). All of this is included in Spanish legislation – and we have already pointed out its weaknesses.

(6) *Vocational training.* The aim of this article of the ESC is to generalize across Europe the right to ongoing vocational training. Effectiveness of vocational training is not a strength of the Spanish labour market, probably because schooling is insufficient and disconnected from job requirements, and retraining unemployed people has been insufficiently focused and made subject to non-economic criteria. Perhaps the ESC will help here.

(7) *Equal treatment for men and women.* The measures provided for in these articles (leave to care for children, protection and safety of pregnant women at the workplace, and so on) have already been introduced in Spain: maternity leave is 16 weeks (Act 3/1989) compared with the minimum of 14 weeks stipulated by the Community directive. A strict application of the ESC could aggravate the employment situation of unemployed women.

(8) *Information, consultation and participation.* The ESC aims to promote increased levels of worker information, consultation and participation in companies, as a means of improving the working atmosphere, increasing efficiency and reducing strife. These rights are already mentioned in the Spanish Constitution, although they have not been significantly developed in legislation. The information given currently by companies is limited, and the trade unions have not made information provision one of their priority claims.

(9) *Health, protection and safety at the workplace.* The ESC aims to harmonize workplace health and safety laws. In Spain, legislation on such matters lagged Community law until Act 31/1995 for the Prevention of Occupational Hazards. However, Act 31/1995 could lead to an increase in costs (for example, creation of Health and Safety Committees) in particular for small and medium-sized companies.

(10) *Protection of children and adolescents.* The Community directives on work of children and adolescents have already been embodied in the Spanish legislation.

(11) *Elderly persons.* The aim is that all workers, and indeed all citizens, have sufficient means to maintain a suitable standard of living at the end of their working life. This objective is already adequately fulfilled in Spain through contributory pensions and the health care provided by Social Security, as well as by non-contributory pensions and medical assistance (Act 26/1990, of 20 December). Although the level of pensions seems to be low in comparison with other advanced economies, one should take into account the lower income levels in Spain and the advisability of implementing these benefits gradually.

(12) *Disabled people.* The ESC encourages their professional and social integration. This issue is already fully developed in Spanish legislation, though there is still much to do in the area of implementation.

The Attitude of Government, Unions, Employers and the Commission

Having analysed the general lines of application of the ESC to Spain, we next consider the attitude of the various social agents to the alignment of the Spanish legal and institutional framework with that of the Community. At the risk of oversimplifying, the following paragraphs summarize the positions of the parties.

The Spanish government has emphasized its commitment to bringing Spanish legislation into line with Community legislation. It seems to have accepted as inevitable that implementation of the ESC in Spain would increase production costs, relying on the modernization of the economy and the generosity of the European Structural Funds to provide the foundations for restoring competitiveness to the Spanish economy. Moreover, the government pushed hard for the Cohesion Funds, approved as part of the Maastricht Treaty. The principle of subsidiarity is not one on which the government wishes to be adamant. However, the Spanish government is now in a difficult political position due to the high rate of unemployment and the high public deficit.

The trade unions wish above all to keep their power and independence and retain the social gains already achieved, such as indefinite contracts, minimum wages, high severance payments, and legal reduction of overtime. For them, the application of the ESC in Spain would allow maximum benefits, without entailing any loss of specific Spanish privileges. The unions are not worried about the transfer of labour policy decision-making to the Community insofar as this enables the standard of living of Northern European workers to be imported (to those remaining in employment). Nor are they perturbed by the possible effects on Spanish competitiveness or unemployment.

For employers the EU legislation is an opportunity to abolish certain pro-union regulations, where Spanish standards are tougher than the Community's, and to bring a considerable degree of rationality to the acts of Spanish unions. Relatedly, they are also in favour of the European social dialogue, but not of supranational industry-wide collective agreements. It should be remembered that the small and medium-sized companies – the ones that may be expected to fare worst in the ESC – are underrepresented in the governing bodies of the CEOE (see above).

The European Commission want Spain to implement the ESC guidelines so that the government will not be induced to promote 'social dumping' measures which can hurt other member states. Hence the Commission's insistence that the recently mooted deregulation of the labour market should not be carried out unilaterally by Spain. The structural funds (including the Cohesion Fund) seem to be the quid pro quo. In theory, the funds are intended to raise the income and opportunities of those countries and regions that have a below-average standard of living, or that have specific problems of unemployment and de-industrialization. In practice they appear to be more a tool to mitigate these problems while minimally impacting the standard of living and competitiveness of the rich countries.

Thus, all the actors are in agreement as regards the implementation of the ESC legislation. However, the reasons given are different in each case, which in turn raises the danger of future deadlocks.

8.5.   Conclusions

Among the present problems of the Spanish economy, the most serious are probably those related to the labour market. In particular, we would point to the high rate of unemployment and its long duration, the inability of the economy to create jobs, and the risk of progressive loss of international competitiveness.

In spite of the reforms attempted since the advent of democracy, the Spanish labour market is still mired in rigidities and inefficiencies. There are several causes of this situation. First, the labour market of the 1980s inherited many of the regulations of Franco's regime. Second, the liberalization attempted in the late 1970s and early 1980s collided with vested interests. Thus, the trade unions attempted to keep all the former 'labour conquests' while seeking to obtain new ones. The regulatory attitude of the bureaucrats and politicians, and the interventionist interpretation of the judiciary were also important, added to which we may cite the government's preference for centralized wage setting, supported by unions and employers' associations alike. Third, a number of noncompetitive factors took root in the labour market during the 1980s, as a result of the political power of the unions: segmentation of the market, low wage differentials among professions and sectors, and the *de facto* indexation of wages and salaries. Last but not least, attempts to gain some flexibility by other means, most notably the development of the underground economy, worsened the situation.

Spanish society and government are certainly now aware of the need for an extensive reform of the labour market, the goals being the attainment of flexibility and lower labour costs. This reform, although limited and insufficient, has been in process since 1994 – but it conflicts with the construction of the European Social Charter.

The conclusions of this chapter are plain. General Franco's regime first put the Spanish labour market into the straitjacket of an interventionist and corporatist legal framework, and the economic, social and political changes of the 1980s did not improve this framework. An important part of Spanish unemployment might thus be said to have an institutional origin, and structural reform is needed, beyond the steps taken in 1994, which although important are still insufficient. However, the ESC may be an obstacle to a more flexible and free labour market. The regulations imposed by the Charter reinforce Spain's current structural rigidities, and support the position of those that resist reform.

Notes

1 For a summary, see Andrés and García (1990, 1992), Bentolila and Toharia (1991), Franks (1995), Pedreño (1992) and Viñals (1992).
2 These are the figures of the *Encuesta de Población Activa* (EPA, Active Population Survey), corresponding to 3 792 800 people unemployed, versus 2 761 200 according to the register of the National Institute of Employment (INEM, *Instituto Nacional de Empleo*). The figures of the EPA are more reliable than those of the INEM, but there is a growing consensus that they are overstated. Alcaide (1995) estimates the error at about 341 000 people at the end of 1994.
3 De Lamo and Dolado (1993) estimate that the non-accelerating inflation rate of unemployment (NAIRU) is around 15% in Spain. This rate has increased by about 5 points since the 1970s and is considerably higher than that reported for other Community member states (Layard *et al.*, 1991).
4 The required number ranges from 1 in firms employing less than 30 through to 2 per thousand in firms employing over 1000 (see Milner and Nombela, 1995).
5 In 1992 the employers paid 24.0% of wages as social security taxes, plus 6.2% as unemployment insurance, 0.6% for vocational training, 0.4% for wage insurance against the risk of insolvency and 1% for industrial accidents insurance. The employees paid 4.8% for social security, 1.1% as unemployment insurance and 0.1% for vocational training (Sanromá 1993).

References

Alba, A. (1991). 'Fixed-term Employment Contracts in Spain: Labour Market Flexibility or Segmentation'. *Working Paper No. 91–29.* Universidad Carlos III de Madrid.

Alcaide, J. (1995). 'La Alta Tasa de Paro Española y sus Expectativas a Medio Plazo'. *Cuadernos de Información Económica,* Madrid: FIES, **105**: 21–28.

Andrés, J. and García, J. (1990). 'La Persistencia del Desempleo en España: Un Enfoque Agregado'. In J. Velarde, J. L. García-Delgado and A. Pedreño (eds), *La Industria Española. Recuperación, Estructura y Mercado de Trabajo.* Madrid: Economistas Libros.

Andrés, J. and García, J. (1992). 'Principales Rasgos del Mercado de Trabajo Español ante 1992'. In J. Viñals (ed.), *La Economía Española ante el Mercado Unico Europeo. Las Claves del Proceso de Integración.* Madrid: Alianza.

Andrés, J. and García, J. (1993). 'Factores Determinantes de los Salarios: Evidencia Para la Industria Española'. In J. J. Dolado, C. Martín and L. Rodríguez-Romero (eds), *La Industria y el Comportamiento de las Empresas Españolas: Ensayos en Homenaje a Gonzalo Mato.* Madrid: Alianza.

Bentolila, S. and Dolado, J. J. (1993). 'La Contratación Temporal y sus Efectos Sobre la Productividad'. *Working Paper No. 9319.* Banco de España.

Bentolila, S. and Dolado, J. J. (1994). 'Labour Flexibility and Wages: Lessons from Spain', CEMFI *Documento de Trabajo* No. 9406.

Bentolila, S. and Saint-Paul, G. (1992). 'The Macroeconomic Impact of Flexible Labour Contracts, with an Application to Spain', *European Economic Review,* **36**: 1013–47.

Bentolila, S. and Toharia, L. (eds) (1991). 'Introducción de los Compiladores', in S. Bentolila and L. Toharia (eds), *Estudios de Economía del Trabajo en España. III: El problema del Paro,* Madrid: Ministerio de Trabajo y Seguridad Social.

Bentolila, S., Segura, J. and Toharia, L. (1992). 'La Contratación Temporal en España', *Moneda y Crédito,* **193**: 225–65.

Calvera, J. L., and Gómez, S. (1994). 'Los Empresarios y los Sindicatos ante una Nueva Realidad Económica y Social'. *Working Paper DPN-29.* IESE.

Confederación Española de Organizaciones Empresariales (1993). 'La Competitividad de la Economía Española en el Horizonte de la Unión Económica y Monetaria: Propuestas del Empresariado Español', *Informes y Estudios,* **69**: 2.

De Lamo, A. R., and Dolado, J. J. (1993). 'Un Modelo del Mercado de Trabajo y la Restricción de Oferta de la Economía Española', *Investigaciones Económicas,* **17**: 87–118.

Draper, M. (1993). 'Indiciación Salarial y Empleo: un Análisis Desagregado Para el Caso Español', *Moneda y Crédito,* **197**: 129–65.

El País (1995). 'Economía Reconoce el Abaratamiento de los Despidos en las Primeras Sentencias Judiciales', 21 October.

Escobedo, M. I. (1992). *La Financiación de la Seguridad Social y sus Efectos Sobre el Empleo. Evidencia Empírica en España (1975–1983),* Madrid: Ministerio de Trabajo y Seguridad Social.

European Economy (1995). *Reports and Studies.* Luxembourg: Office for Official Publications of the European Communities.

Franks, J. R. (1995). 'Unemployment in Spain: Causes and Solutions', *Finance and Development,* **32**: 12–15.

García-Perea, P. and Gómez, R. (1993). 'Aspectos Institucionales del Mercado de Trabajo Español, en Comparación con los Países Comunitarios', Banco de España, *Boletín Económico,* September: 29–47.

Gómez, S. and de la Calle, A. (1995). 'Las Relaciones Laborales en España'. Research Paper No. 297, October. IESE.

Hernando, I. and Vallés, J. (1992). 'Productividad, Estructura de Mercado y Situación Financiera', *Working Paper No. 9227.* Banco de España.

Jimeno, J. F. (1992). 'Las Implicaciones Macroeconómicas de la Negociación Colectiva: El Caso Español', *Moneda y Crédito,* **195**: 223–281.

Jimeno, J. F. (1996). 'Los Efectos Visibles de la Reforma Laboral de 1994'. *Working Paper No. 96–09.* FEDEA.

Jimeno, J. F. and Toharia, L. (1992a). 'The Productivity Effects of Fixed Term Employment Contracts: Are Temporary Workers Less Productive than Permanent Workers?' *Working Paper No. 92–03.* FEDEA.

Jimeno, J. F. and Toharia, L. (1992b). 'Productivity and Wage Effects of Fixed-term Employment: Evidence from Spain'. *Working Paper No. 92–11.* FEDEA.

Layard, R., Nickell, S. and Jackman, R. (1991). *Unemployment.* Oxford: Oxford University Press.

Malo de Molina, J. L. (1983). '¿Rigidez o flexibilidad en el mercado de trabajo? La experiencia española durante la crisis', *Banco de España,* Estudios Económicos No. 34.

Martín, M. J. and Martí, F. (1994). 'Las Prestaciones por Desempleo en España', Banco de España, *Boletín Económico,* February: 31–43.

Milner, S. and Metcalf, D. (1994). 'Spanish Pay Setting Institutions and Performance Outcomes', *Centre for Economic Performance, Discussion Paper No. 198,* June. London School of Economics.

Milner, S. and Nombela, G. (1995). 'Trade Union Strength, Organization and Impact in Spain', *Centre for Economic Performance, Discussion Paper No. 258,* August. London School of Economics.

Milner, S., Metcalf, D. and Nombela, G. (1995). 'Employment Protection Legislation and Labour Market Outcomes in Spain', *Centre for Economic Performance, Discussion Paper No. 244,* May. London School of Economics.

Muro, J., Raymond, J. L., Toharia, L. and Uriel, E. (1986). *Condiciones de Vida y Trabajo en España,* Madrid: Ministerio de Economía y Hacienda, Secretaría General de Economía y Planificación and Centro de Investigaciones Sociológicas.

Pardo, R. and Fernández, J. (1993). 'Grupos de Intereses', in S. del Campo (ed.), *Tendencias sociales en España (1960–1990),* 2: Madrid: Fundación BBV.

Pedreño, A. (1992). 'Desempleo y Actitudes de los Agentes Económicos en el Mercado de Trabajo Español', in J. L. García-Delgado (ed.), *Economía Española, Cultura y Sociedad. Homenaje a Juan Velarde Fuertes,* 2: Madrid: EUDEMA.

Prieto, C. (1993). 'Los Sindicatos', in S. del Campo (ed.), *Tendencias sociales en España (1960–1990),* 2: Madrid: Fundación BBV.

Sanromá, E. (1993). *El Marc Laboral,* Barcelona: Generalitat de Catalunya, Quaderns de Competitivitat No. 15.

Viñals, J. (1992). 'La Economía Española ante el Mercado Unico: Las Claves del Proceso de Integración en la Comunidad Europea', in J. Viñals (ed.), *La economía española ante el Mercado Unico Europeo. Las Claves del Proceso de Integración,* Madrid: Alianza.

Zabalza, A. (1987). 'Los Efectos Económicos de las Cotizaciones a la Seguridad Social'. *Working Paper DGPL-D-87006.* Ministerio de Economía y Hacienda.

9

The European Social Charter and North American Free Trade Agreement: Perspectives from the United States

Jami Mirka and Christopher J. Ruhm

9.1. Introduction

The 'social charter' of the European Community (EC) is of interest to the United States both as a paradigm for government intervention in the operation of labour markets and as a reference for dealing with social and environmental issues in the creation of side agreements to the North American Free Trade Agreement (NAFTA). One useful analogy is to think of the social charter as a further component in developing a 'United States of Europe'. Just as individual states in the US have conflicting and complementary social policy objectives, the same is true of countries in the European Community and even more so for the countries of North America.

The EC and NAFTA are often compared as regional trading areas of similar economic and demographic size – NAFTA members had a combined GDP of $6.3 trillion in 1990 with a population of 363 million, compared to the EC's $5 trillion combined GDP and 375 million people (Lustig *et. al.*, 1992). However, the lessons that can be drawn from the social charter have to be carefully analysed before being applied to the North American Community. Despite parallels between the EC and the North American Community, there are also fundamental differences. The first important contrast is in the current levels of regional integration. The second involves the history of government intervention in social policy, with a more *laissez-faire* approach predominant in the US contrasting with greater public involvement throughout Europe.

9.2. Regional Integration in Europe and North America

Specific terminology has been created to define levels of regional integration. In order from the lowest to highest level of integration there are free trade areas, customs unions, common markets, and economic unions.[1] Different levels of economic integration give rise to different levels of social and environmental integration. It is therefore useful to discuss the levels of integration in Europe and North America, as a framework for considering the European social charter and social/environmental components to NAFTA.

The European Community is moving beyond a customs union (which eliminates internal trade barriers while creating a common trade policy with respect to the rest of the world) to a common market which requires greater integration. Not only are internal barriers to trade removed and common external policies set, but barriers to the free movement of labour and capital are eliminated as well. This creation of a single European market was a major goal of the EC. It appears that the EC is aiming to become an economic union, which requires countries to give up sovereignty in setting exchange rates and monetary and fiscal policies, as well as establishing a unified governmental body which provides a common set of public goods (Grubel, 1981). The United States is often held up as an example of an economic union of independent states.

By contrast, NAFTA falls under the category of a free trade area, the lowest level of integration. In a free trade area, internal barriers to trade are eliminated while each member maintains its own (disparate) restrictions on trade with the rest of the world. The primary focus of the North American Free Trade Agreement is the reduction and ultimate elimination of barriers to trade and investment among Canada, Mexico and the United States. The ratification of NAFTA by the US Congress was delayed because of concerns over its social and environmental impact and US support was partially dependent on the ability of the members to substantially address these issues with side agreements. Although the EC social charter was often held up as a model for these agreements, disparities in the levels of regional integration in North America and Europe, combined with differing histories and approaches toward government intervention, make these lessons less relevant than they might first appear.[2]

9.3.   Regional Integration and the Need for a Social Agenda

Regional integration almost always begins with the elimination of tariff barriers. Baldwin (1970) has likened this process to the draining of a swamp; removal of the water reveals previously hidden branches, stumps, and tires which also must be cleared. The integration process starts with eliminating the most obvious distorting barriers to trade. As these are removed, previously hidden problems appear. Each successive barrier is more difficult to deal with because its distortionary effect is less obvious.

While it is natural for nations to have different levels of social and environmental legislation, these dissimilarities can result in non-tariff barriers which are manipulated to serve a protectionist agenda. Whereas distortionary effects of tariffs and quotas are obvious, it is more difficult to sort out the protectionism imbedded in national choices for social rights, environmental protection, and health or safety regulations. Complicated health and safety standards may make it difficult for foreign producers to enter the domestic market. Regulations on environmental protection may discriminate between foreign and domestic producers, creating another barrier to trade. For example, Ontario, Canada placed a 10% tax on beer cans but not bottles. The tax was for environmental reasons, but some in the USA feels that it discriminates against foreign beer suppliers who usually use cans. In addition, the tax only applies to beer and not to other sorts of cans which would have affected Ontario producers of soups and juices. Therefore, it is necessary to weigh the costs and benefits of any actions under the environmental and social agenda and to be vigilant that they are not being used in a discriminatory manner. Social/environmental standards that are too low are viewed as an 'unfair' competitive advantage. However, standards that are too high can be construed as protectionist.

As the EC strives towards its common market goals, harmonization of social policies is a natural outgrowth. In order to have an efficient common market, all players need to participate under similar rules. Different rules among market members cloud the market mechanism. For example, the EC has been striving for complete mobility of labour among its members. Efficiency is gained as labour moves to areas where the marginal revenue product of labour is high (i.e. high wages based on high productivity). However, the labour market will be affected by the members' social policy choices. National decisions related to health care, working conditions, and unemployment benefits influence the direction of labour flows. It would be a logical outgrowth of the integration process to try to harmonize social policy so that labour flows react to market conditions rather than government policy. Conversely, it is hoped that NAFTA will stem the flow of immigration from Mexico to the USA, not encourage it. Therefore, we expect the social dimension of integration to be more important for Europe than for North America.

Since the level of integration under NAFTA is not high enough to warrant the type of harmonization present in the social charter, the social/environmental agenda attached to NAFTA is more likely to be protectionist in nature. Arguments surrounding the social agenda focus less on improving social conditions in the region than on protecting US labour from low-wage Mexican competition. The global trading environment, however, has become more tightly integrated, even in the absence of formal integration processes, due to increased globalization of corporations, improved technology and communications, and the opening of more developing nations to trade and capital flows. Therefore, social integration may become more necessary both inside and outside regional trading blocs.[3]

When speaking of the social dimension, it is not only the level of regional integration that matters but also the level of economic development among the members. As countries with vastly different levels of economic development are included, concerns over social and environmental differences mount. Nations at similar levels of development tend to have similar wage levels, health and safety standards, environmental regulations, and social safeguards. The higher a nation's standard of living, the higher its taste for safe working conditions and a clean environment. Because Mexico is at a much lower level of economic development than the other members of NAFTA, there is concern that the disparity in social and environmental regulations could have adverse effects on the economies of the USA and Canada. The same was true as the EC expanded to include Greece, Spain and Portugal and it is again becoming a concern as Western Europe contends with the newly evolving market economies of Eastern Europe. The fear is that as the region becomes integrated, differences in standards and wages will alter trade flows, with production in low-wage/low-standard Eastern European nations replacing high-wage/high-standard production in Western European countries and placing pressure on the latter to lower standards in order to remain cost competitive (Mosely, 1990). Developed nations want safeguards built into the agreement to prevent this. It is because of this relationship between integration and the social dimension that many in the USA are looking for lessons from the EC.

9.4.   The European Community and NAFTA

The issue of attaching a social dimension to NAFTA has many similarities with the EC case. The EC-92 (single market) initiative came during a time when nations were experiencing high levels of unemployment and slow economic growth. The creation of a single European market was expected to ameliorate the situation. However, the uncertainty created by the anticipated structural adjustments caused much concern. In order to obtain support for the economic program, it was necessary to present a social safety net to assuage public apprehensions and to gain support for the economic initiative (see Springer, 1992).

Likewise, the Bush administration embraced the idea of NAFTA at a time when unemployment was relatively high. NAFTA was expected to open new markets and to secure economic changes already occurring in Mexico. A stable and strong economy in Mexico would support US business interests, while providing an incentive for Mexican workers to stay at home instead of migrating to the USA. In addition, it was hoped that a united North America would prove politically important in trade negotiations under GATT. However, for many US citizens, economic integration with a low-wage country such as Mexico conjured up images of structural unemployment as US workers would find it difficult to compete with their poorly paid Mexican counterparts.[4] Even more problematic for policy makers were differences in labour costs believed to be a result of disparities in working conditions, occupational safety, and health. Since it is costly for businesses to provide good working conditions, lower requirements in Mexico combined with open international borders raised concerns that US industry would move to Mexico to avoid the cost of regulations or be unable to compete with Mexican production which had an 'unfair' cost advantage.

As the US economy continued to slump during an election year, Bush's opponents pointed to NAFTA as an example of the administration's focus on foreign affairs while ignoring the domestic economy. NAFTA was portrayed as giving away good paying US jobs to businesses in Mexico that exploit workers with low pay and poor working conditions, and that contribute to environmental degradation of the border area as well. The Clinton administration, sensing the mood of the citizens and Congress, believed that NAFTA could be ratified only if social and environmental concerns were sufficiently addressed in side agreements to the treaty. There was also pressure to provide more funds for assistance to those who became unemployed as the economy adjusted to the changes brought about by NAFTA.[5] Once again, support for the economic initiative rested upon the ability of the government to show genuine concern for the social dimension and to make efforts to address that concern. Thus, the need for public support for the integration initiatives pushed the creation of a social component to both the EC and NAFTA.

European and American supporters justify the need for a social agenda as a means for minimizing social dumping. The term dumping refers to the export of a commodity at below cost or at a lower price than the domestic price. Usually, this is a result of a government subsidization of exports. Social dumping involves implicit subsidization, whereby nations take 'unfair' advantage of substandard social regulations and the resulting cost savings to obtain a competitive advantage. (In the case of NAFTA, similar arguments have to be made for 'environmental dumping' based on differences in environmental control costs resulting from disparities in regulations.) The problems associated with social dumping are believed to be threefold. First, production will shift from high to low cost countries. Second, firms will relocate from high social and environmental cost countries to low ones. Third, high cost countries may be tempted to lower their standards to 'even the playing field'. Nations may thus begin competing for trade by using a low social/environmental cost strategy, placing trade above social and environmental concerns.

For the EC, the fear of social dumping was accentuated prior to EC-92, with the addition of Spain and Portugal to the community. When Spain and Portugal were admitted to the EC, in 1986, their per capita GNPs were 40% and 19% of West Germany's (Lustig *et al.*, 1992; see Chapter 10 for the current position). With NAFTA, it is the addition of Mexico to the preferential agreement between the US and Canada that has raised concern. Mexico's per capita GNP is only 12% of that in the USA (Lustig *et al.*, 1992). The social charter seeks to harmonize social regulations to eliminate or greatly reduce the amount of social dumping which could occur under increased integration. The side agreements to NAFTA are attempting to do the same.

However, the existence and nature of social dumping has been exaggerated. Nations at lower levels of economic development join regional trading groups in order to increase their level of development. While differences in social/environmental policies may confer an advantage in the short run, it is doubtful that these nations wish to remain low wage, high pollution havens for developed country exploitation. If social and environmental concerns are normal goods, we expect that wealthier nations will have higher standards, as well as greater ability to enforce these standards. Poorer countries often do not have the money to hire enforcement officers and it is difficult for local officials to shut down a productive company for violations of health or safety regulations when the economic viability of the area depends on that business. A developing nation may not have the resources to support industrialized country health or safety standards and requirements to do so could slow that country's development. One method of improving enforcement is to promote economic growth in less well-off countries. Growth increases the pool of resources which can be used for enforcement purposes and, as job opportunities increase, reduces the willingness of individuals to work under substandard conditions.[6]

Some economists suspect that a protectionist agenda lies behind the current charges that social dumping would be accentuated under NAFTA. Current US antidumping laws have already been under much scrutiny for being used by protectionist interests in US industries such as steel and semiconductors. The antidumping laws allow for trade restrictions to counteract dumping that is found to injure US industry. Often serious antidumping penalties (in the form of duties) are imposed on foreign rivals which force them either to leave the US market or to accept 'voluntary' export restraints. The EC can attest to the protectionist nature of US antidumping penalties regarding the steel industry.

If the USA attaches similar social dumping legislation to NAFTA, there is potential for further abuse. While current antidumping charges often result from foreign subsidies of exports, social dumping charges would have to be based on implied subsidies. For example, US glass producers might say that Mexican producers receive an implied subsidy by not having to meet costly environmental and safety regulations. Social dumping actions would require the calculation of the cost of Mexican glass production if it took place under US regulations, with the difference between that calculation and the actual cost being the implied subsidy. It is easy to see how US industries would have an incentive to use this type of legislation in a protectionist manner. Furthermore, relative costs and benefits are likely to be different in the US and Mexico, making cost comparisons somewhat arbitrary and open for manipulation.

Although social costs are a factor in competitiveness, the decisions nations make regarding the level of desired social and environmental protection are no more 'unfair' than their choice of tax or inflation rates, or their endowment of natural resources. (There are, however, problems with cross-border externalities or in cases where the government is non-democratic.) There is no such thing as a perfectly level playing field in international trade and gains from trade are based on disparities in resources, factor endowments, technology and tastes.

National choices on inflation rates, safety and the environment are usually made for reasons that have little or nothing to do with trade. Nonetheless, these decisions can effect the flows of trade between nations and be manipulated to gain a trade advantage. It is only under deliberate intention to discriminate that these choices become distortionary. These areas, because they are not obviously linked to trade, are difficult to identify and therefore avoid the scrutiny of other sorts of trade barriers. For example, in March 1993, Italy experienced an outbreak of livestock disease traced to Croatia. The EC then put a month long ban on livestock, meat, and dairy products from Eastern Europe, even though some nations reported that they had no problems. The Eastern nations felt that the sanctions were excessive and aimed at protecting EC farmers. It is difficult to separate the level of regulation needed for health and safety from that which is excessive and protectionist in nature. While it is not necessary for the EC and Eastern Europe to harmonize health and safety regulations, it may be prudent to set up procedures to deal with accusations that social and environmental regulations are being manipulated for protectionist interests.

9.5.   Differences Between Europe and North America

While the EC and NAFTA are often compared as regional trading blocs, the level of integration within each group is very different. The EC has been working on integration since the 1958 Treaty of Rome and therefore has a long history of dealing with regional issues. The origins of the social charter date back to the 1970s, with a draft of the charter presented in 1989. Even with this long-standing relationship, the social charter is a very contentious issue. By contrast, the US, Canada and Mexico do not share a history of formal integration. Although there is room for discussing the social agenda, binding side conditions to NAFTA on acceptable standards are probably out of the question. Part of the impetus for NAFTA was the desire of the US to support improved political and economic initiatives in Mexico through stronger trade ties. Efforts to impose a social and environmental agenda on Mexico may be viewed as continued US imperialism and foster resentment.

Another major difference between the social dimensions in the EC and NAFTA is that the completion of the internal market in the EC requires free movement of labour between members whereas NAFTA does not. Free labour mobility requires workers to have full information on the employment opportunities and working conditions of member nations. This information component is included in the social charter with respect to job rights and written contracts detailing the employment relationship in the areas of wages, leave, hours, length of notice, provision of the name of a body determining any collective agreement, advance notice requirements, job vacancies, and international clearing of applications. The absence of free labour mobility makes the harmonization of many types of mandated benefits (e.g. job rights, paid leave, hours restrictions, length of notice etc.) less relevant for NAFTA than for the EC. In fact, it is hoped that the resulting economic gains to Mexico will make it more palatable for Mexican workers to stay at home. As NAFTA increases the mobility of goods and capital among members, there remains a concern over social dumping and the resulting effects on US wages; however, the direct wage effects which would take place under international movements of workers under the EC have a greater impact than the indirect trade effects under NAFTA (Lustig *et. al.*, 1992).

The EC also has a long history of trying to create supra-national institutions to make, implement and enforce EC laws, while balancing members national interests. Conversely, NAFTA members are probably reluctant to relinquish much sovereignty at this stage of integration. The side agreements to NAFTA set up a trilateral committee to ensure that the members adhere to their current (though disparate) social and environmental policies. The focus is on preventing discriminatory manipulation of policy, not on harmonization as under the social charter.

Not only does the level and history of integration preclude NAFTA side agreements similar to the social charter, but so too do US attitudes towards government intervention in labour markets. Attitudes towards labour market legislation in the US are quite different from the prevailing attitudes in the rest of North America and in Europe. For example, with regard to maternity leave, Mexico provides 6 months of leave and Canada mandates 17 weeks (Pastor, 1992) in contrast to the 12 weeks required under recently passed US legislation.[7] Therefore, we next focus on differences in EC and US approaches to this type of government intervention.

9.6.   Employment Legislation in the United States and Europe

The social charter's Action Program establishes a set of common employment practices throughout the EC. Major initiatives adopted include requirements for written contracts specifying details of the employment relationship (i.e. pay, leave, work hours, severance policies), advance notice of mass layoffs, comparable worth (equal pay for work of equal value), paid pregnancy leave, minimum paid vacations, maximum work hours, and limitations on the employment of teenagers (see Chapter 2). Many of these employment mandates were prevalent, in some form, throughout part or all of Europe prior to the social charter.

By contrast, the scope of employment protection has been much less comprehensive in the United States. For example, advance notification of plant closings and mass layoffs was not federally mandated until the passage of the Worker Retraining and Notification Act (WARN) in 1988. Similarly, the Family and Medical Leave Act (FMLA), which legislates unpaid leave for the birth or adoption of a child, did not become law until 1993, and the only federal legislation limiting the right of employers to dismiss individual workers pertains to certain types of discrimination. Corresponding regulation of employers at the state level has also been limited. Only four states passed laws requiring mandatory notice prior to WARN and a small minority offered any type of job protection to new parents before the FMLA.

Relative to their European counterparts, US mandates have also been narrow in scope. Whereas US employees are required to provide 60 days' notice of mass terminations, warnings of 6 months are required in Denmark and 10 months in Greece (Lazear, 1990). Similarly, while the FMLA mandates 12 weeks of unpaid leave for the birth or adoption of a child, leaves of 6 months or more are common in many European countries and at least a portion of the leave is paid. For instance, Sweden guarantees 72 weeks of paid leave, 60 weeks of which are available to either the mother or the father (Ruhm and Teague, 1995). Although the USA has fairly strong laws barring discrimination in pay, hiring, promotions, or terminations, no comparable worth legislation has been passed at the state or national level.

Exemptions are also more pervasive in the USA. For instance, WARN excludes companies employing less than 100 workers, terminating fewer than 500 individuals and less than a third of their workforce, and plant closings resulting from unforeseeable business developments, strikes, lockouts, or because of sale of the business or consolidation within a local area. Firms are also exempt if they are actively seeking new business or if they offer the displaced workers new positions. Similarly, companies employing fewer than 50 workers are exempted from the FMLA and employers are not required to provide parental leave to the highest paid 10% of their workforce or to persons employed for the firm less than 1250 hours during the previous year.

Divergences between the USA and Europe are sufficiently dramatic to suggest that different paradigms are used to evaluate the potential costs and benefits of proposed measures. In Europe, there is relatively widespread acceptance of the need for many types of government intervention in labour markets. By contrast, such interference is viewed with suspicion and used more cautiously in the USA. With this in mind, we next consider the economic arguments for opposing and favouring mandated benefits and attempt to illustrate these positions with specific examples.

9.7. Economic Arguments Against Mandated Benefits

Economic efficiency is generally maximized by allowing working conditions to be freely negotiated between employers and employees, without restrictions like those included in the social charter. The basis of the efficiency argument is that workers and firms will agree to a specified provision only when the benefits exceed the costs of doing so. An example helps to illustrate. Assume that the expected annual cost (to employers) of providing pregnancy leave is £1000 and the expected benefit (to workers) of receiving it is £1500. Workers will then accept a £1000 reduction in pay in exchange for the leave benefit. The company will also be willing to make this exchange because it is no worse off as a result.[8]

Conversely, if the benefit of the leave were only £500, the worker would prefer to receive the extra £1000 in wages and forgo the claim on parental leave. In this situation, mandated leave would require the worker and firm to share the £500 net loss, resulting in both parties being made worse off. If the company is constrained in its ability to reduce wages (e.g. due to minimum wage laws, antidiscrimination legislation, or union wage contracts), total compensation costs (including the expense of the leave benefit) may exceed the worker's marginal product, in which case the employment will be terminated and the loss will far exceed the £500 difference between costs and benefits.

Additional distortions could result, depending on the precise design of the regulation. If fixed costs are associated with the benefit (e.g. employer-provided health insurance in the USA), firms will reduce their use of part-time workers. Conversely, if small firms or part-time workers are exempted, employment will be shifted into these positions. Such concerns are important when considering some of the more contentious issues in the social charter. For example, a regulation requiring firms to provide to part-timers the same vocational training, private pension, and social security benefits offered to full-time employees would discourage firms from hiring part-time workers and probably reduce total employment.

9.8. Economic Arguments in Favour of Mandated Benefits

There are at least two sources of market failure which may make it desirable for the government to intervene in the operation of labour markets (see Summers, 1989; Mitchell, 1990; see also Chapter 3). Broadly defined, these can be categorized as imperfect information and externalities. Information problems can easily cause market outcomes to diverge from the social optimum. For example, individuals who are unaware of their employer's use of toxic chemicals will not demand higher wages as a condition for accepting the risky working conditions. Thus, the employer will have an inadequate incentive to reduce or eliminate the risk.

Government provision of (or requirements that the company provide) the missing information is generally preferable to safety regulation. There are situations, however, where direct intervention may be required. First, it may sometimes be impossible to provide the necessary information. For instance, individuals may lack the technical expertise to understand fully the detrimental consequences of workplace exposure to toxic materials, even when they have full information. Second, some individuals may too sharply discount the costs of risky activities. Thus, government involvement may be justified in the case of youths, since this group is known to undertake risky activities which they regret later in life.

Government intercession may also be desirable when there is asymmetric information (see Chapter 3). Private health insurance provides an illustrative example. Since individuals know more about their health than the insurer, relatively healthy individuals will choose less comprehensive insurance coverage, in order to pay lower premiums. As a result, it is quite possible that individuals with severe illnesses will be unable to purchase insurance at any cost and so will lose the benefits of risk pooling (see Akerlof, 1970, for the initial research here). In this situation, welfare may be improved by placing all individuals in a common insurance pool (although the insurance need not be provided by employers).

Externalities provide a second broad reason for government intervention. An externality exists whenever 'an individual or firm can take an action that directly affects others and for which it neither pays nor receives compensation' (Stiglitz, 1993: 179). Returning to a previous example, if health care is publicly provided, firms and their workers will bear only a portion of the cost of unsafe workplaces. Thus, even when individuals possess complete information, they will be willing to accept greater employment risk than if they were responsible for the full costs of health care. Rules mandating minimum levels of workplace safety may then be welfare enhancing.

Many believe that workers have an absolute right to certain 'merit goods', whether or not they would willingly pay the costs associated with them. For example, advocates of maternity leave often state that it is necessary and desirable in order to place women on an equal footing with men in the workplace (e.g. see Trzcinski, 1991). The merit good argument may include an economic justification, to the extent that it is based on one or more of the sources of market failure discussed above. Without these, however, it represents paternalism and has no economic rationale.

Government involvement in labour markets is also often advocated on equity grounds. Since the demand for fringe benefits and favourable working conditions increases with income, wealthy individuals are likely to receive relatively high levels of nonwage compensation. Although mandated benefits can reduce this dispersion, the side effects of doing so will generally include greater earnings inequality and employment reductions for low-wage workers. Thus, total compensation may become less rather than more equal. Moreover, government policies sometimes discriminate against persons with low earnings potential. For example, in the United States, employer-provided health insurance is not taxed and some pension contributions are tax-deferred. Since highly paid workers typically receive a disproportionately large proportion of their total compensation from these sources, the tax advantages particularly benefit the wealthy. In these cases, mandated benefits may reduce inequality. However, a superior solution would be to uniformly tax all forms of compensation.

9.9.   The Social Charter and Economic Efficiency

The social charter's Action Program has primarily been defended on equity rather than efficiency grounds, without careful consideration of the possibly deleterious effects of interfering with private markets. The economic arguments which are presented typically consist of unsupported suggestions that efficiency will be increased by utilizing human potential in a 'more rational and responsible manner' (see Addison and Siebert, 1994). This section examines whether there are potential efficiency benefits associated with three types of employment mandates: advance notice of mass redundancies, maternity and parental leave policies, and restrictions on individual dismissals from jobs. These are of particular interest, given their central role in the social charter and because of recently enacted regulation in the USA.

Three Council directives pertaining to mass redundancies were passed between 1977 and 1983. The first established uniform definitions of collective redundancies, minimum notification periods, and procedures for implementing mass terminations. The second and third covered transfers of businesses and worker rights in the event of firm insolvencies (see Addison and Siebert, 1991, 1994, for more detail). In 1992, the Council reduced the number of layoffs deemed to constitute a collective redundancy to five. It is again worth emphasizing that (frequently stronger) provisions predated these directives in most European countries. Legislated maternity leave also has a long history in Europe. Germany adopted the first such law in 1878, followed by France in 1928, and Sweden and Finland in 1937 (Cook, 1989). In 1952,

however, the state courts have established an increasing number of exceptions to the employment-at-will rule and, in 1987, Montana became the first state to pass legislation requiring firms to have a 'just reason' to fire a worker.

There are several reasons why legislated limitations of individual dismissals may be desirable. First, it is inappropriate to allow firms to terminate employees when doing so violates public policy – for example, when a worker is fired for refusing to break the law. Second, Krueger (1991) has argued that firms may prefer clearly codified unjust-dismissal legislation, with limited liability, to the greater uncertainty of a common law doctrine; the latter is open to interpretation by the courts and so imposes large legal costs on all parties, as well as the risk of very high damage awards. In this context, the reduction in transaction costs associated with the legislation increases economic efficiency by more than the mandate reduces it. Third, Levine (1991) shows that asymmetric information provides a case for just-cause dismissal regulation, similar to that already discussed for family leave policies.[16]

As far as empirical evidence is concerned on the impact of dismissal regulations, Dertouzos and Karoly (1993) find that just-cause doctrines are associated with reduced employment if punitive as well as compensatory damages can be recovered but have no effect when awards are limited to the latter (see also Chapter 3). Some economists have argued that stagnant European employment growth (compared to the USA – see Chapter 10) is the result of rigid hiring and firing practices. Factors other than employment security could account for this, however, and it is necessary to explain how Japan has largely avoided an unemployment problem, despite having employment practices which are more similar to those of Europe than the United States, before assigning a causal role to the limitations on dismissal rights.

9.10.   Conclusion

Increasing economic integration has led to pressure for greater social and environmental regulation in both the European Community and the North American Free Trade Agreement. Applications of the social charter experience to NAFTA are limited, however, by differences in the level of integration, the potential for abuse by protectionists, and differences in national approaches towards the use of government mandated employment benefits. Given the low level of economic integration and lack of free labour mobility, social charter type legislation probably does not need to accompany NAFTA. While there is little doubt that Mexico has problems in the areas of the environment and social protection, the current debates focus less on improving the lives of Mexican workers and more on protecting US jobs. As tariff barriers are eliminated, previously protected industries are seeking ways to maintain the gains from protection. Social and environmental concerns are currently high on the political agenda. Given their indirect connections to trade, this makes them excellent vehicles for obtaining protection without looking protectionist. As the trading arena becomes more complicated, all members of the international community must be aware of the potential for protectionist abuse of apparently non-trade issues.

Economic analyses of social legislation, either in the EC or NAFTA context, must consider what sources of market failure (if any) they are attempting to remedy and the efficiency consequences of intervening with voluntarily negotiated agreements between employers and workers. Although efficiency arguments can sometimes be made, it is difficult to construct such rationales for many interventions adopted by the EC. Focusing on economic efficiency has the advantage of making these types of trade-offs much more explicit than they otherwise would be. We hope that future debates on the merits and costs of proposed and existing interventions will use this criteria to a greater extent than has been done in the past.

Notes

1 See Balassa (1961) for a discussion of the theory of economic integration. Robson (1984) puts the economics of international integration in the context of contemporary analysis.

2 The EC is often provided as an example for the USA to emulate. For example, Sheldon Friedman (1992) states that the US approach to NAFTA has been taken haphazardly in contrast to the careful concern for the social agenda demonstrated by the EC in order to avoid social damage. He lauds the EC for its creation of a 'social fund', its efforts to retrain and relocate workers injured by restructuring, and for establishing a framework for upward harmonization of policies.

3 Charnovitz (1992) describes how the GATT system is being challenged with respect to trade's social dimension, showing the increased linkages between trade and social issues. Butler (1992) describes the linkages between trade and environmental issues in a multilateral context.

4 In 1990, hourly compensation costs for production workers in Mexico were approximately 12% of those in the USA. By comparison, compensation costs for the EC's poorer members of Portugal, Greece and Spain were 25%, 46%, and 79% of US levels respectively (US Department of Labour, 1991).

5 Studies of the impact of NAFTA on the US labour market by Stern *et al.* (1992) concluded that job losses under NAFTA would be relatively small, in the range of one-tenth of one percent of 1989 US total employment and that there should therefore be no need for large amounts of trade adjustment assistance. Small employment impacts lend credence to the notion that opposition to the agreement is more protectionist in nature, with social and environmental concerns raised as a way to maintain a degree of protection.

6 Grossman and Krueger (1991) suggest that the economic growth for Mexico, resulting from closer economic ties with the US, would tend to improve the environmental conditions in Mexico because nations at higher levels of national income demand a cleaner environment.

7 Although Mexico has an advanced set of labour laws, resembling those in Europe, which regulate everything from union rights and severance pay to mandated employer contributions for worker housing, economic factors frequently preclude enforcement of these regulations (Shorrock, 1992; Morici, 1991).

8 The savvy firm could be made better off by offering a wage reduction of more than £1000 but less than £1500. For instance, if the decrease is £1200, the worker will be £300 better off and the firm's costs will be reduced by £200.

9 This does not imply a complete absence of state activity. For example, more than 125 bills related to plant closing were introduced in 30 states between 1975 and 1983 (Ehrenberg and Jakubson, 1988). However, only four states mandated early notice prior to the national law.

10 Employment spillovers could potentially justify restrictions on job terminations, a much stronger type of regulation than requiring advance notice.

11 Bankruptcy laws would need to be carefully written for mandatory notice requirements to overcome this problem. At a minimum, severance payments would need to be made prior to the claims of other creditors.

12 There may be other, more difficult to quantify, benefits of prenotification. For example,

early warnings could ease the psychological adjustment problems of displaced workers or allow them to find jobs with better working conditions than they otherwise would.

13 For example, Spalter-Roth and Hartmann (1990) claim that the average benefits of parental leave are six times greater than the costs, but fail to discuss why the leave is so rarely provided voluntarily, if there is such a large net gain from doing so. The Organization for Economic Co-operation and Development (1995) provides a useful recent summary of European parental leave policies, with some discussion of efficiency concerns.

14 Leave policy in the USA also covers the care of sick relatives. The same information asymmetry holds in this case.

15 This can be illustrated with an example. Assume that the half of workers are type 'A' individuals and the remainder are type 'B'. The As have a 0.8 probability of needing parental leave, the Bs a 0.2 probability. For all workers, the benefits of leave, if used, are 2 and the costs to the employer are 1. The economy-wide expected benefits are therefore equal to 1 [=(0.5)(0.8)(2)+(0.5)(0.2)(2)], while costs equal 0.5 [=(0.5)(0.8)(1)+ (0.5)(0.2)1], which implies that the benefit is socially desirable. Firms offering leave at a cost to the workers of 0.5 would only attract type A individuals, however, since the expected benefit to the Bs is 0.4 (=0.2×2), which is less than the cost. Since the expected cost of providing the benefit to type A persons is 0.8 (=0.8×1), the firm would also lose money on these individuals. The only way they could offer the leave would be to reduce wages by an amount of 0.8 or more (but less than 1.6). Thus, voluntarily provided leave would never be received by type B individuals.

16 He argues that, even when the benefits of just-cause employment policies exceed the costs, the market will lead to a suboptimal level of worker protection because any firm offering this type of employment security will attract a disproportionate share of workers who provide low effort but are difficult to terminate with cause.

References

Addison, J. T. and Siebert, W. S. (1991). 'The Social Charter of the European Community: Evolution and Controversies'. *Industrial and Labour Relations Review,* **44** (July): 597–625.

Addison, J. T. and Siebert, W. S. (1994). 'Recent Developments in Social Policy in the New European Union'. *Industrial and Labour Relations Review*, **48** (1), October: 5–28.

Akerlof, G. (1970). 'The Market for 'Lemons': Quality Uncertainty and the Market Mechanism'. *Quarterly Journal of Economics*, **84** (3), August: 488–500.

Balassa, B. (1961). *The Theory of Economic Integration*. Homewood, IL: Richard D. Irwin.

Baldwin, R. E. (1970). *Non-tariff Distortions of Trade*. Washington, DC: Brookings Institution.

Butler, A. (1992). 'Environmental Protection and Free Trade: Are They Mutually Exclusive?'. *The Federal Reserve Bank of St. Louis Review*, **74** (3), May/June: 3–16.

Charnovitz, S. (1992). 'Environmental and Labour Standards in Trade'. *The World Economy*, **15** (3), May: 335–56.

Cook, A. H. (1989). 'Public Policies to Help Dual-Earner Families Meet the Demands of the Work World'. *Industrial and Labour Relations Review*, **42** (2), January: 201–15.

Deere, D. R. and Wiggins, S. N. (1989). 'Plant Closings, Advance Notice, and Private Contractual Failure', *mimeo*. Texas: A&M University.

Dertouzos, J. N. and Karoly, L. A. (1993). 'Employment Effects of Worker Protection: Evidence from the United States'. In C. F. Buechtemann (ed.) *Employment Security and Labour Market Behavior*. Ithaca, N.Y: ILR Press, Cornell University.

Ehrenberg, R. G. and Jakubson, G. H. (1988). *Advance Notice Provisions in Plant Closing Legislation*. Kalamazoo, MI: W.E. Upjohn Institute for Employment Research.

Emerson, M. (1988). 'Regulation or Deregulation of the Labour Market: Policy Regimes for the Recruitment and Dismissal of Employees in the Industrialised Countries'. *European Economic Review*, **32** (2), April: 775–817.

Frank, M. and Lipner, R. (1988). 'History of Maternity Leave in Europe and the United States'. In E. Zigler and M. Frank (eds) *The Parental Leave Crisis: Toward a National Policy*. New Haven, CN: Yale University Press.

Friedman, S. (1992). 'NAFTA as Social Dumping'. *Challenge*, **35** (5), September/October: 27–32.

Grossman, G. M. and Krueger, A. B. (1991). 'Environmental Impacts of a North American Free Trade Agreement'. *NBER Working Paper No. 3914*. November.

Grubel, H. G. (1981). *International Economics*. Homewood, ILL: Richard D. Irwin, Inc.

Klerman, J. A. and Leibowitz, A. (1995). 'Labour Supply Effects of Maternity Leave Legislation', *mimeo*, RAND.

Krueger, A. B. (1991). 'The Evolution of Unjust-Dismissal Legislation in the United States'. *Industrial and Labour Relations Review*, **44** (4), July: 644–60.

Lazear, E. P. (1990). 'Job Security Provisions and Employment'. *Quarterly Journal of Economics*, **55** (3), August: 699–726.

Levine, D. I. (1991). 'Just-Cause Employment Policies in the Presence of Worker Adverse Selection'. *Journal of Labour Economics*, **9** (3), July: 294–305

Lustig, N., Bosworth, B. P. and Lawrence, R. Z. (eds) (1992). *North American Free Trade: Assessing the Impact*. Washington, D.C.: The Brookings Institution.

Mitchell, O. S. (1990). 'The Effect of Mandatory Benefit Packages'. In R. Ehrenberg (ed.) *Research in Labour Economics*, **11**: 297–320. Greenwich: CT: JAI Press.

Morici, P. (1991). *Trade Talks with Mexico: A Time for Realism*. Washington, D.C.: National Planning Association.

Mosley, H. G. (1990). 'The Social Dimension of European Integration'. *International Labour Review*, **129** (2): 147–64.

Nord, S. and Ting, Y. (1991). 'The Impact of Advance Notification of Plant Closings on Earnings and the Probability of Reemployment'. *Industrial and Labour Relations Review*, **44** (4): 681–91.

Organization for Economic Co-operation and Development (1995). 'Long-Term Leave for Parents in OECD Countries'. In *Employment Outlook: July 1995*, pp. 171–202. Paris: OECD Department of Economics and Statistics.

Pastor, R. A. (1992). 'NAFTA as the Center of an Integration Process: The Nontrade Issues'. In N. Lustig, B. Bosworth, and R. Lawrence (eds.) *North American Free Trade: Assessing the Impact*. Washington, D.C.: The Brookings Institution.

Robson, P. (1984). *The Economics of International Integration*. Second Edition. London: George Allen & Unwin, Ltd.

Ruhm, C. J. (1992). 'Advance Notice and Postdisplacement Joblessness'. *Journal of Labour Economics*, **10** (1), January: 1–32.

Ruhm, C. J. (1994). 'Advance Notice, Job Search, and Postdisplacement Earnings'. *Journal of Labour Economics*, **12** (1), January: 1–28.

Ruhm, C. J. (1996). 'The Economic Consequences of Parental Leave Mandates: Lessons From Europe'. *National Bureau of Economic Research Working Paper No. 5688* (in press).

Ruhm, C. J. and Teague, J. L. (1996). 'Parental Leave Policies in Europe and North America'. In F. Blau and R. Ehrenberg (eds), *Gender and Family Issues in the Workplace*. New York: Russell Sage Foundation (in press).

Shorrock, T. (1992). 'Mexican Labour law complex, far reaching. (Doing Business in Mexico Under NAFTA)'. *Journal of Commerce and Commercial*, **394** (27866), 3 December: 8C(1).

Spalter-Roth, R. M. and Hartmann, H. I. (1990). *Unnecessary Losses: Costs to Americans of the Lack of Family and Medical Leave*. Washington D.C.: Institute for Women's Policy Research.

Springer, B. (1992). *The Social Dimension of 1992*. New York: Praeger.

Stern, R. M., Deardorff, A. V. and Brown, D. K. (1992). Final Report. 'A U.S.-Mexico-

Canada   Free   Trade   Agreement: Sectoral   Employment   Effects   and
   Regional/Occupational Employment Realignments in the United States', *Submission to
   the National Commission for Employment Policy Through the US Department of Labour*,
   RFP L/A 91–14: Category (2): US–Mexico–Canada Free Trade Zones.
Stiglitz, J. E. (1993). *Economics*. New York: W. W. Norton and Company.
Stoiber, S. A. (1990). 'Family Leave Entitlements in Europe: Lessons for the United States'.
   Compensation and Benefits Management, **6** (2), Winter: 111–16.
Summers, L. H. (1989). 'Some Simple Economics of Mandated Benefits'. *American
   Economic Review*, **79** (2), May: 177–83.
Trzcinski, E. (1991). 'Employers Parental Leave Policies: Does the Labour Market Provide
   Parental Leave'. In J. Hyde and M. Essex (eds.) *Parental Leave & Child Care: Setting A
   Research and Policy Agenda*, pp. 209–28. Philadelphia: Temple University Press.
US Department of Labour. (1991). 'International Comparisons of Hourly Compensation for
   Production Workers in Manufacturing, 1975–1990'. *Bureau of Labour Statistics, Report
   No. 817*. Washington D.C.: U.S. Government Printing Office.
Waldfogel, J. (1996). 'Working Mothers Then and Now: A Cross-Cohort Analysis of the
   Effects of Maternity Leave on Women's Pay'. In F. Blau and R. Ehrenberg (eds), *Gender
   and Family Issues in the Workplace*. New York: Russell Sage Foundation (in press).

10

Overview of European Labour Markets

W. Stanley Siebert

10.1. Introduction

Labour markets in Europe vary widely in terms of wage outcomes, employment growth and unemployment. European states also have widely different traditions of labour market regulation. The aim of this chapter is to describe these differences, making comparisons where possible with Japan and the USA, Europe's main competitors. Such a description will provide pointers as to roots of labour market success. It will also help assessment of the European Union's harmonization project, both by showing the areas in which there is most divergence and the possible consequences of changes in regulation.

First, we will consider the various laws and institutions to which the different European labour markets are subject. Then we will consider the consequences of these laws – the labour market's outputs, as it were – for wages, employment, and unemployment.

10.2. Labour Market Institutions

To anticipate our conclusions, the labour markets of the various member states present quite a highly regulated picture. Within Europe, the UK is least regulated, broadly comparable with the USA, while Japan occupies an intermediate position.

Let us begin with the wage setting framework, aspects of which are summarized in Table 10.1. The first column gives information on whether a minimum wage law applies, and a measure of its 'bite': the ratio of the minimum to manual worker wages in industry. The minimum wage bite is softest in Spain and the USA, at around 40%, and hardest in Belgium, France and Portugal, at about 70%. Japan is in an intermediate position. The minimum wage entries should be read in conjunction with the information on whether the country has machinery for extending collective agreements, since such extended agreements can form, in effect, a wage minimum. (High welfare benefits do the same, but we do not present corresponding estimates because countries' benefit systems cannot be adequately captured in

Wage regulating framework

	Minimum wage (ratio to manual wages in industry, 1993[a])	Union density, 1990[c]	Extension of collective agreements[d]
Belgium	Yes (69%)	51%	Nearly all agreements of the National Labour Council extended
Denmark	No	71	Frequent in the 1980s; central wage negotiations
France	Yes (73%)	10	Frequent – generally on the opinion of the National Collective Bargaining Board
Germany	No	33	Fairly frequent – mainly in industries with many small firms; 10% of workforce affected
Greece	Yes (57%)	34	National agreements directly bind all private sector employers
Ireland	No	52	Joint Labour Committees can set minimum rates of pay; only affects 5% of workforce
Italy	No	39	Industry agreements regarded as generally binding
Netherlands	Yes (60%)	26	Minister of Social Affairs can extend agreements; about 10% of workforce affected
Portugal	Yes (70%)	32	Minister can extend industry agreements
Spain	Yes (40%)	11	There is machinery – though it is rarely used, collective bargaining is highly centralized (see Chapter 8)
Sweden	No	83	No administrative extensions – bargaining is centralized and membership of an employers' association is effectively compulsory[e]
UK	No – except for agriculture	39	No administrative extensions
Japan	Yes (53%[b])	25	Yes, but rare since company collective agreements are the norm[b]
USA	Yes (37%)	16	No administrative extensions

Sources and Notes:
[a] Minimum wage rates (Incomes Data Services, 1993: 12); hourly wages of manual workers in manufacturing (*Eurostat*, 1995: 280).
[b] Sasajima (1993: 163, 173).
[c] OECD (1994: Part II, Table 5.8).
[d] Lecher (1994: Table 1.4); also OECD (1994: Part II, Table 5.11).
[e] Van Waarden (1995: 87).

simple numbers – see Tronti, 1993, on Italy's complex arrangements, for example.)

As can be seen, most countries either have a minimum or some method of extending collective agreements. Britain and Sweden are the only exceptions in the table, but in the case of Sweden this is misleading, because union density in that country is so high, 83%, that collective agreements cover most workers in any case. By the same token, the UK has relatively high union density. Taking all factors together, the USA, Japan, and Spain appear to be the labour markets where there is most scope for wage flexibility.

Turning from wage to employment regulation, Table 10.2 provides data on aspects of dismissals regulation. The first column relates to statutory works councils which are important in this area since they usually have to be consulted, at least, about dismissals and discipline – as shown in the second column. Greece, Portugal and Spain have newly decided to take this route, with the German works councils being the oldest (dating back to the 1920s). The councils tend to work together with unions (see France, Belgium, Germany), and are most prevalent in larger firms. The table shows that most countries in Europe have laws requiring worker representation, with the UK, Ireland, and to some extent Sweden being the odd men out.

The second column of Table 10.2 shows noteworthy aspects of dismissals laws, together with the Grubb and Wells (1993) ranking of the strictness of these laws. The Table only gives high points, because there are many aspects of the laws which do not lend themselves to easy summary; for example, notice periods and severance pay rules vary by broad occupation and length of service. Grubb and Wells rank Portugal and Spain, followed by Italy and Greece, as the countries with most restrictions on dismissal. Indeed, in Portugal, the restrictions are such that firms commonly carry workers on their books who they cannot even pay. As for Spain, restrictive laws here are increasingly avoided by using fixed term contract (that is, temporary) workers, for whom the issue of dismissal does not arise – see below. Within Europe, the UK seems the country with most employment flexibility in this regard. Tenure figures, for what they are worth (since surveys might not be comparable across countries; for example, some consider only full-time, permanent workers) are also low in the UK, 7.9 years. The UK is similar in this respect to the USA, where average tenure is only 6.7 years. Notice, however, that the law is not the only factor determining tenure. In Japan there is the 'lifetime employment system' which, while not apparently legislatively based, is quite pervasive as a philosophy (Sasajima, 1993: 177), and the data show a longer current average tenure value of 10.9 years.

Table 10.3 documents further aspects of employment regulation. The first column relates to the position of temporary work agencies which are in fact forbidden in Greece, Spain, Italy and Sweden. This is interesting as an indicator of the suspicion felt within these countries towards unfettered freedom of contract – and a corresponding faith in government action. The principle is that only the state may operate labour exchanges (IRS, 1990: 46). This suspicion carries over to hours regulation, as shown in the second column. Only the more extreme regulations are shown here for illustrative purposes. We see that it is quite common to ban nightwork for women, to restrict hours, and to limit annual overtime. Belgium, Greece and Spain seem most restrictive in these respects, but all European countries except the UK and Ireland have some restrictions. Interestingly enough, so too do the US and Japan.

It should be remembered, however, that hours and overtime restrictions cannot easily be monitored, for example, in the case of professional and managerial workers (who are in fact excluded from the US law). Hence even strictly regulated countries like Greece and Spain have sizeable proportions of workers – 12% and 8%, respectively – on long hours. Still, the UK, USA and Japan stand out as being the countries where there is most freedom to work long hours. These countries also allow freedom in negotiation of vacations, as shown in the third column. In all the other countries there are mandatory vacation requirements. The final column gives the Grubb/Wells useful summary ranking of countries' restrictions on overall employee work. (This ranking correlates well, $r=0.958$, with their ranking of countries' strictness of dismissal protection shown in column 2 of Table 10.2, but is designed to capture also wider restrictions such as those on hours, overtime, and temporary work agencies.) This statistic credits

Table 10.2. Employment Protection

	Employee representation[a]	Special dismissals protection (ranking)[e] [average tenure][f]
Belgium	Statutory works councils in enterprises >100; union lists for representatives	−(4)
Denmark	Cooperation committees in workplaces >35 in terms of agreement between national employers/trade union confederations; some places reserved for shop stewards	−(2)
France	*Comité d'entreprise* mandatory in companies >50; union lists for representatives; obligation to cooperate (chaired by employer)	Compensation can be 2 or more years pay for unjustified dismissal (5.5) [10.1 years]
Germany	Works councils in plants >5 at worker request	Works Council must be notified, and, if it opposes dismissal, case goes to Labour Court (7) [10.4 years]
Greece	Since 1988, works councils in establishments >50 at worker request	Public Employment Service to be notified, and reinstatement can be ordered (8)
Ireland	Voluntary arrangements only, usually consultative	(3)
Italy	1970 Workers' Statute allows workers to set up workplace union representative structures providing backing for *consiglio di fabbrica* (factory councils); only cover 20% of workforce, mainly in large firms[b]	Provincial Labour Office conciliates, and reinstatement can be ordered (9)
Netherlands	1950 Works Council Act set up works councils chaired by employer in enterprises >100; employer excluded in 1979 and threshold lowered to 35 in 1981[c]	Regional employment office authorization is required (5.5) [7.0 years]
Portugal	Workers' committees emerged after the 1974 revolution, and have been given recognition in the 1976 Constitution	Collective dismissals must be authorized by the Minister of Labour, and individual dismissals are reviewed by an administrative tribunal – many firms have wage arrears[g] (10.5)
Spain	1980 Workers' Statute allows for worker representatives in enterprises <50 and works councils in undertakings >50	Prior authorization by the local Labour Office is required, and reinstatement can be ordered (10.5) [9.8 years]
Sweden	Union workplace 'clubs' rather than works councils represent workers at workplace level; 1977 Codetermination in Working Life Act attempts to increase influence of the clubs[d]	Prior consultation with the local union branch is required, and the Labour Court can order reinstatement (n.a.)
UK	Voluntary arrangements only, usually consultative	−(1) [7.9 years]

Table 10.2. (continued)

	Employee representation[a]	Special dismissals protection (ranking)[e] [average tenure][f]
Japan	Voluntary arrangements only, usually consultative[h]	−(n.a.) [10.9 years]
USA	Voluntary arrangements only, usually consultative	Gender/colour discrimination unlawful, but no general protection (n.a.) [6.7 years]

Sources and Notes:
[a] Lecher (1994: Table 1.10), Mielke *et al*, 1994.
[b] Ferner and Hyman (1992: 552–53), Mielke *et al*. (1994: 206).
[c] Visser (1990: 203–4).
[d] Kjellberg (1992: 121–25).
[e] Grubb and Wells (1993: Table 1): overall ranking of strictness of protection against dismissals amongst EC member states (Japan, USA and Sweden not considered).
[f] OECD (1994: Part II, Table 6.3) (figures relate to wage and salary earners in 1990/1991).
[g] Pinto (1991: 247, 259).
[h] Sasajima (1993: 164).

Table 10.3. Contract regulation, early 1990s

	Restrictions on temporary work agencies	Special restrictions on hours (% working > 45 hours a week)	Statutory paid vacations (weeks)	Restrictions on overall employee work[e]
Belgium	Temporary work agencies restricted	Normal weekly hours restricted to 38; nightwork generally banned (3%)	4	5
Denmark	Limited to office and shop workers	Normal weekly hours restricted to 39; maximum annual overtime 144 hours (6%)	5	2
France	–	Normal weekly hours restricted to 39; nightwork banned for women (8%)	5	6
Germany	Public employment service must authorize contracts	Nightwork banned for women (7%)	3	7
Greece	Temp agencies illegal	Normal weekly hours restricted to 40; nightwork banned for women; maximum annual overtime 135 hours (12%)	4	10
Ireland	–	−(11%)	3	3
Italy	Temp agencies illegal	Nightwork banned for women (8%)	4	8
Netherlands	–	Nightwork generally banned (3%)	4	4

Table 10.3. (continued)

	Restrictions on temporary work agencies	Special restrictions on hours (% working > 45 hours a week)	Statutory paid vacations (weeks)	Restrictions on overall employee work[e]
Portugal	Public employment service must authorize contracts	Nightwork banned for women (9%)	4.4	11
Spain	Temp agencies illegal[b]	Normal weekly hours restricted to 40; maximum annual overtime 80 hours (8%)	5	9
Sweden[a]	Temp agencies illegal	Normal weekly hours restricted to 40; maximum annual overtime 150 hours (3%)	5.4	n.a.
UK	–	–(30%)	No law	1
Japan	–	Normal weekly hours restricted to 44; nightwork banned for women (28%)[c]	10 – 20 days, by service	n.a.
USA	–	Normal weekly hours restricted to 40 except for admin and sales employees earning >given threshold (25%)[d]	No law	(1)

Sources and Notes:
Grubb and Wells (1993: 27, Annex 1), Ehrenberg (1991: Table 2.2), OECD (1994: Part II, Table 6.12).
[a] Nilsson (1993: 255); the 3% figure in the hours column is not comparable with the rest since it gives the proportion of overtime hours in total hours.
[b] In 1994, temp agencies were permitted on certain conditions.
[c] See Sasajima (1993: 167).
[d] See Flanagan (1993: 52).
[e] Grubb and Wells (1993: Table 9); the figures give the rankings of the countries – Sweden, Japan and the USA were not considered, but we have ranked the USA as 1, equal with the UK, for the purposes of the correlations reported in the Appendix.

Portugal, Greece and Spain as most restrictive overall, with the UK and Denmark as least restrictive.

In sum, two broad philosophies are apparent in our brief review of Europe's labour market systems. There is the Anglo-American tradition of free markets, and the social-market view, particularly associated with Germany, which aims to constrain and direct markets. Sometimes the two approaches are labelled 'deregulated' versus 'flexibly coordinated' (Black, 1994: 99). The core European Union states have long taken the social-market view. The more recent entrants – Spain, Portugal, and Greece – have also embraced it, the more enthusiastically, perhaps, because of post-revolutionary fervour. Japan is in an intermediate position. (However, in an interesting study of the reaction of prices to capacity utilization, Japan was found to have the slowest reaction, and the USA by far the fastest, with the main European countries quite similar, and more akin to Japan than the US – see Van Bergeuk et al., 1993.) We next consider some evidence on the performance of the different systems.

Table 10.4. Labour-force statistics

	Labour-force millions 1993[a] (1)	Self employment, 1992[b] (2)	Unemploy-ment, 1994[c] (3)	Employment growth, 1979–90 (private sector growth per capita)[d] (4)	Part-time, 1989[e] (5)	Temporary 1989[f] (6)
Belgium	4.1	10–20%	10.3%	0.1% per year (−0.3)	12%	5%
Denmark	2.9	<10	9.9	0.4 (−0.4)	25	10
France	24.7	<10	11.5	0.2 (−1.0)	12	9
Germany	30.3(w) 9.1(e)	<10	9.3	0.6 (−0.2)	13	11
Greece	4.1	>20	8.9	1.0 (−0.1)	4	17
Ireland	1.4	10–20	17.8	−0.2 (−0.8)	8	9
Italy	22.2	>20	12.0	0.5 (−0.3)	5	6
Netherlands	7.0	<10	10.2	0.4 (−0.6)	31	9
Portugal	4.7	10–20	6.5	−0.4 (−1.4)	4	19
Spain	15.3	10–20	23.3	0.4 (−1.1)	4	27
Sweden	4.3	<10	8.0	0.6 (0.0)	23	10[g]
UK	28.2	10–20	9.9	0.5 (0.1)	23	5
Japan	65.6	10–20	3.2	1.1 (0.3)	20	
USA	124.7	<10	6.0	1.6 (0.8)	15	

Sources and Notes:
[a] *Eurostat* (1995: Table 3.15), *US Bureau of the Census* (1995: Table 1364).
[b] OECD (1994: Part I, Chart 1.3); data relates to self-employment outside agriculture.
[c] EC Employment Observatory (1994: 6), UK Department of Education and Employment (1996: S38).
[d] OECD (1994: Part I, Table 1.1): the private sector includes public enterprises.
[e] Grubb and Wells (1993: Table 4), OECD (1994: Part 1, Table 1.4).
[f] Grubb and Wells (1993: Table 4).
[g] IRS (1991: 43).

10.3. Outcomes

Employment

Let us continue with the employment theme and discuss outcomes, starting with Table 10.4. Columns 1 and 2 give, as background, labour-force sizes and the importance of self-employment (outside agriculture). The latter measure is worth considering in a variety of contexts. Thus high self-employment indicates more scope for the underground economy – as is well known for Greece and Italy. High self-employment also roughly indicates the importance of small firms, which can be both more dynamic than large firms, and more adversely affected by government mandates.

Columns 3 and 4 next give information on unemployment and employment outcomes. Since so many factors influence the unemployment rate (in particular, the generosity or otherwise of unemployment insurance and welfare benefits), the unemployment figures should be considered alongside the employment growth figures given in column 4. The data in the two columns are correlated negatively, $r = -0.405$, as might be expected, but the correlation is not all that close $(p = 0.151)$.[1] (See the Appendix for a full table of correlations.) Thus, even though

Spain has a very high unemployment rate, 23.3%, it has put in quite a respectable employment growth performance of 0.4% a year, 1979–90. The contrast with Portugal is marked. However, it is employment growth allowing for population growth that matters – and this figure, for the private sector, is given in parentheses in column 4. The negative correlation between unemployment and private sector employment growth per capita is quite high and statistically significant, $r=-0.547$ ($p=0.04$). One possible explanation for this negative correlation is that there is some third factor causing both high private sector growth and low unemployment. An alternative is that expansion of the private sector itself works to reduce unemployment.

Since employment growth is such an important indicator of an economy's performance, it is worth looking at the figures in more detail. We see that according to the raw data, that is, not adjusting for population growth, the champions are the USA, Japan, and Greece, all of which have had annual growth rates of 1% or more over 1979–90. The laggards are Portugal, Ireland and Belgium. However, taking private sector employment alone, and allowing for population growth, gives a somewhat different picture. The UK ousts Greece from the top group, which now consists of the UK, USA and Japan. Ireland takes the place of Belgium in the bottom group. (West) Germany turns in a relatively poor performance. However, Sweden, the model of social democracy, continues to do well on this indicator.

Interestingly, there is a high positive correlation, $r=0.574$ ($p=0.032$) between private sector employment growth per capita and the percentage working long hours variable (the variable in column 2 of Table 10.3). It might be argued that working long hours is simply caused by high private sector growth. On the other hand, it should be remembered that hours restrictions raise costs: it is not possible to work existing workers harder by increasing hours when production picks up. Hence there might after all be a causal link between working long hours and private sector employment growth. There is also a high (negative) correlation between private sector employment growth per capita and the Grubb/Wells ranking of countries' strictness of dismissals protection (the variable in the second column of Table 10.2): $r=-0.613$ ($p=0.034$). It may pay to allow freedom to dismiss. At first blush it seems as though the Anglo-American tradition of deregulated markets works well.

The final columns of Table 10.4 relate to part-time work and temporary work. It seems strange that the various economies should differ so much in the importance of these types of contract. In fact the proportion doing part-time work correlates strongly negatively with the Grubb/Wells ranking of countries' overall strictness of regulation of employee work: $r=-0.726$ ($p=0.008$). Greece, Portugal, Spain and Italy are the strictest in regulation of labour contracts, and this appears to discourage part-time work.

Turning to fixed-term 'temporary' workers, we detect signs of an inverse correlation between the proportion of such workers and the proportion of part-timers: $r=-0.489$ ($p=0.106$). The same factors which discourage part-time work seem to encourage temporary work. There is also a high correlation between the Grubb/Wells ranking of countries' strictness of dismissal protection, and the proportion of temporary workers: $r=0.708$ ($p=0.015$). Spain illustrates the reason for this. Temporary work in Spain is a market escape route around Spain's strict dismissals laws (see Chapter 8). It seems as though dismissals protection institutionalizes the very thing – temporary jobs – which it is designed to prevent.

Table 10.5. Earnings and incomes

	GDP per capita, 1993, US$ at PPP[a]	Hourly compensation, production workers mfg, 1993 US$ at 100[b]	Male earnings, 90th/10th percentile, late '80s relative to 1980=100[c] (90th/10th percentile, 1990)[d]	Income distribution: Gini coefficient 1980s[e]
Belgium	19 500	129		23.5
Denmark	19 300	114	100	
France	18 700	97	99 (3.4)	29.6
Germany	18 500	154 (West only)	97 (2.4)[f]	25.0 (West)
Greece	8 800	41		
Ireland	13 900	73		33.0
Italy	17 800	96		31.0
Netherlands	17 600	119		26.8
Portugal	11 900	27		31.0
Spain	13 300	69		32.0
Sweden	16 800	106	100	22.0
Switzerland	23 200	135		32.3
UK	17 000	76	127 (3.2)	30.4
Japan	20 500	114	110 (2.8)	
US	24 300	100	118 (4.1)	34.1

Sources and Notes:

[a] Measured at purchasing power parity (PPP) (*Statistical Abstract of the US*, 1995: Table 1374).

[b] Compensation includes wages plus non-wage benefits such as holidays and pensions, plus employer expenditures for legally required insurance programmes and social security; the US figure for 1993 is approximately $20.00/hour of which wages make up about 66% (*Statistical Abstract of the US*, 1995: Tables 680, 683, 1394).

[c] OECD Jobs Study (1994: Chart 1.5).

[d] Katz *et al.* (1995: Table 1.7).

[e] Atkinson (1996: Figure 4).

[f] Abraham and Houseman (1995: Table 11.1); this figure relates to male full-time, full-year workers in 1989.

Earnings and Incomes

Comparative data on earnings and incomes are given in Table 10.5. The first column gives GDP per capita, a measure of average incomes, that is, average wage plus non-wage receipts including dividends and rents. The second column gives an earnings figure, in this case hourly compensation of production workers, that is, wages plus fringes such as holidays and pensions. The data in the two columns are quite well, but by no means perfectly correlated, $r=0.742$ ($p=0.002$). The correlation is not higher because the figure for average incomes is affected by the incomes of the better-off, whereas the hourly compensation data are relevant more to the man in the street. As can be seen, Greece has the lowest average income, $8800; and Portugal has the lowest production worker compensation, only 27% of the US figure. The USA and Switzerland have the highest incomes, while (West) Germany has the best-off production workers, earning 54% more than their US counterparts.

The important question is what gives high – and evenly distributed – earnings and incomes. We take up the issue of distribution next, but concentrating on levels for

Table 10.6. Trends in earnings inequality (gross real earnings, males)

		Bottom 10%	Median	Top 10%
UK	1970	£136 per week	£209	£336
(1993 prices)	1979	£155	£235	£369
	1993	£175	£305	£567
	Change 1970–79	1.5% p.a.	1.3% p.a.	1.0% p.a.
	Change 1979–93	0.9% p.a.	1.9% p.a.	3.1% p.a.
West Germany	Change 1980–89	1.7% p.a.	0.6% p.a.	1.0% p.a.
France	Change 1979–87	0.6% p.a.	0.6% p.a.	1.0% p.a.
USA	Change 1979–89	−1.3% p.a.	−0.5% p.a.	0.8% p.a.

Sources:
UK: UK Department of Employment, New Earnings Survey, 1970, 1979, 1993; France and US: Katz, *et al*, (1995); Germany: Abraham and Houseman (1995).

the moment, simple correlations with other variables in earlier tables are instructive. As shown in the correlation matrix in the Appendix, incomes and earnings are both lower the larger is the size of the self-employment sector. However, this is likely to be due at least in part to the fact that incomes and earnings are under-stated where there is much self-employment. Lower incomes where there are more small firms should not be taken to mean that small firms are bad for the economy. In fact, self-employment is most prevalent in countries which register highest on the Grubb/Wells indicator of restrictions on overall employee work, perhaps because self-employment is a means of evading such restrictions. Restrictions on overall employee work are negatively correlated with GDP per capita, $r=-0.685$ ($p=0.014$), though less so with earnings, $r=-0.442$ ($p=0.150$). It could therefore be the restrictions on overall employee work which play a causal role in low incomes and earnings. If this speculation is substantiated, it would of course support the Anglo-American tradition of free labour markets.

An important point is that high incomes and private sector employment growth go together, with a correlation of $r=0.569$ ($p=0.034$). High earnings and private sector employment growth are also positively correlated, though less strongly: $r=0.394$ ($p=0.164$). Thus there seems to be a link between incomes/earnings and private sector jobs. This is expressed by the USA and the UK at one end of the spectrum, with Portugal at the other. Exceptions here are France (rich, but with low private sector job creation), and Greece (poor, but quite a good private sector employment record). It is tempting to conclude that private sector employment growth generates the wealth which leads to high income and earnings.

Let us now consider issues of equality in more detail. Some relevant data are contained in the third and fourth columns of Table 10.5. The third column suggests that the earnings distributions of continental European countries were static in the 1980s, while those of Japan, the USA and particularly the UK widened. More detail on the UK, Germany, France and the USA is given in Table 10.6. Here we see that in the 1980s real earnings in (West) Germany rose quickly for the bottom decile of earners, 1.7% per annum, while real earnings for the corresponding group in the USA actually fell by −1.3% per annum. This might be the source of the US jobs 'miracle'.

Interestingly, earnings for the bottom decile in the UK grew quite quickly, 0.9% per annum, in the 1980s. This is hard to explain given the weakening of trade unions and the removal of minimum wages during this period. Earnings of the top decile

Table 10.7. Trends in unemployment inequality (data relate to males 25–55, with figures for women given in brackets)

		Lower secondary or less	Upper secondary or more	Ratio Lower to Upper (ratio for women)
UK	1979	5.4%	2.2%	2.4 (1.4)
	1990	8.7	3.3	2.6 (1.6)
West Germany	1978	4.1	1.8	2.3 (1.2)
	1987	14.6	5.0	2.9 (1.5)
France	1979	3.7	2.6	1.4 (1.3)
	1990	8.3	4.1	2.0 (1.8)
US	1979	6.6	3.2	2.1 (2.0)
	1989	9.7	3.9	2.5 (2.4)

Source and Notes:
OECD (1994: Part I, Table 1.16). Note that a major change in the UK definition of unemployment took place after 1979, so the results for 1979 and 1990 are not strictly comparable, especially for levels.

grew even faster, at 3.1% per annum, much faster than the trend rise in the 1970s, so the distribution as a whole widened. As Table 10.6 shows, earnings of the top decile in the UK have grown much faster than in either Germany or France. Presumably factors such as the deregulation of financial markets in the UK caused the rise in top decile earnings. At any rate it seems that earnings inequality has increased more in deregulated countries such as the UK and USA, than in social-market countries such as Germany and France.

Summary measures of income inequality, Gini coefficients, are given in the last column of Table 10.5. The Gini coefficient can range from zero, for perfect equality, to unity for perfect inequality. As can be seen, the USA is least equal on this measure, followed by Ireland. Sweden, Belgium and Germany are among the most equal. Inspection of the simple correlations in the Appendix reveals that the Gini coefficients are not correlated with GDP per capita. In this sample, the rich countries do not tend to have more equally distributed incomes. However, the Gini coefficients are well correlated, negatively, with production worker hourly compensation, $r = -0.626$ ($p = 0.040$). Countries with well-paid production workers tend to have more equal incomes. This fact might be thought of as supporting the egalitarian, social-market, approach. But we must be careful. The correlation between the Gini coefficients and labour regulation, as measured by the Grubb/Wells indicator of restrictions on overall employee work, is nearly zero, $r = -0.119$ ($p = 0.744$). Hence it cannot be said that those countries with a social-market approach to labour regulation end up with more income equality. At the same time, of course, neither can the deregulation approach be said to be vindicated.

Unemployment

Inequality as measured by unemployment is also worth considering. Data on joblessness in four countries are presented in Table 10.7. Here the unemployment rate of the unskilled, that is, those with a lower secondary education or less, is contrasted with that of the skilled, those with upper secondary education or more. We see that in all four countries unemployment is higher for the unskilled than the skilled. This is to be expected if only because unskilled wages are more subject to minimum wage floors and hence are more inflexible than skilled. However, in all four countries unemployment has worsened relatively for the unskilled. For example, in the UK the ratio of unskilled to skilled male unemployment was 2.4 in 1979, but this had risen to 2.6 by 1990.

The rise in the relative unemployment of the unskilled has been most pronounced in Germany (2.3 to 2.9) and France (1.4 to 2.0). Indeed, in the German case, the reduction in job opportunities for less skilled labour is probably understated by these figures. The better training of less educated German workers should have cushioned them to some extent (this point is made by Abraham and Houseman, 1995: 372; see also Nickell and Bell, 1996: 307). But their labour market outcomes seem to be just as unfavourable. As we have already seen in Table 10.6, in Germany real earnings of the bottom decile have risen much faster than the top decile. Such a rise in unskilled relative pay might explain the relative increase in unskilled unemployment. Again we must be careful, however, because the USA has also experienced a rise in unskilled relative unemployment. The fall in the real pay of the unskilled in the USA, and the accompanying widening of the earnings distribution has not been able to prevent the increase in unskilled unemployment in the USA, or for that matter in the UK. Nevertheless, the rise in unskilled relative unemployment has been less in the USA (and the UK), an outcome to which wage flexibility could have contributed.

10.4.   Conclusions

In this overview of European labour markets we first considered the different legal frameworks and institutions ruling in the various countries. Secondly, we assessed the potential 'outputs' of these institutions in terms of employment, earnings, earnings differentials, unemployment and unemployment differentials. The underlying tension here is between regulation and deregulation. Certainly, we have found that the European norm can be said to be one of regulation, and perhaps increasing regulation. But whether such regulation promotes better and more equal job opportunities and higher earnings/incomes is naturally difficult to decide.

The main patterns we have been able to discern are most simply discussed using the Grubb/Wells index of regulation of overall employee work, which places countries on the regulation spectrum. First, we found that the more regulated a country is, according to this index, the slower is its private sector employment growth, and the lower is its level of average earnings/incomes. These are facts. Whether one wishes to put a causal interpretation on these correlations is of course another matter. Second, we did not find any link, either pro or con, between the regulation index and income inequality. Finally, as regards unemployment inequality, we found that unskilled relative unemployment had increased during the 1980s in all four countries examined (the UK, the USA, France and West Germany), with no obvious advantage for more regulated countries such as West Germany or France.

Note

1 $p=0.151$ means that there is a 15% chance of being wrong in rejecting the null hypothesis that the true correlation is zero.

References

Abraham, K. and Houseman, S. (1995). 'Earnings Inequality in Germany'. In R. B. Freeman and L. F. Katz (eds), *Differences and Changes in Wage Structures*. Chicago: University of Chicago Press.

Atkinson, A. B. (1996). 'Income Distribution in Europe and the United States'. *Oxford Review of Economic Policy*, **12** (Spring): 15–28.

Black, B. (1994). 'Labour Market Incentive Structures and Employee Performance'. *British Journal of Industrial Relations*, **32** (March): 99–114.

EC Employment Obversatory (1994). *Tableau de Bord*. Brussels: DG5 European Commission.

Ehrenberg, R. G. (1991). *Integrating National Economies*. Washington, DC: The Brookings Institution.

Eurostat (1995). *Eurostat Statistical Yearbook*. Luxembourg: Office for Official Publications of the European Communities.

Ferner, A. and Hyman, R. (1992). 'Italy: Between Political Exchange and Micro-corporatism'. In A. Ferner and R. Hyman (eds), *Industrial Relations in the New Europe*. Oxford: Blackwell.

Flanagan, R. (1993). 'The United States: Divided Heterogeneity'. In J. Hartog and J. Theeuwes (eds), *Labour Market Contracts and Institutions*. Amsterdam: North-Holland.

Grubb D. and Wells, W. (1993). 'Employment Regulation and Patterns of Work in EC Countries'. *OECD Economic Studies*, Winter.

IDS (1993). 'Equitable Wages and Minimum Pay Setting'. *Incomes Data Services European Report*, **383** (November): 9–16.

IRS (1989). *Termination of Contract in Europe*. London: Industrial Relations Services.

IRS (1990). *Non-Standard Forms of Employment in Europe*. London: Industrial Relations Services.

IRS (1991). *Working Time in Europe*. London: Industrial Relations Services.

Katz, L., Loveman, G. and Blanchflower, D. (1995). 'A Comparison of Changes in the Structure of Wages in Four OECD Countries'. In R. B. Freeman and L. F. Katz (eds), *Differences and Changes in Wage Structures*. Chicago: University of Chicago Press.

Kjellberg, A. (1992). 'Sweden: Can the Model Survive?'. In A. Ferner and R. Hyman (eds), *Industrial Relations in the New Europe*. Oxford: Blackwell.

Lecher, W. (1994). *Trade Unions in the European Union*. London: Lawrence and Wishart.

Mielke, S., Rutters, P. and Tudyka, K. P. (1994). 'Trade Union Organization and Employee Representation'. In W. Lecher, *Trade Unions in the European Union*, London: Lawrence and Wishart.

Nickell, S. and Bell, B. (1996). 'Changes in the Distribution of Wages in OECD Countries'. *American Economic Review,* **86** (May): 302–08.

Nilsson, C. (1993). 'The Swedish Model: Labour Market Institutions and Contracts'. In J. Hartog and J. Theeuwes (eds), *Labour Market Contracts and Institutions*. Amsterdam: North-Holland.

OECD (1994). *Jobs Study, Parts I and II*. Paris: Organization for Economic Co-operation and Development.

Pinto, M. (1991). 'Trade Union Action and Industrial Relations in Portugal'. In G. Baglioni and C. Crouch (eds), *European Industrial Relations*. London: Sage.

Sasajima, Y. (1993). 'The Japanese Labour Market'. In J. Hartog and J. Theeuwes (eds), *Labour Market Contracts and Institutions*. Amsterdam: North-Holland.

Tronti, L. (1993). 'Employment Security and Labour Market Segmentation: Economic Implications of the Italian Cassa Integrazione Guadagni'. In C. Buechtemann (ed.), *Employment Security and Labour Market Behaviour*. Ithaca: ILR Press.

UK Department for Education and Employment (1996). *Employment Trends,* **104** (March).

UK Department of Employment (1970, 1979, 1993). *New Earnings Survey*. London: HM Stationery Office.

US Bureau of the Census (1995). *Statistical Abstract of the United States*, 115th edn. Washington DC: US Government Printing Office.

Van Bergeuk, P., Haffner, R. and Waasdorp, P. (1993). 'Measuring the Speed of the Invisible Hand: the Macroeconomic Costs of Price Rigidity'. *Kyklos* **46**: 529–44.

Van Waarden, F. (1995). 'Employers and Employers' Associations'. In J. van Ruysseveldt, R. Huiskamp and J. van Hoof, *Comparative Industrial Relations*. London: Sage.

Visser, J. (1990). 'Continuity and Change in Dutch Industrial Relations'. In G. Baglioni and C. Crouch (eds), *European Industrial Relations*. London. Sage.

Appendix: Correlation analysis

Pearson Correlation Coefficients / Prob > |R| under Ho: Rho=0

	U	EG	S	PEG	EGPC	PEGPC	PT	LH	R	RR	T	GDP	HC	GI
U	1.00 / 0.0	-0.405 / 0.151	0.169 / 0.563	-0.475 / 0.086	-0.515 / 0.059	-0.547 / 0.043	-0.370 / 0.183	-0.346 / 0.226	0.272 / 0.393	0.134 / 0.678	0.431 / 0.162	-0.376 / 0.185	-0.184 / 0.529	0.314 / 0.347
EG		1.00 / 0.0	-0.074 / 0.802	0.948 / 0.0001	0.853 / 0.0001	0.858 / 0.0001	0.224 / 0.441	0.528 / 0.052	-0.291 / 0.359	-0.275 / 0.387	-0.015 / 0.963	0.440 / 0.116	0.252 / 0.384	0.086 / 0.802
S			1.00 / 0.0	-0.038 / 0.898	-0.104 / 0.724	-0.077 / 0.793	-0.631 / 0.016	0.161 / 0.583	0.444 / 0.148	0.512 / 0.089	0.153 / 0.635	-0.557 / 0.038	-0.550 / 0.041	0.243 / 0.302
PEG				1.00 / 0.0	0.821 / 0.0003	0.926 / 0.0001	0.277 / 0.337	0.587 / 0.028	-0.425 / 0.168	-0.399 / 0.199	-0.322 / 0.308	0.474 / 0.087	0.316 / 0.271	0.059 / 0.852
EGPC					1.00 / 0.0	0.936 / 0.0001	0.368 / 0.195	0.462 / 0.096	-0.511 / 0.089	-0.458 / 0.134	-0.373 / 0.232	0.540 / 0.046	0.358 / 0.210	-0.190 / 0.577
PEGPC						1.00 / 0.0	0.384 / 0.175	0.574 / 0.032	-0.613 / 0.034	-0.560 / 0.058	-0.560 / 0.059	0.569 / 0.034	0.394 / 0.164	-0.110 / 0.748
PT							1.00 / 0.0	0.108 / 0.714	-0.644 / 0.024	-0.726 / 0.008	-0.489 / 0.106	0.514 / 0.060	0.541 / 0.046	-0.455 / 0.163
LH								1.00 / 0.0	-0.499 / 0.098	-0.463 / 0.130	-0.123 / 0.702	0.269 / 0.352	-0.169 / 0.563	0.588 / 0.057
R									1.00 / 0.0	0.958 / 0.0001	0.708 / 0.015	-0.612 / 0.094	-0.368 / 0.239	-0.057 / 0.876
RR										1.00 / 0.0	0.674 / 0.023	-0.685 / 0.014	-0.442 / 0.150	-0.119 / 0.744
T											1.00 / 0.0	-0.683 / 0.014	-0.537 / 0.072	-0.339 / 0.338
GDP												1.00 / 0.0	0.742 / 0.002	-0.099 / 0.773
HC													1.00 / 0.0	-0.626 / 0.040

Variables:

U=unemployment, 1994 (column 3, Table 10.4); EG=employment growth 1979–90 (column 4, Table 10.4); S=self-employment, 1/2/3=5<10/10–20/>20 (column 2, Table 10.4); PEG=private sector employment growth, 1979–90 (same source as EG); EGPC=employment growth per capita, 1979–90 (same source as EG); PEGPC=private sector employment growth per capita, 1979–90 (column 4, Table 10.4); PT=part-time proportion (column 5, Table 10.4); LH=% working >45 hours a week (column 2, Table 10.2); R=Grubb/Wells ranking of countries' strictness of dismissals protection (column 2, Table 10.2); RR=Grubb/Wells ranking of countries' restrictions on overall employee work (column 4, Table 10.3); T=temporary proportion (column 6, Table 10.4); GDP=GDP per capita (column 1, Table 10.5); HC=hourly compensation, production workers (column 2, Table 10.5); GI=Gini coefficient (column 4, Table 10.5).

Index

Page numbers in **bold** refer to main discussion; page numbers in *italics* refer to tables